GUERRILLA AUDITORS

KREGG HETHERINGTON

GUERRILLA AUDITORS

The Politics of Transparency in Neoliberal Paraguay

DUKE UNIVERSITY PRESS
DURHAM AND LONDON   2011

© 2011 Duke University Press

Printed in the United States of America on
acid-free paper ∞

Designed by Nicole Hayward
Typeset in Quadraat by
Achorn International, Inc.

Library of Congress Cataloging-in-
Publication Data appear on the last printed
page of this book.

For Irene, Loro, Leoncio, and Marcial

CONTENTS

Acknowledgments   ix

Note on Names   xiii

Introduction   1

1   The Transition to Democracy   25

2   Ill-Gotten Land   66

3   Precarious Lots   97

4   Duplicitous Documents   143

5   Populist Transparency   184

Epilogue   223

Notes   233

Bibliography   263

Index   283

ACKNOWLEDGMENTS

I've accrued many debts writing this book, some of which I may someday have the opportunity to repay in kind, most of which are part of complex and ongoing relationships. Some have been dropped in the fog, and still others left hanging under circumstances that I wish were otherwise. It's impossible to conceive of doing research like this without the generosity and openness of incredibly varied interlocutors who contribute to the project at different points and at different registers.

Let's start with money, and get it out of the way. The research for this volume was supported by the Social Sciences and Humanities Research Council of Canada, the Hemispheric Institute of the Americas at the University of California, Davis, the Organization of American States, the Wenner Gren Foundation, and the Catherine Newcombe Foundation. I received institutional support from the University of California, Davis, the Centro de Estudios Rurales Interdisciplinarios in Asunción, the University of Toronto, and Dalhousie University.

Then there's the legal stuff. Parts of chapter 3 originally appeared in *American Ethnologist* (Hetherington 2009) and parts of chapter 5 were first published in the *Journal of Legal Anthropology* (Hetherington 2008). Permission to use several of the pictures was generously granted by Editorial "El Foro" in Asunción, *Última Hora*, and *ABC Color* newspapers.

Permission to reprint the song in chapter 3 was generously granted by the author, Cecilio Mareco.

The backbone of this research, as will be clear from the text, was made possible by the original trust shown to me by Antonio and Jorge Galeano and their families, especially Irene, Derlis, Sonia, Candí, Marisa, Demesia, Leticia, David, Cintia, Romina, and Iván. Similarly, dozens of families in six towns near Vaquería took me in for periods from one night to three weeks, and many more showed me far more trust and compassion than I was due. This is particularly true of Catalo, Eleuterio, Francisco, Franco, Maidana, Mariano, Neri, Ortega, Juan, Juan Antonio, Gilda, Nicolás, Joel, Constancia, Cézar, Herminio, Aristides, Miriam, Silvio, Felicita, Gregorio, and their families. And I never would have even considered Paraguay as a field site if it hadn't been for the generosity of Miguel, Sonia, and Naza.

In Asunción, my work depended on the timely help and friendship of Fabricio Vásquez, Ramón Fógel, Ramona Fischer, Tomás Palau, Juan Bautista Gavilán, Isa Olmedo, Andrés Olmedo, Liliana Vera, and José Nicolás Morínigo. It was also done with the great patience and often active support of dozens of people in the Instituto de Desarrollo Rural y de la Tierra, the Registro Público, Servicio Nacional de Catastro, Ministerio de Agricultura and the Senate, not to mention the Centro de Documentación y Estudio, the Muséo de la Memoria, the Comisión de Derechos Humanos. Marcial Riquelme, Antonio Vicente Castillo, and Noni Florencio all took me in during the harder parts of this journey and treated me like family. Mom and Dad, beyond the rather integral role they had in making me capable of this work, were also extraordinarily supportive at just the right moments during the years of this project and afterward.

Along the way I met fellow travelers in Javiera Rulli, An Maeyens, Reto Sondeggren, Carolina Castillo, John Thiels, Albert Berry, Gustavo Setrini, Christine Folch, and Carlos Pastore Olmedo, all of whom commented on what I thought I was doing. Marco Castillo and Lawrence Morroni, in particular, became excellent interlocutors and advisors.

Hovering in the background of my words are many teachers, at the very least these: David Boyd, Don Donham, Tom Holloway, Alan Klima, Donald Moore, Ben Orlove, Roger Rouse, Suzana Sawyer, Carol Smith, Janet Shibamoto Smith, and Aram Yengoyan. Julie Cottle, Alex Ferry, Chris Kortright, Robyn Krock, Chris Krupa, Fabiana Li, Kristina Lyons, Rossio Motta, Ayesha Nibbe, Gowoon Noh, Patricia Pinho, Michelle Stewart, and Ellen Woodall all made student and intellectual life in general bearable during my dissertation, and all had a hand in the way the project came together. In the later phases, after another border crossing, colleagues at the University of Toronto, Trent, Dalhousie, and St. Mary's have all encouraged me and had their say.

There were listeners in abundance, too many to name, who participated in workshops or as audiences where parts of this book were presented, including the University of Toronto Anthropology Department, the Munk Centre for International Studies, Hemispheric Institute of the Americas, University of California, Davis, Dalhousie, Saint Mary's University, Yale, the American Anthropological Association, and the Canadian Anthropology Society.

My sincere thanks are due to several people who read the entire manuscript at different stages, and offered incisive but encouraging comments. These are Bettina Ng'weno, Tim Choy, Anna Tsing, David Howes, Alex Smith, Donna Young, and two anonymous reviewers at Duke University Press. Others commented on parts of the text along the way: Leticia Barrera, Mario Blaser, Steve Boucher, Jessica Cattaneo, Maggie Cummings, Saul Cohen, Thad Dunning, Drew Gilbert, Alejandra González, Bruce Grant, Matt Hull, Carlota McAllister, Andrea Muelbach, Jim Scott, Krystyna Sieciechowicz, Abigail Sone, Orin Starn, John Thiels, Sandra Widmer, and Laurie Zadnik. At Duke University Press, Valerie Millholland, Miriam Angress, Gisela Fosado, and Neal McTighe have all been extraordinarily helpful during different stages of the editing process.

I have been lucky enough to have two consummate mentors and readers of my work over the past decade. Tania Li, steadfast and always encouraging, has been both an example to follow and amazingly generous with her time. Marisol de la Cadena invested herself fully in making me less stupid. One of my fondest moments with this text took place when I was lying in a hammock with my daughter, listening to Marisol, who was reading my dissertation nearby, occasionally burst out, "I hate it! I hate it!" I hope she still does.

There are several people to whom I won't get a chance to show this work off. Ángel (Loro) Cristaldo and Leoncio Torres, who were murdered during my research, and Marcial Riquelme, who died shortly afterward from ailments that had begun in Stroessner's prison, were all critical to my own perseverance in the field and to the eventual form of this dissertation. Irene Ramírez, who died in 2006, as I was finishing the research, was a constant source of help and of insight, the family rock who not only made Antonio's activism possible, but also made my research possible by making sure, in an unassuming way, that I would always have a place to stumble back to, with cold terere or hot mate as the weather dictated, and chipa or surprising afternoon sweetbreads straight out of the tatakua. She is sorely missed.

Ethnography is a situated reflection on the world, and this text is as much a product of my feeling my way in an aesthetic, ethical, and political world as it is about Paraguay. In that way it is inseparable from the project I am engaged in every day with Danielle, who supported me throughout and whose place in the world defines my own. The text, its leaps, stumbles, and flaws are mine, but its foundation is a joint effort. Sadie has only enriched that effort further.

NOTE ON NAMES

The ethical rule of thumb on ethnographic naming practices is to give pseudonyms to anyone who is not a public figure. The practice requires differentiating between names that are easily substituted and therefore irrelevant to the analysis, names that are already "public" and therefore either impossible to conceal or integral to the analysis, and names that are associated with copyright and must by law be used as markers of ownership of other words. This book, however, complicates this rule immensely. It follows the historical construction of two discursive communities we call publics, and the most important characters in it are men and women who straddle the shifting border between them. Decisions about which names to use or conceal require, therefore, judgments about the specific publics in which each name commonly circulates. Moreover, this text is not isolated, but is already implicated in networks of texts which address their audiences under quite different circumstances than academic publishing. Paraguay's national newspapers and several activist blogs covered events described in this book, using both the names of the participants and the names of the anthropologist who happened to be standing by. Given this history, pseudonyms would offer only a thin veil of anonymity to many of the key characters in my book.

I have therefore settled on a far more idiosyncratic naming practice. With the permission of my primary informants in Vaquería, I have not sought to change their identities; anyone who wished to could figure out who they were anyway. I have not changed the names of most of the communities in which I lived and worked, which could also be easily gleaned from available records. I have, however, changed the names of certain places and of people whom I was not able to ask for permission to reveal. I have concealed the names of most of the people I've called new democrats; since I more often treat these people as tokens of a type, I found it much easier to disguise their identities than those of the specific characters I deal with in the campesino movement. I have also been deliberately vague about people whose politics were at odds with those highlighted in this book, but who were none-theless generous enough to share their time and opinions with me.

The line between what counts as private and public is also difficult to place in relation to state employees and documents. I have avoided naming bureaucrats who agreed to speak to me off the record, and periodically made changes to the narrative or to aspects of their official position so as to make their identities harder to trace. I have changed document numbers for materials to which I was given access but which were not public so as to make them harder to retrieve. In these cases I have also changed the names that appear in the documents. Some of the documents were given to me in photocopied form by activists who treated them as public, and in these cases I followed their example. That is, I have been careful not to leak state documents which I was given permission to view privately in official settings, but I have not tried to conceal those govern-ment documents that already being shared among activists.

I spoke at length with several of the people whose real names appear in these pages about the risks that the text might pose. Some had asked me to use their names when speaking to the media, and asked me to do the same in this book. It is not that people saw no difference between newspaper stories and ethnography, nor that they held simply to some romantic notion of "having their voices heard." Rather, as will become clear, they understood how complex the life of any document can be once it wanders away from its author, but made such documents all the time in the hopes of changing their circumstances, and encouraged me to make my own in that light. The problem of naming is not, in this case or any other, entirely solved by ethnographic convention or "informed consent." Like all of the other words, the names in this book are also irreduc-ibly political.

At the beginning of the twenty-first century, a peculiar
promise held sway in international development circles. Its
central premise was that modern bureaucracies, managing
transparent information, were the key to promoting equality, freedom, and prosperity around the world. This model
of development emerged at the end of the Cold War alongside a host of other projects that have come to be known as
"neoliberalism": structural adjustment programs including
privatization of state industries, outsourcing of public services, deregulation of markets and trade. Most neoliberal
projects, and the premises on which they were based, have
been widely critiqued, and in the wake of financial collapses
in Asia, Latin America, Europe, and the United States, neoliberalism and unfettered deregulation have become unpop-
ular in mainstream political and economic thinking.[1] We
have entered, we are told, the era of "post-neoliberalism."[2]
And yet the model of governance based on bureaucratic
reform remains, and with it many of the catchwords that
were popular in the early 1990s, the heyday of neoliberalism: transparency, accountability, efficiency, anticorruption.
If anything, these promising tropes have thrived and have
been invested with even greater expectation than before.
With deregulation off the table, development is suddenly
to be achieved solely by eliminating waste, streamlining paperwork, making service providers accountable. But if there

is one thing that we should have learned from the twentieth century, it is that simple solutions, premised on simple narratives of development, rarely work out the way they are intended.

The research for this book began during a conflict between peasant farmers and large soybean producers in rural Paraguay, a place and event that might seem far removed from the concerns of bureaucratic reformers or the politics of transparency. But it is precisely on such margins that transparency becomes an interesting research topic. Like many liberal ideas that came before it, transparency presents itself as a universal good that is nonetheless inherently exclusive, and it is people who live inside this contradiction, both embraced and repelled by universal promises, that have the most to tell us about what the phenomenon entails. One of the primary characteristics of being a peasant, or *campesino*, in twenty-first century Paraguay is that while one's poverty and victimization are part of the justification for democratic reforms, one is simultaneously considered a threat to the transparency project. Transparency and democracy are supposed to cure rural poverty, but what most stands in the way of this cure are the rural poor themselves, whose ways of being and thinking are seen by many reformers as inherently undemocratic.

In Paraguay, the word *campesino* usually refers to small farmers with or without land, living in the fertile eastern half of the country. They are numerically important, accounting for at least 20 percent of the population, and at least 83 percent of the farms, although they only own about 4 percent of the total cultivated land.[3] But the real story of the campesinado in Paraguay is about the long struggle of rural people to become involved in national development. People who call themselves campesino today implicitly identify with a struggle for land that has been going on unabated since the early 1960s, when a cotton boom made it possible for smallholders to make some money with family labor, enter the market economy, and become full citizens of their nation.[4] They believed, with rural people all over Latin America, that they and their country could become prosperous if only the vast landholdings of a handful of elites were redistributed to the poor, and if they and their children performed backbreaking work in the cotton fields under a 45°C sun. They were supported in this belief by an intellectual class that believed rural development would eventually bring about democracy, as well as by an authoritarian government that rarely kept its end of the bargain. But as the Cold War ended, the developmental theories of those in power began to shift.

Ever since Paraguay began its post–Cold War experiment, a protracted transition to democracy that lasted from 1989 to 2008, campesinos' attempts to participate politically in their country's development have been regarded by many urban democrats as undermining democracy itself. Campesinos' supposed illiteracy, economic irrationality, and above all their predilection for populist leaders make them a frightening reminder of what democrats think of as the recent authoritarian past, the very thing that transparency reforms are supposed to eliminate. Perhaps most surprising, though, is the fact that most campesinos I know have reacted to this catch-22 not by resisting the ideas of transparency and bureaucratic reform, but by openly embracing them. Many have adopted the very ideas that implicitly exclude them, have tried to make transparency their own, and to adopt new political practices through which they can insinuate themselves into the nooks and crannies of bureaucratic reform. While these legally minded campesino leaders are rarely successful in accomplishing their political ends, their paradoxical existence as unwanted interlopers in a system based on the idea of openness and inclusion serves as a useful vantage point for reexamining the politics of transparency after the Cold War.

TRANSPARENCY AFTER THE COLD WAR

The idea of transparency as a bureaucratic virtue is not entirely new, but in the 1990s it came to prominence as the central idea in at least two international reform projects, one having to do with governance, the other with economic development. The first had its roots in Western criticisms of propaganda and censorship, and state intelligence-gathering in communist countries during the Cold War. The idea that oppressive states manipulated and withheld information from their citizenry was one of the key ideological weapons of the United States during the Cold War, to the point that censorship came to be seen as equivalent to totalitarianism (see Pietz 1988; Franco 2002).[5] The implication was that democracy followed naturally from making "more information" available to the public, and that states which curtailed or distorted information were undemocratic.[6] The arguments made by liberals against propaganda were particularly suggestive, since they implied that public discourse could be divided into two types: that which is transparent, objective, and informative, and that which is deceitful, manipulative, and political. By 1989, the belief that government ought to be based on strong democratic institutions open to its citizenry and streamlined in the way it produced and used information had become the cornerstone of what the World Bank called "good governance" (World Bank 1989; World Bank 1998–1999). This was a stripped-down, procedural model of democracy that was devoid of specific or local content so that it could be patterned into the workings of any state (Diamond 1989). The state became democratic so long as its citizens were adequately informed about their choices, and were free to participate in occasional rituals of choice-making like elections. As such, democracy was in fact formally similar to capitalism—a rule-based playing field on which the rational choices of citizen-consumers equipped with transparent information were to discover and elect optimal governments.

The conceptual similarity between procedural democracy and liberal economics is not coincidental, for transparency's other life began in a branch of microeconomics known as "economics of information," based in part on a rejection of Soviet-style control economies. The principal questions of this economics were laid down by Friedrich Hayek (1945) when he argued that state attempts to control information were not only antidemocratic, but also a drag on the economy.[7] What had begun as a relatively marginal branch of microeconomics during the Cold War came into its own in the 1990s, popularizing the premise that markets cannot achieve efficiency if participants are ill-informed (or asymmetrically informed) about the relative value of the goods that they are buying and selling. Development economists could purportedly find ways of making markets more efficient by improving the availability of information to participants in the market, or by devising end-runs around certain things that were simply unknowable.[8] In a decade where "information technology" was expanding globally and countries were announcing their entry into the "information age," the idea that the production and dissemination of information could have such positive effects was appealing to people of all sorts of political persuasions. Indeed, the strongest advocates of the "information-for-development" approach included conservative disciples of Hayek (e.g., North 1990; de Soto 2000) as well as outspoken critics of neoliberalism (e.g., Stiglitz 1998 and 2002).

During this period, information became the grease of both the market economy and democracy. The failure of democracy and of markets in the Third World were both attributed to a lack of transparent information available to the citizenry.[9] What's most striking about this as a worldview is the way in which it seemed to elude criticism. Even as neoliberalism came under increasingly harsh condemnation in the late 1990s from people within the development apparatus, the argument that information would solve both political and economic ills of all sorts actually increased its influence after hard-edged neoliberalism waned. Explicitly turning away from state-slashing austerity projects, the World Bank suggested in its 1999 World Development Report that investing in "information" and solving multifarious "information problems" were the key to guiding the developing world out of poverty (World Bank 1998–1999).[10] Against the grand projects of the Cold War, in which the World Bank financed massive hydroelectric dams and sought to convert global agriculture to new forms of machine- and chemical-intensive production, there's something almost quaint about the suggestion that what poor people really need is a little more, and a little better, information about their condition.

If development models depend so crucially on this thing called "information," it's worth stepping back and asking what exactly it is. In formal economic models, information is always a kind of pared-down communication, broken down into "signals" with a set value based on the number of different forms a given signal can take—in other words, it is measured as a proportion between actual signals one delivers and the possible signals one might deliver.[11] But in everyday language information is described as a static thing that, even though one cannot touch it, is "contained" in documents and in people's minds. It is an object which circulates in economic systems, a kind of knowledge which economic actors can seek and use, which they can possess, store, share, or hide. That is, information is an object in itself, abstractable in principle from the context in which it is created or interpreted, possessed or lacking; it is knowledge in commodity form, a special kind of object which improves decision-making by helping people to become aware of things beyond a given context. For the most part, information is apprehended discursively, but it is a form of discourse that is overwhelmingly representational. It is not meant to be poetic, to evoke or to stir; it is meant to refer to something in the world, and it is meant to do so truthfully. In a world of confusion and uncertainty, where a rational actor may find it difficult to make decisions, information is certainty itself.[12] In other words, information's value is not intrinsic, but emerges only to the extent that it grants access to something real. The common economic definition of information as "knowledge about values which are important to decision-making" (Rasmusen 1989) says it all—it is the values, which preexist information, that are of interest; information is merely a representation of those values.

Language, of course, does many things other than represent. But it is a peculiar feature of developmental rationality in the twentieth century that the representational qualities of language tends to eclipse other understandings of what language does (Silverstein 2001 [1981]; Crapanzano 1981). Following

Webb Keane (2001), one might say that development discourse is spoken according to a particular "semiotic ideology," the belief that language can, or ought ideally, to work this way. The rise of representationalist ways of thinking can be traced to the Enlightenment, when the work of the mind came to be thought of as separate from the world itself (Foucault 1966; Foucault 1970; Rorty 1979; Hacking 1983). Representationalist governance models matured in the colonial period, an era that ushered in the enduring fascination with mapping (and geometrical space in general), cataloging, registering, building encyclopedias—all in the hopes of building complete representations of the world. As Timothy Mitchell describes these representational practices, they "set up in the social architecture and lived experience of the world what seems an absolute distinction between image (or meaning, or structure) and reality, and thus a distinctive imagination of the real" (2000, 17).

At its height, in the late nineteenth century and early twentieth, British colonial administrators believed that it was possible, at least in principle, to create exhaustive representations of the territories and the peoples they were attempting to rule (see Richards 1992; Mitchell 2002). The entire spectrum of Cold War authoritarian regimes, from the Stalinist Soviet Union to anticommunist Paraguay, exhibited some of the same hubris, a belief that given enough information about the objects of governance, they could run the economy better from a central location. Indeed, part of what ended the Cold War, and made Hayek so prescient in retrospect, was a breakdown in the belief in centralized planning and the aspiration to total knowledge. But if the hubris of complete information control was ultimately abandoned, what remained was a basic semiotic ideology about how communication could ideally work. Transparent representations, too complicated to be known by a central command, merely needed to be dispersed through the whole signaling apparatus that was democratic, market-based society.[13]

If authoritarianism was built on the state's control of information, then democracy is to be built by giving citizens access to, and indeed control over and responsibility for, all information. This ultimately is what a transparent society is supposed to look like: all state knowledge is public knowledge, and citizens can therefore "see" what goes on in government and in the economy, not directly, but by receiving information about it. Transparency is information so complete that it is seems unmediated; it is an access to the real through a medium so perfect as to disappear from the scene it is describing (cf. Morris 2001). This can never be realized, but remains always the ideal: a world of perfect information in which citizens and entrepreneurs can make fully informed decisions about how to organize their society. Capable at last of choosing rationally among political and market options, governments will be held accountable, corruption will decrease accordingly, and markets will become more efficient, leading to better growth, and hoisting developing countries out of poverty.

It is not hard to critique the utopian assumptions of the transparency project, but that ultimately is not the point of this book.[14] My aim is not to critique representational logic, but to treat it as a social fact (cf. Rabinow 1986), as part of the way much of the world now accounts for the real, builds social relationships and institutions, and dreams about the possible. For example, many of the representations described in this book are maps, and maps—even inaccurate, contestable, illegible, distractingly ornate, or dated maps—invite and enable people to do things that they couldn't do otherwise. In rural Paraguay they make a huge difference to how neighbors argue about who owns what piece of land. A map makes it possible to enroll technologies and authorities in support of argument, actors and things that wouldn't otherwise be involved. People without property maps may resort to local knowledge and neighborhood allies to resolve disputes, or if there are hand-written documents, to lawyers who can interpret them. But when a map is added to the relationship, so, too, are surveyors, cadastral agents, and potentially a whole host of public and private technicians, complex technical devices, laws and forms of inscription, development experts, even foreign satellites on which the mapping depends. Though cadastral maps are supposed to make property relations more transparent in the case of conflicts and to make it easier for judges and lawyers to interpret at a distance, their more obvious effect is to dramatically complicate and expand the networks of actors involved in land disputes. Information may not do quite what it is supposed to do in such a case, but it certainly does *something*. As this book shows, the practices of representation that go into creating transparency are saturated at every turn with precisely that aspect of social life that they are meant to get rid of: politics. Indeed, far from stabilizing information, these larger technical networks create new spaces for disagreement and contestation.

A common critique of development in the post–Cold War era is that it is depoliticizing. In a long line of work inspired by Michel Foucault's governmentality lectures (1991), scholars have claimed that the underlying strategy of governance and development is to take political problems and render them technical and bureaucratic.[15] At their simplest, such arguments appear to recapitulate Weber's (1946) old dictum that in modern states bureaucracy becomes an iron cage bereft of human creativity or diversity (see Graeber 2006). But as Tania Li (1999; 2007) has argued, such statements tend to overstate the degree to which developmental projects play out the way they are intended, and everything about the field of these projects remains politicized. I build on this argument by examining a particular aspect of the governmental apparatus—its use of information to promote democracy and economic growth—and suggest that the project has two rather unexpected consequences. First, it creates two classes of citizens: those who are appropriately rational actors in a world of representations, and those who are not. In other words, those who are able to speak in the language of transparency and who are therefore capable of full participation, and those who cannot and can therefore only be governed. This is one of the defining features of campesino life in post–Cold War Paraguay—that no matter how hard campesinos try to become democratic citizens, they are necessarily considered incapable of it. In the post–Cold War era, campesino marginality is justified less in the straightforwardly racial, cultural, and class terms than they used to be, and more in terms of their inability to participate in the information age. Second, though, the relative instability of information leaves immense amounts of room for the politics which it is meant to exclude. Politics may be partially displaced by transparency, from the cotton field and the mayor's living room to the hallways of the public registry in the capital, but it is not diminished.

Perhaps the most notable feature of the politics of transparency is how focused it is on documents. Documents are peculiar sorts of objects which are supposed to contain and organize information. But documents are also bundles of paper (or, increasingly, digital files accessed through expensive, networked computers) whose obdurate materiality undermines the desire for interpretive stability, for transparency. As a burgeoning literature in the anthropology of documents has shown, the meanings made possible by documents are not merely representational, but aesthetic, indexical, and material as well.[16] Documents are always encountered by particular people in particular contexts, and their interpretation is never separable from the contingencies of the encounter. It is via documents that information necessarily comes to be bundled in particular ways, to circulate in particular areas, to be vulnerable to natural disasters and human deception. Most important, it is in the variable interpretive encounters that people create the information that documents supposedly contain.[17] Documents are therefore the place where abstracted representations meet actual, messy contexts, inciting confusion and competing interpretations.

Insofar as they believe information can and should be stable, then, the dream of the transparency reformers is always at some level that documents would just disappear. But the impossibility of this gives rise to bureaucracy's most annoying problem: documents can only ever be fixed by creating more documents, through audits, investigations, and reports.[18]

It is both the underlying exclusivity of the transparency project and the unruliness of documents that give rise to what I call "guerrilla auditing." Guerrilla auditing is the practice of trying to participate in the open flow of government information while being considered a threat to transparency. Very few informational practices actually resemble the idealized version ascribed to them in post–Cold War development practice, but the promise of transparency is more easily achieved when those engaging in information practices are not already marked as ill-suited for the rational space of the public sphere. When guerrilla auditors encounter documents, they unleash undisciplined interpretations and hence novel possibilities into the situations that the documents purport to describe. Moreover, they make obvious that the many different sorts of people who come into contact with the documents, from bureaucrats and lawyers to international reformers and anthropologists, all come to them with very different desires, politics, frames of indexical reference, and habits of interpretation. In these encounters, the proper relationship between representation and reality therefore becomes a terrain of struggle in the sense meant by William Roseberry (1996), the very language in which political projects are articulated and compete with each other.

PARAGUAY'S INFORMATION AGE

The full course of the argument I have just summarized will emerge slowly from a historical and ethnographic description of Paraguayan politics. For those who don't know much about this little country, it bears explaining why the promise of transparency after 1989 was particularly resonant in Paraguay. Until 1989, Paraguay was internationally renowned primarily for the brutality of its secret police, the corruption of its elites, its black market, and the generalized anonymity which attracted all manner of unpleasant characters, from Nazis and fascists to international thieves, exiled dictators, and cult leaders.[19] The country's most accomplished literary figure, Augusto Roa Bastos, had written from exile that "Paraguay is an island surrounded by land," a line that caught on internationally, both among the Paraguayan exile community and among foreigners seeking to understand Paraguay's peculiarity.[20] The popularity of the metaphor showed that Paraguay's isolation had become a existential problem for a certain sector of the population. The image evokes an obscure country yearning for connection. And it is this yearning, for modernity, democracy, and cosmopolitanism, that became one of the defining features of Paraguayan life, particularly in Asunción, after 1989. The post–Cold War world was awash in stories of poverty caused by corruption, crony capitalism, and bureaucratic irregularity, which for many Paraguayans seemed to describe their country's pathology particularly well. In this, the recognition of its universal ailment, Paraguay found its connection to the rest of the world.

Many urban Paraguayans felt that their isolation was economic, cultural, and political. The first problem was a geographical location that conspired to keep it impoverished.[21] It is a small country, with scarcely six million inhabitants as of the last census, and in the late 1990s, over 50 percent of Paraguayans lived outside of major cities, giving it one of the most rural populations in the Western Hemisphere. Paraguay is divided in two parts: 60 percent of the land, from the west bank of the Paraguay River to the border with Bolivia, is desert, and has always been somewhat outside of the national project.[22] What most Paraguayans consider to be the true Paraguay is the eastern half of the country, which comprises extremely fertile land, excellent waterways, and the mestizo population that is iconic of national history. But on the eastern side Paraguay is cut off from the ocean by much larger and more prosperous countries, Argentina and Brazil, which have long seen Paraguay as a backwater and a nuisance. Paraguayans have always felt that their relationship to the rest of the world has been mediated by these giant neighbors, against both of which they fought a famously bloody war in the nineteenth century.[23] Moreover, Paraguay has never had particularly lucrative natural resources, other than those relating to agriculture, nor much of a manufacturing industry. Cold War development schemes largely focused on the production of cash crops, like cotton and tobacco, across the eastern half of the country; these schemes were initially lucrative but quickly became state burdens. In such an economic context, the post–Cold War idea that one might promote economic growth simply by improving information management seemed enormously promising.

A second aspect of the Paraguayan experience which made transparency compelling was the country's linguistic distinctiveness, which caused it to be stigmatized in the rest of Latin America. Paraguay is the only country in the hemisphere in which a majority of the population speaks a single indigenous language, Guaraní, even though they do not politically identify as indigenous.

However, most Paraguayans are to some degree bilingual, in both the indigenous language and in Spanish. In her analysis of Paraguayan bilingualism, Joan Rubin (1968) argued that Spanish and Guaraní have a hierarchical, or "diglossic," relationship.[24] Rubin found that Paraguayans regard Spanish as more formal, prestigious, and rational, and they associate it both with the written form and with urban public spaces. Guaraní, on the other hand, is considered more intimate, vulgar, poetic, oral, and rural. Bilingual Paraguayans address their familiars in Guaraní, but strangers in Spanish. Or, as was often explained to me, Paraguayans regard Guaraní as better for matters of the heart or gut, Spanish as better for matters of the head. Not surprisingly, the differences are also strongly class-based, with elite and middle-class Paraguayans much more likely to speak Spanish as a first language (until recently many such children were forbidden to speak Guaraní at home), while the rural poor encountered Spanish only through schooling (and, more recently, television). In Paraguay this leads to a peculiar linguistic politics: almost all formal state business is conducted and all documents are written in Spanish, a language which the majority find cold, distancing, and snobbish. But most of the hand-shaking, speech-making, and sentimental appeals that make up the bulk of politics are done in Guaraní, a language which much of the elite find lacking in the qualities necessary for rationality and accountability. In other words, Guaraní, the language of choice for a majority of the rural poor, is almost by definition nontransparent to those who now consider themselves to be the managers of Paraguay's new democracy. All liberal democracies are dogged by middle-class fears about the inscrutability of the masses, but in Paraguay the Spanish-speaking elite can actually point to a language to justify this fear.[25]

By far the most important impetus for embracing transparency was the country's historical inability to foster democratic government. In 1989, Paraguay was still ruled by one of the continent's longest-lasting dictators, General Alfredo Stroessner, who had held power since 1954. Internally, Stroessner was immensely powerful, having gained the allegiance of most Paraguayans by collapsing the distinction between the state and his Colorado Party through a huge and increasingly complex system of patronage. Stroessner had a well-deserved reputation for brutality, human-rights abuses, and generally arbitrary ways of governing, but he was supported by the United States through most of his rule for his staunch anticommunist stance (Grow 1981). It is no coincidence, then, that Stroessner saw his support wane through the 1980s, and that he was eventually deposed, as part of a global transition in 1989. The relatively bloodless coup was carried out by Colorado Party insiders, and thus the transition to democracy began with Stroessner's party still in power. The new president, General Andrés Rodríguez, promised to hold free elections in 1992, but whether he would accept electoral defeat remained in doubt. The idea that the coup was the first step toward democracy was therefore pushed most strongly by others: middle-class students and professionals in Asunción, activists, left-wing priests and community organizers in the countryside, and the ex-pats who flooded back into the country in the hopes of rebuilding it. To these people the fact that the Colorado Party retained power was less important than the procedural framework that was being built, a framework for good governance and information distribution which would set the foundations for democracy in the years ahead.

A kind of national euphoria greeted the transitional moment, and especially during the first three years after the coup, rapid political changes and a boom in foreign investment transformed Asunción. A broad coalition opposing the Colorado Party seemed set to create a new country, centered on a new social democratic party called Encuentro Nacional. But the coalition was short-lived, undermined by defeat in the national elections (1993) and the slow fading of the economic miracle. A central argument of this book is that the transition years created two kinds of political subjects in Paraguay, who began as allies in opposition to the Colorado Party, but soon diverged and came to constitute each other as opposites in their aspirations for a national future. The first group were campesinos who found themselves increasingly shut out of the democratic project, and the second, which I call "new democrats," were those who increasingly saw themselves as the sole leaders of the transition. These two groups did not exhaust the identities that one could assume in post–Cold War Paraguay, nor did they form any sort of majority. But they were the two groups that, outside of Colorado *oficialismo*, were most active in the political landscape of the transition. In chapter 1 I explore the history of this divergence in some detail, but here let me sketch their relationship.

Sociologically speaking, new democrats were primarily students and urban professionals tired of the old regime. Most were from relatively elite families in Asunción and were therefore tied in social and familial respects with members of the regime. They shared experiences like attending the Jesuit high school Cristo Rey (often a target of Stroessner's repression) and working as independent scholars, development experts, and artists. A large number had been exiled in successive waves of repression and had returned to Paraguay with a vision of the country that was a product of earlier decades and of a militancy centered on literature, art, and the writing of manifestos. As time went on, this group became far more diverse, joined by ranks of students who were less politically inclined but attracted by the vision of modernity and openness which democracy offered them, and by the business elite that had prospered under Stroessner but now wished to reform their images as supporters of democracy and the new formal economy. The exiles and romantics who yearned for a more socially conscious vision of Paraguay eventually staffed the huge NGO sector that erupted in Asunción in the years after the coup, working as consultants for international agencies. The rest became its professionals, doctors, lawyers, businesspeople, journalists, and entertainers. By the time I did the research for this book, they were less a specific group of people than an identity one could assume, a location from which most of Asunción's middle class and a growing number of rural entrepreneurs thought about the future of their country, aspiring, sometimes despairingly, toward an increasingly far-away democracy.

The specific hope that greater transparency, bureaucratic openness, and elections would eventually lead to a transfer of power was not to be realized for almost two decades. Much to the frustration of new democrats, Colorado candidates won the first four national elections after the transition, even though these elections were seen by the international community as basically fair.[26] But even as the dictator's party stayed in power, the 1990s was a decade of continuous reform in Asunción, of proliferation of information-producing and auditing agencies in Paraguay's capital, from the inauguration of the auditor general's position in the new constitution, to the establishment of a Transparency International office. The national press exploded under its new freedom, reporting daily on corruption scandals at the highest levels of government. Democracy also seemed to bring with it deepening recession and increasing claims by international agencies and Asunción professionals alike that corruption was the primary culprit, and a transparent free market its cure.

But as the transition failed to deliver its promised fruits—new freedoms, new governors, new international respect, new prosperity—those who still invested their political desires in the idea of transparency felt all the more threatened by the various internal forces that kept bringing populist strongmen to power. The fear extended to campesinos, the rural masses who couldn't quite be trusted to participate in rational government, who kept electing the Colorados, and who kept engaging in land invasions and demanding agricultural subsidies out of step with the ideals of the free market. Campesinos had always provided iconic images for a romantic vision of the Paraguayan nation, and as such served as necessary allies to the new democrats. But now they started to look to urbanites like culturally intransigent holdovers from the Cold War, dark, particular, affective, inscrutable, and unreasonable. In short, in this period campesinos came to represent the anachronistic underbelly of a new Paraguayan society, forever impeding the full transition to democracy.

The threat that campesinos pose has been called many things, but perhaps the most convenient term, the one most ripe with liberal ambivalence, is "populism," that aberrant form of politics that seems to threaten democracy everywhere (Panizza 2005; Arditi 2005; Žižek 2006). In Latin America, populism was once considered a "stage" of economic development which preceded liberal democracy (e.g., Germani 1968), but it has continued to resurface since the end of the Cold War as a potential harbinger of transitional failure (Weyland 2003; Demmers et al. 2001). For if liberalism is defined by its basis in the political rationality of individuals, of transparent language and clear rules, then populism is defined by its basis in the irrationality of crowds and leaders who stand outside the law. The defining and most recognizable feature of populism is its use of the category "the people" against elites and institutions (see Laclau 2005). This was precisely the sort of appeal that made Stroessner successful. Focusing his legislative energy on land reform in a country still predominantly rural, he built massive popular support for his regime by promising riches to the rural masses, el pueblo Paraguayo, "the Paraguayan people," a category which connoted rurality, poverty, and Guaraní, and by vowing to protect them against the theft of resources by the landed elite. After the coup, campesino leaders and their supporters continued to promote this vision of the campesinado not only as the marker of a national romantic past, but as the very future of the nation. And it was this very pueblo, remaining after Stroessner was gone in the songs and slogans of the campesino movement, that many new democrats feared in the transition years as the unpredictable fount of political irrationality. As a remainder, el pueblo suggested that campesinos were pathologically nontransparent, for they seemed to move as a mass rather than as individuals, and as such threatened to bring back tyranny and isolation.

GUERRILLA AUDITORS

To understand why this historical situation would give rise to guerrilla auditing, one needs to go to the countryside. I first encountered these activists when I was invited to visit a campesino camp in a settlement called Tekojoja in

BOLIVIA

BRAZIL

PARAGUAY

ARGENTINA

Map
Area

Pedro Juan
Caballero

AMAMBAY

N

CONCEPCIÓN

BRAZIL

Concepción

General Resquín

PRESIDENTE
HAYES

SAN PEDRO

CANINDEYÚ

Paraguay River

Mariscal López

Vaquería

Yhú

CORDILLERA

CAAGUAZÚ

Coronel
Oviedo

Asunción

Caaguazú

Ciudad
del Este

CENTRAL

GUAIRÁ

ALTO
PARANÁ

Villarrica

ARGENTINA

PARAGUARÍ

CAAZAPÁ

ITAPÚA

ÑEEMBUCÚ

MISIONES

Encarnación

ARGENTINA

0   30   60 mi

0   50   100 km

MAP 1. Map of Eastern Paraguay.

the eastern department of Caaguazú. The camp had been built by almost fifty families who had been evicted from their land in the settlement by police paid by larger, richer soybean farmers from a nearby community. The camp was a brutal place to be living, as residents had to huddle against the cold in tarp shelters that the wind was blowing to tatters. The campesinos introduced me to their "kitchen," a single massive pot full of cold rice that had been donated by a friendly neighbor, and showed me where a grove of orange trees had stood until the previous day, when rival farmers had uprooted and dragged away the fruit trees to try to starve them out. They told me about how their gardens had been ploughed, and how much time and money they had put into them before they were destroyed. There was a surprising amount of laughter that day, but it was mostly laughter at what they considered the extremity of their misfortune, as when they told me how quickly they had all contracted diarrhea after moving into the camp, or when they recounted how one friend had been beaten and dragged away by police earlier that morning when he'd been caught stepping back onto the ground from which they had been evicted the week before.

I spent that night in the house of one of the movement's leaders, Jorge Galeano. Jorge was not a squatter himself, nor was he from Tekojoja, but lived in a relatively nice brick house with a well-painted fence on the outskirts of a nearby town called Vaquería. Most surprising was his tiled front room, very clean, with a computer sitting in the corner and a large cabinet full of books and papers, more reminiscent of the lobby of a law office than a campesino hut. Expecting to spend the night listening to more tales of injustice and violence, I found myself instead sitting on a couch going through documents with Jorge, sifting through hundreds of pages of faded photocopies collected over years, of survey maps, legal decisions, and receipts, which to him revealed all the traces of a corrupt state and of a hypocritical legal system. Jorge was living the politics of transparency, the dream that any citizen could access state records and contest them.

Indeed, Jorge's story has the beginnings of a development expert's dream. He and his twin brother, Antonio, were born, in 1960, in the oldest peasant region of the country, just east of Asunción, to a single mother of eight. The family's primary source of income was collecting and selling coconuts. Jorge, the most precocious of his brothers, moved to Asunción, where he put himself through high school by working nights in an alcohol factory. In the 1980s, both brothers moved to the department of Caaguazú, one of the areas of the country being transformed by the land reform. There they met their wives and became involved, through their local church, in the youth movement against Stroessner. Jorge quickly rose in the ranks, and by his early twenties he had become influential in a regional campesino development organization and participated in a number of pressure tactics in Caaguazú to try to force the Stroessner government to redistribute land to landless families. After the coup, Jorge became involved in the Encuentro Nacional alongside opposition politicians from Asunción and was elected to the junta of the department of Caaguazú in the first decentralized elections. There he accumulated experience and accolades and made a fairly good salary.

Jorge had embodied this story of success: he was tall, light-skinned, and always well dressed, and his excellent spoken Spanish meant that he could often pass for a middle-class Asunceño. And yet when I met him, Jorge was destitute once more. The nice front room was all that was left of his wealth—the rest of his house was falling apart. Jorge had left the Encuentro partway through his term on junta because he was disappointed with the party, and he had not been re-elected. For several years he ran small business ventures, did NGO contract work, and tried to start projects with Peace Corps volunteers stationed in Vaquería. He had his local enemies, both those who accused him of corruption while managing NGO projects, and those local Colorado politicians he kept criticizing. But his life was quiet and relatively comfortable. His brother Antonio, meanwhile, had been chased out of a land-reform settlement to the north after mouthing off to local members of the Colorado Party, and had moved his family to Vaquería as well. Somewhere along the line, while Jorge was teaching word-processing to young elites in Vaquería, Antonio implored him to start "working for his people" again.

Antonio, of course, had a story all his own. When I met him, I had no idea that he was Jorge's twin, and wouldn't even have thought they were related. Antonio had embodied an altogether different experience of the democratic transition. He was smaller in stature, darker, more wiry, with fewer teeth. Until I moved in with him, he rarely spoke Spanish, living his life entirely in Guaraní. He had not finished fourth grade, and although he could read enough to get by, he called himself illiterate. He was campesino through-and-through, he would say, che campesinoite,[27] which was both a mark of pride and of self-criticism. And yet Antonio rarely worked in the fields either. He, too, was possessed of an immense charisma, inspiring rare trust among campesinos throughout the district where he lived, and soon in me as well. Antonio was not known for his legal abilities (his shortcomings with technical documents were often repeated to me privately), but rather for being faultlessly selfless in his desire to help others, and fearless in speaking up against injustice. Whereas campesinos would not approach Jorge directly for help any more than they would a Spanish-speaking lawyer (at least until they knew him well), they visited Antonio at all hours of the day or night, for help with land deals, sickness, marital problems, thirst, and death, or simply to report on the movements of soy farmers or the plans of campesinos in nearby communities. He received almost all of them, and regaled them with long speeches and tales to give them the sense that their problems would soon be over.

In 2002, together with a number of their acquaintances from nearby districts, Jorge and Antonio created an organization that they called the Movimiento Agrario y Popular (MAP), aimed at pressuring the government to fulfill the promise of land reform and at improving the economic condition of its members. Jorge abandoned his teaching ventures, and Antonio stopped taking odd jobs for the local cooperative, and in Vaquería they jointly ran the organization. As with most such organizations, the primary goal of MAP was to find and secure land for landless youths on the frontier, and the brothers developed a technique for reconciling land reform with transparency by targeting illegally held estates for expropriation (see chapter 2). But above all else they became known in the area as excellent problem-solvers. Communities from all over Caaguazú with particularly complicated legal or bureaucratic problems would show up to seek the brothers' help and advice. Members called Jorge *orecabaju*, our horse, both because they backed him politically and because he was a tireless worker on their behalf; there was no social, legal, or land problem which he would not try to solve. Antonio, on the other hand, was the trusted face of the organization, and his patio the site of frequent impromptu meetings. His closer acquaintances brought him food, which until I moved into his house and started paying rent was the only dependable income that he, his wife, and his four kids lived on.

Jorge, with his brother backing him up, developed a difficult double life. While living in poverty in Vaquería, he increasingly spent his time in Asunción looking for documents, arguing with bureaucrats and technocrats, trying to figure out the paper trails that linked campesino problems into the archives of the state. Colorados and business interests in Vaquería and Caaguazú hated him for his campaigns against local landowners, and tried to brand him as a guerrilla in the local press. Asunción bureaucrats also couldn't stand him, because he refused to play the roll of the demure campesino requesting help. More often than not, Jorge knew more about the laws and the paperwork than the bureaucrats he encountered, challenging their authority every time he entered an office, producing documents and photocopies of his own that contradicted what they told him to get rid of him. As he became more influential, he began to have run-ins with highly placed technocrats and development experts, who were both intimidated by his abilities and infuriated by the blatantly political tenor of everything he said, as they tried to maintain an image of staid bureaucratic neutrality.

This disapproval of Jorge by elites and bureaucrats is the first thing I mean to evoke with the term "guerrilla auditing." Jorge and others never tried to do anything illegal. In fact, in the spirit of transparency and accountability, they learned the laws, learned how to read bureaucratic documents, gathered documents from state archives, and compiled records of state misdeeds. Jorge did this entirely within his rights as a citizen under the new democratic constitution of 1992, which he knew better than most state employees. I admit I initially found Jorge's approach a somewhat tepid, perhaps safe way of dealing with rural poverty. But, in fact, there was nothing at all easy about it. Jorge had many enemies, from local party bosses and petty criminals to high-ranking members of the government and judiciary. These people regularly threatened him, repeatedly had him arrested on false charges, and on at least one occasion attempted to shoot him, but missed their target and instead killed two of his friends. Jorge's strategy meant that even his supporters didn't entirely understand what he was up to in the countryside, and often worried that he was not actually working in their interests. For this reason he relied on Antonio to give him his grounding, his *base* in the countryside.[28] Jorge always felt this tension, between the hope invested in him and the suspicion that he might lose touch with campesino reality. Being too close in his comportment to urban professionals, Jorge would not have been entirely trusted if not for the fierce loyalty of his campesino twin.

Despite his unthreatening tactics and the manner in which he moved away from his rural beginnings, many new democrats held Jorge in contempt. He had a few supporters in NGOs and activist circles, but development experts, reformers, political analysts, and television reporters treated him like a thug. He embarrassed and annoyed lawyers, judges, and bureaucrats whose profession it was to manipulate documents, and infuriated elites who imagined themselves to have the advantage when it came to legal argumentation. There was only one real difference between Jorge's activities and the kind of scrutiny of public affairs in which new democrats argued all citizens should engage: that his documentary expeditions had an explicit political aim in supporting a sectarian position that new democrats associated with rural populism and authoritarianism. And this is why Jorge's audits were *guerrilla* audits. According to the new democrats, campesino interests were not universal, not unbiased or objective, but sectarian, and immanently violent. If guerrilla auditors saw their actions as a kind of incursion into a world far from their base, new democrats saw that incursion as a threat to the free market and to democracy itself. The blurry line threatened to provincialize new democratic politics, to show them to be interested and political in their own right. In short, new democrats insisted on Jorge's dangerousness so as to maintain the distinction between a universal and a partial public, between the objective reason of liberal democracy and the irrationality of the crowd.

Fortunately, the attempt to exclude from democracy never quite works. Michel de Certeau (1984, 135) once wrote that "reason is written on the no-where of the paper." Guerrilla auditors know that even if the paper contains a nowhere, the paper itself is always necessarily somewhere, and it is that knowledge that underpins their political project. They seek these papers, trace their paths, and reconstruct the processes through which a small group of people have been able to control most of Paraguay's economy. Unlike new democratic auditors, they do not claim to be disinterested professionals in the service of a universal ideal, but understand themselves as an oppressed majority waging a war of position in the archives.[29] Unlike official auditors, they carry out these tasks without subscribing to the representational assumptions of transparency's project. And their view of bureaucracy resembles a war fought with paper, rather than the dispassionate management of information. For that reason, they remain guerrillas in the eyes of political elites, trespassers against civil society, the public sphere, the rule of law, and therefore against the very idea of rational governance.

ETHNOGRAPHIC ENTANGLEMENT

Campesinos and new democrats are characters largely defined by particular kinds of knowledge practices; that is, the primary difference between them is how they claim to know the world. Ethnography is also a knowledge practice, and as such there are conceptual problems that constantly emerge in this sort of analysis. Several exemplary ethnographies of modern knowledge practices have demonstrated that the analysis of such practices runs into a confusion between form and content.[30] In her pathbreaking work on activists who describe what they do through the social-science idiom of "networking," Annelise Riles (2000, 1) says that such phenomena "resist interpretation . . . because they are all too familiar; they share with our interpretive tools a singular aesthetic and set of practices of representation." To describe the activity of such people as "creating networks" would not be to interpret at all, but merely to mimic.[31] I started to feel this same uneasiness early on when, as I attempted to describe what it was to do an ethnography of information-making practices during the transition to democracy, many urban new democrats of my interviewees expressed how happy they were that I would be giving them much-needed information about their society, information which could help them better understand it and thereby improve its chances of becoming more modern and democratic. In other words, they thought that what I was doing was the very thing that I claimed to be studying *others* doing.

This apparent parallelism between what I was doing and what new democrats do all the time often made it difficult to see new democrats as a group apart—they were, as much to me as to themselves, transparent. Similarly, and even more troublingly, both they and I were in the habit of understanding campesinos as a distinct, named cultural object. Indeed, as I will show in chapter 1, rural ethnography and the cultural description of campesinos were always part of the transition project. In other words, the very project of describing how campesinos were marginalized by the culture of transparency participated in the culture of transparency, and therefore in the marginalization itself.

These realizations caused me to change my research in two ways. The first was to name "new democrats," that is, to create a social object which would give the analysis a kind of symmetry which it does not normally have in conversations in Paraguay. New democrats are, in this book, always an analytic interruption in an ethnographic quandary. The second was to try, as well as I could, to adopt Jorge's own research method. Graduate school had primed me very well to look for information before I settled in Paraguay, but it had not prepared me to deal with *documents*. More concretely, it had not prepared me to entangle myself in the infinite interpretive possibilities of a state archive, or even of a small conflict-ridden community, and to cull from those entanglements the details I needed for a provisional account, a useful story.[32]

My apprenticeship reached a crucial turning point in June 2005, seven months after I moved in with Antonio, when I experienced firsthand the effects of being a guerrilla in Paraguay. The event, which occurred in Tekojoja, near the squatter camp I had first visited in 2003, involved another police raid on the community, during which soy farmers destroyed campesino crops and houses. That day ended with a drive-by shooting that killed two people and severely wounded another. Having been asked by acquaintances to photograph the raid, I took pictures from behind a thin orange tree, where, I am told, I cowered rather ludicrously. For better or worse, my ambiguous position in that event temporarily elevated campesino politics to acceptable, national public debate. The first reports about the incident to hit the pages of the national newspaper suggested, despite campesino testimony to the contrary, that campesinos had ambushed soy farmers on a country road and that in the ensuing confrontation two campesinos had been killed, perhaps even shot accidentally by their own idiotic friends. The following day I made my own testimony and pictures available to a rival newspaper, demonstrating that campesinos had been unarmed when they were fired on.[33] It was not until the appearance of my account, which was more transparent to reporters and local prosecutors than the words of campesinos, that the public story changed.

Two things came of this event which are central to this book. The first was that I experienced a fleeting episode of what campesinos call *realidad*, a reality that for campesinos is felt in the body rather than in the transparency-seeking gaze of the new democrat. For me, realidad emerged in bad dreams, in occasional bouts of anger, in skittishness around firecrackers, and in a painful cyst that developed in the back of my throat. I still cannot describe it beyond that, because it is the sort of thing that resists representation or my own powers of evocation, but I was glad when it went away and I could get back to reading and writing. The second, which follows on the first, is that I became implicated in the guerrilla auditors' project in a way that I could not have foreseen. By that I mean simply that I began to produce documents that didn't obey the documentary divide that separated campesinos from the public sphere. I don't claim that any of the articles, pictures, or testimonials I produced had any significant impact on the course of campesino politics, nor am I claiming that this was either good or bad, although I was overwhelmed at the time by the feeling that events had made common research-ethics guidelines largely meaningless. I just mean this as a general statement about how my account is situated, because I consider this book one of any number of documents, few of them authored by me, that emanates from my presence in that orange grove on that cold June afternoon.

I had always seen my relationship to campesinos I met as one of vague solidarity, and I still do. But I think entanglement is a better way of understanding it now, an entanglement made as much by circumstance as by political pre-dilection.[34] My presence in Tekojoja shaped everything about this text. It immediately became impossible for me to speak to many people in the district where I lived, or even to contemplate visiting certain areas, and it changed the ethical and political contours of what I was doing in ways that were out of my control. It destroyed some friendships and strained others. But it also opened up new friendships, conversations, and projects that constituted the rest of my research. Finally, the fact that my name and those of some people I mention in this text are publicly recognized in Paraguay as a result of that event will inevitably shape the way this document is read, where it circulates, and how people engage it.

My circumstantial affinity with certain campesinos should not be mistaken for a celebration of their politics. I don't claim to speak for or to defend campesino projects any more than I intend to repudiate democracy with my critique of certain democratic projects. I'm fully aware, for example, that the very word *campesino* is freighted with a violent, racist, and patriarchal history of its own. This is a problem with any category, including anthropology. I do not dwell there, because those vectors of violence were not the ones that presented themselves to me. This makes my ethnography every bit as partial as Jorge's readings of the land registry. I suspect it will disappoint most new democrats, who will easily find incompleteness, obvious partiality, if not serious representational flaws. It will not provide the kind of information that many people wanted of me.[35] But in the spirit of a guerrilla audit, it's a good enough starting point for an incursion into the discussion of democracy, the changing place of the rural, and the politics of transparency after the Cold War.

1 THE TRANSITION TO DEMOCRACY

When I first visited Paraguay in 1998 and for ten years thereafter, the word democracy was everywhere and always laden
with complicated negative feelings. At the very least, Paraguay was still in a "transition to democracy" which had no
clear end in sight. Since 1989, when the Colorado Party, which
had then been in power for forty-two years, announced that
democracy was coming, Paraguayans had been participating
in open, internationally approved national elections. But the
Colorados had remained in power, and a degree of cynicism
had overtaken most opinions of the transition. Depending
on where and whom I asked, the reasons for these feelings
varied. In Asunción, where most of my conversations were
with middle-class professionals, a longing for democracy
and state reform was still palpable under the deep despair
about the transition, hatred of the Colorados, and fears of a
return to outright dictatorship. In the countryside, or campo,
where I spoke mainly with politically active campesinos,
hatred of the Colorados, often couched in a language of
anti-authoritarianism, was underwritten with ambivalence
about what democracy might actually bring.[1] A common
refrain in the campo was "with Stroessner you couldn't say
what you wanted to say, but you could eat what you wanted
to eat." The politics, aspirations, and worldviews of these
two groups were shaped by the different frustrations of prolonged transition, and they came to be related to each other,

often antagonistically. For while campesinos continued to believe that they epitomized el pueblo Paraguayo, "the Paraguayan people," in Asunción a quite different vision of the country was brewing.

The most powerful actor in Paraguayan politics throughout the transition period remained the Colorado Party, a deep-rooted clientelist network that tied Paraguay's richest families with its poorest and gave the former almost complete control of the military, the judiciary, and the bureaucracy. But if campesinos had carved out their politics in relation to the Colorados throughout the Cold War, they now found they had to negotiate political space with those who increasingly dominated media, business, development organizations, and the school system, and whose primary hope for campesinos was their disappearance. The transition sweeping Paraguay was not about the destruction of traditional campesino culture (although certainly the romantic vision of peasant ways of life reemerged in the debate over these transformations), but rather about the unraveling of a once powerful if fractious historic bloc, organized around a land reform that linked the Colorado Party to campesino economic aspirations. With that unraveling came profound economic and political realignments and a complete overhaul of both the political and the agricultural landscape.

The transition to democracy, whatever else it might have been, was a powerful narrative that organized new democratic politics.[2] The transition produced a publicly legitimated sense of past, present, and future, which in turn created exclusions in time. If the Stroessner government prior to 1989 made a great show of saying that campesinos were the future of the nation, after the coup new democrats increasingly portrayed campesinos as part of the nation's past, and doomed to disappearance. This view of campesino anachronism did not necessarily emerge from overt malevolence toward the rural poor. In the years just after the coup, new democratic politicians, intellectuals, journalists, and social leaders made huge efforts to bring the campesinado into the transition project and to make the narrative of new democratic ascendancy agree with the narrative of rural people's liberation from tyranny. But these projects didn't work out, and over time it became clear that the campesinado simply didn't fit the transitional narrative. Campesinos were eventually held responsible for the continuities associated with a tyrannical past, cultural and bureaucratic elements embarrassingly out of joint with the primary symbols of the coming democracy: transparency, civil society, and the free market.[3] In the worst cases, campesinos were perceived as the frightful masses whose political irrationality might just bring the dictatorship back. At other times they were seen simply to be in the way, a drag on inevitable progress.

CAMPESINOS AND NEW DEMOCRATS

COLD WAR CAMPESINOS

Even in the most dispassionate of analyses, the word *campesino* connotes for Paraguayans a series of cultural, linguistic, and historical associations spanning the gamut between romantic ideals and deeply racist stereotypes.[4] It includes ideas about traditional cultural norms that prevailed among mestizo smallholders in the rural departments closest to Asunción (Caazapá, Guairá, Paraguarí) in the nineteenth century and early twentieth, and the strong populist politics that predominated during Stroessner's reign in the departments that were settled by those same families during the land reform (San Pedro, Caaguazú, Alto Paraná). It also signals a kind of overt identity politics which explicitly retains the stigmatized label to promote a particular view of how the nation should be organized. For those who call themselves campesinos in the twenty-first century, the word is a militant stance against national abandonment and a fierce reiteration of Cold War populism against a political trend away from rural redistribution projects.

The first thing to understand about the stakes of this politics, though, is the degree to which it goes unrecognized as a true politics by most commentaries.[5] For the idea of the campesinado as a passive rabble contains its own theory of what makes campesinos rise up. That theory, formed by liberal fears about the mob's irrationality and potential for violence, goes under the umbrella term *populism*, a style of politics that implies the suspension of rational policymaking in order to pander to the popular masses. In Paraguay, populism is called many things, but most often it goes by the name *caudillismo*, a politics characterized by the leadership of strong men with personal connections to el pueblo Paraguayo, the traditional masses. In the hands of new democrats, caudillismo is a derogatory label for the behavior of acolytes who blindly follow the superficial personalities of *caudillos* (strongmen) instead of the principles of rational deliberation. A comment heard pervasively in analysis of campesino mobilizations is that the majority of people who show up to demonstrations, roadblocks, and land invasions are merely the dupes of cunning, self-interested leaders who know how to attract followers with Guaraní speeches and empty, misleading, or violent rhetoric.

The story of Paraguayan caudillismo goes back at least to the country's independence from Spain, in 1811, after which it was ruled by a succession of the most ruthless dictators in the region.[6] During the transition to democracy, the association of the campesinado with populist leadership evokes the more recent history of land reform that, from 1963 onward, was a central building block of Stroessner's rule. The Colorado Party took power in 1947, during a short but vicious civil war against their traditional rivals, the Liberal Party. General Stroessner, controlling the military wing of the party, assumed the presidency in 1954. He was not personally sympathetic to land reform, which was an idea strongly associated with the Liberals, but other factions in his party were eager to take up the project. Moreover, a regional conversation about land reform throughout Latin America had shifted the debate. Center-left economists from CEPAL (the Economic Commission on Latin America) were arguing that the region's latifundios, vast tracts of land run as private fiefdoms, were "unproductive" and "inefficient" and therefore a drag on the rural economy, and that their redistribution to the rural poor would boost food production and spur national industrialization. The party was fundamentally split on the idea. But by 1960 land reform had been adopted as dogma even by the U.S.-led Alliance for Progress, and Stroessner quickly appointed a proponent of the antilatifundio position to take charge of a colonization project (see Pastore 1972). Juan Manuel Frutos, representing the agrarista wing of the Colorado Party instituted the colonization project that would transform eastern Paraguay and turn the state-granted ten-hectare plot into the defining feature of campesino political life. Frutos enacted the Estatuto Agrario (Paraguay 1963), which established the legal parameters for colonization, and built an institution called the Institute for Rural Welfare (IBR) to carry it out.[7]

For forty years the IBR created colonias throughout the forested eastern half of the country, pioneer settlements intended to grow into thriving peasant communities of titled smallholders. The project, also called the "March to the East," echoed the Brazilian "March to the West," with all its military undertones. (Both were also explicitly modeled on the U.S. frontier of the nineteenth century.) It was seen as a nation-building project which would simultaneously improve the lives of the campesino population and protect the territory from being annexed to Brazil's much larger frontier drive.[8] Between 1963 and 1985, Frutos claimed that the reform had created 661 such colonies, enclosing 130 thousand lotes (plots) on 8.8 million hectares of land (see Frutos 1985, 95). He also claimed that the government had handed out over 400,000 land titles.

Whatever one makes of these numbers, there's no question that the development of the frontier was, alongside the construction of the massive hydroelectric dam at Itaipú, one of the regime's most dramatic economic feats (Roett and Sacks 1991). Families living on very small plots in the central departments of the country headed out to the frontier to take their allotted ten hectares of land, creating new towns, economies, and political organizations. By the time of the coup, in 1989, hundreds of thousands of Paraguayans lived in colonies created by the reform.

The civil war between Liberals and Colorados in the 1940s had severely weakened the Liberal Party in the countryside, and land reform intensified the imbalance, creating an apparatus for rewarding Colorado Party members and for spying on everyone else (see Turner 1993). The Colorado Party became the party of most campesinos, with only a small percentage of Liberal families holding to the opposition party. Stroessner developed a style of fierce anticommunism which served him particularly well during the Cold War. It won him military support from the United States, and in the 1970s, when coups transformed all of Paraguay's neighbors into military dictatorships, it won him allies throughout the region. Despite this it is hard to find much in the Colorado Party's policies to classify it definitively as either Left or Right. What it was was a massive clientelist apparatus that built itself institutionally into the colonial landscape of the frontier.[9]

Even while the party swelled with campesinos, there quickly developed a radical rural politics opposed to the Colorados which further shaped the concept of "campesino." At the outset this was primarily organized around Christian base organizations, collectively called the Ligas Agrarias Cristianas, which claimed land and protested government repression in the 1960s and 1970s (see Fernández 2003; Telesca 2004). Although initially established within the Catholic Church, these followers of liberation theology were increasingly secular, and most of the movement's leaders eventually left the church altogether. The Ligas were violently dismembered in 1976, during a regional crackdown on dissidents.[10] But the influence of liberation theology remained, in the underground Marxist organizations that sprang up in their wake, in the NGOs concerned with human rights and sustainable development, and in the very language of campesino politics as a vindication of "campesino reality" and the "campesino base." As the Stroessner government began to fall apart and was finally overthrown, state commitment to agrarian reform became even more uncertain, and campesino organizations took on the mantle of agrarian reform in protest against the government. These organizations were plagued by infighting, ideological disagreements, and structural frictions, but they all fundamentally stood for a statist model of rural protectionism built on cash-crop production by patriarchal family units in smallholder colonies. In short, the bulk of the campesino movement was never about a wholesale rejection of Stroessner's agenda. Its primary goal was to make the Colorados deliver on their own agrarian promises.

None of this is to downplay the contentiousness of this relationship, or the history of terror, or the violence that Stroessner often meted out to campesino communities that fell out of line. The fearsomeness of Stroessner's military brigades and later police are well documented, and I have heard many stories in the countryside of routine brutality against dissidents and petty thieves, not to mention the daily pall of fear that most people felt about speaking out against the regime.[11] Yet, however violent the dispute between the state and campesino organizations became at different moments during Stroessner's reign, both were committed to a similar strategy for national development. It is on that basis that I suggest one of Stroessner's successes was the creation of a powerful historic bloc based on a singular philosophy of land use, development, and ultimately of the nation-state itself.[12] It is an uncomfortable history for many campesinos, and it certainly doesn't serve them in the present conjuncture, but that strong tie still comes out in conversations even with some of the most vociferously anti-Colorado leaders. One such leader, who was known in the area for making powerful speeches in which he attacked any and all of his opponents for being Stronistas, surprised me during an interview when I asked him to describe the moment of the coup. He and I had been talking about the late 1980s—a time during which he and other landless youths would meet secretly in the local church to avoid Colorado spies—when I asked him how he had felt on hearing that Stroessner had been overthrown. Without pause he answered that it had been one of the scariest moments in his life. "It was so uncertain," he said. "El General was the one who protected us."

Sure enough, the land-reform project began to disintegrate soon after the coup. But in the early twenty-first century that project continues to be the benchmark by which campesinos talk about their economic, political, and cultural aspirations. Simply to call oneself campesino, particularly in the areas affected by the reform, is a sign of the desire and right to live in these colonias. It was this desire that drove the massive pioneering effort that continues today, with young men leaving their parents' homesteads in their late teens to look for their own plot of forest. The premises of the land reform were always highly paternalistic. Campesino rights to land were never simply recognized. Instead, beneficiaries of the reform had to prove their worth as rational economic subjects capable of properly applying their labor to the land, a process through which they would be phased into full ownership and full personhood. But however hierarchical the land reform may have been, it interpellated a massive class of rural people who were eager to live out this process of self-realization.

This narrative about land and self-realization emerged consistently as I spoke to campesinos around Vaquería. Most self-identified campesino men whom I met in Paraguay could either recite a life-story which matched the basic premises of the narrative or expected that at some point they would be able to claim land on the frontier and create a homestead. Even for the many young people (particularly young women) who envisioned a different future opening through educational reform, homesteading remained their fall-back plan. The Estatuto Agrario and the IBR therefore continued to be vital institutions for campesinos. Love it or hate it, all recognized the IBR as the state institution that made these aspirations possible. For several months after the coup, campesinos flooded into IBR headquarters in Asunción, creating a documentary logjam of demands and actually blocking the halls, so that bureaucrats felt they were under siege. While new democrats took over the universities and the media and parts of the courthouse, campesinos headed to that arm of the state that they cherished most. Regional offices of the IBR were taken by force repeatedly during the transition. And even as they become much more familiar with the courthouse, the public registry, and the ministry of agriculture, campesino leaders in the twenty-first century talk about the IBR as the place they gained access to the state, their training ground in dealing with bureaucracy.

For the purposes of this book, therefore, the word *campesino* refers less to a demographic category than to what one might call a *structure of aspiration*, building on Raymond Williams's "structures of feeling" (1977). Nobody ever claims that being campesino is good or easy—a catholic lament about suffering in the present is still a crucial part of what drives campesino orientation toward the future. The campesino narrative combines nationalist ideals with a Christian desire for redemption and a developmentalist sensibility about hard work and economic rewards. Campesinos, in short, are those people who still believe that back-breaking work in cotton fields can or should lead to some kind of betterment in their lives, and that this promise should be backed by the state. When campesinos do abandon this way of thinking, they cease to be campesinos. In my interviews, people were adamant about this language. Those who went to the city were described as *trabajadores* (workers), *prostitutas*, *mendigos* (beggars), or, worse, *tembiguái* (servants or lackeys).

In every community I visited people told me about neighbors who had moved the city and simply disappeared from their social universe. Notably, some people ceased to be campesinos without even moving. Those with land who disso-ciated themselves from campesino organizations and entered into contract agreements with large soy farmers stopped calling themselves campesinos or even *agricultores*, the bureaucratic catchall that most campesinos used to declare their profession when dealing with the state. Most of those planting soybeans on mechanized fields referred to themselves as *productores* rather than campesi-nos. In areas like Vaquería, where the conflict had moved the point of violence, productores insisted on the change of terminology as a political strategy. To these people, campesino was a residual category, soon to be overtaken by a fully capitalist approach to agriculture.[13] Campesino was a sign of backwardness, but more important, of laziness, ignorance, and misdirected militancy.[14] The appearance of productores, along with the movement of many campesinos to the city, simply made many of those who decided to stay all the more militant.

THE RISE OF THE NEW DEMOCRATS

Unlike campesinos, new democrats do not consider themselves to be a group apart. Most would probably not recognize themselves in the description that I will give, and certainly the name is something I've invented whole cloth. New democrats began as a small, educated elite in Asunción, but their increasing influence over news media, social analysis, public criticism, and international relations have positioned them as exceptionally powerful image-makers. But the biggest difficulty in defining new democrats comes from the success they have in positioning their values and politics as universal, and therefore not as socially located in any way. New democrats produce Paraguay's self-analysis, a description from which they have written themselves out.[15] As analysts, they disappear into the normative undercurrent of liberal social science, that con-stituency that desires nothing but the universal good: democracy, freedom, citi-zenship, political transparency, and the sovereignty of a rational public sphere over the arbitrary caprices of corrupt leaders.[16] The primary reason for naming new democrats is to resituate democracy in its specific social history, and to see all of the universalist tropes that arise in their self-description as "engaged universals," ideas whose universality is an effect of their repeated iteration, in quite different forms, in different social, political, and material situations.[17] Democracy is a global project only to the extent that it is associated with citizens who successfully transcend the national.

If campesinos have always been thought of as representing el pueblo Paraguayo, a way of talking about the mass as a repository of national values, then new democrats prefer to think of themselves as *el público*. This is a post-Stroessner construction, present in references to public opinion and public discontent, but more subtly in reference to transparency: for anything to be transparent, it must be so to someone, and that someone is most often "the public," those anonymous eyes that hold vigil over government behavior. Although ideas about public politics have been present since the founding of the Paraguayan republic, nearly two centuries of repression and censorship meant that most Paraguayans identified more strongly with party loyalty than with the kind of individualized citizenship that inhabits a public sphere (see Morínigo and Brítez 2004). During the transition to democracy, however, this began to switch, and el público emerged as an entity which had opinions and political will to which parties were subordinate. It also emerged as the possessor of goods whose appropriation by politicians for private use would be called "corruption."[18]

El público is not an iteration of a universal good suddenly liberated in Paraguay once Stroessner was gone, but a community of discourse that existed before the coup among a narrow but growing group of intellectuals in Asunción and abroad that was able to consolidate its claim to universality after the coup. Like Stroessner's Colorados, these intellectuals were not necessarily of the Left or Right, but a group defined primarily in opposition to Stroessner's clientelist apparatus. They began as artists, critics, and literary figures in Asunción and in the exile communities during the dictatorship, a "community of interpretation" (Cavallo and Chartier 1999) that coalesced around the circulation of particular texts. After the coup, they became dominant in news media and extended their influence out into an increasingly educated urban citizenry, which demanded to be informed about the workings of the government and economy. Their increasingly successful claim to a universal position as liberal citizens of post-Stroessner Paraguay marked a transformation of Paraguayan society which implicated them in a realignment with Colorados and campesinos. Eventually, they ceased to see themselves as a particular constituency allied with foreign interests, and came to see themselves more like the bearers of truly universal values, in contrast to whom everyone else is recognized as driven by particular interests.

This is not to say that new democrats didn't have different political views, that they didn't identify with the left or the right, or ally with other segments of Paraguayan society. Nor did they emerge as some sort of internally formless mass—they too bore the mark of individual successes and failures during the Stroessner regime. Their distinctiveness arose from a new kind of political argumentation that could take many positions but needed to conform to a democratic aesthetic. For example, the two newspapers that dominated news reporting in Paraguay during this period, ABC Color and Última Hora, key venues for the new democratic voice, were owned by extremely wealthy monopolists, economic conservatives who owed much of their wealth to their past and present relationships with the Colorado Party. Nonetheless, with different political inflections, both used their business and media empires to reposition themselves as democrats after the coup, allying with the internationalist values of the anti-Stroessner camp. In particular, by allowing their newspapers to print a range of opinions they could position their own opinions as rational and deliberative, as elements of a properly public opinion about matters of national concern. So while many new democrats held opinions completely at odds with those usually expressed in ABC Color, for example, most recognized them as legitimate opinions, in contrast to the quaint, ignorant, or simply incomprehensible opinions of campesinos.[19]

But the analytic problem of engaged universals runs somewhat deeper for a rural anthropology, because though they do not name themselves as a group, new democrats are very fond of speaking about campesinos as a culture apart. That is, part of what defines them is their facility with playing the anthropologist. New democrats believe that a commitment to political transparency means being as objectively informed as possible about the society they live in, and so tend to talk about Paraguay in social-science terms. And in the portrait they paint, new democrats, and the cosmopolitans they engage with, are the vanishing subject of the objective gaze. The primary characteristic of the new democratic experience in the transitional years is the way they fail to see themselves as a particular group; it is precisely through the objectification of others, in particular "campesinos," that new democrats disappear from their own social descriptions, and often from those written by foreigners.[20]

Though new democrats seem virtually invisible on the streets of Paraguay's cities in the twenty-first century, it is worth remembering that prior to 1989 they were not there at all. Like so many other successful dictators, Stroessner managed to purge much of Paraguay's intellectual opposition in the first decade of his rule (Paredes 2004). The small number that remained in Asunción were usually members of elite families protected by their ties to the regime, but the most spirited intellectual opposition existed abroad.[21] Political exile is a long tradition in Latin America, dating back to before independence, but no country has had a larger proportion of its professionals and intellectuals in exile than Paraguay, which sent hundreds of thousands of Stroessner's opponents to neighboring countries and later to Spain, France, the United States, Sweden, and Costa Rica (see Rowe and Whitfield 1987). But as many of these intellectuals learned in the cafés of Buenos Aires or the art galleries of Madrid, "exile is a University . . . a freeing of boundaries, a place of cross-fertilisations previously impeded by political frontiers which do not correspond to cultural necessities" (ibid., 235). Adding to a spirited underground movement in the country, Paraguayan exiles created an artistic and intellectual tradition out of critiquing their government and developing angry analyses of a history of violence and repression. In comparison to the dictators in neighboring countries, Stroessner was neither particularly violent, nor totalitarian in his ambitions. But the critics of his regime followed a mode of Cold War representation that linked them to the likes of George Orwell and Hannah Arendt. They objectified the dictatorship as a historical block called the "Stronato" and saw it as an iteration of the Cold War's "theoretical anchor, the idea of totalitarianism" (Pietz 1988; see also Guilhot 2005).

By far the best-known critic of Stroessner was the novelist Augusto Roa Bastos, who lived the entire Stronato in exile. In his masterful novel, *Yo el Supremo* (*I the Supreme*), which appeared in 1971, Roa Bastos developed a paranoid and unstable voice meant to reflect the interior of a despotic ruler's mind. The novel is actually about Paraguay's first dictator, José Rodríguez de Francia, who ruled the country from 1811 to 1840 and was renowned for extreme isolationism, quasi-socialistic policies, and violence against foreigners. The novel is written as Francia's internal monologue, and is both a terrifying indictment of totalitarianism and a mockery of it, since the narrator's will to despotism doesn't offer him control even over the narrative "I" which is relentlessly polyphonic, meandering, and even treacherous. One way or another, it establishes the singular fear of Paraguay's liberal intellectual class, the fear of a polity which is coterminous with the unstable mind of its ruler (Franco 2002). Roa Bastos's work admits no outside from which to dispassionately view the political travails of the nation. And yet when people in Asunción casually mention the work, it is usually as a tale of ideology gone awry.[22] It is not the work, then, so much as its reading, that turns it into a standard indictment of totalitarianism, of a will to mind control from which objectivity and rationality is the only true freedom.

The totalitarianism described by works like Yo el Supremo also handily epitomizes another feature of Cold War discourse. Totalitarianism finds its roots in primitivist elements of Paraguayan life, and this is where the campesinado is enrolled in a complicated position. Paraguayan intellectuals have long sought the roots of national popular culture in the link between campesino and indigenous worldviews. From the 1960s onward, this rural mestizo population was the subject of a kind of nationalist anthropology which sought to uncover in their language and customs the essence of the people, or "Paraguay profundo" (deep Paraguay).[23] The most important producers of this anthropology were the Jesuit priests who worked tirelessly with campesinos during the years of the Ligas Agrarias. Familiar cultural traits emerged: communism, anarchy, communitarianism, a wise mythology, a naturalist disposition, and an indomitable survival instinct. But inevitably, these writers and artists also found the roots of Paraguay's seemingly unshakable relationship with authoritarianism in the quasi-primitive, almost presocial worldview of the rural masses. As Roa Bastos came to fear in the later years of the regime, Stroessner was not a singular tyrant but rather the product of a cultural disease. "Like all authoritarian regimes," he wrote, Stroessner's "case leads on to wider questions of social and historical pathology. Its roots are anthropological—that is, cultural—the product of a degraded anti-culture which reflects on the whole of the society in which such phenomena occur, and which are defects in its very nature, part of that 'recurring nightmare that is its history'" (1987: 221–22).

The literary genre that most clearly expressed this view was launched, probably unintentionally, by Saro Vera, a campesino priest whose clerical practice led him to reflect on the most basic of rural character traits, all rooted in the culture of their indigenous forebears. Vera's book, El Paraguayo: Un hombre fuera de su mundo (The Paraguayan: A Man Outside of His World) (1993 [1980]), popularized the three "laws" of Paraguayan behavior, encapsulated in three Guaraní words: vaivai, ñembotavy, and mbarete. Vaivai is a common expression for mediocrity, and the "law" evokes campesino resignation to a life of underachievement and misfortune. Ñembotavy is the practice of acting dumb (literally, "to make oneself stupid"), the idea that campesinos act stupidly in order to avoid responsibility for their actions. And the ley del mbarete, from the Guaraní word for "strength," is the most important of these, expressing the general sentiment that campesinos will respect only the authority of a strongman.

Saro Vera meant all of this quite seriously, and there's an earnestness and even deep respect in the way he treats these familiar tropes about the uncivilized mass as a problem of the Christian educator. But the three laws quickly became staples of a more humorous brand of such books, dubbed *paraguayología* by Helio Vera (no relation), one of the country's best-known satirists. Helio Vera's lampoon of Paraguayan culture, *En busca del hueso perdido* (In Search of the Lost Bone) (1988), became a favorite underground text while it was banned, during the final years of the dictatorship, and a bestseller after the coup. Books and articles of *paraguayología* were written as tongue-in-cheek, self-deprecating looks at a national identity that the authors claimed as their own. But one can easily detect an important separation that the books establish, between literate, Spanish-speaking authors in Asunción, writing for an audience similar to themselves, and the true bearers of Paraguay's backward culture, Guaraní-speaking campesinos with little access to books.[24] Even the title *En busca del hueso perdido* establishes the narrative voice of *paraguayología* as one that looks down from on high. The premise is built around an apocryphal story in which the dictator Francia asks his doctor to conduct tests on Paraguayans to see if they might be missing a bone in their neck that would allow them to hold their head high. Unlike *Yo el Supremo*, which attacks Francia viciously, *paraguayología* adopts his position of bemusement with the masses. The witty, 300-page riff on this and other campesino stereotypes is therefore told from a position of sovereignty and detachment more like that of a despot than a critic or even an educator. And it establishes better than any other the new democratic voice, analyzing the problem of authoritarianism in an objectification of campesino culture from which it stands ironically detached. Indeed, if there is one thing that unites this group more than anything else, it is the ability to speak both earnestly and mockingly about campesinos in these very terms, often with direct reference to these original texts.

New democrats coalesced as a group around these and other critical texts in the late 1980s and early 1990s. Most were still very sympathetic with campesino and indigenous concerns, seeing their problems as due to the dictatorship which needed to be overcome, but always with that hint of anxiety that Roa Bastos had so carefully expressed. New democrats were the seers of a newly objectified national culture, meeting at book launches, concerts, vernissages, and political meetings. The returning exiles, old student leaders, and liberation-theology priests all had an aura of untouchability and incorruptibility for having been victims of the exile, and the group that formed around them came to see themselves as the heirs and leaders of Paraguay's new democracy. The broad consensus among this group in the early days was that the Stronato should be replaced with a kind of inclusive social democracy, an idea that coalesced around a new political party called the Encuentro Nacional, or National Encounter, of which Roa Bastos was a strong and vocal supporter. The Encuentro Nacional was run by new democrats, but it created an umbrella for all who dissented against the regime, including many campesino organizations.

Despite the stereotypes of the campesinado that helped to define the new democratic view of Paraguay, in the years after the coup new democrats viewed campesinos as their natural allies, the humble masses who would embrace their freedom from Stroessner's tyranny. A certain segment of new democrats, often referred to as *campesinistas*, a committed group of social scientists and NGO workers, was at the forefront of this position, and remained so throughout the transition. But by and large new democrats' public opinion was not long in turning against the campesinos. When I spoke to people in Asunción about my research with campesino organizations, I often heard this opinion: that the Ligas Agrarias, the organizations repressed by Stroessner in the 1970s, had fought nobly against the dictatorship, but that now these same organizations were ruining the country. Outside of the small circles of leftist sociologists with whom I planned my research, it was hard to find any sympathy for the marches, roadblocks, and land invasions through which campesinos made it onto the nightly news.

Indeed, by then the face of the new democrats had changed considerably, following a global trend that had emerged at the end of the Cold War. As Nicolas Guilhot (2005) argues, one of the key steps in this transformation was the professionalization of political activism in the form of human-rights and environmentalist NGOs. Throughout in the early 1990s, NGOs multiplied rapidly in Asunción, staffed by new democrats who converted their earlier radical thinking into rights-based thinking that was inoffensive to international donors. The flagship social reform in the early years was not redistributive at all, but rather a World Bank–funded overhaul of the education system run by left-leaning sociologists. The Encuentro Nacional Party fizzled and many of its urban members formed a new party called Patria Querida, dropping their social democratic aspirations and adopting a hard-line free-market approach to reform. By the end of the decade, many businesses, organizations, and government watchdogs had achieved a degree of professionalism previously unheard of, as the new middle class learned to adopt a universalist, new democratic aesthetic.

By the time I began research, in 2004, young new democrats were far less political, aside from a small cadre of university students. In fact, they were less a clearly delineated group than marked by a view of their country's transition shared by most young middle-class Asunceños, their once crisp ideology given over to a vague desire for modernity, professionalism, and cosmopolitanism. But it was not an equal-opportunity position. For instance, well-educated Colorados could easily engage in politics as new democrats by making rational arguments for supporting the regime during polite conversation with middle-class opponents. Conversely, campesinos found it far harder to adopt a new democratic position, even though they were supposed to benefit from the new democratic project. Class, education, physical disposition, language, and the taint of rural populism stood in their way.

This taint even held for older new democratic supporters of campesinos. Among the second generation of new democrats, the campesinistas were looking increasingly dated, and had even come to be known as *setentistas* (seventies-ists), people whose radical ideas had not changed in thirty years and who were a bit of an embarrassment to young professionals. Ángel, a friend of mine in his late thirties, and once an eager student of campesinista literature, described the change bluntly. In the 1990s, he said, "you started realizing that every time you went to a book launch you saw the same people there. We were just talking to each other. . . . But they are out of touch now. Theirs is the politics of victimization, of complaint. . . . My Paraguay has changed. My Paraguay is the businessmen in Asunción, the Mennonites farming milk, the Ukranians producing mate, the Brazilians growing soybeans, the Koreans who run the markets. This is a cosmopolitan country, an urban country. It's not some barefoot guy sitting under his shade tree with his straw hat drinking terere.[25] That's the past." By the twenty-first century, this had become the new orthodoxy of urban new democrats, such that on the middle-class patios of Asunción it was far more common to find Colorados openly but calmly espousing the virtues of their party than it was to find dissidents espousing land reform and a greater political role for campesinos.

Bare feet, terere, straw hats, and shade trees had all, at one point, been icons of Paraguayan nationhood, but they were also icons of a dictatorial pathology, and somewhere in that first fifteen years of transition to democracy the scale had tipped. In the early twenty-first century, the view that campesinos were dupes corrupted by charismatic leaders was often the most generous thing that Asunceños told me about them. More than a few times people brought up Saro

Vera's *ley del mbarete*, the law of strength, both to appeal to my desire for anthropological explanation of their country, and to show why the people weren't necessarily to blame. Under this lay a deep-seated concern that campesinos were, by definition, populist animals, swayed only by strongmen, and therefore incapable of participating fully in political debate. That Stroessner's party still held power fifteen years after the coup was widely blamed on campesinos who were known to vote for it in great numbers.[26]

It should be clear that the new democrats were not the undisputed center of Paraguayan national life during the transition. From their point of view, the state remained largely under the control of old Colorado operatives and their supporters, throwbacks to the Stronato. But if they hadn't yet managed to control the state or large segments of the economy, they had nonetheless staked their ground in a particular view of democratic civil society and developed a way of representing Paraguay which positioned them as the natural successors to Paraguay's tenacious but fading past. They had successfully claimed the principles of freedom, transparency, cosmopolitanism, and public rationality as their own. And in so doing they had vanished as an interest group and become the representatives of a universal civic virtue which rose above the mere politics of campesinos.[27] New democrats were finally fulfilling the cosmopolitan identity that had been bred in exile and brought back to Asunción to take up the fight for liberal universals. It is telling that in 1989, just as he prepared to return to Paraguay after forty years of exile, Augusto Roa Bastos was awarded the Cervantes Prize for Hispanic literature, the highest international honor ever conferred on a Paraguayan artist. But even as he returned to fight alongside the oppressed for a more democratic Paraguay, Roa Bastos and those around him were unintentionally sowing seeds for a new Paraguay free of campesinos. Indeed, Roa Bastos may have been more prescient than anyone cared to admit. Jean Franco argues that implicit in Roa Bastos's 1960 book *Hijo de hombre* is the anxiety "that the intellectual's separation from the people inevitably implies his treachery to their cause" (1987, 276).

THREE TALES OF TRANSITION

The three stories that follow are key episodes of the emergence of this new sphere and the constituency that occupies it. Versions of these stories circulate in newspapers, literature, and around Sunday afternoon *asados* (barbecues) in Asunción, and continue to fuel a publishing industry that holds lavish book launches in Asunción. They are stories of the end of the Stronato, and of professionals and students claiming the historical stage. In short, they are stories of a new nation, and campesinos, once the heart of that nation, are almost absent from the mythology of this ascendant group.

TRANSPARENCY: THE ARCHIVE OF TERROR

The Palacio de Justicia, Paraguay's national courthouse, is a massive building sitting high on the hill in one of Asunción's older suburbs. It is the nerve center of all that the new democrats hate about contemporary Paraguay. Even as the executive and congress made great concessions to some version of democracy throughout the 1990s, the judiciary remained a hide-bound institution ruled by arcane protocols and magistrates appointed by Colorado governments dating back to Stroessner's days. If there were any question about the origin of the building, a giant brass plaque commemorating Stroessner's government still faces the front door. Beyond that, in a large marble lobby, Mary and child stand watch over the small doors to slow, overused elevators. Most of the people coming and going are young white men in suits, either lawyers or *gestores*, those paid to chase documents and put pressure on members of the court. They speak mostly in Spanish, but will address the elevator operator in Guaraní.

But if the rest of the building is a testament to government inefficiency and Colorado influence, there is a room on the first floor which is a glaring exception to that rule. The door is marked "Museo de la justicia," and opening it unleashes a blast of frigid air conditioning and bright lights on a room full of glass cases depicting the barbarity of Paraguay's past correctional practices. Behind this are the documents, known colloquially as the "archivo del terror," preserved from Stroessner's secret police. When I first visited it, the archivo del terror was housed in a nondescript room on the eighth floor, but on any given afternoon it was filled with researchers and high-school classes learning about Stroessner's excesses. The archive housed hundreds of thousands of pages in the form of documents generated by the dictatorship for the sole purpose of keeping track of dissidents. The staff were friendly and happy to give tours of the different kinds of information collected by Stroessner's police, or to help people find files on family members, or even on themselves. At the time, the "archive of terror" was Paraguay's primary instrument of democratic memory-work. It was the new democrats' foothold in the Palacio de Justicia, the monument to their own theory of dictatorship, information, and transparency.

In a suggestive moment toward the end of his Freudian meditation on archives, Derrida (1996) suggests that archives always bear within them a tension between totalitarian and democratic utopias, the tension between patriarchy and parricide. He is musing about the parricidal moment in *Civilization and Its Discontents* (1930) when Freud recounts the birth of society, when the sons of the patriarch rise up and collectively kill their father. That moment marks the death of one form of authority and the birth of a new one which is horizontal rather than hierarchical. This authority "is at best the takeover of the archive by the brothers. The equality and the liberty of brothers. A certain, still vivacious idea of democracy" (Derrida 1996, 195).

Stroessner was just such a patriarch, one of so many symbolically beheaded at the end of the Cold War (Borneman 2004). The quick, virtually bloodless coup which removed him was interpreted by new democrats as a moment of release, not just of a captive citizenry, but also of information. Free expression was one of the defining struggles of the end of the Cold War, in both communist and dictatorial states (Franco 2002), and within days of the coup, Asunceños began to employ their newfound freedom of speech. The presses started up again at ABC *Color*, the cantankerous national newspaper that Stroessner had shut down five years previously, and NGOs used to publishing clandestine leaflets were converted into official presses for the publication of popular political voices. Some of these were explicitly projects of inclusion and alliance-building. Jesuit and campesinista NGOs tried to portray campesinos as victims of the dictatorship and therefore as heirs of the new democracy. The best-known example of this project is the five volumes put out by a Jesuit NGO called CEPAG, between 1990 and 1991.[28] These were simply printed oral testimonials of campesinos who had suffered during Stroessner's repression of the Agrarian Leagues. The last of these was titled *Ko'ãga roñe'ẽta* (Now We Will Speak), and all drew on the image of the oral testimonial as the expression of freedom. But these early documents were more than just speech—they were speech conferred to paper, and they made an implicit demonstration of what sorts of speech counted as free and legitimate. The testimonies were transcribed in Guaraní (a language which everyone could speak but few could read) and followed by their Spanish translation.

This was both a political statement for inclusion and, unintentionally, an affirmation that free speech was also fundamentally the freedom to write. For new democrats, writing is the preferred medium for making speech public and historical, and it is virtually impossible in Guaraní because Guaraní remains, more than a language, an index of orality.[29] The attempt to make Guaraní writing public in works like those of CEPAG was therefore highly significant, but it was only an interim step. The Spanish translation was necessary for the testimonials to be read. And this is what marks one of the unacknowledged companions of the right to free speech, not the right to speak or write, but the far more complicated right to *read*. It was reading more than speaking that defined the new public sphere as the arena in which citizens could be informed and vigilant about the actions of the state or other corporate bodies around them (see Hultin 2007). Legitimate public opinion is informed opinion, limited by the ability to read and the level of interest in reading.

Paraguay's constitution of 1992 represented the new democrats' first institutionalization of the right to read as a core democratic principle.[30] Article 135, "Habeas Data," adapted from the Brazilian constitution of 1988, was, at the moment when it was enacted, the strongest privacy of information provision in the world.[31] Article 135 allowed people to solicit, at no cost, access to any data about themselves contained in any archive, to be made aware of the purpose of this data, and to contest its veracity. Heralded as an adaptation to the Information Age by some (e.g., Guadamuz 2001), its symbolic importance in Latin America clearly had more to do with the history of secret police activity during dictatorships and with that growing buzzword of procedural democracy, *transparency*.

The great narrative flourish was added when, only months after the adoption of the constitution, a Habeas Data writ was used to unearth the most extensive known archive of police brutality in Latin America, laying bare the excesses of Stroessner's regime, and also dramatizing the extent to which the private control of documents can lead to the control of people (see Blanton 2008, 63). The discovery came as part of a lawsuit filed against the government by a doctor named Martín Almada for the persecution he had suffered under the regime. It was in late 1992, in the dense political moment between the signing of the constitution and the first democratic elections, that Judge José Agustín Fernández announced that he had discovered a massive cache of documents in an obscure suburban police station. Reflecting on the moment, Almada called the discovery of the documents Paraguay's "storming of the Bastille" (Boccia Paz, González, and Aguilar 1994, 26). It's an interesting metaphor. In the original storming of the Bastille, an angry mob attacked a prison and liberated inmates unjustly held by the king. But in the Paraguayan version, it is a judge flanked by reporters who represents the people, and rather than liberating prisoners,

FIGURE 1. Sorting the *Archivo del terror*. (Courtesy of *ABC Color*)

the Paraguayan storming liberated nearly two tons of documents, making them available to be read by anyone with the time and education to do so.

The story of power revealed by the archive is one wherein to inscribe is to know, and to know makes it possible to kill. Stroessner's control of information achieved through spying and torture was one of the keys to his regime of fear, where anyone could be a *pyrague* (hairy-foot, or spy), and informants' reports were known to travel up through the Colorado Party's *seccionales* (a hierarchical system of local committees and police linked to the ministry of the interior). The information was used by the department of technical matters, la Técnica, the euphemistically named interrogation headquarters in downtown Asunción. As the regime solidified, through the 1950s and 1960s, so, too, did its ability to gather information, and with every success, the archive grew and became more organized. By the mid-1970s, under the maniacal tutelage of Pastor Coronel (known among activists as the Pastor of Death), the department had grown from an ad hoc depository of snitching into a professional investigative unit, with full-time police investigators and a massive network of trusted informants. They recorded everything, from the suspicions of *seccionaleros* in the interior, to the photographs of campesino activists who had died of "acute pulmonary oedema" in the bathtub in the corner of the department itself (Boccia Paz, González, and Aguilar 1994).

After the documents were rescued from the bowels of the Lambaré police station, they were moved into the Palacio de Justicia where they became the archivo del terror. The archive's new home marked the transfer of documents from one regime of political value to another. In the first, they could be consulted by police and party operatives to find and silence dissidents, while in the second they could be used by anyone to investigate past injustices of the regime itself. This was not only the apparatus of Stroessner's brutal repression laid out for all to see, but was also the demonstration of a particular will to representational power. The archivo was built slowly through a particular fantasy of exhaustively knowing and thereby controlling a territory and populace.[32] The conviction that to archive is to know, and to know is to rule was apparently so strong that many of Stroessner's cronies could not bring themselves to destroy the archive, even three years after he was deposed, a refusal which ultimately compromised many of them.[33]

The informational fantasy proposed by the archivo was that the ability to document the excesses of the regime would ensure control over it. Far from confirming Stroessner's regime as one of improvised brutality, as most people assumed it had been, the archivo constructed a new view of the regime as a calculating and efficient user of information. It showed, like nothing else, the single-mindedness of the regime, and reinforced the idea of the Stronato as a logical, totalitarian complex, a complete and systematic controller of information and violence.[34] In allowing new democrats this reading, the documents collected for the purposes of state terror didn't disappear, but inaugurated a new kind of power. The secrecy that made documents capable of channeling sovereign power now made them capable of channeling the new democracy. Democracy was just as invested in the possibility of knowledge through documentation as was the view of totalitarianism against which they presented themselves. The very possibility of public democracy resided in an image of totalitarian secrecy as its antithesis.

In the years after its discovery, the archive would move to the new symbolic center of popular sovereignty, the judicial branch, charged with enforcing the rule of law. Even the U.S. government was able to get in on the symbolic transfer of power. Having previously worked with the secret police to keep records on communist agitators, the embassy now helped to fund the study and preservation of the archivo through a grant from the United States Agency for International Development (USAID). USAID was also behind the later creation of the Museum of Justice, which would move the archives again to the first floor, spruce up the waiting room, and pay for the extreme air conditioning. All this reinforced the notion that democracy was underpinned by transparent information, offering a stable store of data about the country as sign of the existence of a public sphere.[35]

Until it moved, there was no single room in Paraguay that inspired confidence in the notion of transparency like the archivo. Its friendly staff and efficient, computerized database made an odd contrast with the grainy black-and-white pictures of arrests and mangled corpses displayed on the walls, let alone the eerie contents of the hundreds of boxes and binders lining the shelves. In the world of new democrats it was this ability to connect a memory with a document that made truth, and that generated the legitimacy of the public sphere. Ironically, it was once the archive moved to the museum that it ceased to seem so efficient or orderly. For even as the front face of the museum gained a new sheen, the documents became caught up in a bureaucratic mess involving the attempt to pay indemnities to the victims of the dictatorship. That is, until someone tried to use the information systematically, no one had realized just how costly, time-consuming, and open to multiple interpretations and misreadings such documents could be. The commission charged with investigating victims' claims in the archivo was bogged down for years, and the back rooms of the museum came to be clogged with campesino families trying to find the documents they were sure were there. At that point, the archivo began to look more like the rest of Paraguay's information institutions—outside of the static museum piece, transparency is the object of complex political haggling. For the first decade of its existence, the archivo served as a monument to transparent justice, even one so displaced in time, to the possibility of the rule of law. But the rule of law that the archivo performed was always law in relation to the past and worked best when not examined too closely; when opened to the present, the documents, and the information they were supposed to contain, began to take on a new life.

The archivo del terror inaugurated a new political language, and through it a new understanding of citizenship as a community of readers, ever vigilant of their leaders. After the opening of the archivo, the three major national newspapers devoted five pages a day for six months to simply printing its contents (López 2003). And therein lies the beginning of a critique of the political economy of transparency, for these national newspapers, whose circulation consolidates the new public sphere as a community of readers, were in short supply in the campo. During my fieldwork, only a dozen or so copies of the three daily papers, combined, made it to the whole district of Vaquería.[36] Even committed readers of national politics like Jorge Galeano rarely saw one in the campo unless he or I went early to buy it off the bus. Older campesinos whom I interviewed about the experience of repression under Stroessner often asked me about the archivo, or asked me to look up their files, making it clear that they would never go there themselves. Campesinos, though well represented in the archivo as objects of torture, were not part of its public. That new relationship of exclusion would harden further when the new community of urban readers, the idealized civil society of a transparent modern democracy, met its first major test almost a decade later.

CIVIL SOCIETY: *EL MARZO PARAGUAYO*

In January 1999, at the height of a new round of political turmoil, I visited my friend Marta, a wealthy and progressive young law student who epitomized the hope of Asunción's up-and-coming new democrats.[37] Her television was on, and the former general Lino Oviedo was giving a speech to a raucous crowd on the streets of Asunción. Oviedo, at that time, was the most popular and feared character in Paraguayan politics. His popularity had been steadily increasing since 1989, particularly among campesinos and the urban poor, who saw him as their only hope to solve a deepening recession. In 1996 he had attempted another coup against the sitting president, and had been stripped of any official position by the courts. Thereafter he had become something of a wanderer, giving increasingly brazen public speeches to adoring masses. That night, dressed in the red kerchief of the Colorado Party, the diminutive general was in top form, sweating, waving his arms, and screaming in Guaraní to his appreciative audience, decrying a recent decision by the Supreme Court to have him thrown in jail. Marta sat to listen to what he was saying, and after the news clip was over, I asked for a translation. I couldn't yet understand Guaraní, and although Marta claimed that she couldn't either, like so many wealthy Asunceños, she seemed quite capable of understanding it when it mattered. "He says he's going to bury the Supreme Court justices," she said somberly. My reaction was not as strong as she'd expected, so she continued, "It's hard to translate. It sounds much scarier in Guaraní."

It had been an entire decade since Stroessner's deposition, and most new democrats still found it hard to call their country democratic. The constituent assembly of 1992, and the unearthing of the archivo del terror, had added symbolic legitimacy to the new state. A short-lived investment boom had begun to transform the face of Asunción, and returning exiles had set up residence in the new suburbs of the city and built shopping malls, the new public spaces of the nascent professional class.[38] Freedom of the press, new human-rights NGOs, and a massive educational reform funded by the World Bank seemed poised to make over the Paraguayan masses in the image of the urban middle class. But the Colorado Party remained handily in power. If anything, political corruption seemed to be on the rise. Paraguay's first elected president, Juan Carlos Wasmosy, a consensus candidate between warring factions of the Colorado Party, was a man without any political vision or vocation, and seemed to see the office only as a means of enriching his various construction and engineering firms.[39]

Most troubling about this was the feeling among new democrats that their democracy was extremely fragile and could easily revert to dictatorship. That fear centered on the figure of General Lino Oviedo. Oviedo had been a key player in the coup against Stroessner, and he soon became the first political figure to grace democratic Paraguay with many of Stroessner's impressive personal qualities. He was a military leader capable of attracting fanatical adoration among throngs of otherwise disillusioned supporters, capable of capitalizing on the growing hatred of President Wasmosy, with whom he publicly warred. He openly flouted the law and got away with it, and he seemed to have no end of wealth with which to fund his political gift-giving. His appeal was neither rational nor reasonable, but unsettlingly messianic, and he was able to convince people that his rise to power would unequivocally lead to the nation's salvation.[40] In short, he was a classic caudillo, generating powerful links between his own blustery charisma, the masses, the military, and vested business interests who wanted to jump on the right bandwagon in case the transition to democracy failed.[41]

One of the discourses that General Oviedo was most able to capitalize on was "corruption." The new democrats' project of creating transparency as an antidote to corruption had brought Wasmosy's dealings to light in a way that shocked much of the population. By all accounts, Oviedo played the same game, only better. Whether apocryphally or not, campesinos in the northern Caaguazú settlement of Sidepar tell a story in which Wasmosy arrives in a helicopter and publicly hands money out to all the residents, only to have Oviedo show up in a helicopter a week later and give out more. It's not clear what Oviedo was actually worth, but the resources he commanded weren't really his anyway. He ran much of the national military as his own political and commercial machine, mobilizing entire platoons to fix roads, install electricity, and perhaps smuggle drugs and other contraband in and out of the country. If one accepts the common definition of corruption as "application of public property or license for private gain" (Tulchin and Espach 2000, 4), then Oviedo was one of its most successful practitioners. And yet for much of the population, Oviedo owned the anticorruption platform. This was Oviedo's gift, and his great lesson from the Stroessner era: knowing that, in effect, corruption wasn't about ethical behavior, but about accusation. Whoever accused their enemy most loudly won the battle on the terrain of political ethics.[42]

A decade and a half after Stroessner was exiled, leaving behind a gigantic structure of wealth and power based on contraband, political gifts, and appropriation of state resources, even some new democrats were susceptible to the argument that the old regime wasn't corrupt. I remember one night driving across Asunción with a friend, a lawyer who had spent most of the dictatorship in Europe, after being brutally tortured for his participation in student demonstrations. Like so many of his colleagues, he had returned to the country after the coup to try to rebuild, still bearing the scars that Stroessner's police had inflicted. He was trying to impress on me just how terrible the elected governments had been, when he said, "Stroessner was terrible, but at least he wasn't corrupt like the people who succeeded him." It seemed at the time the most peculiar thing for him to say. But if one takes corruption to be the blurring of the boundary between public and private by state officials (Bratsis 2003), one could argue that Stroessner could not have been corrupt since the entire state was treated as a private enterprise (see Nickson and Lambert 2002). Indeed, there cannot be modern corruption until there are public goods to be misappropriated. Oviedo's claim to not being corrupt, a claim accepted by a huge percentage of Paraguayans at the time, was simply a denial that el público had ever come into being. Instead, Oviedo used a different meaning of corruption, accusing political leaders of reneging on private promises to followers. In using this strategy, Oviedo understood that if people believed in his charismatic aura enough, and trusted that he would direct resources toward them, he would be impervious to the accusations of corruption that he slung at his opponents.[43] He even named his political movement (and later his breakaway party) Unión

Nacional de Colorados Éticos (UNACE, Union of Ethical Colorados). When Oviedo orchestrated a failed coup against Wasmosy, in 1996, and still managed to get himself named minister of defense a few months later, there could be no question of his untouchability, and the fact that he would make good on his promise to win the next election.

In Asunción, new democrats called him a dictator and a fascist, and claimed that he was recycling the tactics of the Stronato. But they were not his audience, and that was part of the point. For Oviedo's followers, he was in fact the only person capable of breaking Stroessner's influence in Paraguay—for if the evils of the Stronato emanated from the man at the helm, only a similar strongman in the executive position, a man who had defined himself as Stroessner's enemy, could change the course of things. Wasmosy made similar claims, noting that Oviedo had once been Stroessner's crony. But he had not proved his parricidal mettle, as Oviedo had in the coup. A vote against Oviedo was a vote for Stroessner. In effect both pro- and anti-Oviedistas claimed the same political ground: they were transparent and their enemies corrupt, and they were everything that Stroessner was not. However, while Oviedistas saw the key to the transition in a new populist figurehead, anti-Oviedistas claimed that the root problem was populism itself. For Oviedo and his followers, ethics was a personal trait emanating from a strong leader; for new democrats, ethics was institutional, something that had to be built into the state through institutional reform, and Oviedo was frightening because he threatened to overwhelm that institutional ethics by channeling the apparent irrationality of the masses living in the perpetually troubling campo. In populism lies the threat of mob rule. So long as the educational reform hadn't worked its magic on this mob, which stumbled around in the darkness of the primitive *ley del mbarete*, the threat of a new dictatorship lay just around the corner. Oviedo confirmed these fears at every turn. He promised that after his election campesinos would "retake the reins of the nation" (Morínigo 1999, 66), and in return he received massive support across the countryside.

Between 1996 and the general elections in 1998, Oviedo's appeal and power only increased as popular opinion of Wasmosy declined and as the cotton market, the backbone of the smallholder economy, spiraled into a new crisis. Following the coup attempt, Oviedo won the Colorado Party's presidential nomination contest (a process that was more important in deciding the president than were the national elections),[44] accompanied by vice-presidential candidate Raúl Cubas, an extremely wealthy engineer.[45] His chief rival for the nomination, and Wasmosy's candidate of choice, was Luís María Argaña, former president of the supreme court during the Stroessner regime. He was given the consolation prize of heading the party's list for senate.[46] Before the general election, Wasmosy finally had Oviedo convicted for the coup attempt and thrown in jail, making it impossible for him to run. According to electoral rules, Cubas became the presidential candidate, and his arch-rival, Argaña, went on the ticket as vice president. The image of his persecution at the hands of a corrupt elite only increased Oviedo's popularity, and Cubas easily won the 1998 election on the slogan "Cubas in office, Oviedo in power." His single electoral promise was to pardon Oviedo.

Cubas made good on his promise to free Oviedo even though the Supreme Court ruled the pardon unconstitutional several months later. From the moment of his release, Oviedo was a loose cannon on the streets of Asunción—institutionally without power, yet publicly manipulating both his allies and his enemies. Cubas was a relatively ineffective president. For the first months of his tenure, the government divided into two warring factions, one led by Oviedo from the streets of Asunción, the other by Argaña, who tried to form a coalition with the opposition to check Oviedo's power. The speech I watched with Marta that summer was one of many in which Oviedo promised that his victory was imminent, and that his enemies would pay dearly, especially Argaña. Oviedo's repeated public threats tore the party apart, and kept the new democrats sitting on the edge of their seats.

On Tuesday, 23 March of that year, political tensions finally came to a head, when Argaña was ambushed and assassinated along with his chauffeur. It has never been clear who exactly carried out the attack, but it remains a topic of considerable intrigue, as are the three days that followed the assassination. That week was the single most important period of the transition, a clash so laden with symbolism as to generate multiple retellings and conflicting narratives. A group of students originally organized in opposition to the Oviedo coup of 1996 called up its network to protest the assassination and demand Cubas's resignation and Oviedo's arrest. They marched down to the central Plaza de Armas in front of the Congress building just a few hours after the assassination. Later that day, the small group of student pro-democracy demonstrators swelled exponentially when it was joined by Argaña's Colorado supporters and by tens of thousands of campesinos who happened to be in Asunción that day demonstrating for cotton subsidies. The three groups merged their demands and took over the plaza in front of the government buildings, where they were later confronted by a much smaller group of Oviedistas out to support Cubas. The pro- and anti-Oviedo sides spent days hurling insults at each other over a thick police barricade. Power struggles in both the army and the police led to periodic repression of the students and campesinos, until finally on Friday night, gunmen positioned on buildings around the plaza opened fire on the crowd, miraculously killing only seven demonstrators while wounding around two hundred (see Bareiro 1999). In the aftermath, Cubas resigned and went to Brazil, and Oviedo fled to Buenos Aires. The head of the senate, Luís González Macchi, assumed the presidency as per the constitution.[47]

These events were quickly memorialized as "el Marzo Paraguayo," the Paraguayan (month of) March, a defining moment in the coming of age of a new democratic Paraguay. In the years following Cubas's overthrow, González Macchi would come to be reviled as the most incompetent and corrupt president in Paraguay's history. But the events that got him into power were nonetheless remembered by new democrats as a redemptive moment, when the foundations of a fledgling civil society showed itself to be more robust than the trembling state.[48] The national newspapers Última Hora and Notícias did much of the work of memorializing in this way, as did NGOs like the Centro de Documentación y Estudio and the Comité de Iglesias (see Centro de Documentación y Estudio 1999; Rivarola et al. 2001; López 2003).[49] The key here was that the protagonists were almost uniformly seen as urban students and the free press fighting against dictatorship (see Morínigo 1999), the youth vanguard of the new democrats.

The preceding story, about the Marzo Paraguayo in Asunción, was told to me repeatedly. It's a compelling story. The biggest problem with it, though, is the difficulty it has explaining the role of the Federación Nacional Campesina, or FNC, one of the country's largest campesino organizations, which actually provided the majority of protestors on the anti-Oviedo side of the conflict. The student march became what it was because it joined with campesinos who had been bused into Asunción for a completely unrelated event. The particularly low price of cotton that year had brought record numbers of campesinos (around twenty thousand) to the capital the night before to rally for subsidies. News of the assassination arrived just as they were about to start their march toward the Congress. They held the march anyway, but changed their route and set up a protest camp in a square adjoining that occupied by the students. When they joined forces, the now massive demonstration adopted a peculiar hybrid project: they would remain in the plaza until Cubas resigned *and* the cotton debt of all FNC members was forgiven. The FNC leadership sold this plan to its followers as a tactical short-term alliance, although most campesinos told me in hindsight that they hadn't really known what the student demands had been. In fact, most of the FNC members I met who had been in the plaza that week considered themselves Oviedo's supporters, and many felt they had been misled during the march.

The narrative ambiguity of the campesino presence at the protests comes out clearly in a fictionalized retelling of the event by Andrés Colmán Guttiérrez (2004). A highly respected journalist with Última Hora, Colmán reported on the conflict as it was unfolding and later reminisced about his experience in a sentimental novella called El país en una plaza (The Country in a Plaza). The story follows the adventures of a cynical middle-aged reporter who is sent against his better judgment to cover the demonstrations. As the story begins, he is on "vacation" in Yhu, an isolated and extremely impoverished town in eastern Paraguay. What kind of vacation he is having there is never clear, but his co-workers enjoy making fun of him for it, and there is never any indication that he or any of the other staff at his paper have any connection to the country-side besides this inexplicable leisure activity.[50] During the four days he is in the plaza, he meets the six valiant students and one campesino who will later die in the shootings, and comes to understand that there is something fundamentally revolutionary about the demonstration he is witnessing. He slowly gets drawn into the action, using his media connections to get information in and out of the plaza and ultimately to help out the "side of the democrats," as he calls it, coming to see in the students the future of his beloved country, and fulfilling the journalistic responsibility of making the government's actions "transparent" (transparentar las acciones). Even as he reflects, five years later, on the political disaster of President González Macchi, he knows that in that plaza he had seen the model society that portends Paraguay's potential.

Several key characterizations anchor this new vision of Paraguay. The first is the character who for the narrator epitomizes the youthful rebellion. When he introduces her, she is sitting off to one side of the action,

carefully constructing little arrows out of recycled office paper. She was dark and thin [morocha y flaquita], still a teenager, 16 or 17 at the most. She wore faded jeans and a white T-shirt with the words "Dictatorship never again" [dictadura nunca más] written across the chest. She had red, white, and blue paint on both her eyebrows, the colors of the national flag, which danced every time she smiled and revealed her marvelous dimples. She also wore a cloth flag on her back, tied around her neck like a cape. (16)

The image distills all the romantic elements of the narrator's newfound national fantasy. The girl's dark skin and the arrows she constructs retain the indigenous element of Paraguayan mestizaje. Her youth, the fact that she cannot yet vote, sets her up as the future of the nation. On her face are the colors of the flag, the same colors traditionally worn during nonpartisan campesino protests, which were painted all over the students in the plaza on the day of the protest (and which differentiated them from the monochromatic red of the Oviedistas). The jeans and the cape are modern elements. For the first two-thirds of the book, the narrator doesn't even know the girl's name, so he refers to her as Batgirl (Batichica). And all of this is tied into a simple discursive utterance: dictadura nunca más, as the singular political desire of the new national subject. The girl is fully objectified as a beautiful, young woman, and in fact, as the novel progresses, the sexual undertone of this first contact becomes overt. She repeatedly offers herself to the narrator, and he, the responsible father figure, shows restraint. He is troubled by his sexual feelings for the girl, but not too much, and he allows himself to kiss her before the book ends. Still, he manages to hold off just enough to convey the quintessential patriarchal image of the nation as female purity incapable of protecting herself and in need of a dominant male figure. In this case, the purity which Batichica symbolizes—and which the narrator can possess, even if not sexually—is neither blood (from the dominant racial myth) nor earth (in the agrarian and military views of the nation), but democracy itself as an abstract ideal.

The first figures to provide symbolic contrast to Batichica are the campesinos, rendered with all the awkwardness that their role in the story deserves. During the demonstration, the students and campesinos take up positions in separate but adjoining plazas, and meet only when the students are chased by police toward the campesinos. The students encounter an impenetrable mass which will not let them in. A famous actor tries to force his way into the space.

When they saw what he was up to, without a single word, as if obeying a telepathic order, the farmers [agricultores] stood firm. Keeping thirty centimeters between each of them, they raised their sticks and kept them at waist height, horizontally, end to end, forming what appeared to be single long bar. The students advanced until they hit the obstacle. The farmers made a perfectly synchronized arm movement, pushing the sticks forward so that the mass of demonstrators was thrown back into the street, many of them falling at the feet of the police. (25)

The campesinos eventually allow the students in, but make their political position clear—they are only there for an economic "class interest" (in contrast to the universalist demands of the students). In short, campesinos are vital to the story but not protagonists in it. Not only do they act as a militarized horde, but their communication is telepathic, invisible, and indecipherable to the new democratic observer.

The final players in Colmán's drama are the Oviedistas who are fighting the students for control of the plaza. They are an unruly and violent mob whose primary motivation for the counterdemonstration is the free gifts being handed out from the Linobar, a refrigerated truck well stocked with cans of beer. The Oviedistas are never scary, though; if anything, they provide the book's comic relief, falling over themselves and yelling idiocies. Moreover, their poverty is everywhere apparent, as they call out for their "líder pynandi," or "barefoot leader."[51] What is most notable about these barefoot Oviedistas is the Guaraní they use. The students inflect their Spanish speech with the occasional token of Guaraní slang, while the campesinos use a controlled Guaraní which switches into Spanish whenever the dialogue gets too involved. But the Oviedistas are always speaking in a low register of Guaraní, and never in more than short, violent, or confused snatches. When one of the characters, a private detective, wants to pass as an Oviedista, he adopts this language, obsequiously begging a corrupt police officer for alcohol and money.

Even though it's clear that most of them are poor people from the campo, Colmán is careful not to call the Oviedistas "campesinos." Nonetheless, their portrayal leaves open an important ambiguity. Unlike the Oviedistas, the campesinos are disciplined and dignified, both physically and linguistically. But they are neither heroic nor entirely trustworthy. One can't help get the impression that given a slightly different field of force, they might have been on the other side. In this telling, the "country in the plaza" respects them, thanks them for their efforts, but from a distance. Their role is accidental and a bit dangerous, and as campesinos they symbolize neither democracy nor dictatorship, but an alien force, an anachronism, fortuitously out of place. Most of the scholarly analysis suggests the same thing.[52] The Marzo Paraguayo was a student victory against tyranny whose campesino foot soldiers were little more than accidental helpers in a scene which came to epitomize the transition to democracy. As José Nicolás Morínigo and Edwin Brítez put it in their analysis of the formation of public opinion during the transition, "The 'marzo paraguayo' activated a process which substituted affective loyalty to parties for loyalty to a series of values and a cause, and would radically change the Paraguayan political system" (2004, 264).

Colmán captures the new democratic sentiment about the meaning of Marzo Paraguayo, and completely ignores the deep ambivalence with which the event is remembered in the countryside. I met dozens of campesinos who had been at the demonstrations, and none spoke to me about it as a victory for democracy. They did talk with pride about toppling the government, and in this sense it was seen as a victory and a sign of campesino strength. But to most campesinos the event was not about the power of ideas so much as the potential power of mass mobilization. During large demonstrations in the years I was there, campesinos made frequent reference to Marzo Paraguayo, suggesting that they could win their demands by bringing the government to the brink of collapse. But in other contexts they referred to Marzo Paraguayo as one of the main reasons that so many campesinos left the Federación Nacional Campesina in 2000 and stopped participating in the annual cotton demonstration. Many felt as though they had been duped. By no means were all campesinos I knew Oviedistas, but those who were deeply resented what they saw as their unwitting participation in the overthrow of their political savior. And they read it as yet another symptom of their increasing marginalization within a system which included them only when it found them useful, and otherwise derided them as backward and fearsome.

FREE MARKET: SOYBEANS

As the transition consolidated, campesinos were excluded from both new democratic redemption narratives, the archivo del terror, and the Marzo Paraguayo, and eventually found themselves on the outside of the transition project. But the most devastating aspect of this exclusion happened as new democrats developed an interest in the central object of campesino politics: land. Until the late 1990s, democracy had been largely an urban affair, and the rural figured as a space to be transformed through paternalist interventions. But by the time I arrived in Vaquería to do fieldwork, at the end of 2004, an unprecedented transformation was occurring in the economy and on the landscape. For those who were attuned to it, particularly landless campesinos still looking for a place to settle, the change looked like nothing less than a massive green blanket of soybeans being rolled over their communities. It had started to the east, first in the departments of Itapúa and Canindeyú, bordering Brazil, later moving westward into Caaguazú. By the time it reached Vaquería, it was halfway between the Brazilian border and Asunción, and spreading so rapidly that many could imagine a time when all agricultural land would be taken up with the beans. From high points just north and east of Vaquería the new rural economy was a terrifying sight. When campesinos took me up there they could point eastward to bare green hills and tell me where whole campesino towns had once stood: San Roque, Pariri, Vera Kue, and Yvypytã. To the southeast, just outside of the campesino settlement of Zapatini Kue, a shiny new Cargill silo glinted in the afternoon sun. The takeover had been going on for several years, but had recently accelerated so much that it completely dominated local campesino politics.

The beans figured into the transition narrative by providing new democrats with a story of *economic* redemption. The archivo del terror and the Marzo Paraguayo had signaled the potential for a new kind of sovereignty, generated a new public sphere, and produced a new citizen ready to take on the mantle of democratic governance based on transparency and a self-organizing civil society. But the new democrats had yet to show that they could fix the economy. In the years following the close of the Cold War, the internationally recognized formula for underwriting democracy was the free market, publicly regulated by professional technicians. Many of the reformists who believed in some sort of social democracy right after the coup quickly hardened into promoters of free-market solutions who all but vilified the state itself as imminently corruptible. According to these reformists, the only appropriate role of the state was as a technical institution, an arbiter of the kind of open transaction rules that they believed made regularized capitalist growth possible. New democrats would experience serious setbacks in their attempts to institute a technocratic economic model, but economic recovery was key to their argument that they could manage not only Paraguayan politics better than Stroessner had, but also its finances.

Marzo Paraguayo had brought to office President González Macchi, a man whose tenure would be remembered for nothing but disappointment, the withdrawal of international development support, gross mismanagement in almost every aspect of governance, and a failed attempt to privatize public enterprises. By the time his controversial time in office came to an end, in 2003, the Paraguayan economy was eight years into a deep recession known almost affectionately as *la crisis*. La crisis affected everyone in the country. Although people blamed it on different sectors, depending on their position, la crisis became one of those communal experiences of loss and suffering which Paraguayans of almost all stripes stoically related to a history of lost wars, imperial manipulation, and political brutality. Because la crisis was contemporaneous with the rising visibility of "corruption," the two were always associated. People were poor because their leaders were stealing from them.[53]

But la crisis had much deeper roots in economic planning. Paraguay's economy had arguably been in pretty rough shape since 1982. During the 1970s, the country had posted some of the most impressive growth in the hemisphere as several of Stroessner's development projects paid off (see Weisskoff 1991; Baer and Birch 1984). There were three prongs to this economic boom. The first was an opening of the economy.[54] Stroessner built roads to the borders and established trading towns, turning the country into a vigorous importer and exporter, a duty-free zone that funneled goods from East Asia and the Middle East into Brazil and Argentina. The second was the construction of the largest hydroelectric dam in the world, a project so huge in this tiny agricultural country that it easily became the largest single employer and the largest buyer of industrial goods for a decade. And the third was the growth in agricultural exports through peasant colonization of the forested eastern frontier during the land reform. Paraguay's production of lumber, tobacco, and especially cotton grew at unprecedented rates during this period.

In some respects these strategies followed standard development orthodoxy of the time. But as growth goes, the miracle of the 1970s was comparatively "cheap," in that it didn't require much in the way of government investment or planning (Albert Berry 2010b). The dam, paid for and designed by Brazil, probably had the biggest short-term payoff. The infrastructure for importing and exporting was easy to build, and virtually nonexistent taxation and regulation provided great incentives for immigration and border-town entrepreneurship. The largest import-export growth was not in the formal economy at all, but in the expanding black market for which Paraguay was to become infamous. These conditions made the growth of the state itself impossible, since it didn't collect the revenue necessary to expand its regulatory capacity. Agriculture was similar, in the sense that once invited, campesinos were more than happy to do almost all the work of establishing agricultural colonies on the extremely fertile red soils of the Atlantic forest. High fertility, low endemic diseases, and excellent commodities prices, alongside the free labor of hundreds of thousands of pioneers, made the state's role in providing infrastructure and technical aid for agricultural development negligible.[55]

For these reasons growth was both cheap and not particularly stable, relying almost entirely on exogenous factors, and not surprisingly, it came to a dramatic halt, in 1982, with the simultaneous completion of the Itaipú Dam and the global crash in agricultural prices. Stroessner was able to manipulate the numbers for some years after that, but his inability to turn the recession around caused different economic sectors to slowly turn against him. Moreover, as other countries in the region, like Argentina, Uruguay, and Brazil, began to elect nominally democratic governments, Stroessner was becoming an increasing embarrassment to international trading partners and creditors, who soon withdrew the loans that made the party and military viable. This is the main reason his party eventually ousted him (Roett and Sacks 1991).

As the country reinvented itself in Stroessner's absence, after 1989, the economy briefly seemed to recover, a great boon to the new democratic narrative. The return of professional émigrés and the new confidence of international banks precipitated new investments, particularly in the urban economy. But that trend was short-lived, and with no serious industrial production or regulation to buttress the economy against difficulties like droughts and banking crises, the economy was by 1995 again spiraling into recession; this one, la crisis, was so deep as to get its own personal name.[56] That stage of the recession only deepened under González Macchi, and was seen as a major challenge to the idea that democracy would necessarily bring prosperity (see Borda 2010).

In 2003 several changes suggested that la crisis was coming to an end. The first was the election of President Nicanor Duarte Frutos, soon just "Nicanor." An old hand in Colorado Party politics, Nicanor had positioned himself perfectly over the previous decade. He was allied with the Argañista wing of the party, which became dominant after Argaña's assassination and Oviedo's departure. He had also performed well as education minister under the failed consensus government, giving him some standing with the new democrats. By the time the election came around, Nicanor could sell himself as a young Colorado reformist, someone who combined some of the populist charisma of Oviedo with a kind of professionalism and liberal credentials in the education portfolio that convinced outsiders he might make a good manager (Lambert 2005).[57] Even before assuming office, Nicanor had begun to act as president, running a parallel government in an office building blocks away from the palace where González Macchi and his cabinet had ceased functioning altogether.

Despite the fact that the colors in the presidential palace did not change, new democrats believed that the new administration might finally begin transforming the one-party privatized state into a technocratic public state. Nicanor's boldest move in this direction was in hiring Dionisio Borda as his finance minister. Borda was one of the country's most respected economists, and a harsh critic of the Colorado Party. His appointment caused major problems for Nicanor within the party, but it paid off with new democrats. In short order, Borda was able to reactivate an IMF standby loan that had been suspended for close to a decade.[58] With the loan came a structural-adjustment program which included a number of surprisingly progressive elements, particularly in the area of taxation reform, including a progressive land tax.[59] Other elements included the professionalization of the civil service and the privatization of the state development bank, which would slowly chip away at thousands of state jobs created as patronage appointments and regularize the use of funds that the party used for populist handouts in the countryside during conflicts.

In the style of economic interpretation that became popular in the 1990s, economic booms are the result of entrepreneurial genius, while busts are due to improper state management. González Macchi's regime was not the only one at this time to be blamed for economic recessions across the globe. He had assumed power just after the crash in Southeast Asia and coincided with major currency devaluations in Argentina and Brazil. While many interpretations of these failures were possible, the one that was attributed to places like Paraguay was that crashes were the result of "crony capitalism," a kind of business practice that distorted markets by taking advantage of corrupt officials (e.g., Haber 2002; Marcus-Delgado 2003). This critique of the porousness of public regulatory bodies accompanied the rise of what Peck and Tickell (2002) call "roll-out neoliberalism," a form of free-market regulation that is increasingly involved in institutional reform. In the years after the crash, the IMF was interested not just in governments willing to liberalize trade, but in serious managers who promised to keep corruption in line with stiff regulation and newly auditable institutions. In the new model, not only would attracting investors with lax regulations create growth, but so too would curbing the corruption of parasitic officials through the institutionalized vigilance of the public sphere.

Borda promised all of this, and as he slowly instituted the IMF's prescribed reforms, the economy posted its first positive growth in close to a decade. Paraguay's gross domestic product (GDP) grew by 2.7 percent in 2003, not quite enough to break even with population growth, but a decent improvement on o percent, which is where it had been wallowing. In subsequent years, the IMF continued to renew the standby loan solely on the basis of positive growth. Despite their hatred of Nicanor for being Colorado and for making inflammatory speeches in Guaraní, new democrats grudgingly admitted that his economic management was on the right track. There was a remarkable change of tone in economic sections of the newspaper, on television news shows, and among sociologists, economists, and lawyers around Asunción.

But while better economic management and investor confidence were credited for turning around Paraguay's economic fortunes in 2003, the most significant change came again from unforeseeable exogenous conditions. Although it could be easily folded into a story about new democratic triumph, most of the credit for Paraguay's economic recovery was due not to people, but to beans. In the late 1990s, soybeans seemed to suddenly dominate the Paraguayan economy, even if it was still difficult to see from Asunción what they were doing to the landscape. They had been a steadily growing part of the economy since the late 1970s, but had remained segregated from smallholder cotton and subsistence production areas, and hence from the standard image of rural Paraguay.

The segregation was a product of convenience rather than of design. The same land agency that had begun to resettle campesinos on the frontier moving eastward from Asunción had started giving large land grants to military generals in the far eastern border region of the country. Many of them would quickly resell their parcels to Brazilian speculators and medium-sized farmers (Kleinpenning 1987; Nickson 1981). Even though these migrants were marginal to the Brazilian national economy (see Wagner 1990), they were outfitted with better technical know-how, access to capital and equipment, and a very different conception of farming than campesinos.[60] Brazilian pioneers, or *brasiguayos*, quickly colonized most of the three border departments of Canindeyú, Alto Paraná, and Itapúa (see Souchaud 2002; Fogel and Riquelme 2005). As early as 1981, Andrew Nickson (1981) predicted that these two frontiers would soon clash, causing a serious land crisis. But for close to two decades, they remained more or less distinct. Both groups had sufficient land to expand onto and quite different methods for appropriating and exploiting it. They were tied into different commodity chains with distinct geographies: cotton, tobacco, and sugarcane made their way through middlemen to regional processing facilities on the campesino side; and in Brazilian areas, mint was processed at first, later to be taken over entirely by soybeans (rotated with corn and wheat), which would be sold to silos and shipped raw to Brazil. These commodity chains established not only different commercial networks, but different geographies of transportation, technical support, and input distribution, along with strong regional distinctions in land markets (Souchaud 2002). Until the late 1990s, the soy sector remained relatively separate from the rest of the rural economy, and registered only in Asunción as an important but secondary commodity in Paraguay's export repertoire.

By 2004, however, Paraguay had become the world's fourth-largest producer of soybeans, after Brazil, Argentina, and the United States. Moreover, soybeans alone accounted for almost 11 percent of GDP, and their phenomenal growth in 2001 and 2002 accounted almost entirely for the economic recovery. In other words, Paraguay's economic growth depended on a single export commodity. It created lopsided wealth and almost no employment, while increasing the value of the national currency and thereby damaging other export industries.[61] More important, it voraciously consumed land, the one resource which had generated the most cash employment in Paraguay, through the cotton sector, but also fed the underemployed rural poor. Between 1995 and 2005, the area covered by soybeans had doubled from one to two million hectares, all of which were taken either from the small patches of remaining Atlantic forest or from smallholder communities.[62]

To further aggravate the land problem, soybean production remained concentrated and controlled by Brazilian migrant communities. By 2004, most of the districts along the border were run by brasiguayos, with Portuguese as the language of choice. In some places, brasiguayos controlled the municipality and could call on the technical help of the Brazilian ministry of agriculture in their fields (see Marcial Riquelme 2005). There was some outcry about this among campesinistas, who lamented the loss of "sovereignty" to the Brazilians who were taking over eastern Paraguay. In their edited volume on the subject, Ramón Fogel and Marcial Riquelme (2004) described the displacement of Guaraní and even Spanish from schools, the use of Portuguese in municipal government, and Brazilian country music at rural parties. The cultural displacement, they argued, was linked to the physical displacement of campesinos, who were now increasingly disfavored by employers, their peasant way of life threatened by mechanized agriculture and rising land prices. But these authors failed to spark the sort of public debate they had hoped for, and I heard their work dismissed repeatedly for being too nationalist and too Marxist, for being out of touch with the current generation. Theirs was a lament of setentistas.

It is impossible to overstate the degree to which soybeans were destroying the campesino landscape, a transformation as devastating to campesinos as their own arrival had been to indigenous groups living in the forests of eastern Paraguay in the 1960s. This was the scene that we could see from the high points around Vaquería, as fields of monocultured beans replaced small settlements of houses, mixed fields, and patches of forest left for firewood. The displacement process was well known. It began with Brazilians offering unprecedented prices for a few plots, often ten times what campesinos expected to pay for land.[63] Some families, with possibilities for finding land in other settlements close to relatives, jumped at the opportunity and left. The first speculators were often quite welcome, paying locals to strip the forest and take out the trunks, often allowing campesinos to make and sell charcoal out of whatever wood was lying around. But after the first year, the new owners, rather than building houses, appeared on tractors to plant soybeans, spraying Roundup and 2–4D on their crops from the safety of air-conditioned machinery. Few of them respected environmental regulations, which stipulated that barriers of vegetation be planted between the spraying and houses or public spaces, but were never enforced, and so the chemicals wafted into the homes and patios, schools and churches of the community. And while everyone from Monsanto representatives to the minister of agriculture claimed that these chemicals were completely benign, there was no disputing that for several days after the neighbors sprayed, the whole town smelled like a rotting carcass and residents experienced headaches and nausea. Even soy farmers joked with me about how noxious these chemicals were.[64] As the smell of the dispersed chemicals increased, more campesinos decided to sell their plots and look elsewhere for land. With cotton fields and forests went the cycles of high-paying jobs, so rapidly that in the three years before I arrived, daily wages for agricultural work had fallen from 15,000 guaranis (just over two dollars) to 8,000 in districts neighboring the soy fields.

This economic process, devastating to campesino families across the region, was the worst blow yet to hopes that they might continue their current lifestyle and eventually be invited to participate as full citizens in their country's new democracy. In May of 2005 and 2006, shortly after the failed cotton harvests of those years, when soy farmers were on the hunt for land for the coming year, it was not uncommon to see two or more trucks a day, loaded with furniture, children, and a few small animals, heading down the road past Antonio's house. Though no employment awaited them in the city, they had been convinced that the prospects were better there, and I found it hard to blame them. But those I was living with and spending most of my time with saw these moves as nothing less than a capitulation to a new form of corruption, a new form of state violence, and a new economy that didn't even deign to exploit them.

The accidental soy boom may have provided new democrats with the most important chapter of their narrative of ascendance. It is also the chapter which most clearly defines the difference between new democratic aspirations and those of campesinos. If campesinos are absent or ambiguously allied in the first two stories, in the last they are absolutely extraneous, and their only role is to be expunged from the landscape. Soy made the idea of land reform as a path to economic growth seem not only dated, but completely counterproductive. It is in the face of soy, and the new economic miracle, that I heard employees of the ministry of agriculture referring to campesinos as kapi'atĩ—an invasive burr that is almost impossible to remove from a field. Kapi'atĩ sticks to your clothes, cuts your fingers, and when you try to whack at the stalks with a machete, its sharp thorns spring into your face.

To campesino organizers, their relegation to the backside of history and the receiving end of the soy frontier is nothing but an accelerated project of dispossession, displacement, and death. I do not use these terms lightly—they are the words that campesinos themselves often used to describe their current situation to me. Soybeans, and for many of them democracy itself, had brought with it deepening economic desperation and even hunger, seemed to close off avenues for future aspirations, and appeared to make inevitable the withering away of land, of the nation, of life itself. In taking up that language, I do not mean to make an empirical claim about the multifaceted violence of the frontier, although violence there is. I mean to evoke something of the smallness and the fear that one feels when standing over the wreckage of a well that took a week to dig but two minutes to destroy, or trying to salvage a bagful of manioc roots from a garden that has been maliciously ploughed over, or crouching behind a thin orange tree watching bullets fly at you from the back of a truck normally used to carry soybeans.

It is in those moments that campesinos, and anyone who cares to stand by, realize how deeply the narrative of progress that sustained campesino aspirations is being supplanted by another one. Campesino organizers like Jorge Galeano talk about this as being victimized by "neoliberal hegemony," and I don't think that's a bad analytic beginning. I have used similar Gramscian language to underline that I see the campesino frontier, and the soy frontier engulfing it, as terrains of political struggle which closely link these shifts in worldview to the material conditions of people's existence on the Paraguayan frontier. But I also use it to highlight the precariousness of the arrangements one calls hegemonic. Just as the alliance with campesinos that propped up Stroessner through thirty-five years came to a sudden end at the close of the Cold War, the new democratic vision, as campesinos know, is a delicately woven system of fickle relations sustained by bits of paper that circulate between lawyers and bureaucrats, a community whose edges are secured by violence. In that somber appreciation of how campesinos have come to be shut out of the nation's official democratic future, there is also the reason for sustaining hope. By this, I don't mean to romanticize the campesino project, but merely to evoke something of the sense of history that one feels in those moments after the trucks have passed and the funerals are over, when you begin to rebuild your neighbor's hut, to dig the third well in as many years, or to join a group of fifty campesinos pulling soybeans out of the ground with hoes and making room, again, for manioc. It is on that spark of hope that campesino organizations continue to thrive, to change, and to develop the new politics that will help redefine their role in Paraguay's future.

In May 2006, a public forum organized by the Paraguayan Comisión de Verdad y Justicia (Truth and Justice Commission) was the site of a confrontation between one of the country's best-known campesino leaders and a representative of the Colorado Party. The forum was called "Campesinos y tierra malhabida,"[1] which roughly translates as "peasants and ill-gotten land." The forum was one of the few gatherings to which campesinos were invited by a consortium of new democratic NGOs and government sponsors to give their own narrative accounts of the dictatorship. Highly mediated though it was, the invitation was quite unusual, for it encouraged campesinos to address their concerns about land in the publicly recognized idiom of torture survival. However, that address was tightly regulated. The figure of "tierra malhabida" condensed arguments about the relationship between authoritarianism and land, and in certain contexts could express a deep campesino sense of injustice. But in the official public forum of the Comisión de Verdad y Justicia, its use showcased above all the degree to which campesino politics remained constrained in public discourse.

Held in Caaguazú, the capital of the combative interior department of the same name, the public forum was one of a series of events in which survivors were invited to tell their stories to that public that had been built around the archivo del terror.[2] On this occasion, no one's testimony was more eagerly anticipated than that of Victoriano Centurión. A passionate and poetic Guaraní speaker, Centurión recounted harrowing episodes from his already well-known story of imprisonment and torture, and of the strange circumstances that ultimately allowed him to escape into exile in Panama, in 1980. Centú, as he is affectionately known in the campo, had commandeered a passenger bus outside of Caaguazú, in 1980, with twenty other armed campesinos. In the campesino version of the story, they had not planned to take the bus by force, but had found no other way of getting to Coronel Oviedo for a meeting with the governor. The ill-fated decision to draw arms had made Centú easily one of the best-known characters of campesino political lore. After leaving the bus, the group was hunted into the forest by Stroessner's police, where nine of the twenty were shot. Ten were imprisoned and tortured for years. Only Centú managed to escape, evading several encounters with police cordons and party informants, and earning a quiet reputation for witchcraft among detractors. He returned to Paraguay, in 1990, to exoneration, compensation, and a life of telling his story to all those who would listen.[3]

At the forum in Caaguazú, Centú added a new chapter to this story. He had recently visited the area where nine of his friends had been killed, a field not far from the city of Repatriación. To add insult to a history of injustice, the land, he discovered, had been bought up by Brazilian farmers and covered over with transgenic soybeans. If the comisión were to live up to its name, he said, that land needed to be returned to campesinos, so they could build a community and commemorative monument—it was tierra malhabida and needed to be reverted to campesino hands. The story combined three elements that are key to understanding what campesinos mean when they use the words tierra malhabida. With the story, Centú linked the arbitrary violence of the dictatorship with the current takeover of the landscape by soybeans, and he opposed both to a continuous campesino struggle for land. Tierra malhabida in his usage expressed campesinos' sense of rural injustice, which downplayed the transition to democracy as a dramatic historical rupture. In other words, Centú's story built a specifically campesino version of history which overlaps with the new democratic narrative, but unsettles it by removing its central historical moment.

It was at this point in his story that Centú was interrupted by a member of the otherwise unobtrusive comisión seated behind the podium where he was standing. Miguel Ángel Aquino was the only member of the comisión from the

Colorado Party, a position which he proudly displayed by wearing the party's traditional bright red shirt. Aquino had originally been part of a a dissident wing of the party that had been exiled by Stroessner. Returning after the coup, he and others like him had helped the Colorados to rebrand themselves as victims as well, a position from which they could claim to be in alliance with new democratic projects. Aquino became the first leader of legislature during the transition, and in later years gained genuine respect among new democrats for his work in the comisión (Paredes 2001). In this event, Aquino showed some of his old political fire. He interrupted Centú's speech at the mention of land, saying that it was inappropriate for speakers to advocate the "violation of private property." There followed a heated exchange between the two men, at the end of which Centú left the stage, saying he wasn't interested in a fight.

Those I spoke with in the audience downplayed the incident. This was, after all, an event of public remembrance, and not a place to pitch political battles in the present. Besides, they said, both of the men had a point, and both were known for their hot-headedness—it was a minor dispute which would be resolved by cooler tempers in a more appropriate environment. But Centurión's small defeat that day mirrored much larger defeats I had been tracking over the past two years in the department of Caaguazú. The interchange dramatized one of the most difficult negotiations the campesino movement had encountered in its attempts to realign its politics with new democratic political morality. As with all things having to do with tierra malhabida, the confrontation of that afternoon was about campesino political encounters with legal liberalism, their adoption of the language of anticorruption, and their strained adjustment to the rule of law. More to the point, it was about campesinos learning the pitfalls and concessions involved in addressing the public sphere and the new democrats who define its morality. Indeed, as Don Handelman (2004) might put it, this was a public event intended to assert a bureaucratic logic over the grievances of citizens.

Of interest here is not the Comisión de Verdad y Justicia per se, but the way that campesino politics is translated in their occasional alliance with new democrats. The new democratic transitional narrative, which authorizes certain forms of public discourse, like those of torture survival and anticorruption, gives campesinos a language through which to address the public sphere. That authorization also entails a violent translation that removes campesino temporality from politics insofar as it reaffirms the public sphere as a singular space of legitimate political discourse. In the campo, tierra malhabida evokes a rich history of injustice which continues to dwell in the landscape over which campesinos are constantly struggling. But in its authorized public form, tierra malhabida remains a celebration of an incomplete transition and of the rise of new democrats. It is a statement about the legitimacy of a new liberalism which affirms the law as the most appropriate language for public discourse. In so doing, it repeats the new founding myth of Paraguayan democracy rather than the narrative of ongoing campesino struggle.

TWO ILL-GOTTEN NARRATIVES

I heard two quite different uses of tierra malhabida in the heady spring of 2004, when I began my research. The first usage occurred in the campo and, much like Centú's story, helped organize a diffuse sense of injustice about land distribution. It was a catalyst for anger, hope, and identification, a structure of feeling rather than an explanation of how land distribution works. Among campesinos I knew around Vaquería, tierra malhabida was so self-evident that it was hard at times for me to elicit a definition. In everyday speech it was always a denunciation, but it could refer to any concentration of land that campesinos deemed illegitimate, often connected to an argument about Colorado (or other forms of elite) corruption. Vaquería was surrounded by tierra malhabida or its vestiges, and when I asked people to identify it specifically, many responded that all of the land was to some degree tierra malhabida. To the northwest were the vast stretches of Financiera Picollo and Ka'iho, the products of crooked dealings that had eventually been taken over by government slush funds.[4] Directly across the bog to the southwest was a tract of land belonging to an old friend of Stroessner's, and it had recently been bought up by a supernaturally rich Mennonite teenager, who flew into the property every day to oversee logging operations. To the west was land owned by the front company of former president Wasmosy. Due north, beyond the defunct runway, was a quickly growing soybean field belonging to the wife of a congressman whom no one ever saw.

Some of this land had been repossessed by banks, and some redistributed by the IBR in the years shortly after the coup, but all retained a history and taint of misappropriation. There were the old forests to the southeast that Colonel Zapatini had appropriated in the 1970s by forcibly evicting the residents of an old communal pasture, now a thriving, if rough, IBR colony known as Zapatini Kue.[5] To the northeast were the lands of Coronel Vera, redistributed to campesinos after the coup, and Cataldi, the surveyor who appropriated stretches of forest that he identified as unclaimed while measuring land for his military bosses. Despite this recuperation of some tierra malhabida shortly after the coup, misappropriation was still occurring all around them. Campesinos spoke about Santa Clara and Pariri, the land that had been sold illegally to Brazilian migrants by speculators in the 1970s, as malhabida, as well as land in Tekojoja that these same Brazilians had recently bought from land-reform beneficiaries against the citizenship requirements codified in the land-reform law.

Campesinos were liable to consider most large estates malhabida if they were owned by people with whom they had no patronage relationships. A ranch owner who provided employment to his neighbors was less likely to be branded as owners of malhabida property. Brazilians and soybean farmers, absentee landlords and police were more likely to have their land considered malhabida. Specific estates with histories of violence and misappropriation, abuse or disappearance were all deemed malhabida, since few campesinos with relations of dependence and reciprocity were around to defend their owners. Tierra malhabida was also used to describe farms where deforestation, pesticide dumping, or aerial fumigation threatened air and water quality in surrounding villages. From the most radical perspective, all private property was malhabida. In other words, the term expressed a moral indictment about land use that often had little to do with the specific legal history of land, a sometimes vague but always deeply felt sense of injustice about the way that land was distributed and used in eastern Paraguay. It was as much an argument about violence, fear, ill-health, and powerlessness as it was about law.[6]

For new democrats I spoke to, in contrast, tierra malhabida organized a clear *explanatory* denunciation of corruption and dictatorial abuses of power. This usage, formatted for public denunciations, was part of a diagnosis of the evils of Stroessner's regime—it was primarily a figure from the past, which survived in the present *to the extent that the transition remained incomplete*. The phrase was first used by new democrats in the late years of the regime, then repeatedly appeared in print in 1989 and 1990 as a way for new democrats to express their solidarity with campesino struggle against the dictatorship. It was a way of talking about land that saw everywhere on the Paraguayan territory the mark of powerful elites' violation of the public trust and failure to obey the rule of law. It was a story that one could find in the beginning of almost any book about land written in the 1990s in Paraguay, and elements surfaced in newspaper stories during the same period.

The new democratic narrative of tierra malhabida reaches back to the nineteenth century and goes something like this: Paraguay has always been an agrarian nation, blessed with some of the most fertile lands on earth, a true natural abundance for its relatively small population. And yet Paraguayan history was marred by a famous double-cross when, in the heyday of late-nineteenth-century liberalism, the government privatized almost the entire territory. These were the decades following the War of the Triple Alliance, during which Paraguay had been all but destroyed by the combined armies of Brazil, Argentina, and Uruguay. The new Paraguayan government, formed in the image of the Argentine state by occupying forces, had paid its reparations debt to its three enemies by selling off land by the square league. The investors were primarily European, many of them forming consortia with the politicians who authored the laws, including President Bernardino Caballero, founder of the Colorado Party, whose Industrial Paraguaya bought 8 percent of the national territory. The eastern part of the country came to be dominated by a handful of companies which lackadaisically produced wood and yerba mate (the tea leaf that goes into mate and terere) on several million hectares of the subtropical Atlantic forest (Pastore 1972; Kleinpenning 1992; Caballero Aquino 1985).

Strong opposition to this economic strategy emerged as early as 1887. The majority of the lands had been sold by then, and Congress was already looking for new ways to raise cash for remaining reparations debt. A cartoon in El Látigo in September 1887 depicted Paraguay as a naked woman named Patria, who, "outraged and dishonoured, weeps to see her principal lands sold and divided by her evil sons" (Warren and Warren 1985). This personification of a nation abused by the dishonesty and juvenility of politicians remains one of the most common graphic representations of corruption and political incompetence today. Not surprisingly, the symbolics of a betrayed mother, and even of rape, continue to serve as common metaphors for what politicians have done to the land in different periods.[7] Land and country remain passive and feminized, even while called "patria," and the many political interests that abuse or save her are almost always male.

The cartoon in El Látigo reflected the elite disagreement of its time, a disagreement which the opposition eventually won. The sale of state land in this first Colorado period is now a well-known part of Paraguayan history, universally condemned as a betrayal of the nation, a named historical era everyone recognizes as "La venta de las tierras públicas." The story of the sale of public lands served the Liberals in their defeat of the Colorados in the early 1900s, then served the Febrerista Party in their 1936 coup against the Liberals. The story eventually served the Colorados themselves during the Cold War, when they reinvented themselves as land reformers and denied their connections to the party that had sold the lands in the first place. The story continues to be used by Colorados, now to distance themselves from Stroessner, as well as by new democrats and Liberals trying to chip away at the Colorados.

It was Stroessner, however, who was best served by the story of the venta de las tierras públicas. In the period between the U.S. invasion of Guatemala and the inauguration of the Alliance for Progress at Punta del Este, in 1961, land reform had become a development tool open to even the most vociferously anti-communistic regimes, including that of Stroessner.[8] Carefully excising the term *land reform* from his government for sounding a little too socialist, Stroessner renamed his land agency the Institute for Rural Welfare (IBR) and installed one of his most ardent and loyal bureaucrats, Juan Manuel Frutos, at its head (see Pastore 1971). Opening in 1963, with a fresh new Estatuto Agrario, copied in large part from the proceedings of the Punta del Este charter, the IBR would become the cornerstone of Stronista populism, at once the center of state be-neficence and of anticommunist strategizing for rural areas (see Arnold 1971). Frutos, demagogue and policy architect, would become one of the most power-ful characters in shaping nationalist ideology in the campo, and in producing the campesino subjects who continue to fight to deepen the reform. Whatever else might be said for the Paraguayan land reform (comparative analysts like Peter Dorner [1992] and William Thiesenhusen [1995] call it "reform light" and, ultimately, an utter failure), there is no question that it completely trans-formed the eastern half of Paraguay. It became the backbone of the contentious but strong historic bloc between Stroessner's Colorados and the campesinado, just as it supplied the ideological material of campesino dissent.

The Estatuto Agrario, the legal regime that governed the reform process, es-tablished guidelines for how the government was to expropriate unused lands from people and companies on the frontier and redistribute it to campesinos in need of their own land. According to the economics of the day, this was supposed not only to help landless campesinos, but also to boost the national economy, which was being dragged down by inefficient and unproductive large *latifundios*.[9] Unlike in other parts of Latin America, where large extensions of land tended to be owned as hacienda ranches run by rich families and worked by sharecroppers, Paraguayan latifundios were large extensions of unused land which tended to have few people living on them. Land reform was therefore far less conflictive. The tracts would be expropriated from individuals, many of them barely more than European names inscribed in the public registry by international brokers in the late nineteenth century. Each tract would then be sold to solicitors at fixed, below-market prices on credit to be paid back over ten years. The overarching idea was that unproductive land owned by uninterested companies would be made productive by smallholders, not only reducing rural poverty, but ultimately boosting the economy and helping to underwrite national development. The plan fostered two new forms of land tenure segregated into two distinct forms of colonies: "agricultural colonies" populated by smallholders, and "ranching colonies" for wealthier ranchers.

In order to control land speculation, there were several restrictions on who could buy land in either of these categories, and three of these restrictions would become particularly important later: (1) lands designated as "ranching colonies" would be divided in the eastern region into fractions of three hundred to one thousand five hundred hectares; (2) beneficiaries of land grants had to be *agricultores* by profession, that is, people who dedicated themselves to agriculture; and (3) beneficiaries could not already own more than fifty hectares of land.[10] Together, these three provisions should have prevented civil servants and industrialists from buying up unlimited supplies of land for logging or resale, and ranchers from using the regulated prices to acquire more than 1500 hectares. These limitations were generous by any standards, a fact which reflected the government's certainty about the abundance of land on its eastern frontier. But the laxity of these limitations, much groaned about by critics of the Colorados, hardly mattered, since they were rarely enforced anyway. In practice, the IBR facilitated rather than restricted the concentration of land, and became one of the official instruments for handing out executive favors.

In a country with no strong tradition of capitalist investment, powerful figures converted their political capital into real estate, and their money into cattle, chainsaws, and day-wages. High-ranking military officers who met none of the above requisites were the most notorious beneficiaries of the program, controlling from afar small fiefdoms throughout the eastern region.[11] But they were certainly not alone. Stroessner's family itself took possession of thousands of hectares of land, as did Frutos and dozens of other high-ranking party operatives. Many of them retain possession of their land to this day and wield considerable power in the senate, which continues to be dominated by large landowners, "beneficiaries" of Stroessner's rural welfare program. All of this led to the amazing fact that despite the government's claim to have distributed nearly one million property titles during the regime (Frutos 1985), Paraguay still had one of the most uneven distributions of land in the world.[12] Later studies showed that 74 percent of the land redistributed by the government went to 2.8 percent of the beneficiaries of the reform (Morínigo 2005).

It was this land, distributed by Colorados in contravention of their own laws, that new democrats called tierra malhabida after the dictatorship fell. It linked their critique of Stroessner to the historical critique of the venta de las tierra públicas, and in a moment of political alliance-seeking allowed them to connect their struggle for democracy with campesinos' struggle for land. For the first time since the crushing repression of the Ligas Agrarias (the Paraguayan Christian base organizations), in 1976, campesinos had a public language with which to vent their outrage at having been left out of the land reform, while others appropriated land with impunity. Newspaper articles, roundtables by leftist academics, and campesino leaders began to pose the question of poor distribution again, pointing out that in statistical terms, the actual distribution of landownership had not changed at all, even though the landscape of property had been revolutionized. In damning newspaper reports Stroessner's bureaucrats were called on to justify their more egregious excesses.

But while it brought into public debate campesinos' long-repressed sense of rural injustice, even in the early days after the coup tierra malhabida enabled a subtle translation of that rage into something considerably tamer. For tierra malhabida, in new democratic usage, was an argument about bureaucratic mismanagement and Colorados' manipulation of the law, completely eliding the question of whether rural inequality was in itself wrong. Even Juan Manuel Frutos, architect of the IBR project and clearly a party to its duplicity, understood this right away. Shortly after the coup he was pointedly asked to explain why Anastasio Somosa, the Nicaraguan dictator who had been given asylum in Paraguay, in 1980, had qualified for land under the land reform. In his first response, Frutos denied having anything to do with Somosa's grant. Less than a week later, he changed his answer, admitting that he had granted Somosa the land, but claiming that the grant had been completely legal within the terms of the Estatuto Agrario (see Salazar 2003). He understood that the arguments against him and his participation in the dictatorship's moral turpitude (dramatized in Stroessner's friendship with Somosa and other unseemly international characters) could be defused with reference to law. The political language of the new democrats was a celebration of the universal good of constitutional law, bureaucratic transparency, and depoliticized proceduralism. As such, it necessarily excluded the passions and sectarian interests of those enraged with the Colorado Party or the rural elite more generally. Those passions, themselves unseemly in the new democrats' staid public rationality, would be left to dwell in the countryside.

TIERRA MALHABIDA ON PAPER

In late 2004, stories about tierra malhabida came to life again in the national press as the result of a report, by the opposition congressman Efraín Alegre, which claimed to systematically document over 1.5 million hectares of ill-gotten lands dating to 1950. Alegre's Liberal Party was hardly free of historical taint itself. As a traditional party dating back to the late nineteenth century, it had a structure and tactics quite similar to those of the Colorado Party.[13] Liberal attempts to position themselves as allies of the new democrats and the proper governors of democratic Paraguay were not that different in form from that of dissident Colorados, and like Aquino's rise to prominence within the Colorado establishment, Liberal ascendancy was built primarily on denunciations of past Colorado corruption and claims of victimization. The Liberals were never a particularly rural party (historically, the Colorados were the communitarian *agrarista* party, while the Liberals were the party of urban intellectuals and industrialists), and Alegre's report was not primarily created to forge ties with campesinos, but to boost the moral authority of his party. As such it was a quintessential new democratic document, which, like the archivo del terror, laid claim to a moral space opened by the transition.

Alegre's document offered proof, in the form of tables and graphs, for the new democratic narrative of tierra malhabida. Like most official versions of this story, the document focused on the excesses of the dictatorship, and it also aimed to show that the Colorado Party had continued, after the coup, to act in a dictatorial manner. The IBR, and the arbitrariness with which it produced and kept documents, were offered as proof that Colorado patronage, corruption, and authoritarianism were alive and well. The document gathered names of party members and military operatives and gave quantitative coherence to their corruption, with lists of owners, numbers of hectares, and laws broken. It was only narrowly connected to the campesino sense of tierra malhabida, and made no reference at all to Brazilian investors, soybeans, broken promises, pesticides, or rural unemployment. Most striking, it finished the purification of the malhabida story by completely eliding the question of unequal land distribution.

But while Alegre's document was not attempting to reach out to campesinos, it was taken up by them. Because it was engineered to link the Liberal Party to the anticorruption politics of the new democrats, campesinos and their allies found the document extremely useful for getting their claims about rural injustices heard by a public that often ignored them. It allowed that sense of campesino injustice, the ambiguous force that fuels rural populism, to briefly speak in the words of the redemptive narrative of Paraguayan democracy and in the cold safety of legal rationality, and to be on the side of bureaucratic reform and transparency. Through Alegre's document, campesinos could claim new democratic legitimacy and address the public sphere. The document therefore had two lives, the first in its service to Alegre's politics, the second as a translator of campesino anger into new democratic language.[14]

I heard two versions of the story of how Efraín Alegre put together his report on tierra malhabida. The first was that he had hired a well-known *gestor* to get the information for him. Gestores are members of the unofficial second layer of Paraguayan bureaucracy, a private, parasitic service sector that lives off the inefficiencies of all public institutions. Flatteringly translated by the World Bank (2005) as "special agents," gestores tend to be current or former public employees, people who understand enough of the inner workings of the bureaucracy in question to be able to find information or force a bureaucratic procedure to completion. In some institutions, such as the police's Identificaciones office, gestores are an open and brazen group, hanging out on the front steps demanding exorbitant fees for services which are supposed to be provided free inside. In others, like the courthouse and the national cadastre, they are middlemen and -women, mediating most of the negotiations over documents between clients, notaries, lawyers, and bureaucrats. The gestores who work the IBR, where Alegre's research was carried out, are more specialized, since most of the IBR's clients cannot afford to pay for their services. Instead, they serve politicians and researchers who need to systematically retrieve from the institution documents that can only be found with specialized knowledge of where to look and whom to bribe. The person Alegre is purported to have hired was well known among researchers, a disgruntled former employee of the IBR who left shortly after the fall of the dictatorship and who boasted, with proven results, of being able to obtain any and all information from the IBR, for a price.

The second version of the story, given by Alegre and his assistants, involved no such shady characters, only documents lying in the basement of the IBR that needed to be found and coaxed out of the institution. This story is interesting because of its echoes with the story of the discovery of the archivo del terror: a series of documents detailing dictatorial abuses emerges from a hidden executive archive to be paraded in front of the public in an easily digestible form. In his own account of the work, published some years later, Alegre himself made this comparison explicit: "While turning these pages the reader might feel like a new archive of terror is being discovered and made public. And with good reason. The data we are presenting possess, in terms of their transcendent importance, something that we could well call 'the *Archive of Terror of the surrender of national territory* [patrimonio].' . . . And these data are scary" (Alegre and Orué 2008, 18; emphasis in original). In other words, the dictatorship's documentary practices left material deposits that had a life of their own, returning in the transitional moment to incriminate their producers. Just as with the *archivo*, the documents discovered by Alegre's assistants showed that the IBR had kept records on its own abuses of the law, and it was possible in Paraguay's new democracy to discover and lay bare these abuses. The story of the documents cropping up is presented as a tale of the victory of information over corruption, pointing to the final unassailability of the law and of the new democrats' drive for transparency.

A small team of Alegre's assistants worked over the documents for almost three weeks to produce a breakdown, by department, of land grants which violated any of the three articles of the Estatuto Agrario addressing the size of ranching colonies, the agricultural commitment of beneficiaries, and the maximum amount of land a beneficiary could already own. In the end, they produced a PowerPoint presentation for the Congress, presented on 30 September 2004, which generated a few good days of scandal for the media. More important, they sent a public letter to the procurer general and the auditor general, along with a forty-page report on their findings, requesting a full investigation of the IBR. The document included lists of illicit landowners, the numbers of hectares they had been given, and pie charts showing the percentage of the IBR's land grants that had been processed irregularly or illegally. The document follows a crude quantitative logic that breaks down the agrarian history of Colorado rule into numbers: Paraguay has 41 million hectares of land. In the period between 1950 and 2000, 11.9 million hectares (29 percent) were distributed by the state through the IBR. Of this, 1.5 million hectares (12.6 percent) were granted in contravention of the Estatuto Agrario, with 480,000 of those hectares being located in the combative eastern half of the country. Most of this illegal land granting happened during the dictatorship, but the practice had continued without much change under new Colorado governments in the

1990s. The document told a story of democratic transition deferred, of the continuity of corruption in the present, and called for strengthening of the rule of law against unscrupulous Colorado agents.

The congressman's project ended with the public letters and the report. After scoring some excellent points with the media, proving himself once again to be the champion of democracy and transparency, Alegre seemed to drop the subject altogether. He went on to run a damning campaign to expose corruption in the running of the Itaipú Dam (the great cash cow of the Stroessner regime). To a number of researchers (including myself), it seemed at the time that the topic of corrupt land grants had simply disappeared. Lawyers asked Alegre for access to the fabled malhabida documents, but he simply ignored their requests (nor did he show interest in being interviewed on the subject by a foreign anthropologist). And when the issue did reappear it was with little of the public spectacle of the first report. The comptroller general and auditor general published reports of their own studies, which confirmed the view that the IBR was beset with irregularities and poor record-keeping[15] but beyond these procedural matters had little to say about the actual land-distribution figures Alegre had created. Four years later, when Alegre became minister of public works under a new government, he published a book-length version of his report meant as an embarrassing expose on sixty-one years of Colorado rule (Alegre and Orué 2008), but like any great critic, he knew when to withdraw from controversy he had initiated. Transparency's political value was unleashed through denunciation, and its medium was the document. But after the performance of making once-hidden documents visible was finished, there was very little political gain to be had without difficult and controversial efforts.

After his retreat, though, Alegre's report began to circulate on its own. Loosed into the public sphere during the media spectacle, it soon found its way into the hands of campesinos, with political consequences presumably unimagined while it was being produced. Although campesinos were not present at Alegre's presentation, sociologists advising the senate commission on land reform made copies of the document and distributed them among intellectuals in Asunción and campesino leaders in the campo, where they continued to be replicated in the campesino photocopy economy. The document struck the imaginations of campesinista intellectuals, who began referring to it in interviews with the press. It also hit a nerve with leaders of a large campesino group called the Mesa Coordinadora Nacional de Organizaciones Campesinas (MCNOC), which was planning a series of demonstrations over land distribution for later

PAIS	TOTAL HAS Y PERS.	PORCENTAJES	HAS X PE
TOTAL HECTAREAS	11.883.262	100%	
TOTAL PERSONAS	164.550	100%	
HAS	8.826.576	74,28%	
	3.056.686	26,12%	
PERSONAS	4.086	2,48%	
PERSONAS	160.467	97,52%	

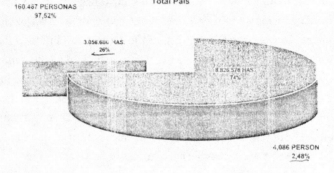

Total Pais

160.467 PERSONAS
97,52%

3.056.686 HAS.
26%

8.826.576 HAS.
74%

4.086 PERSON
2,48%

74,28 % HAS.	PERSONAS X IBR	PROMEDIO 110 HAS	PERS. EXC
8.826.576	4.086	152.280	

PERSONAS EXCLUIDAS POR LA MALA DISTRIBUCION DE TIERRAS

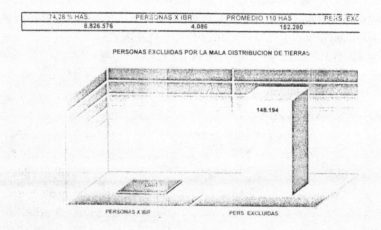

148.194

PERSONAS X IBR   PERS. EXCLUIDAS

FIGURE 2. Document about tierra malhabida as it circulated among campesino activists.

that year. Still quite fresh to the campesino movement, I first encountered the report, in November of that year, at a protest camp, where a copy was held up as proof of the government's misdeeds and the history of injustice suffered by campesinos. I would later see barely legible photocopies of photocopies of the document in the files of other campesino leaders and on the desks of campesinista sociologists.

Both of these groups—the spokespeople of large national movements like the MCNOC, and their campesinista sympathizers in the universities and NGOs of Asunción—together revived the discourse of tierra malhabida. Acting as brokers between the felt injustice of the countryside and the rationality of publicly recognizable political speech, they took to the document immediately. If in the campo I heard references to tierra malhabida as a diffuse moral taint on the landscape and a general sense of malaise and anger, in zones of political production tierra malhabida came to be a direct reference to "el documento de Alegre." The physicality of it, the apparent objectivity of all those numbers and charts, lent a new kind of authority to campesino grievances.

Even when people stopped mentioning Alegre himself during talk about tierra malhabida, the document was implied in the reiterations of one number: in the wake of Alegre's document, tierra malhabida was definitively quantified at 11 million hectares. I heard this number long before I knew where it had come from (and I also heard it grow over time to 12 and finally 13 million). As it turns out, the number came from a misreading of Alegre's report. The number 11.9 million referred to the *total* amount of land distributed by the IBR over a fifty-year period; in other words, that quantity included all land distributed in small parcels to campesinos. In the fertile eastern lands, Alegre had in fact concluded that only 480,000 hectares of land in the contentious eastern region had been illegally distributed to large landholdings. It took me a while to figure this out because the document, although it looks impressive, is actually put together quite poorly, and it is not always clear what the numbers mean. Therefore, very few people read it closely. While the document performed tierra malhabida as an objective fact, it did not make that fact particularly rigid, and it remained open to interpretation. As far as I can tell, the popular interpretation of the document was not produced by campesinos any more than it was by Alegre. It first appeared in *ABC Color*, in a report about the original presentation to the senate, wherein the newspaper states that the IBR had distributed 11.9 million hectares of land "without appropriate procedural control."[16] Always of the position that agrarian reform had been a flop and that the IBR had to be done away with as soon as possible, ABC Color made no distinction as to whether the land was distributed to political elites wanting to bank their wealth in real estate or to landless campesino families entering the cotton economy. To ABC Color, Alegre's document was an indictment of the entire project of land reform, not just of elite corruption. Whereas campesinos decried corruption in the land reform they continued to desire, many new democrats saw corruption as inseparable from land reform and from rural populism more generally. Nonetheless, it was ABC Color's interpretation that stuck, circulated alongside copies of the document itself, eventually making its way into the published writings of campesinista sociologists (e.g., Palau Viladesau 2005).

On closer inspection, there is another way in which Alegre's document appears to defy the narrative that circulates around it: the word *malhabida* never once appears in it. Nevertheless, the document, its graphs and tables, and especially the number 11 million were enlisted almost immediately into campesino public discourse in the name of tierra malhabida because it did what so few official documents seem to do: it appeared to express a rare recognition of campesino experience, and to link that experience to the new democratic cries for institutional reform and transparency. But recognition is also cunning (see Povinelli 2002). Alegre's denunciation bolstered and publicized the campesino sense of injustice, but it did so by subtly filtering out campesinos as subjects of that injustice. In this iteration, the injustice of tierra malhabida is no longer about material distribution in the campo, about a history of deprivation suffered by campesino neighbors of wealthy landlords. Instead, it is a crime of theft, abuse of power, and bureaucratic mismanagement, inherent in the very idea of land reform, which offends liberal morality by breaking its laws.

In the months after Alegre's report began to circulate, campesinos discovered that while the document could be used to create effective public spectacle, it did not make a particularly effective legal instrument. Public condemnation of the misappropriation of land by Colorado operatives did not necessarily lead to a redistribution (or reversión, as campesinos put it) of those lands to smallholders. If anything, it deepened the new democrats' distrust of the idea of land reform itself and renewed calls for scrapping the project altogether. And it reinforced the idea that private property, so long as it had been bought according to the complicated land laws of the republic, was inviolable. Owning a half-million hectares of land in this argument was not in itself a problem, but owning ten hectares of land without papers in order was morally wrong.

This very problem became a point of tension between the two largest national campesino organizations, the MCNOC and the FNC. The latter argued that the legality of land ownership didn't matter, only the size, and declared that any property larger than 3,000 hectares could be seized by its members. At stake in this dispute was the political tension between seeking recognition or redistribution.[17] The strategy favored by the FNC appealed to a redistributive ethic that stood outside of the law, and could impose itself on civil society through militant action. The MCNOC, by contrast, translated campesino morality into terms consonant with Paraguayan civil law, and in so doing became subject to that law. Arguing as though before a court, MCNOC representatives were forced to adopt a sort of legal positivism which accepts law as given and is incapable of questioning injustice of the law itself. What they argued for was not redistributive justice, but the rule of law, or *estado de derecho*, an argument that by definition sees law as the container of legitimate struggle in liberal democracy.[18] The more campesinos became enamored of Alegre's document, and the version of tierra malhabida that enabled them to argue publicly, the more they embraced this form of argument.

INSIDE THE LAW

I don't want to overstate the degree to which campesino organizations submitted to the rule of law here. Each of the country's major campesino organizations put forward a slightly different opinion, none of which completely ruled out illegal tactics. For example, the FNC decried tierra malhabida publicly, but maintained its claim that properties larger than 3,000 hectares were always illegitimate and subject to squatter invasions by their members. As a result, it was excluded from official public negotiations with the government. The MCNOC was more careful, stating that it would claim only land that was malhabida, but one of its justifications was that tierra malhabida was "irrationally exploited," an economic argument of the 1960s that had been all but erased from the new version of the Estatuto Agrario. Even Jorge and Antonio's Movimiento Agrario y Popular (MAP), the law-abiding group that dominated campesino politics in and around Vaquería, refused to wait for the courts to finish their deliberations. While MAP never invaded land without first filing legal charges against the owners, it backed up its charges with actions that were specifically prohibited by the Estatuto Agrario and the Civil Code, and for which its members were routinely arrested and persecuted.

What I am talking about is at best a tendency that emerged as campesinos attempted tactical alliances with new democrats. The pragmatics of alliance making led to tensions not unlike those they had campesinos had encountered in their earlier alliance with Stroessner's government. The original Estatuto Agrario was the nexus for a contentious historic bloc that linked Stroessner's Colorados to campesinos by giving both a common language for the rural future. But the link between campesinos and Colorados was also fractious and violent, and by no means equal. If many campesino groups adopted the language of the Estatuto Agrario as an expression of their own political desires, they protested bitterly when the government failed to live up to its own policies. For this they were violently repressed in wave after wave of police action and subjected to targeted torture and assassination; liberation theology priests sympathetic to the movement were expelled. These repressions were strongest between 1976 and 1981, a period which destroyed the Ligas Agrarias and sent the campesino movement underground. The antiestablishment militancy of the FNC is largely a product of 1980s underground organizing, which adopted a hardened Marxist stance in the face of its total exclusion from public politics. In that period, the contentious relationship was between campesinos and the populist rule of the dictator over which they had very little control. Campesinos seeking strategic alliances with new democrats encountered a similar problem by publicly supporting the rule of law. Insofar as they abandoned strategies that violated the law, they also gave up any leverage they might have over the law itself.

Campesinos learned this lesson forcefully during their failed attempts to foment a general strike, or paro cívico, in November 2004, shortly after the release of Alegre's report, when they tried to combine the legalism of tierra malhabida with a show of force. Massive demonstrations, marches, land invasions, and roadblocks have, since the early 1990s, been campesinos' primary extrajudicial tool for affecting government policy. These tactics were successful in pressuring the government to redistribute land or increase cotton subsidies on several occasions in 1989 and 1990, and then again in 1999 (during the Marzo Paraguayo) and 2002. In 2004 they seemed set for an even larger campaign. A new coordinating body called the Frente Nacional por la Defensa de la Soberanía y la Vida (National Front for the Defense of Sovereignty and Life) brought together a number of campesino groups (primarily the MCNOC and the MAP) with urban labor unions, and began a series of three national days of action in August, September, and November.[19] The Frente Nacional had a litany of demands, but chief among them were stopping the privatization of the national credit banks and the redistribution of tierra malhabida.[20] It was unclear how many people the group would be able to bring out for a demonstration, but it was certainly the broadest political agglomeration to emerge in years. As the stakes escalated, the executive also developed new tactics for dealing with it. President Nicanor called together a Gabinete de Crisis Rural, headed by Vice President Castiglioni, and sat down to dialogue with the leaders in frequent meetings over several months.[21] The president also readied the police and military to deal with the conflict.

The first mobilization, in mid-August, got the government to the table. Blocking some roads and invading key properties in different areas of the country, leaders claimed that this was a training event for their members and stood down as soon as the government agreed to dialogue. In mid-September, campesino leaders called their constituents to the roads again, organizing an impressive three-day march in multiple areas of country, along with periodic roadblocks and land invasions. They claimed that the Gabinete de Crisis was negotiating in bad faith, which required forcing its hand on several key issues, and they added to the list of demands that protestors jailed during the first demonstration be released. They called off the mobilization once they had received executive promises that 240 campesino organizers detained without trial would be released, that the privatization of the national bank would be delayed, and, most important, that the IBR would expropriate 15,000 hectares of tierra malhabida for redistribution to campesino groups.

This second demonstration was much larger, and many people later described it as the most inspiring demonstration they had ever taken part in. The media portrayed it as a large popular uprising, giving real credence to the possibility that the Frente Nacional would succeed where other coordinating attempts had failed. On the strength of these marches, campesino spokespeople gave the government sixty days to comply with its promises before calling a paro cívico, by which they promised to paralyze the entire country until the conditions of the agreement were met. As the sixty days ticked by, it became clear that none of the government's three promises would bear fruit in short order. Only a handful of campesino prisoners were released. The privatization of the bank was fumbling along, and it seemed as though the negotiators hadn't had the authority to even negotiate on the issue. But the 15,000 hectares proved to be the biggest sticking point. The Gabinete de Crisis turned out to have jurisdictional problems which deprived it of the authority to make budgetary promises. President Nicanor tried to fix the situation by promising to find money in the Instituto de Previsión Social (IPS), but this also proved unsuccessful.

In a last-minute deal breaker, the president had to retract his offer of IPS money because his finance minister, Dionisio Borda, came out against the plan. This development was particularly complicated for campesinos because Borda was, at the time, the most highly placed new democrat in government and one of the few members of the executive whom campesino leaders respected or trusted. During the 1980s, Borda had been one of a small number of outspoken campesinistas who publicly championed the campesino movement against the dictatorship and produced economic arguments for land redistribution. Exiled in the late 1980s, he had gone to study economics in the United States, and returned as a champion of institutional reform and governmental transparency. He had also been a vocal critic of the Colorado Party throughout the 1990s. So when President Nicanor had appointed him finance minister, it was seen as one of his boldest moves, part of a sincere attempt to generate alliances with the new democrats and open up channels to international credit.

But in moments of crisis, Borda showed that his training in economics and his belief in institutional reform trumped whatever sympathy he might have had for campesino politics. In the lead-up to the paro cívico, Borda argued that caving into campesino demands would constitute a breach of the public trust, because it would require a last-minute diversion of funds for what he considered purely populist ends. In other words, the promise to redistribute land to campesinos was deemed to be arbitrary and out of touch with the rule of law. He argued that whatever deal the executive had reached with campesinos was an extension of an old style of politics, which he, as monitor of the public trust, could not be a party to. In the fallout of this breakdown in negotiations, only Borda remained unscathed in the press, and even campesino leaders were later unable to find fault with him. When Borda resigned, in 2005, it was taken by economists, journalists, campesinos, and campesinistas alike as a sign that the executive was slipping back into populism. And yet in the short term he was also their most pressing problem, for it was Borda's assiduous guarding of the national purse strings that made it impossible for campesinos to achieve any of their political goals.

And so on 16 November, a day of torrential spring rains, the clock ticked out and the paro cívico commenced. The beginnings were anything but impressive: small knots of demonstrators huddled under tarps in the capital; students burned tires on the highway out by the national university; and a few hundred state employees walked out of their jobs. In the countryside, only the most ardent made it out on that first day, setting up tarps in the mud and chanting through bullhorns into the sheets of rain. But while the urban demonstrations lasted only hours before union leaders cut a deal with their political patrons, the mobilization in the countryside continued to grow over the next few days. When I arrived at the camp near Caaguazú, on 17 November, almost a thousand people were there, and the camp was still expanding along the southern edge of the country's most important highway.[22] People and supplies arrived by the truckload, met by cheers and the waving of sticks. Flags went up, a sound system was assembled, toilets were dug, and kitchens were built. A constant stream of campesino leaders from the region made speeches on the sound system in the center of the camp, yelling out radical slogans, defying the government and police to do anything, and invoking the great bloodbaths of Paraguayan history.

Yet there was also a measured undertone to the proceedings. This would be a model camp, they kept repeating. They would be disciplined and peaceful; there would be no drinking, no fighting, no display of weapons. It was time for campesinos to take the high ground against a government known for cheating and lying, with a long history of theft and injustice. They would win this fight to reclaim the rule of law by obeying the rule of law, and in so doing reestablish the dignity of the nation and the constitution. In refusing to engage in any sort of contravention of the law, the campesinos made an explicit move away from tactics which might lead to violence.

There was of course disagreement about this in the camp and between organizational members of the Frente Nacional. The camp had resolved itself into different areas corresponding to different regions and organizations. At the western end of the camp was the dominant group from the MAP, with several large tents full of people from in and around Vaquería and their allies from further west along the edges of the department of Caaguazú. Their primary spokesperson was Jorge Galeano, who represented the MAP and was also head of the departmental wing of the Frente Nacional. The rest of the camp was broken up into small regional organizations, most of them members of the MCNOC or its allies. The national rural women's organization (CONAMURI) also had a presence, along with a small indigenous group that had already been camped by the road for months, having been evicted from land in the north. Added to this contingent were those who wove in and out of the proceedings, from members of urban squatter organizations living in the shantytown bordering Caaguazú to leaders from the radical political party Patria Libre who would later be implicated in a high-profile kidnapping.[23] The most conspicuous absence was the FNC, which disagreed in principle with the legal tactics being used.

Breakout discussions between leaders became rancorous over the issue of whether or not to block the highway, a clearly illegal activity. One of the radical contingents had smuggled hundreds of long knives into the camp, and its representatives were going from tent to tent, quietly advocating armed confrontation with the police. Young men sized each other up, asking where they would stand "when the moment comes." But the moderates, those who held most strongly to the legal line, won out, primarily through Jorge's tireless efforts to convince people and the impressive mastery of the law that he demonstrated in his speeches to the crowd. As the police set up their own camp on the northern side of the highway, with an imposing force of several hundred *cascos azules* (blue-helmeted riot police), horses, water cannons, and armored vehicles, the growing consensus in the camp was to do nothing that would vindicate the state's obvious overreaction. When the government threatened to mobilize the army to move out the demonstrators, the Frente Nacional responded by challenging the constitutionality of such an act.[24] Even on 19 November, when protestors in a second camp in the northern department of San Pedro were viciously beaten by riot police, Jorge was able to convince campesinos in the Caaguazú camp that by sticking to legal principles they could vanquish the arbitrary use of force.[25]

Beyond the arguments made within the restricted public of the camp, a game of cat-and-mouse developed between demonstrators and police on the borderline of the highway. Campesinos occasionally ran up to the side of the road in defiance of the police lined up on the other side, causing them to move in formation. People dared each other to make the police trot about in this way, but the primary effect of these games was to show that beyond the edges of legal demonstration stood an impressive capacity for state violence. It remained abundantly clear who was in control. Meanwhile, leaders like Jorge periodically crossed the road to make sure that what they were doing was legal. They negotiated to march on half of the highway, obtaining police permission to march from their camp into the city of Caaguazú, to surround the IBR office, then return to the camp. During the march, camp organizers kept protestors in three files, carefully regimenting them so that no one fell out of line and to demonstrate their conformity.

FIGURE 3. Paro cívico march. Caaguazú, November 2004.

The most immediate outcome of this discipline was that riot police were able to easily surround us on all sides. I participated in two marches, and I stayed outside for several others, and this dual perspective gave me a remarkable view of what was going on. On the inside, it was possible to feel the strength of hundreds marching down the road. Antonio walked up and down between our ranks, barking out orders and leading chants. But it was also strangely claustrophobic in there, and the world outside, that world which our chants were supposed to address, was completely flanked off by the police. Even though there was general consensus among campesinos that the police looked ridiculous using so much force to guide a compliant mass, one also felt on the inside that if things were to go wrong, the demonstrations would be crushed handily. Indeed, from the outside, the marches themselves looked laughable, tiny parades hidden behind a wall of blue. While the police made these marches legal and legitimate, they also limited what the protestors could do and say to a restricted enactment of the legal.

The camp suffered from the same problem. Most of us were convinced, at least for the first few days, that what we were doing was having a national impact, that the brutality and injustice of the regime were being exposed, and that an outpouring of popular support was imminent. Leaders like Jorge had managed to instill in most of the camp a sense of immanent victory, but in retrospect that sense lasted as long as it did only because so little news reached the camp. Our tent had a battery-powered radio which the owner listened to intently for news, but he could rarely get good enough reception to be sure what was going on. I once bought a newspaper, but it proved to be a slow news day as far as the camps were concerned. So we listened to what the most charismatic people in the camp were saying. A radio announcer from Vaquería, who had left his broadcasts to a friend, dominated campfire discussion near our tent and often took the microphone in the middle of the camp as well. He told everyone that the country had come to a virtual standstill as people awaited the outcome of the demonstrations. He even said that the national anticipation and general depression had reached such a level that radio stations had stopped playing music out of respect for those in the camps. When organizers started talking about the possibility of a march on the capital—a walk that would have taken at least three or four days from where we were camped—there was no doubt in anyone's minds that it would come to this, and that it would spell the end of the government.[26] The law-abiding masses could by their very legality bring the government's dictatorial tendencies to the surface, and so vanquish it. Nicanor was getting more and more dictatorial every day, and was on the point of falling under the weight of his lies and his theft. It was the campesinos' historic duty to restore the rule of law.

In trying so hard to build their camp not as a space of exception to the law but as a performance of it, they had created a little world, enclosed by their harsh self-imposed limitations to action. From inside the camp, this looked like a symmetrical confrontation between long-standing adversaries, and this was exactly how most campesinos experienced it. Around the campfire at night I heard stories of past demonstrations and land invasions in which the cascos azules had shown up. Many of those in the camp had been beaten and arrested, or chased and driven off their land by the police. The contingent from Tekojoja had recently had their houses burned to the ground in a police raid, and many more could recount such stories going back to the early 1980s. Even if they respected the policemen individually, they saw their presence as an abstract representation of state forces ranged against them. That symmetry allowed them the conceit of claiming to be right.

But the desire to make the camp an example of legal protest undermined this position, because the only way to validate the legality of the campesinos' actions was to ask permission from the police. The police were happy to meet them halfway, offering them one side of the road, or telling them they could keep the bullhorn going until ten o'clock at night (the law normally prohibited that kind of noise in public places after eight o'clock). The irony is that for all their references to upholding the constitution, the law was not some pre-given code that campesinos were simply respecting in the camp. Instead, the law was being made in these encounters with police, and not symmetrically. The rules of protest were improvised, and they were legal only because police consent made them so. In other words, the campesino protest not only reinforced the law as the only legitimate terrain of struggle, but also revealed the law as subject to the dictate of violence. The rule of law was whatever the police said it was.

Unable to move or do anything that amounted to real force, the camp was slowly crushed by its own insistence on legality. Food became scarce. The toilets filled up. Colds and diarrhea swept through the tents, and several people were taken to a nearby hospital with a dangerous gastrointestinal illness. By the fourth day, organizers had asked the police for permission to collect money by the side of the road for two hours a day. Even as the government accused campesinos of being funded by international terrorist organizations, protesters in Caaguazú were holding out hats and bags on the roadside, with the police directing traffic. The radical groups, their tactics voted down in leaders' assemblies, left the camp. More people arrived, but numbers were nevertheless flagging.

On the ninth day of the paro cívico, the camps were dismantled, and people slowly headed home, pooling for trucks or begging for bus fare. The leadership had come to a minimal face-saving agreement with the Gabinete de Crisis, in which the latter agreed to continue with its ineffectual plan to buy land for campesinos (now saying that it would do so in the following fiscal year) and agreeing to treat the campesino prisoners expeditiously—in short, conceding nothing at all. Tierra malhabida had been conjured repeatedly, and in this way campesinos had acquired a sort of legal recognition for their struggle that they hadn't had before, but that recognition had come at a high price. If legality was the compromise through which campesinos tried to address the public sphere, it was legality that silenced them as well. The law, still produced in negotiations with the Colorado Party and the security apparatuses which they controlled, strangled them off. And the new democrats, simply not interested enough in the plight of campesinos to be outraged by this routine arbitrariness, barely noticed. In the following two years the Frente Nacional slowly disbanded, and the campesino movement again fractured into regional organizations. In the monthly meetings of the Movimiento Agrario in Vaquería, any suggestion of organizing a march or demonstration was met with resistance from local leaders fearful of losing credibility. The failed paro cívico was not mentioned for many months, and when I started hearing about it again, it was as a cautionary tale about the problems of poorly planned mobilizations.

The marches in the paro cívico, as seen from the outside, showed the degree to which a public spectacle of coordinated dissent could be coopted and transformed by the police into a show of state orderliness. If campesinos thought that the show of force looked authoritarian, they underestimated the degree to which orderly and controlled force is necessary to the new democratic understanding bureaucratic regularity. As Don Handelman (2004) argues, public events orchestrated by the state can serve one of two purposes, and usually serve both. The first, much talked about, is the display of nationalism, to elicit common feeling among citizens. But the second is what Handelman calls "bureaucratic logic," which shows that the state is capable of creating order out of chaos, of controlling unruly flows with the proper application of regulation and policing. Indeed, the paro cívico, and the repercussions it had over the next six months, may well have constituted President Nicanor's finest hour, for he managed to show new democrats that if nothing else, he was not incompetent. After Borda made campesino demands seem unreasonable, populist, and economically unjustifiable, Nicanor's overwhelming control of the demonstrations seemed appropriate to many people in Asunción. Indeed, it was the very thing that government is all about—to allow dissent but not disruption, to consider arguments and to reasonably refuse them, and to do everything possible to stop things from getting out of hand. On the basis of this show of bureaucratic logic, Nicanor spent much of the rest of his mandate militarizing the campo with very little protest in Asunción, setting up military posts which could be called on to aid the police, and eventually even creating civilian parapolice units to control campesino organizations.

GENERAL STRIKES FROM THE INSIDE

Let me return for a moment to the Comisión de Verdad y Justicia event held in May 2006, a year and a half after the paro cívico. As I left it, Victoriano Centurión—hero of the campesino armed struggle of the 1980s—had stood down from a debate over tierra malhabida, defeated by the simple statement "We can't violate private property." The comisión had been a tepid affair from

the outset. In keeping with many such institutions, it had little retributive function (although its investigations could, in principle, lead to criminal charges
against perpetrators), and was mainly packaged as a healing exercise.[27] In this
sense it was meant to account for the past, but not necessarily to hold anyone
accountable, and to inaugurate (again) the present as a radical departure from
the past. That rupture, by the time the hearings began, in 2004, had already
been established by demographic changes. Paraguay's high birthrate meant
that over 50 percent of the population was under fifteen, and thus had not been
alive during Stroessner's time. Like other spaces of new democratic remembrance in Paraguay, the comisión was beginning to look like an affair of the old,
and the bodies which attended it were marked not only by torture, but by age.

This is why the introduction of tierra malhabida to the comisión's discourse
marked a minor but palpable danger. The unusual idea had come from Digno
Brítez, a lawyer and famed campesinista rabble-rouser who had been helping
campesino organizations in all matters legal since the early 1980s. He now
worked for a well-endowed NGO in Asunción and only occasionally went to
the countryside, preferring to help out on the bureaucratic end of things. He
was the keynote speaker at this chapter of comisión hearings and had given
the event its name, "Campesinos y Tierra Malhabida." The title was a self-
conscious attempt to link the struggles of his old friends in the Stroessner resistance to current land struggles and to the politics of campesinos who had
taken up Alegre's document and tried to march with it in the paro cívico. In a
carefully constructed exhibit to the side of the stage, Brítez's NGO had hung
pictures of Stroessner's torture victims culled from the archivo del terror next
to pictures of current land disputes, including some I had taken only months
earlier in Tekojoja. In his speech, and in the exhibit, tierra malhabida linked
past injustices to the injustices of the present, to the impossibility of accessing land on the frontier, the droughts, pesticides, and unemployment which
infect campesino communities, and the terror created by local parapolice units
formed to protect private property from campesino invasions.

When Brítez, a card-carrying new democrat with glossy pictures and legal
credentials, brought these topics up, reading from a prepared speech in Spanish, these ideas were accepted as part of the public performance. This was
unusual, the sort of discourse that only a small group of campesinista intellectuals in Asunción ever engaged in, and their opinions were, to most new
democrats and Colorados, distasteful but innocuous. But when Centurión, the
campesino leader with wild eyes and wilder Guaraní, with stories less abstract,

more intimate, and more situated, tried to say the same things, he was shouted down by the Colorado member present, Miguel Ángel Aquino. The interchange dramatized the degree to which campesino participation in public politics was conditioned by the transition. Campesinos were invited to participate in discussions of tierra malhabida so long as the conversation remained focused on the historical shortcomings of the dictatorship or the Colorado Party. They could not turn the conversation into one about actual land and people living in the present, those ingredients that conjured something outside of legal deliberation and polite remembering, campesino politics in its popular danger. Brítez, Aquino, and Centurión, although as close together ideologically as such people ever came, nonetheless played the roles of new democrat, Colorado, and campesino perfectly. The first two eyed each other carefully and respectfully as they negotiated a historical transition for their country, while the third was forced to voice his opinion only briefly and without becoming too rowdy.

Tierra malhabida came into campesino politics in the early 1990s and again in the 2000s as a discourse borrowed from the new democrats and as a way of addressing a new public obsessed with legality and transparency as the condition for its own existence. Borrowing the concept involved submitting it to a translation that turned that deep campesino sense of historical wrong into a legal argument. And that translation caused campesinos to affirm rather than question the directionality of modern democracy's official narrative, the temporality which made the constitution, the rule of law, and the eventual hegemony of new democrats possible. It made campesinos subaltern to the new democrats just as they had been subaltern to Stroessner's Colorados. They received recognition as a population with needs, as a constituency to be mobilized, as bundles of rights that had been violated, but not as citizens of the present capable of participating in public debate on the direction of law.[28] For campesinos, the rule of law was absolute—they were either subjects to it or in violation of it, but they were never its authors. As such, anticorruption and tierra malhabida were not idioms of legal contestation. They were reiterations of the mythic grounds of a new democratic rule from which campesinos remained excluded.

Paraguayan campesinos are not the only people to confront the duplicity of the "rule of law" in the post–Cold War world. One could see tierra malhabida as a symptom of the global decline of traditional radical politics in favor of pursuing rights and law-based strategies to progressive projects. A number of critics have pointed out that this celebration of the rule of law tends to confine progressive ethics to a kind of legal positivism, that position that sees law as the will of the sovereign and a separate sphere from the actual making of law itself (see Brown and Halley 2002; Borneman 1997). Consider Talal Asad's commentary on the Universal Declaration of Human Rights: "The declaration seems to assume a direct convergence of the 'rule of law' . . . with social justice. . . . If that is the case, *the rule called law* effectively usurps the entire universe of moral discourse" (2004, 138; emphasis in original). Anticorruption arguments seem to be prone to the same problem, of abandoning the transformative potential of social justice struggles by equating ethics with law.

But the argument that law usurps moral discourse only works if it elides the negotiation that takes place, not only in creating the rule called law, but also in interpreting it in the political tussle of legal battles. Unless one subscribes to a kind of legal literalism (see Crapanzano 2000) that sees the universe of the legal as preestablished by some external sovereignty, then the rule of law need not be understood as a moral prison. For new democrats, this is what the transition in Paraguay was all about—the simultaneous establishment of the rule of law and decentering of sovereignty from the dictator to the public sphere. Campesinos experienced the rule of law as a trap, not because it necessarily needed to be so, but because they were its perpetual subjects. During the transition, new democrats owned law's morality, and the Colorados owned its violence. Campesinos had neither, and thus were enveloped by it.

The campesinos' self-defeating attempt at a general strike in the name of the rule of law is the perfect demonstration of this impossible position. In this direct action against the government, one of their first concerted coordinations with urban unions, campesinos employed a political tactic with a storied history, but may have turned the logic of the general strike against itself. The paradox of the paro cívico recalls Walter Benjamin's discussion of strikes in his "Critique of Violence" (1978 [1920]). The right to strike, Benjamin asserts, presents an exception to the prohibition on private violence in democratic states, and as such blurs the line between what he calls foundational and conservative forms of violence. In the right to strike, the state's monopoly on legitimate violence (of the sort that preserves the rule of law) makes limited room for a form of extortion (striking) that has the capacity to found contracts. Following Georges Sorel (1910), Benjamin claims that the (emancipatory) danger of the strike lies in the possibility of the *general* strike, which focuses its foundational violence on the state itself, and therefore exists outside of the law. The contract which a general strike aims to found is a constitution, the very beginning of law.

The possibility of structural upheaval was definitely on the minds of campesinos in the paro cívico, at least in the first few days. Campfire discussions and repartee over the terere gourd were inevitably about the waning legitimacy of the current state, and about the dawn of a new order led by a solid campesino sense of justice. The public face of the march, on the other hand, was always presented in liberalisms' own language of critique—the critique of corruption. In this iteration, the injustice of the state is not the injustice of its laws, but of a few unscrupulous elites charged with positions of power. And since campesinos cannot speak the law, they need confirmation of their legality. Hence the absurd negotiations during the paro cívico. Campesinos claimed to be standing up for the rule of law and the constitution against their government's egregious abuses. But to remain true to this principle, they steadfastly refused to break the law, and the only way to assure that they were acting legally was to check with the law's most proximate official representatives, the police. Although they faced off across a highway with police as antagonists, when they wanted to make sure that they weren't contravening any laws, campesino leaders would cross the road to get permission for their actions.

In evoking tierra malhabida campesinos participate in another even more pernicious ritual of new democratic mythmaking. For them, tierra malhabida evokes an injustice felt in the present and inscribed almost everywhere on the landscape. This resonates with the general feeling that if anything has changed in the campo since Stroessner's time, it has changed for the worse. But as translated into the legally recognizable language of Efraín Alegre's exposé, tierra malhabida has redemptive temporality. From this perspective, tierra malhabida represents an injustice committed overwhelmingly in the past, a past irreconcilable with the democratic future. This past is objectified in documents which speak for themselves, precisely the way evidence is supposed to speak for itself in law. Like the Comisión de Verdad y Justicia and the archivo del terror, Alegre's performance sustains the promise of transparent, procedural democracy by creating a dismal past in which the rule called law barely held. Alegre's indictment might be directed at the Colorado Party still in power, but it is fundamentally an indictment of a past system, a past land reform, a past populism, a past to which campesino politics properly belongs.

This, finally, is the key to the emergence of the new democrats, which relies on the 1992 constitution as a definitive rupture in the country's history. In Paraguay it is not quite enough to claim that the constitution was a "friendly liquidation of the past," to use Donna Lee Van Cott's memorable phrase (2000).

Nor is it sufficient to point to the inadequate forms of retribution meted out by the comisión, as John Borneman (1997) and Richard Wilson (2001) have done for Eastern Europe and South Africa, respectively. Both of these institutions play a key role not in erasing past injustice, but in repositioning it in relation to the present. In Paraguay's post–Cold War constitutional democracy, *the past serves new democrats as the safe receptacle for the very concept of injustice.* Traditional Liberal politicians, businesspeople, members of the judiciary, and even high-ranking members of the Colorado Party like Aquino and President Nicanor can ally with new democrats so long as they adopt this temporality. But campesinos, creatures of the past, cannot.

Nineteen eighty-nine was supposed to be the end of history.[29] That argument, that liberal democracy had won out as the only possible frame for global politics, for all its empirical shortcomings, *was* an effective description of the liberal political project for the post–Cold War world, and of the new democratic hopes for Paraguay. This is also why rituals of new democratic affirmation, such as the comisión and denunciations of corruption, are also rituals for the control of populism, which thrives on the injustices of the present. New democrats fear even more the irrational quality of campesino subjects, at once the victims of past totalitarianism and the vectors of its reemergence in the present. Tierra malhabida, and the recognition it confers on campesino politics, is at least as much a form of control as it is a spark, smuggling as it does a note of liberal triumphalism into the politics of those for whom no democratic transition ever really happened, and whose sense of injustice is out of joint with the new rule of law.

Joel Jara was the first person I met in rural Paraguay who really challenged my understanding of the word *privatiza-tion*. We were sitting out on his parents' front patio, pass-ing around a terere gourd with his cousin, talking about the upcoming cotton harvest. Drought had seriously damaged everyone's crops that year, and it was unlikely they would be able to pay off their debts, much less make any money. What was most troubling about this, for Joel, was that the end of the harvest was moving season, when some families used their extra cash to move elsewhere or to send their kids abroad in search of work. In the recent years of failing har-vests, the pattern had been changing. Every April and May, bankrupt campesinos had been selling their land to Brazil-ian soy farmers from down the road just east of where we were sitting, expanding what had become huge fields of soy-beans into the edges of Joel's community. The fear was that this season's drought would bring many more land sales. Complaining loudly about the Brazilians' push into what he considered peasant cotton country, Joel declaimed, "Opriva-tizapase la oreyvy!" (They want to privatize all of our land!).

At the time, this comment made little sense to me. Joel said it on what I considered his parents' private property, a homestead they had cut out of the bush during the campesino settlement of the area in 1978, when cotton crops promised to make everyone rich. Joel himself had been born here.

I had already spoken at length to his father about the land. He had long ago managed to pay the IBR for full title, but in the intervening years he had lost his paper copy of the title, and he was terrified to ask anyone official about it, for fear they might evict him. I thought at the time that this was unlikely, but I could understand the serious menace that soybeans represented to the farm. From the cotton field behind the house, the horizon to the northeast looked like a green blanket. The Jaras were among the most adamant on their road that no one should sell their farms to Brazilians or even plant soybeans, but they knew well that communities where the process had started had quickly become unlivable to those who insisted on staying. With soybeans came deforestation, pesticides, and machinery, and in several cases they also brought police and vigilante groups ready to threaten the diehards to sell. But was *privatization* the right name for this process of violently forcing people to sell their own, titled property?

Over the following two years, I frequently encountered people using the word *privatization* in this way. I came to see it as a complex commentary on economic changes facing the country, but also of a profound reimagining of the role of law throughout Latin America after the end of the Cold War. It was a subtle legal transition that seemed literally to be creeping across the land from the east, following a tide of beans and engulfing those areas that had been part of the populist legal regime of the land reform. What Joel called privatization was therefore quite different from the better-known cases of privatization of customary land or postsocialist state land happening in other parts of the world.[1] But it was related to those transitions, part of a global move in the post–Cold War period to rethink the governance of property relations. For with the advancing beans came de facto legal shifts which subtly reformulated not just *who* owned land, but *how* land was owned.

This peculiar war against the "privatization" of what the state already considered private property came about in large part because of contradictions in Paraguayan law. But despite recent attempts at simplifying property law, through new democratic schemes like public registry streamlining and rapid titling, I argue that these contradictions cannot simply be legislated away. Rather, they speak to a long-standing tension in liberal forms of property between a conception of right as an abstract relation between people, and another conception in which right is a relation between people mediated by material things. That is, liberal legal traditions oscillate between holding to a purist understanding of property as a purely legal principle, and a more pragmatic understanding that acknowledges that property is constantly made and struggled over as people interact with each other and the things they wish to possess. Holding to this latter position, campesinos offer a biting challenge to the hypocrisy of elite lawmakers and to theories currently popular among new democrats and international development practitioners about the need to create increasingly abstract systems of property ownership in order to improve governance and agricultural performance. Indeed, as the fight for one community, Tekojoja, progressed, campesinos increasingly saw it as a fight against legislative reform, against the Inter-American Development Bank (IDB), and against lawmakers enamored of a new approach to property registration promoted by international development guru Hernando de Soto (2000).

My argument unfolds in three parts. First, I describe campesino notions of property as a material product of their work and explain why they see "private property" as something quite different. It is this difference that allows campesinos to see certain kinds of private transactions on the land as "privatization," but not others. Second, I show how this divide in property forms has solidified into a territorial division, blocking off campesino territories from "private" territories, leaving each with their own laws, bureaucracies, and modes of relating to the land. I focus on a conflict that happened in the community of Tekojoja, at the border between those two territories, and show how privatization works to harden highly exclusive notions of citizenship and legitimate politics. In the last section, I show how the idea of the "precarious lot," a stigmatizing description of campesino living conditions used in legal and bureaucratic documents, undermines even the idea that private property is an abstract right divorced from the material conditions of those who possess it. In short, even those who advocate a purified notion of property rights implicitly advance or withhold those rights on the basis of wealth. The campesino fight against privatization is a fight not so much against the idea of private land ownership, but against the hypocrisy of an increasingly influential conception of property rights that tacitly excludes the poor.

TWO KINDS OF PROPERTY

In some respects, the argument ahead seems like a relatively straightforward exercise in economic anthropology—that is, describing the economic thoughts and practices of a group of people who call themselves campesinos, and analyzing their difference from more familiar liberal conceptions. But immediately the way is blocked by the very word *campesino*, because this demographic or class designation doesn't seem to lend itself to an analysis of economic thought. In fact, I have as much trouble making this argument theoretically as campesinos have trouble making it politically. The trouble stems both from the fact that there are few explicit attempts in anthropology to systematize the difference between campesino economic thought and institutionalized political economy and from the related suspicion that, unlike indigenous people, campesinos aren't different in the way they need to be to be conceptualized as something apart. Peasants, according to most scholarship, do not cohere in their differ-ence from modern thinking the way indigenous people do, but cohere only in their articulation to larger systems defined by others.

This is particularly problematic in anthropology and the related post–Cold War politics of liberal multiculturalism. Both are due at least in part to a histori-cal division of labor demarcated by the word *indigenous*.[2] Indigeneity, which by definition marks a postcolonial difference from the colonizer, produced a se-ries of theoretical markers for that difference, from "culture" to "ethnicity," all of which became highly politicized in the second half of the twentieth century. Depending on the moment and perspective, this difference has been under-stood as a superficial aesthetic one, as a container of beliefs about the world, or as a radically divergent ontology. *Peasant* or *campesino*, on the other hand, has been used to specifically deny that difference, even while it debases and stigmatizes. Fundamental to the concept of the nation, rural food producers are marked by their marginality to, but not historically valid difference from, national economic and political processes (e.g., Chakrabarty 2002). The rich literature on Latin American peasantries has thus been almost exclusively po-litical and economic in its focus, describing structures of exploitation and the partial articulations between impoverished rural populations and national or international economies.[3]

As Michael Kearney (1996) argues in his excellent genealogy, the academic distinction between peasant and indigenous is marked by a parallel division rooted in Cold War politics. While many groups may qualify equally as indig-enous and peasant, and may even switch between one and the other, the labels mark different political modes which rarely overlap (see de la Cadena 2000; Boyer 2003; Collier 1994). During most of the twentieth century, with indige-neity still firmly excluded from the modern nation, many of these populations were conscripted to peasanthood as they became the constituencies of Mao-ist parties, national populist movements, dependency theorists, and finally the rural development projects that sprang up in the 1960s around the Alliance for

Progress. The much ballyhooed "disappearance of the peasantry" toward the end of the Cold War was in part due to economic restructuring and rural-urban migration, but also to a different politics of identification that emerged to meet new development orthodoxies and the waning of leftist politics in general.

The devaluation of a certain brand of agrarian populism in Latin American politics was accompanied by a slim and still highly circumscribed opening for ethnicity as a realm of authorized difference under new multicultural forms of governance. Hence the surge of indigenous politics in a number of different national contexts, such as Ecuador (Sawyer 2004), Bolivia (Postero 2007), Guatemala (Hale 2006), and Brazil (Warren 2001). New multicultural constitutions sprang up throughout Latin America during the 1990s, many of them claiming to dramatically open up official politics to these culturally distinct groups (van Cott 2000). But multiculturalism is limited and constrained. Many of these movements argue that even while citizenship has been formally extended to indigenous populations, it is a hollow extension that does not come with the full gamut of rights that define participation in liberal democracy (Dagnino 2003; Yashar 2005). Citizenship itself has therefore become a terrain of struggle on which indigenous groups can critique their exclusion from states that claim to be newly inclusive. This struggle over indigenous citizenship in other parts of Latin America has opened up enough of a crack in the exclusive walls of the public sphere that large numbers of people who once called themselves "campesinos" have begun calling themselves "indígenas."[4]

But for campesinos who cannot make a claim to indigeneity, the argument about citizenship remains harder to access, in part because their exclusion from formal politics has never been as explicit as it was with indigenous people. Most campesinos are, after all, citizens. They have identity papers, serve in the army, and vote in elections. Yet their inability to be taken seriously in national public discourse underscores the fact that their inclusion is a purely formal one. Their grievances are harder to articulate because their exclusion has always been tacit rather than legally explicit. This is certainly the case in Paraguay, where the stakes of the campesino-indigenous divide are such that it is highly unlikely that peasants would take on the mantle of indigenous politics.[5] The populist project begun by Stroessner in the 1960s adopted the rural masses as its primary constituency, anchoring a new vision of the nation in a massive land-reform project. This did not make campesinos full citizens—land reform was the means through which they might *eventually* achieve citizenship—but it did continually affirm their belonging to the nation in a way that it never did for indígenas. If anything, campesinos were entrusted with policing the borders of this modern nation, as the colonization program brought them increasingly into contact with indigenous populations on the country's frontier.[6] That bloody encounter, now only a generation or two old, cemented a rural antagonism that still plays a large role in structuring campesino aspirations to full citizenship. It was, after all, indigenous land which provided the blank slate for the campesino land reform, and the few stands of forest left for them to live and hunt in remain targets of campesino expansionist aspirations. More recently, some of the language of multiculturalism has made its way into the campesino movement, and there has been an important softening of antagonisms between campesinos and indígenas, laying the groundwork for a number of strategic political alliances. But I have met very few who would go so far as to claim indigeneity for themselves, and it remains far more common to hear people speaking in patently racist terms about their indigenous neighbors.

Campesino aspirations to citizenship were produced by land reform, the political anchor of the historic bloc between Stroessner's Colorado Party and the campesinado. Despite a history of struggle between campesino organizations and Stroessner's party, by the 1970s both groups were at least speaking the same language, and both professed to be building a nation out of campesino labor. That historic bloc, along with land reform, broke down after the coup that deposed Stroessner, in 1989, leaving campesinos to ponder their role in the emergent public sphere of Paraguay's new democracy. Campesinos remain committed to the idea of building a modern nation, but as they find themselves increasingly excluded by their country's new elite, they, too, have tried to adopt a politics of difference—not of ethnicity, but of economic thought. So combative has this identity become in Paraguay that even the word *campesino* connotes a very particular relationship to preserving the goals of Stroessner's land reform. Without that political project, campesinos cease to be campesinos.

This is why the category campesino is so slippery in Paraguay: to be campesino is to propose a national project that is at odds with the transitional narrative of new democrats. And this problem is not only confined to identity politics, but influences the very manner in which the state works. The most threatening aspect of campesino economics is the way that it understands the relationship between land, rights, and documents. Solutions to land problems favored by new democrats rely on a theory of representation that denies, or tries to mitigate against, the materiality of documents. But campesinos understand the material production of documents as an economic activity linked to land use, and the circulation of these documents as a fundamental aspect of citizenship. Just as they understand the exclusionary networks of documentary circulation to be the basis for the injustices they are fighting against, they also see their way out as involving the creation and circulation of their own documents in the interest of building a new and better nation.

The one work that has come close to understanding this difference is an idiosyncratic volume by Stephen Gudeman and Alberto Rivera, *Conversations in Colombia* (1990), which seeks to describe the logic of campesino economic thinking in Colombia in the 1980s. They call this system the "economics of the base," in which the patriarchal household or homestead serves an as anchoring unit around which all economic behavior is organized. They suggest that the Colombian campesino homestead is built through the cumulative investment of annual surpluses derived from family labor and the divine productivity of nature, and that market exchange, labor migration, and the use of money are all subordinated to the construction of this base. From this, Gudeman and Rivera build a complex synchronic picture of campesino economic thought, which they claim is inherited from the Physiocracy of the eighteenth century.[7] This language is strikingly similar to how campesinos in Paraguay speak about their own economic activity in the early twenty-first century. They use the Spanish word *base* in both Spanish and Guaraní to talk about their economic activities, and young men pioneering on the frontier or starting a new family say they are starting *chebase* (my base). For campesino households in most of eastern Paraguay, the production of cotton, supported by state extension agencies, was critical to sustaining this cycle between the mid-1960s and the early 2000s (see Bray and Borda 1988). Profits from the sale of cotton in April and May are immediately invested in improving the home, buying tools, drums of oil, fencing, and clothes. As the cotton economy continues its annual decline, an increasing portion of investments goes to schooling and to sending children off in search of work.

Gudeman's and Rivera's book, along with Gudeman's later and more formalistic work on the economy of the base (2001; 2008), provides excellent tools for understanding Paraguayan campesino economics. But the conclusions they draw undermine the historical significance of what they have encountered. The homology between their own model and that of eighteenth-century economics is interesting, but by focusing on that alone, the authors short-cut Colombia's independent history entirely, and end up providing a "rural folk" economics that is profoundly ahistorical and apolitical. In their attempt to disrupt the marginalization of campesino economics they recognize its complexity and coherence, but they do so by relegating campesino thinking to the distant past with their suggestion that "what is now the margin was once a wellspring of ideas for the center" (17). The temporality accorded to campesinos in this model is not "traditional" in the sense of indigenous and timeless, the wedge that is necessary for ethnic politics. Instead, it is just plain anachronistic, belonging to the West's intellectual past, and their analysis in no way treats campesino thinking as coeval or potentially symmetrical with that of the various kinds of economists who oppose it. Most surprisingly, the book never mentions the multiple land reforms or the long history of violent struggle over land as a possible source of thinking about land.[8]

My argument here has quite different ends, and the picture of campesino economic thinking I mean to present is dynamic and contested, at least as much the product of 1960s populism as any previous intellectual tradition which has been preserved by the "rural folk." What this suggests is that the relationship between an economics of the base and a more "current" market economics is far more variable and politicized than Gudeman allows. Gudeman's project (esp. 2008) is to find the economy of the base in a particular tension between an embedded community and an abstract market (conjuring echoes of Karl Polanyi [1944]). I do not contest his argument, but as I read them in Paraguay, such terms as mercado, base, and comunidad are entirely contingent and are taken up as available languages for economic struggle in ways that might easily be reversed or fought differently. The market is, of course, a kind of community, just as communities and "the base" itself are abstractions. The relation between these is not one to be negotiated by a Polanyian pendulum, but a language in which economic actors position themselves in relation to each other. I contend that the way that base is used in Paraguay, whatever its similarities to eighteenth-century economics, is at its core an expression of Cold War development theories promoted by Stroessner's government, which campesinos now adopt as a form of critique against emerging development projects from which they feel excluded.

For campesinos the "base" is not only a homestead but also the beginning of political subjectivity. In the populist rhetoric of the land reform, progressive "improvement" of the base was part of the improvement of people, a slow building of political clout and recognition for the rural poor. Just as families worked the land to build crops and surpluses for investment in their houses, they also worked on acquiring land titles from the land-reform agency, material objects which connected them as citizens to the state. The idea that land rights were material goods acquired through labor was therefore linked to the idea of the development of political subjectivity through labor. Cold War Colorado propaganda was explicit about this link, arguing that to give campesinos land was to give them full personhood and thus the possibility of participating in the national project: labor built the household base, created political subjects, and ultimately built a whole new nation.[9] By the 1990s, the project of acquiring political membership through land rights had become a deeply felt way of reckoning campesino identity and of structuring the aspirations of young men like Joel. In this there was an alternate conception of property at work than that of new democrats. If the latter saw property as an abstract right agreed on by the public and documented in a national registry, campesinos saw property as the endpoint of labor on the land and the starting point for the very possibility of public life.

The link between investment in the base and membership in the nation is clearer when one looks at conceptions of property at work in land-reform colonies. Land ownership in *colonias* was governed by the Estatuto Agrario, which came into effect in 1963 and was amended in 2002, and all services related to the land reform were run out of the office of the IBR. In areas of concentrated land resettlement during that period, most campesinos lived and worked in such colonias or in the periphery of small towns, and until recently, almost all were dependent on the economic cycle of cotton (see Nikiphoroff 1994). In the early twenty-first century campesinos in Paraguay's eastern colonias owned and traded land in three distinct ways. Depending on their position in the pioneer narrative, campesinos own their land as *mejoras* (improvements), *derecheras* (rights), or *títulos* (titles). And although campesinos saw títulos as the best form of property, all three were part of a spectrum of forms that were different in degree, but not in kind. For the campesinos I knew, the mejora was the most fundamental form of ownership, the baseline on which other forms of property were built.

MEJORAS

When campesinos talk about land transfers in the colonias, they usually refer to these as sales of mejoras, or "improvements," to the land, rather than of land itself. The legislative precedent for this is straightforward enough. The land reform initiated in the 1960s retracted the rights of possession of unproductive latifundios, which owned vast tracts of forest without doing much with them.

It also implicitly disqualified indigenous hunters and gatherers from making claims. Prior to the colonization, most economic activity on the frontier fell into one of these two categories, with most latifundios existing for low-intensity extraction (of valuable woods and yerba mate) and using occasional indigenous labor to carry it out (see Domínguez 1995 [1967]; Kleinpenning 1992; Reed 1995). Campesinos wanting to participate in the colonization had only to find land that was not being intensively used for agriculture. Inside the colonies, land that was already being used, regardless of its legal status, could be bought by campesinos from the person who was working it at an informally arranged price. What was being bought, then, was not the land itself but the mejora, the human intervention on the land, including clearings, structures, wells, and gardens.

In the early years of most colonies, young men found, improved, and sold plots frequently, making their living out of clearing forest, selling wood, and then moving on to find new land, selling mejoras to a new wave of settlers. Tekojoja, a colony begun by pioneers in 1975 and officially expropriated by the state two years later, has almost no descendants from those early pioneers still living in it. Besides a handful of original families, the oldest group of settlers is part of the second or third wave, people who bought mejoras in 1976 and 1977 from young men who did little more than clear trees with axes. The clearing constituted their stake, and it was this that they sold to others.[10] In these cases, nothing formal traded hands, except occasionally a piece of paper written up and signed by both parties. In general, a handshake sufficed to seal the deal, and the transfer was conducted *arriero porte*, informally. In Guaraní, to do something arriero porte means to do it "in the manner of a young man," not a bad campesino equivalent of "gentlemanly agreement"—the kind of consensual transaction that does not require formalization.

DERECHERAS

Although Stroessner liked to sell the March to the East as a land reform and resettlement program, almost none of the resettlement that occurred was planned or coordinated beyond the building of roads (see Vázquez 2006; Sánchez González 1997). The main activity of the IBR was to provide state recognition to settlements achieved "spontaneously" by pioneers seeking land on the frontier and then to help out by establishing an IBR office, measuring plots, and marketing cotton (all the things that allowed the state to extract some of the profits from pioneering). Because all of this land was claimed by somebody, even if only very tenuously, successful claims of this sort involved either ex-propriation by decree or purchase from the owner. Communities like Tekojoja were bureaucratically straightforward in this regard. The land was owned by a Colorado Party operative who had likely bought it only a few years earlier know-ing that the state would soon be buying. So when campesino laborers living on the outskirts of a nearby Mennonite settlement told the IBR they wanted to start a colony there, it only took two years to get the paperwork settled. Payment simply had to be transferred from state coffers to the owner, and the IBR could begin to formalize the colonization.

Many colonies remained unofficial long after they were first settled, usually because for political reasons it was difficult for the IBR to expropriate them. A landowner tied to the Colorado Party might be asking too much for the land, or there might be competing claims on the original title, making it hard to trans-fer. Most of these colonies were allowed to flourish in the hopes that the prob-lem would simply resolve itself, and in some cases the IBR even established offices, measured plots, and began accepting payments for plots before they were technically available for sale (this was going on in two of the seven com-munities I studied). The presence of the IBR in any of these communities pro-moted the understanding that, however long it might take, the expropriation and redistribution of land was a foregone conclusion.

The logic of the land reform set a very soft line between "land invasion" and the organized resettlement of idle frontier land, and tacitly let campesinos judge for themselves what land could be expropriated. The process was often antagonistic, with landowner organizations objecting to the way it was done.[11] But since, at the beginning of the process, the vast majority of the land was owned by foreign companies with very little interest in it, most land invasions led relatively smoothly to expropriation and settlement.[12]

Even if they remained unofficial after a few years, once colonies began to look somewhat permanent, and as families began to settle on particular plots, the sale of mejoras usually slowed. The second step of settlement was to so-licit state recognition for the properties, both individually and collectively. The standard procedure was for the IBR to do an initial measurement of the colony and any roads that residents had already cut, and then to issue nontransferable "occupancy permits" to solicitants. The Estatuto Agrario restricted who could solicit these permits: they had to be Paraguayan nationals, agricultores (mean-ing that they devoted their lives to farming), and landless, and they could not solicit a plot if they had already been granted one and abandoned it. There were also size restrictions and an absolute prohibition on buying and selling permits. However, these rules were not enforced until well into the transition.

The rights conferred by this interaction with the IBR were colloquially called *derecheras*, a word which until quite recently had not appeared in any legal documentation.[13] Campesinos and bureaucrats used the term to describe both the rights and the document on which they were inscribed, a one-page form with the name of the occupant and the lot number written on them, and they were the first documentary evidence of ownership. Even the issuance of this paper took a long time, as campesino requests for recognition wandered back and forth from the local office to the regional office in Caaguazú to the central office in Asunción, but eventually owners received a sheet of paper with a number on it. When it arrived, the paper facilitated a new relationship between campesinos and the state, a relationship that allowed the payment of yearly quotas on the land around the time of the cotton harvest. The permits granted campesinos access to a brown folder that remained with the IBR. These fragile brown folders, which detailed any transactions (including measurement, disputes, and especially payment to the IBR) performed on the land, also snaked their way between the offices with every addition, collecting receipts, notes, staples, stamps, signatures, and tears along the way. But delicate as it was, it was this connection between solicitants and a bundle of papers somewhere in the IBR system that made landownership official.

It was technically illegal to sell derecheras.[14] Nonetheless, until recently it was in practice only slightly harder to sell derecheras than it was to sell mejoras. Usually the transfer could be accomplished with a local bureaucrat as witness. Almost anyone would do, from a notary to the local justice of the peace, priest, or school principal, but the local IBR representative was preferred. The transfers were officially entered into the books as one person forfeiting their rights and another soliciting them. The new solicitants had to prove that they met the requirements of the beneficiary, and the process began again. Buyer and seller still said they were trading mejoras, but it was understood that having some form of documentation added value to the land. In other words, the legal status of the land, and the paper that came with it, was a form of mejora, an indication of personal or community investment in the legal status of the land.

TÍTULOS

Once derecheras were completely paid off, campesinos received a land title, but with certain limitations. For one thing, following the nontransferability of the derecheras, there was a ten-year moratorium on the sale of new titles, as part of an attempt to limit campesino "self-dispossession" through rapid sale.[15] After the ten-year period, the title ceased to fall under the jurisdiction of the Estatuto Agrario. In principle, it would move from the IBR to the Registro Publico and be governed by the Civil Code. There is no question that campesinos highly valued these títulos. But they did not generally see the conferral of the title as a transformation in the legal status of their rights. When I first started interviewing campesinos, no one talked about the way in which a title effectively signaled his or her own transfer from one legal community to another one, and few had much sense of the relationship between the Estatuto Agrario and the Civil Code.

From the campesino point of view, the conferral of property titles by the IBR was more mundane. It basically meant swapping the brown cover of the permit, which by then had accumulated years' worth of receipts, stamps, and notes, as well as a staggering quantity of staples, for a fresh new folder made of yellow cardboard. Campesinos referred to both permits and titles as kuatia, papers, and as with derecheras, used the word to refer to both the paper and the rights it represented. There's no question, however, that títulos were a highly valued form of paper, and that they had a special role to play in the pioneer narrative. I almost never saw one of these yellow papers, in part because of their rarity in the areas in which I worked, but also because people guarded them so carefully. Several heads of households refused outright to show me theirs, and those who did would often fetch them out of locked briefcases hidden in the bottom of locked cabinets.

Campesinos mainly wanted titles as a form of "security," most often security against the police taking the land away from them, or as a symbol of their achievements. Those who were closer to acquiring titles also recognized the credit possibilities that such titles opened for them. With derecheras, the only way to get credit was through the government Crédito Agrícola, or through local lenders who accepted motorbikes or cattle as collateral.[16] A title made credit cheaper, although many people with titles either never went into hock or did so once and vowed never to do it again after fighting their way out of debt. The title also meant that, in principle, campesinos were liberated from their relationship with the IBR and would henceforth deal solely with the public registry, where their titles were housed, and any notary public could witness transactions in accordance with the Civil Code. In practice, however, this almost never happened, since the IBR office remained the most proximate representative of the state, and campesinos continued to conduct most official business through them. Besides, the official relationship between the IBR's own property registry and the public registry was ill-defined. The ten-year moratorium against sale led to widespread confusion about the status and location of titles, and many papers got lost in the traffic between the IBR, the public registry, and the second office of the IBR housed inside the public registry.

So while titles were considered a desirable goal, both by policymakers and by campesinos, the latter didn't necessarily consider titled land to be of a different sort than untitled land. Land with kuatia was better than that without. Derecheras accompanied by receipts of some quota payments was better than just the simple occupancy permit. A title was better than either of these. Each of these steps was a proof of hard work, investment in the base, and by virtue of that investment provided a more solid stake in the land. I asked a number of people to explain the difference between buying mejoras and buying títulos, and all replied that títulos were a kind of mejora. The difference was one of degree and price, rather than of kind; the título was merely a material improvement that took the form of a piece of paper and a newly formalized network with local state representatives, and was therefore harder to take away.

That titles were ultimately considered a kind of mejora—similar to tilling a field, digging a well, or building a hut—shows just how ephemeral the notion of titling remained in the campo. Tilled fields grow over, wells fill in, and huts burn down. The difference between simple mejoras and titles was analogous to (and often correlated with) the difference between houses with dirt floors and houses with concrete or tile floors. That concrete is an improvement over dirt does not make the house completely permanent or invulnerable to natural disasters or capricious people. I met almost as many campesino families who had once had title and had lost it, either in fire, legal battles, botched inheritances, or through simple theft (usually by notaries hired to carry out land transactions) as families who still had their titles. That most of these families could probably have solicited and received a new copy of the title, which in principle remained in the registry or the IBR, didn't matter. The loss of the material evidence of title was considered the equivalent of losing it altogether, and while some expressed to me the idea that in the abstract they might still hold title, like Joel's father they were so uncertain of this as to avoid approaching anyone official, for fear of being evicted.

Paper titles are achieved with pride and maintained with pride, preserved and protected the same way that whitewash is constantly painted over house boards to keep them gleaming. This is a crucial point, not because it is so strange but because the commonsensicality of it challenges the view of post–Cold War bureaucratic reformers and of the logic of property law expressed in the Civil Code. In fact, it reverses the basic tenets of current conventions in land management. For campesinos, titles are the endpoint of property, the form to which one aspires. For middle-class urbanites, soy farmers, and international experts advising the government on land governance, all of whom subscribe to the legal precepts of the Civil Code, the title is a representation that makes property possible. It is the very beginning of property, and anything less is a feeble and mongrel form of ownership.

PROPIEDAD PRIVADA

In the words of the Estatuto Agrario, the central document of land reform, all of these stages of ownership were steps toward private ownership. Officially, the IBR saw the title conferred at the end of this process as merely a certificate of the absolute right of private property. The land reform followed a standard liberal rationale in suggesting that giving campesinos private title to their land would not only spur economic production, but also produce rational citizens for the nation. The first article of the Estatuto Agrario proclaimed that private property rights would be the basis for all rural development, both for economic advancement and for the incorporation of the campesinado into the nation. The Estatuto Agrario and the IBR were meant to be transitional institutions which would be dissolved when the campesinado had all acquired property and the economic conditions that prevented them from becoming full members of the nation had disappeared. But forty years later, the institution had not disappeared, and the language of private property, the supposed endpoint of the reform, had not become part of the reform process. In the actual process of colonizing, soliciting, improving, and gaining derecheras, few of the beneficiaries of the reform actually thought of the land titles they possessed or desired as being "private property." This is because the term *propiedad privada* was reserved for an entirely different sort of relation to land than the one to which campesinos aspired.

Campesinos referred to their land as *cheyvy* (my land), *chelote* (my lot), or *chelote titulado* (my titled lot). They even sometimes ironically called it *chelote precario* (my precarious lot). Those people in colonias who did call their land "propiedad privada" were small farmers who had taken on a whole new way of thinking about their land, and who as a consequence had started calling themselves productores, rather than campesinos. Rather than seeing land as a "base," they saw it as capital, a commodity that could be bought and sold in the interest of accumulating more capital and modernizing production. Most important, to call oneself a productor was to signal a change in politics and vision of the future of farming. In the area in and around Tekojoja, this was a small minority of farmers. The rest, those who continued calling themselves campesinos, used the term propiedad privada simply to refer to large tracts of land that were off-limits.

Brian Turner (1993, 180–81), in a nuanced political ethnography of rural politics on another part of the Paraguayan frontier, claims that there were two forms of property operating in the town of Minga Guazu in the late 1980s: propiedad privada meant alienable property, while the Guaraní possessive form, chelote or cheyvy, referred to inalienable property. My own reading of these terms is quite different. To talk about land as being inalienable on the frontier is somewhat absurd; in fact, many campesinistas describe the problem of frontier land as one of too much mobility, too much buying and selling with or without clear title.[17] In 2004, a few communities, like Joel's organized neighborhood groups, were trying to prohibit the sale of land to soy farmers, but these were new ideas, based on the fear that communities were disappearing and that the frontier had filled up. Until then no one had had trouble buying, selling, or subdividing plots and the labor invested in them. If anything it was propiedad privada which they considered inalienable, at least for certain people. Propiedad privada was precisely the label given to land from which the speaker was definitively excluded—it might be tradable, but only on a market to which campesinos had almost no access. Unlike land rights in the colonies, built on campesino labor, private property was an exclusionary practice backed by police violence. When I asked for a definition of private property, several campesinos gave the succinct answer: "ndojeikekuaai" (you can't enter).

The largest single landholding in a ten-kilometer radius to Tekojoja, which had changed hands three times since people began settling the area, was known as "la propiedad privada" or just "la privada," because of the signs that had been posted along the length of the fence after the last attempted land invasion, in 1990. Everyone I spoke with agreed that the property was nicknamed after the signs were put up, but there were a number of versions of what happened afterward. For some, the property was a place nobody dare enter throughout the 1990s, guarded as it was by a burly German with a huge dog, and with roads crisscrossing the forest so the police could be called in to go after poachers. For those who worked at the sawmill on the property and respected the German owner, the property was a legitimate holding because the owner gave work to campesinos. Even when campesinos did not harbor an explicit desire for the land in question, to talk about private property was to recognize the owners' ability to exclude, either through client allies in the local community or by mustering police violence. For these reasons, propiedad privada was almost never a target of land invasions, and as soon as it became a target, it would be renamed or qualified as tierra ociosa (idle land) or tierra del estado (state land).

In 2004 there were many signs that campesinos' relationship to private property was changing. For instance, the newest category which propiedad privada could turn into was tierra malhabida, considered an illegitimate holding, which while privately claimed was still properly state land. In fact, ever since la privada had been sold, in 2002, to a young Mennonite who lived far away and hired very few locals, there were rumors that it, too, was malhabida, at least partially. But perhaps the most striking sign of this shift, this rethinking of what private property meant to campesinos, was the smash success of "Propiedad privada," a purahéi jahe'o (lament song) sung in Guaraní. Written by Cecilio Mareco, and originally performed by a band called Odilio Román y los Románticos, it was covered repeatedly throughout the next two years, as it continued to be the song most played on country radio. It built on the patriarchal metaphor comparing lost land and lost love to offer advice about land conflict in the countryside.

PROPIEDAD PRIVADA
Propiedad privada nimboraka'e la che ahayhuva
Aikuaami'ỹre chemba'e roguaicha amokunu'ũ
Chupente ahayhuva, ambojerovia iporãvehaicha
Mamoiko aimo'ãta ijaratee oguerekoha

Chorus

Mba'eiko ajapota, mamoiko ahata, che yvoty ahayhuva, oumi hağua,
Ku ka'aruetevo, aha'arõiteva, aikuaa porãha, mba'e ahenoha.
Ko'ağa aikuama mba'epa ovale propiedad privada
Naimo'ãietene pe ahayhueteva che hegui oipe'a
Cheaño apyta ajeplaguea, ku tyre'ỹmicha,
mba'erepa peicha ha'e ndavy'aigui añekonsola.
Ağui añeha'ata ama'ẽporã pe cheraperare
Anive hağuama propiedad privadape aju aikeve

Porque ambyasy, añerepenti cherembiapokuere
Nachepohãveima, japerdetema, ahayhuva che.

PRIVATE PROPERTY
It turned out that the one I loved was private property
I didn't know it and treated her as though she were mine
I loved only her, and did everything she wanted as best I could
But never imagined that she had another owner.[18]

Chorus

What will I do, where will I go, to make my flower come to me?
In the afternoons I wait and I long, even though I know she is someone
    else's.
Now I know the real value of private property.
I had no idea that the one I loved so much could be taken from me.
I ended up alone, crying like an orphan.
How could it be? I say to console myself in my misery.
From now on I will try to stay on the right path
So as never to enter private property again
Because I am sorry and repent what I did [my past work].
There's no cure for me—I've definitely lost that which I love.

The purahéi jahe'o genre is sung almost exclusively by men. Nonetheless, because the Guaraní is not gendered in the third person, and because the speaker is rarely required to use pronouns, the object in most of the song is indirect. What I have translated here as "her" and "she" is actually better translated as the indirect "that which I loved" (*ahayhuva*), "that which was had" (*oguerekoha*), and "someone else's belonging" (*mba'e ahéno*). The indirect reference works with the song's patriarchal objectification of the woman in question, but it also enhances the canny use of the metaphor of land ownership which accounts for much of the song's appeal. For the song is both about lost love and about changing property regimes in rural Paraguay. While it is clear that the object of the singer's affections is a woman, there is only one moment in the entire song where this is necessarily so, when he refers to her as "flower," a common metaphor for girlfriend.

Although popular Guaraní is peppered with Spanish loanwords, their pronunciation and integration into the grammar of sentences marks some of them as borrowings. While words like *ajeno*, *valer*, *plaguear*, and *repentir* are all recognizably Spanish words, they are common forms used in standard Guaraní speech and are not immediately recognized by speakers as loans.[19] The term *propiedad privada*, however, pronounced as it would be in Spanish, is set apart as a noun, and the narrative thrust of the song is about learning the "value" of this foreign concept. The concept is presented here as a powerful force that takes the protagonist completely by surprise, and following another common trope of campesino songs and stories, the narrative is not about overcoming or vanquishing that force, but about learning to accept it. Not to put too fine a point on it, it is not the woman/land that the song's narrators laments losing in the end, but his actions or work (*tembiapo*). He is resigned to having lost his labor and has learned his lesson not to "enter" (*aike*) private property. In addition to the obvious gendered connotation of "entry" here, *aike* is a verb used euphemistically for land invasions, as in to "enter private property," and the key verb used to describe private property in the phrase *ndojeikekuaai* (you can't enter). The singer's sense of injustice about this inability to enter remains in the melodramatic final lines.[20] Private property, in this song and in other common uses I heard in the campo, was as much a potential theft of the value of labor as a relation of spatial exclusion.

THE ANTI-PRIVATIZATION TRENCH

Two quite different forms of property exist on the Paraguayan frontier. On the one hand is campesino property, conceptualized as three different forms of mejora, and on the other hand is private property, a form of alienation to which campesinos have no access. Soybeans brought these differences into sharp relief. The expansion of the campesino frontier created by the colonization scheme in 1963 slowed down in the 1980s and 1990s, and by 2000 had more or less halted. New campesino communities continued to be established, but they were hard won, small, and usually on poor land. The booming soy industry, meanwhile, began to take over campesino colonies in the 1980s, and accelerated into the 1990s and 2000s (see Nickson 1981; Souchaud 2002; Fogel and Riquelme 2005). In areas where these two frontiers met, there was a clear distinction between the two territories. To the west were the remaining smallholdings characteristic of campesino agriculture, mixed fields and fruit trees with large stretches set aside for cotton, corn, manioc, or other cash crops. Land ownership in these areas was still governed by the IBR, out of district offices, under the terms set out by the Estatuto Agrario. To the east were holdings of 50 to 50,000 hectares, treeless and mechanized, covered in rotating soy, corn, and wheat crops, and mostly owned by Brazilian immigrants. These holdings rarely fell under the auspices of the IBR, and instead were governed by the general property laws laid out in Paraguay's Civil Code. The division was rarely this stark, but in communities like Ocho de diciembre, where Joel grew up, and Tekojoja, where he moved to, it had radicalized into trench-like separation and an open war between defenders of the two models.

Between 2002 and 2006, a group of several hundred campesinos in Tekojoja from the Movimiento Agrario y Popular were embroiled in a violent struggle with a handful of Brazilian soy producers from the nearby community of Santa Clara. The immediate stakes were simple enough: both groups were trying to control about 200 hectares of arable land, scattered in ten separate plots throughout the settlement. But despite the relatively small area—similar conflicts for much more land had been taking place in Paraguay for decades—both sides managed to harness high-profile supporters, lawyers, organizations, politicians, and media, which saw the struggle as symbolic of fundamental shifts in Paraguayan society.

What made Tekojoja such an important case, and what made it a fight against privatization per se, was that it was one of the first high-profile land conflicts to occur *within* an IBR colony. The Paraguayan frontier, as are all frontiers, had always been a violent and tough place. But campesinos were protagonists of the expansion—violence was directed outward at the moment of conquering more land. Subsequently, there tended to be little internal conflict over land in the colonias because the landless wing of campesino organizations was always focused on the creation of new colonies elsewhere, on finding state land, or on invading large estates. Tekojoja sat in the middle of a network of such colonies which stretched for at least eighty kilometers in all directions, land that until 1975 was almost completely covered with dense Atlantic forest. Until very recently, it had been a relatively quiet place. People were afraid of snakes, jaguars, and well-known families of *bandidos*, who lived by taking advantage of people in the area, but there was little reason to fight over land. Campesinos respected each others' stakes in the land whether or not these were formalized as titles.

Privatization, in Tekojoja, specifically referred to the appearance in the colony of a new kind of land buyer. According to the campesino version of the story, the conflict started when a group of ten Brazilians led by a man named Ademir Opperman began buying up land rights in Tekojoja, in 2002. The Brazilians already owned land across the river, in Santa Clara, and were looking to expand their soy farms after a bumper crop in 2001. They showed up looking for people who wanted to sell their plots, and they soon found ten families who were moving out. One family had a title, but the rest had derecheras in various stages of payment. The Brazilians bought all of these rights, ratifying them either through the local IBR representative or the justice of the peace. They then solicited and received occupancy permits from the IBR and began paying them off as quickly as possible to convert them into titles.

Such transfers were commonplace, even though technically illegal. What made this instance different was that a group of landless campesinos from neighboring colonies objected. The group was called together by Jorge Galeano, whose idea it was to try to stop the transfers. About 150 young men and women, most of them seeking land for themselves, decided to move on to the disputed plots to prevent the transfers from happening.[21] Their fear was not of living side by side with Brazilians, but of a takeover of the community, even the entire smallholder area, by soybeans, which they had already seen happen in communities farther east, like Pariri and San Roque. In each of those places soy farmers had arrived offering open-market prices for the land, as much as thirty times what campesinos could expect to get from each other for colony land.[22] Many families were looking for ways of leaving the countryside anyway and were thus easily convinced to sell their plots after hearing these offers.[23] As soon as the soy farmers were established, neighbors were under greater pressure to sell because the unregulated use of herbicides during soy season made the communities extremely unpleasant to live in. Moreover, in many places the contamination of air and water and the destruction of crops and small animals bordering on soyfields was supplemented by direct intimidation and violence.

This is a familiar frontier story, about pioneer waves being progressively supplanted by more concentrated forms of capitalist agriculture (e.g., Foweraker 1981). In that narrative, privatization might simply be the name given to an inevitable process of legal formalization of frontier land, and Tekojoja might have been just a small footnote in an unpleasant but rapid transformation of the landscape in the district. But Jorge and his followers argued that Tekojoja was a line in the sand, a trinchera between two national cultures and economic ways of thinking that needed to be held. They petitioned the IBR to recognize that the Brazilians had no right to the land, and asked that the lots be granted to landless campesinos instead. Following the standard procedure for requesting expropriation, they moved onto the disputed plots and began to build shelters. When I first met Jorge and his companions, in 2003, the shelters had just been burned down and the group was camped out under ragged tents in the garden of a sympathetic neighbor. They stayed there waiting for the IBR to make a decision while tractors worked daily on the plots ripping out fruit trees from which the camp was getting much of its food.

The IBR eventually conceded that the occupancy permits were illegal. It revoked them and awarded new ones to the campesino families in the tents. Working through a lawyer in Asunción, the Brazilians appealed the decision to the Supreme Court, and a temporary ban on "innovations" (the legal term for mejoras) was assessed against both parties, meaning that neither could cultivate the land. Campesinos, who were by then living on the land and feeding themselves from their gardens, took the ban to be absurd and continued to build. But over the next three years, as the case made its way to the Supreme Court, the Brazilians convinced police on three different occasions to evict the campesinos from the site, burn their houses down, and plough their crops under. Many of those who had initially participated in the occupation abandoned the effort due to hardship, and went elsewhere to settle. They were replaced by others, like Joel, who had heard about the fight and wanted to join in.

Not everyone living on undisputed plots in Tekojoja supported the campesino cause. Many of course had economic or family relationships with the soy farmers, and many, now calling themselves productores, rented out parts of their land for beans. The priest in Vaquería also established a cooperative which made it easier for small farmers to rent equipment and access credit for soy planting, and some had begun trying this themselves. Colorado operatives liked the soy farmers, as did merchants, real-estate speculators, mechanics, and gas-station owners who lived along the main road connecting Tekojoja to Vaquería. But when push came to shove, hundreds of people turned out to help the squatters in any way possible. The families who remained in the camp simply tried to hang on to whatever they had and keep an eye open for new attacks. Jorge and two other local leaders did most of the bureaucratic work, traveling between Tekojoja and Asunción, lining up help from lawyers and anyone else they could to press the case in the Supreme Court while formulating their own grievances about the violence perpetrated against them. And although they were not successful in getting these grievances addressed, they managed to generate enough controversy that various entities distanced themselves from

Opperman and the Brazilians: first the IBR representatives, then the district attorney and local police.

The tensions came to a head after three years, on a frigid morning in June 2005, in which an accident of history changed the course of the story in campesinos' favor. Opperman had convinced a district attorney named Nelly Varela from the regional attorney's office in Coronel Oviedo to carry out a third eviction of campesinos from the disputed plots. Two truckloads of riot police showed up at five o'clock in the morning and began pulling people out of bed. They loaded the trucks with over a hundred campesinos, including Joel and his wife (who was then eight months pregnant), and drove them to the regional jail while Opperman's gang drove through the community on tractors, demolishing houses and setting them on fire. Then, as Opperman was leaving the location, he spotted a group of about fifty campesinos, some of whom had hidden during the evictions, some of whom had gathered in solidarity to discuss a reaction. As his convoy drove past, men in the trucks opened fire on the campesinos with shotguns, killing two young men and severely wounding another.

The incident was not unprecedented, but Jorge was a media-savvy leader, and it was only a few hours before news of the drive-by shootings was percolating through the talk-radio circuit locally and in Asunción. The next morning, the first newspaper to pick up the story, *ABC Color*, framed it as a confrontation between two armed groups.[24] And this is probably how the story would have remained, as so often happened, were it not for the fact that I had been present, taking pictures, several of which proved that the campesinos had been unarmed when they were attacked. Around the campfire that night at the site of the murders, campesinos urged me to release the pictures to the media. Two days later, when the pictures reached the front page of *Última Hora*, public opinion turned on the soy farmers, thoroughly compromising their legal position.[25] This set the stage for a Supreme Court ruling which favored the campesino land claim.[26]

Tekojoja was an unusual and highly significant victory for campesinos, but it was not an unqualified one, and some of the details are very telling. The court ruling in their favor came with one important caveat: of the ten plots in question, the campesinos won nine, but they lost the plot that had been titled by the IBR one year before it was sold to the soy farmer. The court upheld the nontransferability of derecheras, but decided to allow the title to be sold, even though, technically, this meant violating the ten-year moratorium on its transfer. In other words, the court chose to treat the titled land as private property; transactions on the title would be governed by the Civil Code, and any restrictions placed on it by the IBR in awarding the title were deemed irrelevant. The court effectively moved the land from one legal regime into another to award it to the soy farmers, and it used the title to do so. Although I had been hearing about privatization for months from campesinos, it was in the public discussion that followed the ruling that I first heard people talk about land titles themselves as a tool (rather than a representation) of privatization, a sort of documentary trap that allowed land to be taken away from campesinos after they had put so much work into it. In Tekojoja, people suggested that land titles could be used to destroy the IBR and the very nation-building project of which they all believed themselves to be a part. In short, land titles were now seen as a threat to campesinos' remaining institutional foothold in the state, so much so that, in the following year, campesinos even organized against laws that would have allowed them to trade in their derecheras for titles free of charge, something that, until that point, would have been quite appealing to them.[27]

This sudden shift in campesino politics, from desiring to fearing land titles, speaks to a long-standing tension in liberal thinking about the relationship between property, law, and citizenship. Take, for instance, one of the founding liberal narratives of private property, that of John Locke. Locke believed that "in the beginning," and on new frontiers, men could reasonably appropriate those elements of nature that they improved with their own labor. He saw as a principle of natural law that property followed from the extension of the owner's body into the land on which he worked (see Radin 1993). But Locke saw this form of appropriation as ultimately limited and likely to generate conflict as people multiplied and resources became scarce. That conflict led to the invention of land titles, an institution created by contract for the mutual benefit of all those contracting in. Once land titles came into effect, labor in itself was not enough to justify appropriation of a resource, and property moved into the realm of abstract rights tacitly agreed on by members of society.

Like other contract stories (see Pateman 1988; Rose 1994), the narrative that grounds the Lockean understanding of property describes the birth of civilization in the moment of the founding of a consensual abstraction. Locke's story tells of a radical historical break between a moment when human relations were governed by direct human interaction with material things through labor and the moment when relations came to be governed by the higher order of the social contract. Without taking the Lockean view of abstraction as an analytic premise, one can nevertheless see that in Paraguay property struggles are saturated with Lockean language. In other words, people on all sides understand the conflict to be in part about the relation between the material and the abstract. For bureaucrats, soy farmers, and reformers, the invocation of codes and efficiency imply the superiority of abstraction over the material, whereas campesinos' invocations of mejoras and their insistence on rights as kuatia, or papers, suggest that abstractions are an outgrowth of material processes. The language of contention within which these positions are articulated is internal to long-standing liberal notions of property that have informed the land reform and the projects that succeeded it.[28]

The Lockean narrative reemerges in proposals both for and against the land reform, with proponents and opponents arguing that for Paraguay to become fully modern (in the style of Western democracies), it must create institutions that supersede the material and allow for governance to be conducted at the level of nationally recognized representations of ownership rights (titles) and legal contracts. Paraguay's original land reformers always equated campesino development with the acquisition of titles, suggesting that titling signaled campesino incorporation into the modern body politic. Post–Cold War opponents of the land reform suggest that the convoluted bureaucracy of the IBR is keeping the campesinado in a premodern state and that only by improving the documentation of property can Paraguayan agriculture really flourish.[29] The difference between these two positions is where they place the representational rift in relation to the present. For land reformers, the full formalization of the legal code had yet to be achieved, and campesinos were encouraged to improve land on the open frontier as part of creating the modern nation. The people now seeking to overturn the land reform see the Civil Code as a contractual fait accompli and those still clinging to the materiality of property rights as troublesome reminders of Paraguay's not-quite-modernity.

The consequences of this difference lie in how land reformers and their detractors define the limits of the social, for social contracts are built not on sudden emergence of consensus, but on the violence of constitutive exclusion.[30] In a telling aside to this discussion in the *Second Treatise on Government* (1963 [1689]), Locke uses the example of the Americas: "There are still great Tracts of Ground to be found, which (the Inhabitants thereof not having joyned with the rest of Mankind, in the consent for the Use of their common Money) lie waste, and are more than the People, who dwell on it, do, or can make use of, and so still lie in common" (341). In other words, some land uses were tantamount to waste, because the inhabitants of those lands had not consented to the legal order established by "Mankind." The opening of the campesino frontier in the 1960s had as its goal the founding of a new nation, slowly to be built by campesino labor on that frontier. It is not hard, in retrospect, to see that project's exclusions, which were similar to those implicit in the Lockean view of the "empty" American frontier.[31] The hundreds of indigenous people inhabiting Paraguay's eastern forests were simply considered not to exist. They were dispossessed of everything and, until the late 1970s, had no recourse at all to protect themselves from being hunted and massacred (see Arens 1976; Reed 1995). But the new counter-reform also has its exclusions. In the reconfiguration of law and territory, it is campesinos who sit outside the social sphere delimited by the Civil Code. And just as the Estatuto Agrario was never explicit about its exclusions, so too does one need to read between the lines of the Civil Code to see how campesinos fall outside of the sphere it governs.

The conflict between the waning Estatuto Agrario and the ascendant Civil Code was palpable in several bureaucratic encounters I witnessed. It was most explicit in an exchange between Jorge and Lourdes, a senior IBR bureaucrat, in the IBR office in Caaguazú shortly after the court victory was announced in Tekojoja. The encounter had quickly become heated, with Lourdes accusing Jorge of strong-arming and Jorge accusing Lourdes of corruption. They were arguing over the case of Pariri, a community adjacent to Tekojoja, in which soybeans already predominated. Campesinos wanted to take back several of the fields that they knew had been bought by soy farmers as derecheras, and they were asking Lourdes for an inspection of the land records. In the middle of the discussion, Lourdes turned to Jorge and said simply, "It wouldn't matter if the land had been bought illegally. If there are soybeans in the field, I am obligated by the Civil Code to treat that as an act of possession." Jorge replied by naming articles of the law from memory: "It doesn't matter what the Civil Code says. You are bound by Article 17 of the Estatuto Agrario, which says that in the colonias nobody can solicit more than one agricultural lot. It says lots can only be sold to naturalized Paraguayans who do not already own land. And furthermore it is illegal to sell derecheras, and you know that you and your staff are responsible for helping to sell them." At this, Lourdes reminded Jorge that the Civil Code overrode the Estatuto Agrario, but she didn't push the point further, and they proceeded to schedule her visit to Pariri.

I later asked Jorge about this exchange. He confirmed the existing legal contradiction, and he even admitted that Lourdes had been right. "Technically she's right that the Civil Code overrides the Estatuto. They are always bringing up that inconsistency. But that is incoherent of them—the Estatuto is their document, how can they claim that it is invalid? If you go by the Civil Code all the time, then the land reform is over."

The government had, indeed, in 2002, passed a law (the revised Estatuto Agrario) that contradicted central tenets of that drafted in 1985 (the revised Civil Code), and it had continued to make minor amendments to both laws without ever touching on this fundamental inconsistency. So long as the two bodies of law were thought of as separate, pertaining to distinct territories, and not subjected to court challenges, the contradiction did not much matter. Because, for the most part, land was either in a colony, and therefore governed by the IBR, or not, the question of the legal overlap was not pertinent. In the process of privatization, though, the Civil Code was used to override the IBR within the colonies. Rights, built up with campesino labor according to one set of rules, were being sold into another legal regime in which past campesino labor did not matter as much as current "acts of possession." Jorge's point was that the more troubling part of the dispute was not the legal inconsistency, but that bureaucrats hired to administer one set of laws were making recourse to another set to justify their own complicity in the first law's failure. When pressed further, though, Jorge had much deeper critiques of the way the Civil Code was wielded.

THE MATERIALITY OF RIGHTS

Thus far I've depicted two ways of reckoning property rights, each emerging in relation to the other and echoing profound tensions in liberal thought, and each increasingly associated with opposing territories on Paraguay's rapidly closing frontier. In one of these views, property is governed by the idea that rights are a progressive result of human labor on the land; in the other, property rights are understood as a result of legal recognition in an abstract code. In legal argumentation like that between Lourdes and Jorge, the neatness of this distinction seems to hold, and one might easily argue that Lourdes's position is a more pragmatic one on which to govern and that campesinos should simply submit to this practicality. That is the express view of organizations like the IDB and the World Bank, both of which have, in the name of good governance, market efficiency, and conflict reduction, supported projects that would transform all derecheras into titles that could be openly traded. The question for them is not which of these systems to support, or whether they can both be upheld simultaneously, but how to make the transition to a single, unified property system smoother and ultimately dissolve the IBR and its peculiar way of reckoning ownership.[32]

This particular solution to the land problem became known in Asunción as the "de Soto solution" because of a campaign by *ABC Color*, which ran a series of interviews with the Peruvian economist Hernando de Soto.[33] De Soto (2000) is well known for arguing that Third World poverty stems from three related causes: unclear property rights, lack of "information" (i.e., a transparent registry of all property), and inefficient bureaucracy. For all of its obvious flaws, the de Soto solution is very seductive, and is only the most simplified version of what has come to be a land-policy orthodoxy among major lenders (e.g., Deininger 2003). It is seductive because it is parsimonious, cheap, and because it takes redistribution completely off the table and offers a purely "market solution" to rural poverty. In Asunción it also offered new democrats a strategy for dealing with land problems that bypassed the IBR, a notoriously impenetrable institution for bureaucratic reformers, and for dealing with the problem entirely in the national cadastre and the public registry.

The *ABC Color* columns in favor of the de Soto solution came out in September 2004 and again in 2005, and the ideas they expressed were often repeated by politicians like the Liberal senator Alfredo Luís Jaeggli and Nicanor's vice president, Luís Castiglioni. Both had been involved for years behind the scenes trying to legislate the IBR out of existence by reforming the Estatuto Agrario. But by the time the new estatuto passed into law, in 2002, it was so watered down by campesinista advisors and rural senators (who favored the land-reform status quo) that it allowed the IBR to function as it always had, with only a name change.[34] Instead, Jaeggli and Castiglioni decided to introduce what they called a "rapid titling" law, which would override the Estatuto Agrario altogether, allowing campesinos in all colonies to trade in their derecheras for titles. Jaeggli's bill was short and to the point: every campesino would receive a final title to their land, free of charge and without conditions, effective immediately. Titles would be handled by the public registry and governed by the Civil Code.[35] Implicit in this sort of project is the new democratic dismissal of campesino forms of property as incoherent. For this group, campesino property is just a mongrel form of private property, what they would call *lotes precarios*. Precarious property was land that, due to campesino backwardness, bureaucratic sloth, and improperly executed land reform, had yet to become properly private.

There is, however, another way of seeing the relation between these two positions, one that reverses its premises completely. For campesinos, the view that the Civil Code is more consistent is hypocritical, because, although the criteria it establishes for adjudicating property are abstract, the tacit criteria for dealing in abstractions are themselves material. The question is not whether the Civil Code has a better claim to universalizability than the Estatuto Agrario, but, rather, which one is able to more effectively call state violence to its aid in shoring up the borders of its jurisdiction. The Civil Code, campesinos argue, is not divorced from a material context that props it up; rather, the legal practice of adjudicating rights depends on a prior, unacknowledged conception of material advancement. They assert that bureaucrats and lawyers tacitly rely on a position that is in fact similar to the campesino view of property, but that they garb its slight differences in the apparent universality of an abstract code. To campesinos, in other words, it is the new democrats who peddle an aberrant form of property equivalent to rigging the books in their favor.

In the French legal tradition which Paraguay follows, the Civil and Penal Codes lend legal coherence to the republic by systematizing its laws. The laws of the Civil Code are contractual, based on internally coherent principles for resolution of disputes, and not on prior or natural principles.[36] The principle of the "mejora" is inoperative. The absence of title is considered an aberration, but can be corrected through the issuance of a new title, based on a descending hierarchy of "acts of possession," which signal the claimant's intent to own the land. Unlike the Estatuto Agrario, which treats the title as the desirable end of labor on the land, the Civil Code treats all land as though it were already titled, either formally or through an "act of possession," a communication of intent. Title isn't a mejora, but an ideal type of market signal, and in its absence, the code looks for other markers (a fence, a sign, a notch on a trunk, a field of beans) which can stand in for a title.

The key is that the Civil Code assumes full membership in civil society. It is designed to work as a set of predetermined rules for an exclusive club which internally determines the tacit threshold of communicative success. Property is a matter of recognition, both of membership in the club and of individual acts of communication by those members, and labor is only a marker of possession if "society" understands it as such. And this is precisely why the Civil Code didn't work before the land reform and, campesinos argue, cannot work now. For if official membership in society is supposed to be guaranteed with citizenship, the success of communication is still adjudicated by elites who have always seen campesinos, like indigenous people, as being inscrutable and irrational. In other words, campesino claims are unrecognizable without translation—a mejora doesn't count as property unless it can be translated into an act of possession. On their own, campesino communicative acts are not transparent to the law. Campesinos know that their attempts at communicating possession are not as strong as the attempts of soy farmers, and that more often than not their possession markers are disqualified simply because they themselves made them. Huts, tents, and manioc gardens do not signal possession as successfully as a nice field of beans planted in straight rows. This, campesinos claim, is the ultimate hypocrisy of their political opponents: it is poverty which disqualifies them from participating in a system where the material is not supposed to count.[37]

To illustrate this claim, I return to Tekojoja, where these processes of material disqualification were laid bare in court documents. Three years into the struggle, the lives of affected campesino families had become saturated with legal language. Although they held the ground physically, their plans, their desires, and even their lives seemed to hang on the whims of judges and lawyers in the faraway rooms of the Supreme Court. Everything they did, every small decision or act, was capable of affecting the outcome of the trial adversely. Jorge would advise people at monthly meetings on the many ways they could improve or harm their chances of winning their land claims, from planting vegetable gardens (which improved their chances) to avoiding talking to local politicians (which invariably harmed them). The level to which these legal considerations had infused everyday life was clarified for me one day when I encountered a friend on the road leading out of Tekojoja. "Come by my *rancho* [hut]," he told me. "There's something I want to show you." Then he corrected himself, switching into a more formal register: "I mean my *'óga* [house]." When I responded, I used the word *rancho* to assure him that, despite my appearance and accent, my Guaraní was good enough to know what he had meant by the informal term. But it turned out that was not why he had corrected himself at all. "Oh," he said, "Jorge wants us to stop using that word. He says it could hurt our chances in the case. It's sometimes hard to remember—we've always just said, 'That's my rancho.'"

What Jorge was worried about was that different words connoted different levels of material improvement. Campesinos use the word *rancho* to express humility about the homes, but ranchers and soy farmers use the word to describe temporary or secondary dwellings. According to Jorge's argument, if campesinos kept using the word *rancho*, the designation could make its way into media reports and court testimony and be read as a lack of seriousness about the structure of the house. He preferred they use *'óga*, the Guaraní term for dwelling, and stop adding the ubiquitous diminutive -'i, as in *'óga'i* and *rancho'i*, which connoted the same lack of seriousness. This careful use of language was part of a campaign that also encouraged campesinos to clean properties, paint houses, build wooden outhouses, and plant trees in front yards. If outsiders came by to take pictures, material improvements helped residents' case by turning ranchos into *'ógas* to signal a more permanent stake on the land.

Jorge had good reason to believe specific words made a difference. When asked for an example, he pointed out how in legal documents soy farmers and their lawyers used the term *lote precario* (precarious lot), the same term which reformers used to justify titling procedures. The Spanish word *precario* has an interesting double meaning, not unlike the English word *insecure*. When used as a modifier for *tierra* (land), *lote* (plot), or *tenencia* (holding), it serves as a legal term referring to untitled holdings. But when used to describe a way of life, it indicates poverty, as in the English "precarious condition." Unfortunately, one sense of the word connotes the other—poverty easily becomes a sign of illegality.

The term *lote precario* has been in common usage in Paraguay at least since the 1950s, when it was used by political enemies of the proposed land reform to deride campesino land use (Pastore 1972). By the 1980s it was being used primarily by campesinistas, intellectual allies of campesinos who claimed that the government was not fulfilling its titling obligations and abandoning campesinos owning only lotes precarios (see Fogel 1990; Borda 1990; Quintín Riquelme 2003). *Lotes precarios* continues to be used as a descriptor by government agencies, NGOs, foreign experts on land reform writing reports about rural Paraguay, Marxist and neoliberal policy wonks, lawyers, police, ranchers, and even campesinos themselves to describe both states: extreme poverty *and* lack of title. In both of these usages, lote precario stands as a a self-evident sign of failure, with people differing only on whether it is the state or the campesinos themselves who are responsible for that failure. Either the government has failed to produce titles and rural services, or campesinos have failed to drag themselves out of poverty and are therefore incapable of acceding to legal title. With different political goals and causal reasoning, the lote precario is an idea that links wealth to legality.

One can argue incessantly over the significance of definitive land titles, until someone actually tries to take them away. At that point, definitive title is supposed to ensure that the state is on your side in the dispute. The argument offered throughout the 1990s and 2000s by economists, that the Paraguayan state needs to issue definitive titles or else find themselves incapable of protecting the poor in land disputes, is, from another perspective, also an argument that the state ought not be responsible for protecting the rights of those without definitive title.[38] These are commonsensical and not specifically legal interpretations of the Civil Code, but they have their effects on bureaucrats and judges adjudicating land conflicts. In places where a marker of possessorial intent is sufficient to claim land as private property, the acts associated with lotes precarios are simply not considered adequate markers. Derecheras still have some legal weight in Paraguay, but only in the legal realm of the Estatuto Agrario, and as the estatuto loses credibility in the face of the Civil Code, the stakes of living on a lote precario increase. Living on a lote precario is no longer a sign of slow advancement or an indictment of the state, but rather a sign of not fitting with the new legal regime. It is fundamentally *not* an act of possession in the same way that a fresh field of soybeans *is*.

In Tekojoja, as Jorge pointed out, soy farmers exploited this ambiguity in their deposition against the campesinos. They were keen to underline the difference between their claims and the precarious claims of the campesinos, a difference they backed up with pictures of the campesino dwellings. They hired a lawyer to accompany them to the site and generate a description of the land based on purely "ocular inspection," and spent an hour or so driving around the settlement, taking pictures and generating descriptions of the disputed lots.

> In Mr. ———'s lot are seen 4 (four) small, very precarious houses [casitas muy precarias] presumably constructed by the accused. By the side of the road the clandestine installation of electrical wires is observed. . . . On the other side of the road, in Mr. ———'s lot, we see 3 (three) small, precarious houses occupied by the accused. . . . In Mr. ———'s lot are 5 (five) precarious huts [ranchitos]. . . . In Mr. ———'s lot are seen 4 (four) small, rustic houses by the road. . . . In Mr. ———'s lot is observed the clandestine installation of electricity using precarious electrical wires.[39]

Although the foregoing is presented as a visual narration of the lots, to be accompanied by legal documents, the descriptions are already loaded with implicit legal indictments and, moreover, tacitly accept the soy farmers' property claims ("Mr. ———'s lot"). More significant, the squalid living conditions of the campesinos is advanced in support of the claim that they are living there illegally. Together with images that speak for themselves, the words *precarious* and *clandestine* evoke the common assumption shared by rural elites and legal professionals that the poor are by definition incapable of having full rights to land.

THE MATERIALITY OF REPRESENTATION

That there is a close link between the acknowledgment of property rights, the status of solicitants and the aesthetic condition of properties should come as no surprise. North Americans are certainly familiar with the kinds of lawn-mowing and fence-painting activities that serve no purpose except to proclaim to the world "this is mine, and I deserve it." Still, one principle of titling schemes is to make it more difficult to remove property rights on the basis of class or any other marker of distinction. When de Soto (2000) or Klaus Deininger (2003) or even Milton Friedman (Friedman and Friedman 1962) talk about tenure security, they do mean security for *anyone*. Recognized property rights can only be revocable on the basis of market principles or violations of the law, and having a small house should not therefore present a risk. New democrats would make the argument that the exclusion of the poor from participation in the legal economy is one of the things that the de Soto solution is supposed to guard against. By making property rights clearer, representing them in forms that are increasingly regularized and removed from the material domain that they represent, new democrats are trying to prevent what they would regard as feudal status concerns from trumping the law in land disputes. But from a campesino perspective there is another problem beyond the issue of rapid titling, and that is precisely the fact that the proclaimed abstraction of property in the Civil Code model makes it impossible to talk about the materiality of claims and counterclaims. Campesinos may be at a disadvantage in this material history based on wealth, but they are altogether absent from the history of coded representations—campesinos may have made feeble personal imprints on the land, but they have made few if any in the public registry, and they aren't even sure how to access those that they have made. The logic of the Estatuto Agrario, however flawed, is that by which they work their way into the body politic as citizens capable of making such imprints.

That process of achieving citizenship never quite ends for campesinos. To them, titles are fragile, held together by material and social processes that require constant maintenance. The most obvious reason this is true has to do with the materiality of paper, kuatia. The work of improving rights from derecheras to titles is reflected in an improvement in the quality of the paper on which the right is printed, a progression that leads from informal notes scrawled on pages torn from spiral notebooks, to occupancy permits with brown newsprint covers, to titles with thick yellow covers. These are correlated very closely to the conditions of the houses. When I asked people to show me their documents, I could often predict what sort of titles they would be by the conditions in which they were kept. Whereas the lesser papers often emerged from plastic bags squirreled under mattresses, titles were more often secured in locked briefcases and wooden chests. The conditions of storage said as much about the houses and the (more or less precarious) economic condition of the inhabitants than it did about their desire to keep the documents safe, and that is precisely the point. The material security of the paper itself tended to improve as the quality of the paper improved and as the legal security that the paper represented increased.

The material fragility of campesino land rights was reinforced rather than diminished during the conflict in Tekojoja, when campesino houses were burned down during successive evictions. Because the houses were made of boards and thatch, they burned very quickly, and while everyone was able to escape, each time the campesinos lost all their documents, including those they needed to prove that they had rights to live there in the first place. (The only house that didn't suffer this fate was a brick house that the police couldn't bring themselves to destroy. An officer was overheard telling people not to destroy it because it "would make a good police station," but it was clear to all of us that the job would also have been a lot more difficult and would have violated the police's tacit sense of what sorts of structures they could legitimately destroy.) Those who lost their documents in the fires also lost their identity cards, marriage certificates, and their children's birth certificates, making it all the more difficult to plead their cases. In fact, despite concerted efforts by Jorge, myself, a senator, a bishop, and a human-rights lawyer to file a suit against the government for the evictions, we were hamstrung by the lack of documents after the fire. Transporting everyone from Tekojoja to the civil registry to acquire replacements and generate power-of-attorney papers, and then to the courthouse to give testimony and file claims was so expensive and time consuming that everyone agreed in the end to spend their time rebuilding houses instead. This underlines the fact that such documents are not just representations of legal rights—they *are* rights, and poverty is what keeps most people from acquiring them.

To add insult to injury, a year and a half after burning down campesino houses for the first time, the Brazilian claimants were back again, using photographs of the "ranchitos precarios" built out of burnt planks and twisted tin roofing to prove that the residents couldn't possibly deserve to be there. What this points to is not just the problem of protecting representations of property, but the capacity, also economic, of producing them. If the key to creating property rights is generating authoritative representations of those rights which can be recognized by others, then part of the maintenance of property rights is to continuously produce such authoritative representations. This again belies de Soto's claim that solving rural poverty is just a matter of securing property rights by producing representations of what is owned. It is not, as he claims, the lack of clear representations that causes poverty, but poverty that causes the lack of representations.

From the moment I first arrived in Tekojoja, I was called on to help people create representations which would appear authoritative under bureaucratic and legal scrutiny. Jorge and other members of the Movimiento Agrario would approach me to photograph conditions in the village as proof of the persecution they were suffering, of the effects of agrotoxins, and of people guarding their tractors with weapons. What they saw in me was a chance to create a photographic record of their own, complete with interpretive captions, which could provide legitimacy for their legal claims. But it went further than this. I was frequently asked to edit letters to state officials and to make these letters look as professional as possible. Since it was almost impossible to obtain actual legal representation, the most effective outlet for these texts and images was the newspaper, and much energy was put into trying to get local stories into print. These small acts of representation cumulatively helped to bolster the legitimacy of campesino legal claims, but they never produced stable objects, instead, the representations had to be constantly made and remade. Newspaper stories and letters were relatively cheap ways into the public sphere, but they had short shelf-lives which required constant renewal. And they were feeble documents when compared with the weighty court dockets, covered in important stamps on expensive paper, bandied about by the soy farmers.

The problem of distance from the centers of power was also manifest in the quality of the documents that campesinos produced and possessed. Just as the letters were often signed with shaky, grade-school signatures, sometimes even with highly stigmatizing thumbprints, so, too, were the copies of documents they received from the centers of power marked by many passes through rural photocopiers. Jorge's archive, a treasure trove of laws, manifestos, and court documents, included thousands of pages of faded copies. The copies I have of depositions and warrants related to Tekojoja are illegible in places, the pages mixed up. The houses were not only precarious in their construction, but in their reproduction, the images so degraded as to lose all distinctiveness. The most curious of these images are pictures of grainy houses with well-dressed men posing on the road in front of the lots. The photographs have been copied so many times that they verge on being unrecognizable, but they are clearly of the claimants. While the pictures were initially meant to give the viewer an immediate connection to the claimants and the object of their claims, along with a picture of campesino precariousness, the mediation of the photocopiers adds another depth of meaning. This is a conversation happening far away between wealthy people whose words and intentions can only be gleaned in partial snippets through careful eavesdropping.

Copies such as these exist in the margins of the network of documentary circulation that creates the public sphere, and so new democratic citizenship. Campesinos who have attempted to contest property claims in court know that elite cliques mirror on a small scale the larger networks of circulation and privilege out of which civil codes, public registries, and abstraction itself are built. The campesinos engaged in this work have developed strategies for infiltrating documentary networks in an attempt to subvert them. But they also build networks of their own, which mimic in many instances the strategies of privilege and exclusion of those they seek to break. Jorge's archive was the center of one such network, and those privileged few who had access to it had an indispensable tool in trying to argue legal land cases. He made a point of circulating copies from the archive to designated representatives in places like Tekojoja, and gave documents to people in other communities, and to journalists and other potential allies as a way of enlisting them to his cause. In that slowly growing network of circulating documents, the very rare original prints, notarized copies, even those copies that bore someone's stamp had an unquestionable value, and even people who had trouble reading the text could tell how important documents were. I was given immediate access to the archive as a way of inviting me into the group, but it wasn't until a year after my arrival that I started receiving such semi-authentic copies as gifts, a sign of my growing importance and acceptance.

This concern with authenticity, with closeness to the site of production, and with the perishability of authoritative representations was best illustrated by

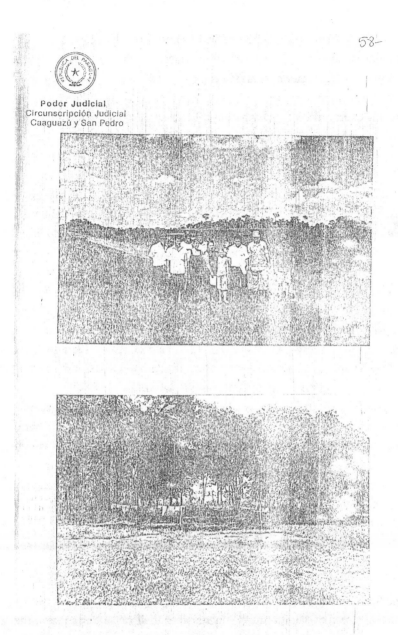

Poder Judicial
Circunscripción Judicial
Caaguazú y San Pedro

FIGURE 4. Photocopy of pictures filed in court docket showing claimants posing in front of "ranchitos precarios."

the fate of the letterhead that the MAP had devised for all of its correspondence with official entities. The MAP had not managed to get official recognition as a community organization, because people with criminal records were barred from representing organizations publicly, and all of MAP's leaders were undergoing court proceedings for having resisted eviction and for other charges cooked up by foes.[40] The situation was not unlike the catch-22 of the burned documents, in the sense that people were incapable of defending themselves legally for the very fact of having been charged with an offense. Given the impossibility of gaining official recognition, Jorge and others felt that the MAP must be particularly careful to produce an aesthetic worthy of an official organization. They formed a dedicated committee, which spent days developing a logo and discussing the symbolism of each of its elements, down to the color scheme. At a moment when many of the organization's members had had money available, they had paid for a ream of paper to be printed with a striking graphic at the top.[41] By the time they ran out of paper, the two-bit printing company they had used had lost the originals, and the membership couldn't muster enough money—it was in the middle of a drought—to recreate them. They were reduced to photocopying the logo in black and white, and that copy soon degraded after the original copy was misplaced.

All of these efforts to create and hand out documents, to forge connections with official letters, paid off in different ways, most dramatically after the third police attack in Tekojoja. By then, a variety of intellectuals and NGOs, as well as one leftist senator, had developed an interest in the community due to the MAP's constant communication. Campesinos had slowly built a public for their demands and desires, a public comprising representatives of the Colorado state and of new democratic civil society. Perhaps most important, the local district attorney and police captain were sufficiently aware of the details of the case, and of the campesinos' allies, that they refused to participate in the third eviction. The soy farmers trying to force their claim to the land had had to go further afield to find members of the state apparatus who didn't belong to that community. They ultimately recruited to their cause Nelly Varela, the district attorney from Coronel Oviedo, who agreed, based on the deposition quoted above (and in apparent ignorance of the legal fallout of the first two police actions in the town), to order a third eviction—the one that ended in two deaths.

The speed with which the MAP was able to call up these networks after the attack was the most impressive result of all their work. By the following morning, they had sympathetic members of the police making statements in their favor, had been visited by a senator, the bishop, a prominent sociologist, and reporters from Última Hora. Campesinos used the pictures I'd taken of the incident and asked me to give the newspaper my version of the events. This made a difference, too, not because I said anything different from campesinos, but because I said it in Spanish rather than in Guaraní, and, more to the point, because I wasn't campesino. My version simply counted differently. These elements made for a front-page spread in the Sunday paper, and captivated several pages of the paper for days thereafter. The story quickly showed up on websites of international organizations. Tekojoja was the subject of choice for national talk radio for most of a week, and Jorge was even invited to make his case on the Humberto Rubín television show, the country's best-known political talk show. Symbolizing one of those few irruptions of the campesinado into the public sphere, Jorge spoke defiantly in Guaraní in what was almost exclusively a Spanish arena.[42]

I am not suggesting that Tekojoja marked an unqualified "victory" for campesinos. The process was long and hard, and the families involved suffered immeasurably as a result. Months and years of court cases later, they did eventually win recognition for their derecheras, and some of the shooters even spent time in jail awaiting a trial that never happened. In short, the campesinos won the right to remain exactly as they had always assumed they could, and were given assurances, once more, that they would be allowed to rebuild from the fires of their homes. But the fact that the incident went to trial, the fact that the case became a matter for official political and public discussion, and quite likely the fact that they won in the end resulted from a concerted effort to build recognition through labor.

There were those who continued to see the case of Tekojoja as an argument for sweeping reform in the way that property is represented, rather than as an object lesson about how Paraguayan elites believe that poverty implies illegality. Humberto Rubín, in a frustrated rant at the end of his show with Jorge, expressed the new democrats' point of view that the old IBR was at fault and that the lack of clarity in property rights had created the situation. The sooner the IBR was destroyed, he said, the better. Nelly Varela, whose signature was most conspicuous on the eviction warrants, gave the lie to Rubín's position with a telling choice of words. A month after the eviction and murders, she appeared before the senate human-rights commission to explain her actions, a performance in which she appeared both arrogant and ignorant of the actual laws pertaining to the case. She was asked to corroborate earlier testimony by a young woman from one of the evicted families who claimed that she had run out of her house with a copy of the IBR derecheras to explain that they had the right to be there. The young woman testified that the police had thrown the paper on the ground, saying that it wasn't worth anything, and had then pulled her by the hair toward the truck. When Varela was asked if any of the evictees had had "papers," she replied, "They didn't even have toilet paper" (No tenían ni papel higiénico).

The joke, good for laughs in certain more sympathetic contexts, echoes a story of elite adventures in the countryside which I heard at least four times in Paraguay, from both campesinos and elites. In this story about encounters between elites and campesinos, an unsuspecting lawyer, journalist, or anthropologist finds it necessary to pull their car to side of the road and ask to use a campesino latrine. Since the latrine lacks toilet paper, they sheepishly ask for instructions, at which point they are pointed to the pile of dried corn cobs sitting beside the hole. Corn cobs versus toilet paper serves as one of those visceral markers of class and cultural distinction, more amenable to expressions of contempt and revulsion than are stories about language and food. So while it was technically true that Tekojoja's latrines were not equipped with middle-class amenities, it was Varela's linkage of toilet paper to all paper that restated the automatic indictment of the poor as incapable of possessing property rights, regardless of what bureaucratic inscriptions they might wave at the police at the last minute. Varela was implying that she could read a person's legal status from the condition of their latrines, and that any "paper" presented in that context would have been beneath her contempt. According to that perspective, private property is only a sign of the owner's capacity to access (or buy) state violence. "Abstract right" is only a marker distinguishing those whose documentary networks give them access to such violence from those whose documentary networks remain marginal to the law.

According to supporters of the de Soto solution, of course, Varela's actions constituted "corruption," and the fact that she was not disciplined for them was a symptom of the very bureaucratic irregularity that produced derecheras in the first place. Varela, in her support of violence and in her embarrassing views of the victims of that violence, could be dismissed by new democrats as part of a team of bad (Colorado) apples, and by foreigners as par for the course in a fundamentally rotten barrel. And of course campesinos, too, were quite happy to damage her reputation in any way they could. It was widely rumored that the judicial chain of command reached up to the attorney general's office. Certainly, Varela was not investigated for wrongdoing, and in an early interview, before the alibis converged, she herself mentioned that she was working with direct orders from that office. Those of us involved in the case wound up with feelings of distaste from our experience with the justice system. When I gave my testimony to the district attorney assigned to investigate the murders, right down the hall from where Varela sat unscathed at her desk, the regional superintendent listened in, though he was not officially part of the proceedings. In the narrow office, he sat behind me, where I couldn't see him, and shouted out questions that undermined my testimony. The same man had been seen on a number of occasions driving around Tekojoja with soy farmers in the month before the raid.

New democrats, and particularly the economists and planners sent by the World Bank and IDB to create the conditions for rapid titling schemes, didn't like to consider themselves bedfellows of such petty provincial crooks. Claiming to represent a purer understanding of the law, they separated themselves from Colorados in the judiciary and the prosecutor's office through a discourse of corruption.[43] The argument of the reformers was that a more transparent set of rules could prevent this kind of behavior, and thereby would have benefited the campesinos in this case. In effect, they claimed, Varela would not have been able to carry out such an irregular raid had the rules of property law and judicial engagement in rural disputes been clearer. And at times the campesinos agreed with this argument. Jorge, who spent much of his time arguing over legal inconsistencies with bureaucrats, for example, often told me that more specific laws would have been an improvement. But, he said, this was only if the system better reflected campesino interests, something that the Civil Code, on its own, failed to do. From his perspective, institutions like the Civil Code were themselves built by elite political interests with no interest in campesinos. They were no more universal than the partisan interests of the Colorados. The Civil Code and public registry were created through the production and circulation of representations of property among a small group of elites. Clarification, they claimed, was all about migrating campesino property from a jurisdiction where they had some control to one where they did not. Hence "privatization," the hardening of boundaries around a documentary network named "public," to which campesinos did not belong.

CONCLUSION

If the campesino struggle against the privatization of the already private seems contradictory, it is only because it straddles a contradiction within liberal legal tradition, between a conception of property as relations between people heavily conditioned by material circumstances and a conception of property as an abstract relation predicated on a tacit social contract backed by state violence. The Keynesian policies adopted in places like Paraguay during most of the Cold War embraced the first of these tendencies, but since then the pendulum has shifted hard in the opposite direction. This push toward abstract legalism is not just part of radical neoliberal development policies. Everything from the rise of microeconomics in development planning (Carter 1997), to the push toward market-driven notions of good governance (Abrahamsen 2000), to the saturation of leftist politics with rights discourse (Brown and Halley 2002) and the pull in liberal philosophy from redistribution to recognition (Fraser and Honneth 2003), all tend in the same direction. At their broadest, campesino critiques of privatization suggest that all of these moves are fundamentally problematic, because they harden the distinction between the material basis of rights and an abstract conception whose exclusions are harder to pinpoint and more difficult to fight.

A week after the shootings in Tekojoja, I returned to the site of the murders, the shrines that had been built where the two bodies had fallen, and the camp of sticks and wind-frayed tarpaulins that grew as truckloads of supporters arrived. By then, the displaced families had been joined by at least a hundred more campesinos from other communities on the frontier, who wished to express their solidarity, and more were arriving all the time. There was already a certain ambivalence to the mood. On the one hand was a deep feeling of dread and weariness, especially in the residents, who had lost everything they owned for the third time in two years. Many of those who had witnessed the murders, including me, were still shaken, prone to occasional tears or other unexplained signs of distress, like talking too loud or not talking at all. At night, as the young men in the camp took shifts patrolling the perimeter, with makeshift wooden nightsticks, children could be heard crying in their tents. The first signs of gastroenteritis were sweeping through several tents, soon to affect everyone in the camp.

On the other hand, the solidarity had raised people's spirits, and that strange feeling of revolutionary potential that can accrue in spaces of extreme liminality, not unlike the paro cívico, coexisted with the generalized depression. In the hours after I arrived, two more truckloads of sympathizers showed up, one carrying a sound system which would serve as entertainment for the next several months, pumping out Kachaka music and getting people to dance.[44] The other truck brought a family of singers who were well known in the area for their rousing rendition of country standards and old protest songs. Jumping down from the truck, they took up a position in the middle of the field, not far from the two shrines, and began to sing a trio of favorites: "General Stroessner," "María Escobar," and the most popular song on the radio, "Propiedad privada." Until then, every time I had heard "Propiedad privada" played, it had been well received. But on this occasion it was precisely the wrong song; as soon as the singers finished, the crowd dispersed and walked away. No one spoke about what bothered them in that moment. But I remember the feeling well. Carlos, a normally jovial person who was standing right next to me, turned away from the singers and actually kicked the ground (lightly) with his giant bare foot, muttering "propiedad privada."

The media fury did generate some arrests, but by the time of the first anniversary of the shootings, all but one of the murder charges had been dropped. Opperman, the one suspect who still faced charges, had escaped from a rather porous house arrest, and another group of soy producers was trying to intimidate people into selling their land. By 2006, most of the families in Tekojoja had managed to rebuild yet more precarious houses out of burned boards and twisted tin roofs. But the contradictions in land laws, and in government responses to campesinos, were becoming all the more obvious. On the one hand, the government finally attempted to resolve the campesinos' troubles in the most material way it could manage, with the Supreme Court ruling in favor of the campesinos again that summer, finally sealing the question of who had the right to the land. To lend credence to the decision, and to deflect the accusation that it was just a victory "on paper," a representative of the president's office promised to rebuild the houses at the government's expense, this time with bricks, so that they would be harder to burn down. Many campesinos considered this to be a more important victory than the court decision itself, for it was recognition in the language of material durability, rather than in legal proclamations.

On the other hand, it was in 2006 that Jaeggli and Castiglioni introduced their rapid titling bills to the senate with much media hype. With the newfound security in their own homes, campesinos in Tekojoja began to organize against these bills, arguing that their passage could spell the end of the land reform.[45] They understood that had the bills been passed before the confrontation in Teko-joja, they would not have been able to win their legal case. Most were convinced that even if the bills passed, the government had neither the resources nor the organizational will to actually distribute the titles. But they were adamant that the plan was a double-cross. A title that hasn't been worked for simply isn't a title, they would claim, but a trick that then makes it easier to take your land away.[46] Privatization would mean the end of the pact between campesinos and the IBR. It would undermine campesino politics, halt their attempts to colo-nize new land, and undercut the relationship between work and ownership, the very relationship on which the aspiration to national inclusion rests.

To campesinos, official national politics has always been structured around the production and circulation of documents among a small cabal of elites. Fo-cusing on colonial and early independent Latin America, Angel Rama (1996) called this phenomenon the "lettered city," in which wealth and citizenship were tightly connected to the ability to participate in a literate culture in the cen-ter of capital cities. And while the mid-twentieth century did see the boundaries of the lettered city degrade (Franco 2002), the idea that poverty is a self-evident sign of nonmembership in public life is alive and well (Guano 2002). Evelina Dagnino (2005, 7) puts it succinctly: "Poverty is a sin of inferiority, a way of be-ing in which individuals become unable to exercise their rights. This cultural deprivation imposed by the absolute absence of rights—which ultimately ex-presses itself as a suppression of human dignity—becomes then constitutive of material deprivation and political exclusion."

Even if it was never expressed in these terms, this ideological shore of the lettered city was one of the targets of land reform from its inception. For all the critiques of agrarian populism, its current erosion provides an opportunity to reassess some of the radical possibilities (and they were only ever possibili-ties) that it opened. Land reform created a completely different set of relations between the state, the poor, and documents. By irretrievably blurring the na-ture of property rights in land, even if unintentionally, the IBR also blurred the line of tacit exclusion between campesinos and the aspiration to full citizen-ship. It is not that campesinos believe that the land reform was complete or successful or that it exhausted all of the possibilities for improvement of their situation—if anything, it is the very political arrangement within which state-backed improvement becomes imaginable as a limitless possibility. And it is this blurriness, this opening to the aspiration of landownership, the refusal of contractual closure around social membership, that campesinos are desperate to preserve. Land reform cannot succeed on its own terms because its very success would destroy it, but the space of striving that it opens keeps the idea of land use and distribution within the realm of political contestation. Unlike the titles offered by the IBR, the new titles bear all the hallmarks of exclusionary power and of building the documentary walls higher.[47]

Furthermore, there is no multicultural compromise to be had here which might authorize difference and inscribe it on territory—the kind of legislation that Paraguay and many other countries use to recognize indigenous land rights, for example. In another flawed attempt at rural governance, and again with the help of the World Bank, Paraguay began in the 1990s to set aside indigenous "reserves" out of which it is supposedly impossible to sell land.[48] But such a system could never work for campesinos, whose project is expansive and whose difference is not authorized as difference. That partial recognition of indigeneity that seems built into neoliberal political restructuring is highly limited, but it provides the wedge into which radical new conceptions of political participation might make their way into mainstream politics. But the campesino project I've outlined may be even more unsettling to neoliberal conceptions of land and property. The problem is that campesinos don't ask for recognition and couldn't be authorized anyway because they don't obey the temporality of difference. As far as land is concerned, indigenous people are traditional and different, and peasants are just backward, an embarrassing reminder of the not-distant-enough past.

So the struggle for and against privatization is a territorial struggle, but also a temporal one, between neoliberal time and campesino time, each positing a future nation that is profoundly in conflict with the other. Neoliberal reform posits a separation between the material and the abstract, which builds on a particular narrative of law. Their utilitarian approach sees in legal reform a means to the end of maximizing a narrow conception of the good. But such a view of the law as means is also built on a form of legal positivism—the argument that right is nothing but the will of the sovereign. To argue that it is possible to tinker with the law in order to produce a social end is to assume that sovereignty is already a fait accompli. And this is precisely what the campesino movement rejects. For campesinos see property not as an abstract instrument at the sovereign's disposal, but as the basis for a *sovereignty in-the-making*. The story of campesino families building a nation out of the land is their story of progress, and in that story, the law is not the basis for improvement—it is the result of it. If reform builds on an already existing sovereignty, it can be nothing more than the codification and legalization of police thuggery, the material processes which have always excluded them from full citizenship.

For campesinos, land titles are material objects produced through labor and struggle, a view of documents that is fundamental to the way that they understand their relation to the state. This is a straightforward enough argument, which helps explain how campesinos organize their legal incursions on land. Privatization, from this perspective, is a system for abstracting land titles from the labor that produced them and placing them in the realm governed by the Civil Code, a document addressed to a public that tacitly excludes campesinos. On the margins of this public sphere, in those places where campesinos have begun to challenge privatization's advances, the abstract arguments made in defense of the Civil Code break down as elites enlist increasingly materialist common sense to support their claims.

But this basic understanding of documents is not exclusive to land titles; it extends to all sorts of paper artifacts with which campesinos collectively engage the state in the post–Cold War period. Just as new democratic privatizers began to imagine campesino territory as potential capital in the abstract and governance as a technical matter of managing information, campesinos began to look past the politics of land titles and to see the whole bureaucracy as a series of material entanglements built around papers. As the new masters of the lettered city worked to extend their representational hold on rural Paraguay, campesinos began to tinker with the technologies of representation on which that mastery was built.

At the center of this story is the group of young men and women I call "guerrilla auditors," a small group of campesino activists from around Vaquería who form the MAP's leadership. The MAP shared many characteristics with the FNC and the MCNOC, and other smaller regional organizations, such as the community "bases" inherited from the Ligas Agrarias of the 1970s. They were also involved in some creative political activity that while quite novel in 2002, when they started, was soon adopted by other organizations. Unlike the larger organizations that had important sources of funding, either from large, dues-paying membership (the FNC) or from international support from groups like Via Campesina (the MCNOC), the MAP could not afford lawyers, and so they had to teach themselves enough about the law to be able to make their own cases to bureaucrats and judges. The more literate members of the regional leadership spent a great deal of time retrieving and familiarizing themselves with documents from bureaucracies in Asunción. They were led in this project by Jorge Galeano.

Jorge and those he worked with never spoke about what they did as "audit." In fact, they rarely spoke about it as a separate activity at all, and it took me some time to understand the complexity of what they were doing on their periodic trips to the city. In the first few months of research, I considered my field site to be rural, and spent as much time as I could getting to know people in the various communities around Vaquería, where the Movimiento Agrario was working. I attended meetings of the local and regional chapters of the organization, conducted interviews with as many members as I could, and desperately tried to find ways to be useful. I spent much of my free time looking at the archive that Jorge was building in his house, thousands of pages of photocopied documents of all sorts pertaining to the land they were fighting over. I mulled over these pages for hours, often understanding very little of what they said, trying to cross-reference the texts with old copies of the Código Civil and the Estatuto Agrario, which Jorge also had ready at hand, and in this way I eventually acquired a rudimentary understanding of Paraguayan land law. But in retrospect, it is clear that during that whole period I never really saw the documents *as documents*. As a researcher, I considered it fortuitous that Jorge had collected all of this information in one place, and indeed, this is how Jorge first presented his archive to me, as a handy tool to help in my research. When I asked Jorge how he had come to possess a particular document, he gave me an imperious look and said that all of this was public information in the IBR. You simply had to go and ask for it.

My perspective changed as I watched the archive mature over time. It grew until the old cabinet that Jorge had acquired in his days on government salary was unable to contain all the paper any more. Three of Jorge's close acquaintances added to the archive fairly regularly, but Jorge himself was the primary contributor. He traveled to Asunción every two weeks, usually to meet with other national campesino leaders, and invariably came back with a folder full of photocopies. There was also a young woman named Sonia, trained as a nurse but now living with her parents in Tekojoja, who occasionally accompanied Jorge, but also attended meetings on her own. And there was Derlis, who lived on twenty hectares without electricity in the quasi-legal settlement of Mariscal López, who also showed up with documents every now and then. The documents in question usually came from the IBR, photocopies that detailed the progress of different kinds of legal and bureaucratic proceedings, new maps and measurements of land they were interested in, and dossiers filed by other claimants on the land. During meetings that could last well into the night, top representatives of the Movimiento Agrario would pore over these documents for information about how particular bureaucratic processes were unfolding. At least that is how I read it at first, because what they were doing looked an awful lot to me like what I was doing: research. They consulted the archive as I would for information.

I was disabused of this impression when Jorge sent me to retrieve a file at the IBR office in Caaguazú. I had casually told him that I was going into town and asked whether he needed anything. As it turned out, he said, he needed a copy of a file, or *expediente*, pertaining to a plot in Tekojoja that he referred to simply as *lote diés*, lot 10. The expediente in question had been created to deal with a request by campesinos in Tekojoja to review the conditions under which the lot had been sold to Brazilian investors. The request had not yet been filled, but the MAP wanted to see if the *trámites* (bureaucratic procedures) were proceeding, or if they had just been stalled. Jorge gave me clear instructions. Walk into the IBR office in Caaguazú and ask to see expediente number 27013/04. If the bureaucrats gave me any trouble, I was to speak to someone named Lourdes, tell her that I'd been sent by Jorge, and she would retrieve the file for me. If possible, I was to make a copy of the final page. If not, I could just read it and see if any decision had been reached, or at least note what trámites had recently been effected on the file.

Nothing seemed simpler. When I entered the IBR, I encountered a sour-faced secretary who told me simply that the file I was looking for didn't exist. When I asked to speak to Lourdes, I was told that Lourdes was in the field that day, but that I could speak to her assistant. The assistant was friendly enough, but balked when I told her who had sent me to retrieve the file. Then she opened up the ledger on Lourdes's desk and apparently finding the number I was looking for among pages and pages of handwritten numbers, written down in the order in which they were processed (rather than the numerical order), she told me that the expediente had indeed been in the office, but had been sent on to Asunción. If I wanted to see it, I had to go to the head office in the capital.

The IBR's head office in Asunción is a massive warren of hallways on three floors, taking up much of a city block. At the front desk, the receptionists told me to search for the expediente in the office of the general secretary, but the secretary in that office told me he had never seen it. When I returned to the front desk, the attendants told me that I wasn't authorized to see the document anyway. After much persuasion, they admitted that the expediente was actually up in the planning department, but when I got there, I was told it had been sent to the "office of decentralization," which had sent it back to Caaguazú. In each office I encountered the same thing: a young secretary with a long ledger book detailing the movements of expedientes all over the sprawling institution, inscribed in the order in which they were received in each department. Some of these movements were computerized (particularly the intake at the front desk), but most were not. The only way to find a document was by following its trail and the traces it left on other documents in its wake.

A little annoyed to find out that the file had been in Caaguazú all along, but nonetheless certain that I had tracked my quarry successfully, I called Jorge and told him that while I didn't have the expediente, I knew where it was, and I knew that it had been moving. Clearly, I reasoned, if it had been sent back to Caaguazú, this meant that some decisions had been made, and the trámites must be proceeding. Jorge said little on the phone, only huffed his skepticism about my report and said that he would check Caaguazú again. Two days later I ran into him in Asunción outside the IBR office. When I asked, he told me that he had not bothered going to the office in Caaguazú after all, but had come straight to the head office, where he had found the expediente exactly where he had left it two months before, in the office of the general secretary. It had not moved since then. Jorge had taken the opportunity to tell the general secretary (whom I had not even been able to meet) that he needed to attend to the file, and the document had risen to the top of a deep expediente pile on the desk, where Jorge felt there was at least a chance it would be processed. With that, he headed back to Vaquería and waited, and started saving bus fare for the next incursion.

Jorge never did explain to me exactly what it was he had done to retrieve the paper that had completely eluded me. I felt certain he hadn't bribed anyone, since I knew how much money he was carrying with him at any given time, and he had no discretionary funds for bribes.[1] I realized I was in the presence of a political art that I had completely overlooked until that point. I also came to understand this episode as a test of my abilities and perseverance, a test that I failed miserably on both fronts. I had seen Jorge send Sonia and Derlis on these sorts of errands, and over the next few years, I would see him send at least a dozen other people on similar missions, always with clear instructions. Those who returned with the document in hand would slowly become involved in his inner circle of confidants, taking on more and more complex documentary tasks over time. Those who returned empty-handed found it much harder to earn his confidence. My own peculiar position eventually enabled me to overcome this setback, and over the next several months, I followed Jorge and others into the IBR whenever they would deign to let me tag along and watch them at work.

At first I assumed that what I would learn from this apprenticeship would be how to deal with bureaucrats, how to persuade them to cough up information or to do one favors inside government institutions. At the time, my understanding of how bureaucracy worked was not far from the Weberian description which permeates international development thinking about "good governance" (Weber 1946). I imagined it as a procedural apparatus in which the movement of files was instrumental to the deeper function of managing information about the relationships between citizens and the state. And the infuriating, Kafkaesque stories that Paraguayans told about their encounters with bureaucracy I assumed to result from a combination of inefficiency, corruption, mismanagement, and the maddening, calculated indifference with which bureaucrats imperfectly perform the separation between public and private (Herzfeld 1992). In other words, before I entered the warren of the IBR, I still imagined that it was useful to think of it in terms of its deviance from an ideal type. Since all I wanted to do at the beginning was read a little in the archive, I understood all of these difficulties as simple impediments to the process of collecting information—in this case different versions of the histories of particular land conflicts. Annoying as they were, the bureaucratic stumbling blocks were literally *immaterial* to my research. But I couldn't keep up this distinction for long, as I soon realized that there was no clear separation between the information contained in archives and the art of finding documents.

By far the most consequential lesson I learned in these early encounters was about how to read, and that the most important aspect of bureaucratic activity lies in its peculiar approach to creating and reading inscriptions on paper. I had been reading government documents all wrong. For months I skimmed Jorge's archive for content, ignoring signatures and stamps, rhetorical flourishes, and the many pages describing where the documents had been. I passed over lists of names looking for histories. I skimmed the records of requests by stakeholders to have the documents reformatted, unbound, or photocopied, and I looked instead for narrative passages outlining legal arguments or describing conditions in a given community at a particular time. But in meetings, Jorge and others would always draw attention to the marginal details I found unimportant. To be sure, they read the content, looking for inconsistencies, lies, or elisions in the text. But they also read as auditors might, analyzing the traces of documentary transactions, precisely the stamps and signatures I found so uninteresting. How, they always asked, was this document made? This strategy had provided a huge early breakthrough in Tekojoja, when they realized that the IBR had stopped authorizing transfers of derecheras to Brazilians, and that the latter had simply gone to other bureaucrats—the local justice of the peace and notaries from a neighboring district—to stamp the papers they had created to officialize the illegal transfers. Legal documents that had snaked their way through the courts or the IBR were far more intricate; their marginalia described networks of people and personalities, offices, money, laws, and motives that explained how things were getting done inside government.

This sort of reading built on an intimate practical knowledge of the institutions concerned, a familiarity with the people involved and with the forms of transactions in which they engaged that Jorge insisted campesino leaders needed to develop in order to be effective. It was also, of course, the sort of reading practiced by bureaucrats, even those who explained what they did in terms of transparency.[2] Reading this way was also necessary for acquiring more documents to read, and this is why it was a critical component of research to engage in the same practices. For instance, the first thing I learned was that it was pointless to enter the IBR without an expediente number. There was no way to find documents about a given community, case, or person unless you had a corresponding file number or were lucky enough to meet someone who knew it. But every file, if read carefully, would reveal more numbers, and therefore more files. The second thing I learned was that unless you entered into a clientelistic relationship with someone on staff, the only way to get access to files was to start a file of your own, and thereby get a number. Far from being impersonal, the bureaucracy worked as an economy of favors, most of which involved moving paper. Usually you needed both—a personal relationship and a file.[3]

Like the expediente I had sought for Jorge, my file began with a letter to the president of the institution, deposited at the front desk, requesting access to information and documents within the institution. My letter was given a number, a stamp, and a cover sheet, and set on a pile, and I was told to return in two days to get my answer. Two weeks later, after five visits to the front desk, I received an approval from the president, and my expediente was closed. This was my first mistake: since the file was closed before it had acquired any other numbers, it no longer had any function in the agency, and no bureaucrat to whom I showed it knew what to do with it.

I opened another expediente, which stayed open, but I lost track of the file. Since at the beginning I was trying to do this part of my work during short visits to Asunción, the file eluded me for weeks. When I finally caught up with it, my problems only became more complicated; in the office of the secretary general, I was told that the office could not handle my request, that such requests were handled by a different office. This was probably sincere (the people I was talking with didn't have a protocol for handling foreign anthropologists). But in every office I received the same response: the problem was explained to me, and the expediente was stamped and placed on another pile moving to another office. Each time my expediente encountered a problem in interpretation—that is, the bureaucrats looking at it couldn't make sense of it within the context of their office—they would forward it to another office, in the hope that a different reading would help. In the process, I did learn much about the structure of the IBR, but my file and my request refused to accrue any meaning. Without me standing over the desk, no one would even bother to read it, and the file would not move, and moving the expediente, I realized, was one way to change the reading in the hopes that something might open up.

Much of what happened in the IBR was simply that, moving documents around until they encountered a context in which they could be effectively interpreted. As it happened, my document found its meaning in entirely arbitrary circumstances: a secretary for the director of planning recognized my face from the newspaper (after the events in Tekojoja) and alerted her boss that someone of interest was coming to visit him. The director turned out to be a friendly and professional bureaucrat, with a degree in human geography, who was prone to boredom on the job. He was one of the few people in the IBR with a new democratic sensibility (though, like all other highly placed bureaucrats, he was also a Colorado Party member) and was interested in having a conversation. Thus, while that expediente never got me into the archives, it did help me to create a relationship with a high-ranking bureaucrat, who helped me craft the next expediente.

I had envisioned the IBR as a massive store of information managed through filing and the movement of files. My mistake was to imagine that there was something called information that was separate from files in such a way that files might give one access to it. In retrospect, it seems odd that I assumed information to be separate, something "contained" by files, but in fact this is a central assumption guiding governmental practice from at least the mid-twentieth century onward.[4] My breakthrough, however mundane it may seem at first, was to realize that the files were all there was. What people referred to as information followed rather than preceded the encounter with documents. One did not gain access to information through files, but in the encounter with files, information, in the sense of becoming informed, sometimes happened. My initial approach to the institution was predicated on an objectified view of information, as though the ideal relationship to information were one in which the movement of documents themselves was invisible. Armed with the same assumptions about representation as new democrats, I found myself approaching the archives with the same semiotic naïveté and zeal of international development economists, hoping to find, or somehow manufacture, transparency.

It was hard to explain this problem to people like Jorge, who simply didn't labor under the assumption that the system ought to work differently. Those to whom my problem made sense were new democrats, sociologists I knew who had for years been trying to compile reliable statistics about the land reform, pro bono lawyers, and the staff of NGOs and media concerns who believed in the new democratic project for transparency. Most of them continued to hunt for information. Some of the high-ranking bureaucrats I befriended, especially those who described their jobs as contributing to "development," would tell me that Paraguay's biggest problem was its lack of information. Many of them, as representatives of institutions like the IBR, were in the unenviable position of being called on by media, NGO, or governmental watchdogs to provide information, as though this were a simple procedure of mining the archives, when they knew it to be an arduous task of investigation, extrapolation, interpretation, and translation that they found almost impossible to perform. They were split on whether the requests were simply out of touch with the institutions, or whether the difficulty was a fault of the institution for not properly storing this thing, information, so sought by reformers. But for campesinos and most of the civil service, the materiality of expedientes was so obvious as to make my insistence on representational information nearly incomprehensible.

Guerrilla auditing is made possible by the understanding that, at its core, the state functions through the creation, circulation, and endless interpretation of documents. For campesinos, documents do not store information so much as make it possible, and state power is therefore not about seeing or inscribing so much as it is about controlling who reads what and under what circumstances. Information, in other words, is the quality of a document that always belongs to the document's future as a form of possibility. The power of the land title, for example, lies in the possibility that it gives the owner to fend off potential claims or attacks against his or her land. Expedientes circulating in the IBR, and even the Estatuto Agrario, the Código Civil, and the Constitution function in much the same way: they are powerful insofar as they enable political action. The work of guerrilla auditors like Jorge is to create files, find others, keep track of the movements of multiple related documents, and control their interpretation as they show up in different contexts.

But they are not alone in this project. In the early twenty-first century, two different kinds of political actors began to infiltrate Paraguay's government archives. The first group were allies of the new democrats, whose project to make the government more transparent was based on an understanding of documents as mere vehicles for information. These "transparency projects," as I call them, saw information as something separate from documents and thus aimed to streamline the way that the government stores and retrieves it. They relied on audit rituals being built into institutions, but the projects were not about audit per se; they were about top-down rethinking of how governments ought to organize communication and interpretation. The second group were those campesinos I have been calling guerrilla auditors, whose work to win land for campesinos on the frontier was focused on documents as material forms. Both positions arose from opposing ideologies of meaning and hence gave rise to different understandings of the possibilities for the bureaucratic future.

In October 2006 the Paraguayan government contracted the national consulting firm MCS Grupo Consultor, known for its studies of the Paraguayan economy, to look into a study of corruption produced by Transparency International. An international NGO funded in large part by USAID, Transparency International had been stirring the political pot in Paraguay for years with its annual *Corruption Perception Index*, which rated countries around the world according to the degree to which their citizens perceived them to be corrupt. Every year when the index was published, some version of the following headline would appear in the country's crankiest newspaper, *ABC Color*: "Paraguay is the third most corrupt country on earth!"[5] The government, explaining the contract to MCS, claimed that Transparency International's index was not a "fair reflection of reality," and that they wanted this to be proven scientifically so as to boost Paraguay's image in the eyes of would-be investors. *ABC Color* quickly printed the story, denouncing it as another sign of government corruption. Their headline read: "The government wants to deny what is visible to everyone."[6] In other words, it was transparent to "everyone" that the Paraguayan government's attempt to show that Transparency International's index was itself nontransparent was merely a symptom of its own lack of transparency.

If nothing else, this story should serve as a caution about the conceptual muck surrounding the words *transparency* and *corruption*. Corruption is, above all, a kind of accusation that politicians lob at each other. That strategy is often associated with a kind of caudillismo, as when President Wasmosy and his nemesis Lino Oviedo used it to shout each other down during Wasmosy's term. But the transition to democracy complicated the notion of corruption. For new democrats, and for the international organizations, like Transparency International, that supported them, corruption came to be opposed to transparency. The pairing mirrors familiar discourses about contamination and purity, in which corruption appears as a hidden rot in some governmental body, while transparency denotes its absence (see Verkaaik 2001; Gupta 1995). It's hard to overstate the degree to which this idea took hold in Paraguay in the 1990s. In the transition to democracy, most of the country's ills could be linked back to some form of "corruption," an increasingly nebulous category that basically connoted public malfeasance. At the same time, the word *transparency* found its niche, in an equally nebulous way claiming to be the cure for all of these ills.

Still, the pairing is a bit of an odd one since transparency and corruption are rather different sorts of things: corruption is an ethical lapse, while transparency is the visual quality that an object is said to have if one can see beyond it to something of greater interest—in this case, information.[7] Nonetheless, both words tend to be used to describe a measurable quality and a quick look at even the most basic metrics used to confirm suspicions about corruption and transparency shows just what a peculiar diagnostic tool they are. Take the *Corruption Perception Index*. *ABC Color*, like other media outlets around the world, reports on the index as though the perception of corruption (gleaned by interviewing citizens about how corrupt they think their governments are) were equivalent to corruption itself. The producers of the index surely understand that this is a false conflation, but do nothing to counteract this approach to reporting it. However, if the primary purpose of putting out the report is to encourage newspapers to report on corruption, then the index is merely a self-referential political loop, producing precisely the phenomenon which it will return the following year to measure (see Marcus-Delgado 2003).[8]

But the problem goes deeper than this. The claim that transparency decreases corruption is undermined by the method used to produce the index, since the increase in transparency should, in principle, increase corruption-perception. In other words, Transparency International's political claim is that corruption decreases to the extent that it is perceived by the populace, and yet its measure of corruption suggests that corruption and its perception are equivalent. In an unrelated case in Canada, for instance, the press made a big deal about how Canada had slipped several places on Transparency International's 2004 index during a kickback scandal that implicated the governing party and the prime minister. Just as in Paraguay, Canada's rise on the index was initially taken as international condemnation of Canadian political corruption, even though the slip—that is, the change in Canadians' perception of corruption—happened precisely because corrupt politicians had been caught by the auditor general and taken to court. In that case, given a nationalist press corps keen to defend Canada's "international reputation," it was eventually pointed out that increased corruption-perception actually indicated a healthy and transparent audit system.

From this point of view, the Paraguayan government's position that the index is misleading seems entirely legitimate. But unlike in Canada, the press in Paraguay sees its main role as trying to embarrass the government for its public and for international audiences, and the reporting has gone in the opposite direction. In fact, the most striking feature of the interchange between the government and Transparency International is how the language of transparency had itself become the only critical language available for attacking Transparency International's methods. In their riposte, and in their contract with MCS, the government claimed that Transparency International's index was itself nontransparent. Transparency International's success, in other words, lies not simply in the way that it can destabilize politicians by playing the corruption-accusation game, but in the way that it has managed to reformat the language of political critique. The very idea of transparency has usurped the field of political virtue, and failure to create perfect correspondence between representation and reality has come to be understood as a sign of ineptitude or duplicity.

Here one sees in part why transparency is such a productive language in the post–Cold War era, for it makes it possible to easily elide corruption with politics, interests, and partiality. This is not Transparency International's doing alone, of course. That organization and the politics from which it takes its name are symptomatic of a critical episteme that reaches far beyond Paraguay. The modern era is awash in a kind of semiotic ideology which privileges representational forms of language over others. As Timothy Mitchell (2000; 2002) and others have noted, it is a peculiar feature of this way of knowing that one tends to divide the world into the real, on the one hand, and a picture of the real on the other hand. The two spheres remain separate, and true knowledge inheres in the correspondence between the two. The bulk of modernist anxiety derives from the feeling that this correspondence is never quite as good as it should be. Statements, rather than being understood as necessarily situated, pragmatic, and interested, are judged instead by their deviation from an ideal truth, becoming a potential lie or grave mistake.[9] This particular view of the role of representations is as true of most social sciences as it is of popular understandings of how development intervenes in the present and how governments catalogue that which they govern. Popular views of transparency derive very much from the brand of empiricism bred in the social sciences: the assumption that scientific methods are all about producing representations of the world which are more accurate, and therefore more transparent, than other representations.[10]

Indeed, the back-and-forth between the Paraguayan government and *ABC Color* is not dissimilar from arguments made in anthropology and critical theory. The talismanic claims that transparency cures corruption has predictably given rise to anthropological analyses invoking magic, fetishism, and ideology. Transparency, some authors claim, is the new fetish of economic development.[11] The appeal of this analytic is obvious. For burgeoning nineteenth-century liberals, the fetish was the opposite of transparency, the site of representational confusion, and it was Marx's rhetorical ploy to put the fetish at the center of liberalism's most rational sphere, the market.[12] In the 1980s and 1990s anthropologists used the fetish to deconstruct the state, arguing that the state is not a proper object but a metaphysical projection of power relations which gets confused with an object.[13] Finally, the critique of the state is displaced to the document itself and to speculation about the fetishization of state paper. Documents such as identification cards and land titles, the sort of papers that materialize state practice, have a special role to play in this reification, since they serve as constant reminders of the state's existence, and so appear to be fetishes in their own right (Gordillo 2006; Wogan 2003). Some analysts suggest that transparency is only the name given to a magical and illusory quality attributed (or denied) to state documents (West 2003).

This sort of critique offers a good corrective to the easy ethics of Transparency International, but it only goes so far. The reason why it has become possible to talk about the state in these terms is that Marx's fetish has been refracted through poststructuralist semiology (Pietz 1993). In this reading, the fetish-object is equivalent to a floating signifier whose salient property is "to register the representation rather than the being represented, the mode of signification at the expense of the thing being signified" (Taussig 1997, quoted in Gordillo 2006, 172).[14] In other words, the fetish is a sort of opacity that obscures, rather than enabling the viewer to see "the thing being signified." It is this fetish, solidly grounded in representationalist theory, that has found its way into the anthropological critique of transparency. The problem is immediately apparent when people start describing transparency as a mask ("transparency conceals") and critique becomes an act of simple inversion. Both the project and the critique are couched in similar semiotic ideologies (cf. Keane 2005).

In other words, like the Paraguayan government's attempt to escape the accusation of nontransparency, the fetish argument in anthropology seems incapable of escaping a tit-for-tat about visibility. The critique either implies the possibility of a different, truer transparency or rests its case about the impossibility of transparency on the known noncorrespondence between language and the real. In its most sophisticated, self-reflexive iterations, transparency itself becomes a kind of social pathology of rebounding accusations (see, e.g., Žižek 1997; Nelson 2009). But none of these options offers much purchase for a situated or ethnographic appreciation of the effects that the particular practices associated with transparency politics have in the world, nor does it help to unravel what bureaucrats, campesinos, anthropologists, or new democratic reformers think they are actually doing as they spend so much time and energy with these documents.

One way to get past this analytic impasse is to step a little closer to the phenomenon that discourses of transparency claim to be describing or giving people access to: "information." Transparency as the key tool of political reform in the post–Cold War era built on a longer discussion in economics about the role information plays in markets. Transparency made it possible for citizens to make better decisions about their governments, only because politics now worked like a market, in which it had long been argued that better distributions of information made economic actors more rational.

Following an anticommunist argument made by Friedrich Hayek in 1945, economists had been arguing since the 1960s that information, traded between participants in an open market, played a special role in ensuring that economic transactions achieve maximal efficiency (Levine and Lippman 1995). In early iterations of this tradition, prices were considered the pure signals of the market, which distilled all the information that actors needed to make decisions, but economists soon began to argue that there were more kinds of information that went into economic decisions, information about quality, reliability, competitive products, market conditions, other consumers, and so on.[15] It stood to reason that not everyone always had the information they needed to make rational economic choices, and that this negatively affected market outcomes.[16] Following a logic similar to that of transparency, economists of information suggested that market outcomes could be measured against an ideal of "perfect information" (even if impossible to achieve), in which all actors had complete knowledge of everything that affected transactions and therefore found the most optimal distribution of goods possible. All markets were therefore somewhat "imperfect," but by improving information one could create the possibility of improving economic outcomes.[17] Yet even in this fairly vast literature it remains surprisingly unclear what "information" actually is.[18] The definition of information tends to tack between being simple, accurate representations of the world as it is, and being signals between parts of a system that have predictable effects. Neither of these definitions is entirely compatible with the other, and neither explains how, outside of abstract theoretical models, one actually knows if one is in the possession of information or not. Indeed, one of the main things that information seems to create for people wanting to reform markets and bureaucracies is anxiety about its very existence, which is one of the reasons why so much of the literature concentrates on information which is missing, imperfect, incomplete, and unreliable.[19] The sense of inadequacy which follows information around is often correlated with (but not easily identified with) the confusion that abounds in places like a state agency.

Despite confusion about what it meant, the idea that information might act as a panacea to all sorts of economic inefficiencies became far-reaching in the 1990s, embraced by experts on all sides of the international development community, from neoliberal efficiency-maximizers (e.g., North 1990; de Soto 2000) to advocates of a softer reformist approach like Joseph Stiglitz (2000), who made the link between information and transparency explicit in his grand claims about the possibility of information for the Third World. In the increasingly popular works of development writers, information came to be understood as something that was straightforward to create and unquestionably good. The fall of the Soviet Union and the poverty of the Third World were blamed on information problems (Stiglitz 1994; Shane 1994), and the coming "information superhighway" was supposed to improve economies worldwide. In 1999 the World Bank issued a *World Development Report* that likened the information problems of sharecroppers to those of Third World plant breeders and manufacturers who were blocked by patents from acquiring engineering data.[20] In both cases, more information was predicted to generate more wealth for the poor by promoting equitable growth. Even those reports that were not directly about information, like the 2008 *World Development Report* on agriculture, implied that many of the Third World's economic problems could be solved by collecting and disseminating information on market conditions, and every proposal in the 2008 report included components for the creation of "evidence-based research" in planning (Hetherington 2009). Because none of this literature fully resolves what "information" is, most of the early development projects that resulted from it were simply about producing representations of things that seemed to be useful to people in making economic decisions. As with the archiving projects of new democracies and the NGO projects to "give voice to the voiceless," the primary result of these arguments was an explosion in the number of documents and copies of documents circulating through different networks.

In Paraguay, the most influential version of this argument was Hernando de Soto's *The Mystery of Capital* (2000). De Soto's version of this argument, that the problem of the Third World was the "problem of missing information," is simplistic, but that is what gives it force, and one doesn't have to go far in Paraguay to find bureaucrats, new democrats, and foreign consultants using his ideas as explanations for what they do. Elaborating on his claims about missing information, de Soto says that in the Third World capital is "dead" because assets do not have a "representational life" which would allow them to be taken to market. The primary example of this is land titling. Land needs to be represented so that one can go to market with the documentation about the land (rather than the land itself, which is stubbornly immobile). This argument is misleading because it implies that titling or registering is simply about creating representations that are "missing." In fact, land-titling and land-registration schemes never merely create representations where before there were none. Almost all of the land markets that the de Soto solution has set about reforming already have property registries and cadastres of one form or another. The problem with these representational systems is not that they don't exist, but that they are, in de Soto's opinion, inefficient, unreliable, and contentious, and therefore don't do what they are intended to do. But of course they cannot be thrown out, because they are the only record of what anyone owns. So what reformers do when they say they are creating information is really *translate* existing representations into new forms of representation that supposedly contain more or better information. The archives created by de Soto's ideas are not new representations of previously dead assets, but new documents about old documents, on the argument that the new documents do something the old documents could not: produce an efficient land market. Information is no longer a thing, but the description of an effect. Documents contain information if they produce the effect desired by development experts (efficient land markets) and they don't contain information if they fail to produce this effect. More precisely, and circularly, information is the thing that a document is said to contain if the document has the effect that economic models have previously attributed to information.

One of the problems with this way of seeing things is that documentary systems can be inefficient for having too many documents, and bureaucratic reforms always add to these documents. For this reason, there is a very fine line for the reformers themselves between projects that merely add pages to what are already overstuffed archives that impede information and projects that are said to actually create information where before there was none. The difference is in the details that are glossed over by the neutral language about creating information: the key to making sure your documents contain information is really reducing inefficiency, unreliability, and, above all, contentiousness. Creating information is all about disciplining the interpretation of documents. Despite all this, the reigning explanation remains the same: a document is good if it truthfully represents something in the world other than itself. The document by necessity exists in one place, a mundane problem which bureaucracies are always dealing with, but the reality to which it refers is something stable, apolitical, disinterested. In fact, what bureaucratic reformers do is what all auditors do: report on the consistency of things found in other documents. And as Michael Power (1997) has pointed out, all audit reports are limited in their authority by the same thing that makes them necessary in the first place: the suspicion that documents can never quite capture what they are supposed to. De Soto's popularity is attributable precisely to the rise of what Power calls "audit society" in Paraguay, that feeling that all existing representations of assets are suspicious, but that the only way of making them trustworthy is by creating new representations of the suspicious ones. Like the back-and-forth between the Paraguayan government and Transparency International, or the analytic debunking by modernist anthropologists, the "information" game is all about commanding the authority to represent the real. In a climate of suspicion of all things representational, transparency is the ability to claim, however briefly, that unlike anyone else's, one's own representations of past attempts at representing provide a glimpse of the *really real*.

Transparency and information, whether in Paraguayan politics, bureaucratic reform, or social science itself, are part of a trap that linguistic anthropologists have been warning about for some time. The disciplines which have given rise to these kinds of thinking are by and large still stuck in a peculiar episteme that "gives ideological priority to the referential function of language and to the text understood as an objectification of that function" (Crapanzano 1981, 123; Silverstein 1979). The linguists' answer to this problem goes through the Peircian view of language, in which "signs give rise to new signs in an unending process of signification" (Keane 2005, 187). From this perspective, documents, like any other signifying device, cannot have stable meanings. They do not contain information at all. What we call information are the radically contingent meanings actualized in the process of reading in a given context. This model of signification is far closer to the strategic approach that campesinos and most Paraguayan bureaucrats use to negotiate their relationship with the state than is anything that reformers call information.

In eastern Paraguay there is a strong critique of documents that one hears all the time outside of the upper ranks of campesino leadership: "Ndojeganai mba'eve kuatia'ári" (You can't win anything on paper). Guerrilla auditors are an exception to this rule. But the majority of campesinos I spoke to were fiercely skeptical of the claims made about modern bureaucratic documents. Phrases like "Pe'a kuatiánte" (That's only paper) or "Kuatia ndovalei" (Paper is worthless) express this sense of the uselessness of documents.

The reason campesinos disdain such papers is exemplified by the differences between medical practitioners in the campo. Natural doctors (*médico ñana*) and witch doctors (*médico paje*) recite and incant, handing out objects with curative or other powers, including religious images and prayers which hold important powers in people's homes. But modern doctors (*médico*) offer only prescriptions, which are at best seen as an annoying trick for increasing their own revenue. Although many campesinos desire and have faith in the modern medicines themselves, they see doctors as mere dispensers of prescriptions, scraps of paper whose only apparent function is to limit patients' direct access to medicines in the pharmacy. Documents are a form of superfluous mediation inserted by elites into otherwise straightforward transactions. The charge that doctors levy for the "service" of writing out the prescription is considered unjustified, but given the control doctors have over the flow of drugs, campesinos recognize their dependency on the service. Documents like prescriptions are really just a method elites use to continuously bilk the poor. This kind of critique is easily extended to land transactions, which seem to get more complicated and costly with every new documentary layer that gets added to the system. Each document, to some degree, both fortifies the walls of the lettered city and creates a vector of exploitation by which bureaucrats can demand small payments from the poor for the privilege of the city's protection.

And yet despite refrains about the uselessness of paper, certain documents are also held in great reverence by their owners: almost every political activity that I engaged in during research involved trying to win things on paper. Most of these struggles were over land, and no one ever considered themselves to have won land until its possession was materialized by paper of some sort. Those who already possessed such documents, or some version thereof, kept them carefully protected, often with identity documents and family photographs. Some people refused to show me their titles and derecheras, fearing that my seeing them might cause problems, while others would proudly display them, waiting while I read over the details on the page. Early in my research, I was intent on attributing the aura of property titles and other documents to a history of state education. They often reminded me of pictures on documents produced by the land agency in the 1960s, 1970s, and 1980s, which depicted campesino men holding up documents as the ultimate expression of inclusion in the republic.[21] The iconic image of the young campesino displaying a piece of paper was also frequently echoed in meetings, where campesinos would present papers as proof of bureaucratic victories, as when Jorge returned from Asunción to show us all what he'd accomplished by opening a folder full of photocopies. The new campesino leader, holding papers in defiance of authority, was both an extension and a reversal of the campesino subject created by the land reform. The campesinos no longer held up titles; instead, the documents used as props in such speeches were about bureaucratic procedures, newspaper clippings about government corruption, or angry letters addressed to the president. These documentary gestures made claims about battles and partial victories on paper. Campesinos also produced documents and adopted documentary practices from modern bureaucracy, like writing out highly detailed and protocol-oriented minutes of their meetings. The FNC even produced identity cards for its members similar to those handed out by political parties.

In the simultaneous desire for and dismissal of documents lay a fundamental tension over how to engage in politics. This was one point of friction between Jorge and his brother Antonio, for instance. The latter was simply not literate enough to participate in the auditing side of their joint operation, and when Jorge failed to produce results in his documentary ventures, Antonio would complain that you can't win anything on paper, or that "la kuatia ricomba'e" (documents are the things of the rich). When handling documents, campesinos were in the presence of the lettered city. Antonio was not the only one to voice these concerns when Jorge or Sonia returned from the archives in Asunción to find people fending off physical attacks on their land. Jorge personally struggled with the persistent feeling that his friends thought he was becoming too distant, too much part of the world of Asunción, and losing his base. This question of how, when, and how much to engage documents was debated at every level of the organization, and permeated all of its activities.

It was during one of my forays to the IBR with Jorge that I realized just how complex and perilous the negotiation with documents really was. Jorge had

invited me to a meeting, along with five other members of the MAP, some of who were entering the IBR for the first time. We had all met the night before, and Jorge had prepared us for the meeting, outfitting each of us with a folder full of documents that would be important for the event. With the help of two other leaders and Digno Brítez, the Asunción lawyer who worked for a Jesuit legal-aid organization, Jorge had managed to book a meeting with the IBR's *gerente general*, or general manager. The gerente had an interesting status in the agency; although his office was one of the largest in the building and had the largest waiting room, which was always full of people, his position didn't formally appear on the organization's structural plan. Legally, at least according to the procedural law governing the IBR's functioning, there was no gerente general.[22] But in practice his role was critical, extending into all the operations. The person who had previously held the position had gone on to become president of the institution. Problem cases and unusual requests (like anthropologists asking for archival access) always passed through this office at one point or another. Expedientes were sent there when bureaucrats with more specific job descriptions couldn't figure out what to do with them. And it was a real sign of being a repeat customer that Jorge had managed to book an appointment.

Jorge and his colleagues had been granted an audience to discuss six different and intractable cases. All of the cases involved land with multiple claims. Two, including Tekojoja, had recent counterclaims, while the others dated back twenty to thirty years. These were the sorts of cases that often fell under the category of tierra malhabida: land which had been settled by squatters, but which had never been fully redistributed to them because the history of ownership was too tangled for the agency to fix with a simple expropriation or buyout. The communities living on such lands were under constant fear of being evicted by former claimants, and with soybeans now pushing up the value of land in the area, many of these owners, or more often their heirs, were threatening to do just that. Resolution for these cases rested on the government settling an account or forcing a legal decision, and in each case the IBR had waffled for years, the expedientes multiplying and growing. As long as the IBR failed to address and close the expedientes, the legal situation remained confused enough that violence of the sort we had all seen in Tekojoja remained a possibility.

The room, while large, was an awkward fit for the fifteen people at the meeting, and one of the campesinos squatted by the door through most of it, getting up every two or three minutes to let people in and out. The gerente sat behind a large desk, which was the only piece of furniture in the room other than a handful of chairs and shelves stacked with expedientes. Three secretaries stood behind the desk and were dispatched on errands every few minutes, while two lawyers from legal aid took turns on a single metal chair. The rest of us, eight men and one woman, stood around the opposite side of the wall, also taking turns on three chairs. A pattern developed for each of the discussions. Jorge would announce the name of the community we were to discuss, along with the number and title of the corresponding expediente. The gerente would send one of his assistants to find the file, and one of the campesinos, usually helped by Jorge, would begin to explain the case. She or he would explain details of the documentary trails from memory, explaining to the gerente what he would find in his own file and detailing the bureaucratic action required to resolve the case, making reference to laws of possession and land distribution. Usually the campesinos advised the gerente to send a representative on a site visit to witness the falsity of claims made by their opponents or previous bureaucrats.

These interventions were all prefaces to reading: they prepared the gerente to interpret the expedientes in particular ways. At the beginning, the documents themselves seemed to play only an ornamental role. As we talked about the cases, the gerente's assistants returned with expedientes, often huge and withered packages of documents, hundreds or thousands of pages held together by staples, tape, and string. The gerente glanced at them, but did not attempt to read them or to corroborate any of the accounts that he was being given orally. Occasionally one of the assistants would begin leafing through the stack, but whatever they found there did not make it into the wider discussion in the room. The only people who were capable of speaking authoritatively about the documents on the gerente's side were the legal-aid lawyers, who had prior experience with two of the cases in particular. In fact, while documents were central to this entire political meeting, both as aesthetic props for indicating authority and bureaucratic agility, and as referents in discussions, the documents themselves were not consulted directly. Their contents were useful only insofar as they had been committed to memory in a highly digested and interested form. And as Jorge and one of the lawyers showed, arguments made about the contents of the expedientes always straddled a line between what was in the documents and what lay outside of them. That is, they presented the contents as already relational with things that the documents made no mention of—stories about what was going on at the site, metastories about how the documents were created, complaints about past treatment at the hands of bureaucrats.

It was in recognition of the slipperiness of these stories that the fields of authority and strength in the room had been so carefully orchestrated. While the meeting was framed as a conversation about technical matters, Jorge was explicit from the beginning that it was also a calculated political confrontation. On the one hand, the gerente and his staff clearly used the desk and the mounds of paper to bolster their authority. In all of these conversations, authority rested with the expediente, and the gerente made it clear that the documents were part of their realm. Since all of the expedientes were written in Spanish, the staff behind the desk muttered to each other in Spanish, marking out a site of linguistic authority as well. In response to this, Jorge had balanced the power dynamics by giving campesinos folders of their own and instructing them on how to speak about them authoritatively. Even more important, though, he had sought to fill the room with as many campesino bodies as possible, throwing in a lawyer and an anthropologist for good measure, and having several of us stand through the entire meeting. This also meant that the conversation would be conducted, for the most part, in Guaraní. While the gerente understood Guaraní, he was able to speak it only haltingly, and was thereby forced into a deferential position when speaking. This made Jorge the most fluently bilingual person in the room, and he could switch back and forth strategically to help or hinder communication according to the mood. Those around the gerente spoke no Guaraní at all, and so barely participated in the larger conversation, remaining quietly behind the desk, with only one of the women from the legal department periodically, and quite aggressively, questioning Jorge in Spanish.

The strategy was explained to me in the same way as marches and roadblocks were explained: without breaking any laws, campesinos would try to force their position into official conversations through gentle intimidation. Campesinos would not question the authority of the expedientes, but would create a climate in the room whereby their own interpretations of those expedientes dominated the conversation as it led up to an official reading. Once the gerente was ready to make a pronouncement, he would ask his assistant to draw up a new document, detailing a course of action, which he would then stamp and sign and attach to the growing expediente. Most of these "courses of action" were orders for legal aid to reread the expedientes in light of what had been learned from campesinos or from field visits, and to add these new interpretations to the expediente, thus making it possible for the president of the land agency to make a ruling in the case.

In other words, the conversation, which made constant reference to reading, was actually about writing—it was not about consulting the archive, but about adding to its sediment. This is part of campesinos' documentary strategy—interpretation, they know, is only politically effective insofar as it produces more paper. This suggests something both about campesino views of materiality and about how Paraguayan bureaucracy functions. For campesinos, it shows how there can be a fairly seamless connection between agricultural labor, political labor, land titles, and other sorts of bureaucratic documents. When campesinos engage with such documents, they produce more documents, and thus produce the legal landscape around them. For bureaucrats, it underscores the incongruousness of suggesting that the documents "store" information or give access to information. Instead, it suggests that information is a potential quality of documents as material objects that produce more material objects.

I use the word quality to draw attention to the single most important aspect of the document's materiality. To say that information is a quality of documents is not dissimilar from saying that redness is a quality of apples, and this, as Webb Keane (2001; 2005) notes, means that redness is always connected materially to other qualities so as to resist our interpretive attempts to reduce them.

> Qualities must be embodied in something in particular. But as soon as they are, they are actually, and often contingently (rather than by logical necessity), bound up with other qualities—redness in an apple comes along with spherical shape, light weight, sweet flavor, a tendency to rot, and so forth. In practice, there is no way entirely to eliminate that factor of copresence, or what we might call bundling. This points to one of the obvious, but important, effects of materiality: redness cannot be manifest without some embodiment that inescapably binds it to some other qualities as well, which can become contingent but real factors in its social life. Bundling is one of the conditions of possibility for what Kopytoff (1986) and Appadurai (1986) called the biography of things, as the qualities bundled together in any object will shift in their relative salience, value, utility, and relevance across contexts. (Keane 2005, 188)

The information, always multiple, and always part of the document's future, is bundled with decay and fire, with tears and theft and loss. The stamps and signatures may or may not connect the document to parallel biographies of bureaucrats past and present, themselves being amended between readings, disconnected and reconnected to new networks and political entanglements. As the document grows, all sorts of contingencies can intercede in its growth to open up new interpretive possibilities and close down others. Lost pages, accidental or otherwise, are part of the document's surprises, as is future legislative reform, which may entirely amend the document's qualities. Its size may affect how it is handled, whether it can be carried across a room during a debate, or even read at all. And the very presence of written words may, when they encounter a particular semiotic ideology of transparency, compel people to read in search of a definitive interpretation.

Documents are artifacts with many qualities which can be momentarily actualized as information in the multiple readings, negotiations, and tussles into which they are introduced. The insight of guerrilla auditors is to never see documents as the end point, but as the site of possibility, not a store of information as a static thing but as a tool for making it as a political effect. And perhaps this is the point around which guerrilla auditors depart absolutely from the documentary pedagogy of Stronista populism. The pictures put out by the regime of campesinos holding up documents, like the dozens of books written by Juan Manuel Frutos enumerating the titles that had been handed out to campesinos, were intended to show the effects of the regime's good works. It is to this hollow victory that even Jorge would use the words "You can't win land on paper." But like brick houses, fruit trees, shotguns, and cellular phones, a well-made document, carefully managed, can open up possibilities in the endless struggle over land.

DON'T APPROACH THE TABLE

Over time, I came to see the artful manipulation and production of documents as the primary skill of guerrilla auditors, and the sessions in Jorge's living room as a form of apprenticeship for campesinos from a dozen neighboring communities. The stamped letters and photographs about Tekojoja, the reproduction and discussion of Alegre's report on IBR mismanagement, and the folders that Jorge assembled to bring into the gerente general's office, all were attempts to shepherd documents into configurations that helped campesino political goals. I say artful manipulation, because this was by no means *mastery* in the sense that they could impose their will definitively over the documents themselves. The way they saw it, no one had mastered the documents. The strategic commitment to the documents' materiality meant negotiating the bundled qualities that documents brought with them.

Toward the end of the meeting in the gerente's office, an episode took place that highlighted one of the difficulties that campesinos often encountered when they use documents this way. The case was that of Yro'ysã, a squatter community which had been fighting since the early 1990s to get papers for the land they lived on. The story I had gleaned from a meeting between Jorge and Julián Pérez, the main campesino representative from Yro'ysã, went something like this: Campesinos had originally petitioned the IBR in 1993 for the expropriation of three fractions of land belonging to three landowners who had fallen under suspicion after the 1989 coup. The request had resulted in an expediente that called for the IBR to examine the properties of Generals Amarilla and Gómez and of the businessman Luciano Olivieri, and thus to send a team to verify that there was a fully functioning squatter settlement named Yro'ysã on the land. The petitioners felt certain that this would result in a "reversion" of the tierra malhabida to the squatters. In such cases the quickest resolution for the IBR was to buy the proprietors out as quickly as possible, divide the fractions into campesino lots, and begin the long process of colonization and titling. Gómez and Amarilla soon added letters to the expediente indicating their willingness to sell at 350,000 guaranis per hectare, and after two years of trámites, their two farms had been transferred to the institution and parceled out to resident campesinos. Olivieri also wrote a letter to the IBR agreeing to the same conditions of sale. But there were questions about the legality of the title which complicated negotiations, since the institution didn't want to pay for land that wasn't legally owned. At a certain point the expediente dealing with Gómez and Amarilla was separated from the Olivieri case so that the former could go ahead, and the new expediente for Olivieri went into limbo. The supposed owner and the campesinos living there had quarreled for years, accusing each other of theft, false claims, and violent threats. The IBR was called in repeatedly and sent teams to the area in efforts to make sense of the conflict, each time returning with maps and pictures, but no clear solution to the problem.

The newest round of negotiations was happening with Olivieri's widow. After her husband's death, in 2000, she sent a letter to the institution offering to sell the land for 800,000 guaranis per hectare. A series of studies and surveys were carried out, but again the transaction stalled. In 2004, Pérez, leading a new group of campesinos associated with the MAP, wrote a letter to the IBR demanding that the case be resolved, and the expediente was dredged up once again. This time the IBR took the initiative and wrote to Olivieri's widow, asking her if she was still willing to sell. The reply was favorable, but she said given the new rural situation (i.e., the increased value of the land due to soybean expansion), the price of the land would be 2.6 million guaranis per hectare.[23] The IBR was willing to buy, but couldn't immediately raise the funds. Moreover, a new problem had emerged, as a Colorado Party boss by the name of Castillo had fenced off a piece of the property, claiming that the IBR had awarded it to him. The thrust of the campesinos' agenda for the meeting I attended was to convince the gerente to speed up the process of buying the land once and for all. They seemed close to an agreement, and the hope was that they could force a resolution by impressing on the gerente the political necessity of the action.

All of this was known, in more or less detail, to the campesinos standing in the room that day, but the gerente and his assistants knew almost nothing about it. The job of telling the story fell to Julián Pérez, who, although not particularly charismatic, could talk for hours about the problem and its history. His land, he said, the piece of the Olivieri fraction that he had been living on for about ten years, was being threatened by Castillo, and he understood that

there was no way of solving that problem unless the legality of the larger fraction was resolved by the IBR. He made the case quite clearly, but the gerente's
office seemed to make him nervous, and he kept getting lost in the details of
Castillo's role, which, though important to him, was peripheral to the case at
hand. He also kept looking down at a document in his hand, a photocopy of
one of several property maps that the IBR had produced in the last ten years.
Eventually he saw that the gerente was eyeing the folder as well. So he got up
and moved toward the table, to show him the paper, rather than try to explain
it himself.

As soon as he did this, the mood in the room changed. While three people
behind the desk huddled with Pérez over the paper, the energy drained out
of the rest of the room. We could no longer hear what was being said, so we
were excluded from the conversation, which was now being conducted mostly
in Spanish. Pérez and the gerente were no longer looking each other in the
eye, but down at the paper, and the gerente kept turning pages, lingering over
stamps and signatures and marginal figures, reading text in Spanish to his
staff. Those around me became unsure what to do with the space. This continued for almost five minutes before Jorge approached the table, after a few
seconds retreating to the wall with Pérez and proclaiming, "All of these details
will be worked out once the land has been bought." We then moved on to the
last two cases. But Pérez's act of deference, his relinquishment of Guaraní, of
his interpretation of documents and his story from the campo had affected the
dynamics. The campesinos had lost the upper hand that they had so carefully
maintained through the rest of the meeting. With regard to the case of Toro
Kangue, the gerente's assistant came back claiming that she could not find the
expediente, and the gerente merely resolved to keep looking for it. And with
regard to the Tekojoja case, Jorge nearly got into a yelling match with the lawyer
from legal aid, who claimed that Jorge was the primary source of the problem
in that community.

When I asked Jorge how he felt about the meeting, he said he was thrilled
that they had managed to pack so many campesinos into the room and had tied
up so many bureaucrats for two hours. The only problem, he said, was Pérez's
mistake. "You can never approach the table," he said. "As soon as someone approaches the table like that, the meeting is lost." I would hear this sentiment
many more times, both as an admonition against people and in planning for
meetings. I witnessed one meeting with the president of the land agency break
down when people started approaching the table with specific requests relating

to documents they held in their hands, usually receipts, maps, or occupancy permits issued by bureaucrats years before. It was clear that bureaucrats relished these moments, as campesinos ceded interpretive authority to them. It alleviated the pressure, collapsed the space of negotiation, and allowed them to defuse loud speeches and avoid making eye contact with aggressive campesino leaders. But more importantly, it reestablished what for bureaucrats was the proper social hierarchy around the documents, which put the technocrats of the lettered city back in control of interpretation.

The case of Yro'ysã was settled later that year, but the resolution had little to do with what had been read off the expediente during the meeting. If the meeting had any effect, it was that it moved the expediente into the orbit of the right people in the institution. At the other end, Olivieri's widow was more persistent than her late husband had been. In April, Olivieri's lawyers had shown up one last time, with pictures purporting to demonstrate the urgency of the situation (pictures of campesino houses with captions about how the campesinos were invaders on private property). By keeping the expediente circulating and adding fresh pages, the Yro'ysã case was kept on the informal priorities list of bureaucrats. This may have been as simple as the expediente remaining at the right depth of the right pile at the right time, because the real break came when the government received an $80 million grant from the Taiwanese government to help resolve rural conflicts, and Yro'ysã made it onto the list.

At this point, when the general secretary decided to authorize the purchase, the expediente moved into a new tier of the bureaucracy and a new speed of circulation. The gerente's order came with the proviso that he needed three more trámites performed on the file. First, with at least ten maps and measurements of the property, which varied in size from the original 398 hectares to 405 hectares, on file, the gerente dispatched a topographer to produce another map, now with the GPS, which had been newly habilitated in the area; the new measurement came back at 413 hectares, the largest so far. Second, being uncomfortable with the newest asking price of 2.6 million guaranis per hectare, he commissioned an estimate of the property value, which came back at 3.5 million guaranis per hectare, and was quickly rising, as soy farmers in the area were entering a buying phase. Seeing how much higher its own estimates were, the IBR quietly agreed to the asking price for 398 hectares. But another problem had come to light: a pesky receipt from the archive suggested that somewhere in the system was an outstanding debt on the property. The third order of business, then, was to send one of the lawyers to look into the problem so that the books could be cleared.

A week later, the lawyer submitted a fascinating report. According to her reading of the documentary trail, Olivieri had originally bought the property from a colonel named Julio Rojas, who had been awarded the land by the IBR in 1975. But Rojas had never finished paying the IBR for the land, which meant that it was technically nontransferable when he sold it to Olivieri, a detail that had gone unnoticed at the time. This situation proved difficult to navigate, because the IBR was currently mired in controversies in which their own lack of consistency about this particular rule was blamed for much of the problem of land irregularity on the frontier itself.[24] Technically, Olivieri's sale couldn't proceed, since the discovery of the illegality of the previous sale meant that it would be nullified. The title would be returned to Rojas, wherever he might be, who would then be held accountable for his debt to the very institution that was now considering buying it from someone else. In her striking conclusion to this report, the lawyer revealed her own frustration in a page-long sentence, which I will translate in part (with appropriate English punctuation). If the institution tried to repossess the land, she said,

> the heirs of Luciano Olivieri could claim to have bought the property in good faith, which could lead the whole thing to be decided against the interests of the institute. But even if this were to come out favorably, as has been noted, circumstances would be rewound to the moment of the initial transfer. In other words, Rojas would be the proprietor and we could demand payment. Ergo ALL of the judicial action taken since then would have been a waste of time and resources. It is therefore preferable that the institution move ahead, on the basis of the current conditions, with the appropriate procedures for the purchase of the property, paying the total value of the property at the time of the transfer. This is my pronouncement.

In other words, her reading of the documents led her to the conclusion that if the IBR proceeded in accordance with what the documents indicated, it would end up turning the very reading of the documents into a waste of time. The documents could not be allowed to impose their past on the trámites of the present. It was therefore best to proceed as if the documents didn't exist. Luckily, another document could be summoned for this purpose. Article 123, section G, of the new law of public contracts allowed executives of certain agencies to forgo the legal niceties of acquiring property if there was a sufficiently urgent "social problem" that would be solved by the acquisition.[25] Once again, and even more strikingly, the outcome, favorable in the short term to everyone involved, was not the result of a simple reading of the documents. Rather, it was due to a creative juxtaposition of different documents, bringing them into relation with each other by creating new documents which quoted and otherwise indexed the previous ones. The legal decision exploited some interpretations of the archive, pragmatically excluding others, so as to produce a new one. At best, this new interpretation was a layer of potential provided to future auditors, bureaucrats, and contexts.

Lawyers employed by the IBR shared with guerrilla auditors this appreciation of documents' materiality and the understanding that it was never entirely advisable to let documents "speak for themselves." Consider again Jorge's instruction not to approach the table. This was a contextual instruction, built on the knowledge that, as Keane puts it, "the qualities bundled together in any object will shift in their relative salience, value, utility, and relevance across contexts" (2005, 188). As such, it was a repudiation of the document's transparency, because what Pérez might read off the document in Jorge's living room with a close group of confidants was completely different from what he might read off of the same document in a head-to-head encounter with the gerente general of the IBR. Trying to read the document in that context had changed the relational dynamics in the room in which the document had been introduced. Pérez approached the table because he believed at that moment that the document in his hand could say better what he intended than his mouth could—what he was really doing was relinquishing the power to interpret. Campesinos had carefully established a space of negotiation in which their intimidating numbers and clear oral fluency had given them an upper hand in creating meaning in the room. Approaching the table collapsed this space and unleashed the excessive potential of the document to create meaning. Left to its own devices, the document did what one would expect: it created a space in which bureaucratic expertise trumped campesino knowledge, in which Spanish and reading took precedence over speaking in Guaraní. In this new space, the gerente and his staff could pick through the indexical traces of past interpretive attempts, overlook anything Pérez might have to say, and come up with their own interpretations.

When given a chance to express themselves, the expedientes merely expressed a sort of uncontainable excess. Their inscriptions were always too open for simple consensus, and so could not be expected to "speak for themselves" in political confrontations. And while this created problems for the campesinos, it was also the condition of possibility for guerrilla auditing. The documents' excesses *were* the terrain of struggle for confrontations in the gerente's office, as well as in Lourdes's office. These excesses were what made possible the entire debacle over land in Tekojoja and dozens of other communities across eastern Paraguay. They facilitated Efraín Alegre and his gestor in the pursuit of incriminating evidence against the Colorado Party, and the many who took up his document for their own purposes thereafter. They gave ABC *Color* endless material to interpret and digest in their attempts to embarrass the government. Each of these activities was an attempt to create a stable interpretation of documents that contradicted the official interpretation.

Information was not contained or carried by such documents; it was only one quality of those documents, a potential that emerged as bureaucrats, campesinos, lawyers, or anthropologists encountered them. These were highly indeterminate objects that made information possible, but never in a direct or even predictable way. The documents refused, in short, to merely represent. They were radically open, and hence the centerpieces for all sorts of disputes about land, about the role of the state, about the relations that the state facilitates. The documents were resting places for signs, yet they were not places where signs could become stable—just where they were held in trust for further deployment into new relational spheres.

WHO'S GOING TO READ ALL OF THIS?

The dizzying ambiguity of IBR files meant that they were rarely closed, often spending years sitting on shelves before being requested and brought back into play during some conflict. After almost twelve years of negotiations on a single expediente, the IBR finally settled on a price with Olivieri's heir. But even this decision created closure only in a narrow legal sense. On 19 September, the day that the IBR paid Olivieri's widow 80 percent of the price of the property, the amount that was required to effect the transfer, Pérez and Galeano sent a note to the agency requesting immediate action on Castillo's activities in the area. This opened up another expediente, as would Olivieri's complaint, several months later, that the IBR was stalling on the last 20 percent of the payment. The final page of the original expediente when I saw it, some six months later, was my letter asking for a photocopy of the file, creating one of the documentary conditions of possibility for this chapter.

To guerrilla auditors, this is just how the state works, and most administrative lawyers basically agree with them. But there are many who think that this isn't the way it ought to be. To new democrats, such bureaucracies are a throwback to a past that needs to be modernized with more systematic information technologies and procedures; they are deviations from a bureaucratic ideal, and the documents are deviations from the pure vessels of information that would make the state transparent. New democrats, along with a number of powerful news sources and funding institutions, believe that a modernizing overhaul of the bureaucracy would transform the Paraguayan state, stamp out corruption, and solve the problem of rural poverty. Based on the representational ideologies of de Soto and the World Bank, these proposals are built on the premise that it is possible, and desirable, to render the documents invisible and to let the information be seen unencumbered. The most salient of these projects while I was doing my research was led by the IDB, and the architects of that project referred me to de Soto as a source of inspiration.[26] Nothing vexed these technical advisors more than the IBR, the site of constant documentary negotiations. To the reformers, these maneuvers are transaction costs that ought to be minimized for the sake of efficiency and the benefit of everyone involved.

The IBR's system is undeniably confusing and frustrating by any standard. But it is into this confusion that guerrilla auditors have found a way to insert themselves, generating a politics inside the technocratic wall of the state. The new democratic dream of transparency, then, is not only to streamline the bureaucracy, trim the civil service, and speed up rural economic transactions, but also to remove campesino politics from the equation altogether. This is why the IBR would be the first agency to be closed if the new democrats had their way; from their perspective, the IBR serves no purpose except to slow down commerce and to invite campesinos and other populist relics into a process that ought to be carried out by technicians. The institutions of the state, new democrats believe, should work like a machine in which the documents carry only one possible interpretation and the possibility for politics disappears. If the documents *could* speak for themselves, campesinos would have no purchase in the bureaucracy at all.

But if that is the utopia presented by visionaries like de Soto, the actual mechanics of transitioning toward it are more mundane and confusing. The IDB's project to reform Paraguay's property-registry system is a case in point. Having repeatedly encountered institutional inefficiencies, the IDB loaned the Paraguayan government $9 million to hire experts who would streamline its entire property-registry system, introduce new documentary protocols, and digitize most of the system (see Inter-American Development Bank 2002).[27] The original project called for an overhaul of the public registry, the national cadastre, and the IBR, but after two years of planning, the IBR pulled out because the IDB insisted that they drop the nontransferability clause from their titling program. Still, the loan went ahead, in revised form. The project now required technicians, hired by the bank, to systematize millions of expedientes housed in the public registry and the national cadastre. Even at the national cadastre, the technicians encountered a profoundly complex documentary situation that refused to conform to their desires for routinizable information. From conversations with IDB staff and the head bureaucrats involved in the process, I learned that it was a monumentally frustrating task.

To give a sense of what they must have been confronting, let me relate my own story of trying to systematize information in the public registry. After months of attending meetings like the one between the campesinos and the gerente, of going to demonstrations and participating in land invasions on the frontier, I was still having trouble untangling exactly how things had come to be so complicated. I had a great deal of trouble understanding the cases as they were unfolding before me, and I thought it might help if I sat down for a few days with some of the key documents that everyone was referring to all the time to see if I might make sense of them. I was, as so many times in my fieldwork, approaching the table, still hoping that in a quieter setting the documents might speak for themselves. My project was therefore formulated in reverse: while I sincerely thought I was looking for definitive history, what I was really doing was trying to create one that would satisfy my need for stability. A good new democrat by temperament, I believed I could do what professional auditors claim to do—somehow translate the long, tedious encounters with mounds of papers into a definitive (transparent) representation of each of these conflicts.

I eventually ended up in the public registry, the cavern below the Palacio de Justicia which was supposed to house copies of all official registered land titles in the country. At the bottom of the stairs, in neatly printed black type on the white walls, was a simple request: "Respeta la Institución: No ensucie los paredes" (Respect the Institution: Don't dirty the walls). The floor which housed the registry was divided into eighteen "sections," where the documents sat alongside six to twelve functionaries, each room corresponding to an area of the country. Even the hallways were bustling with activity. This was the realm of the gestores, almost all of them young men paid by lawyers and other clients

FIGURE 6.
Inside of the Public Registry.

to look for documents, keep up to date with the functionaries' work, and otherwise stick their noses into the bureaucrats' business.[28]

Inside section 15, where I spent about two weeks, it was a little different, quiet except during World Cup games, when the director brought in a television and we all ordered fast food. The room was long and skinny, perhaps thirty meters deep, with every wall covered floor to ceiling by piles of browning property titles. There were over 100,000 rural titles, some of them 500 pages thick, organized into bound packets of five titles called *finqueros* (literally, "farmers"). When I wanted a particular title, it was the job of the youngest man in the room to climb on a chair and get it down for me. I read dozens of titles, dating back to the 1930s, that described a legal and legislative history of the area I lived in. But I quickly found that this mode of understanding history was no easier than that of contested oral claims I heard in the campo. Written in highly specialized legal jargon in long flowing script, the documents were so aesthetically peculiar as to make it difficult to find my bearings in them. It took several days, and much help from the director, to even begin to understand how to read them. For me, still guided as I was by a representationist ideology, reading these documents was a fight against form, against the irreducible bundling of signs and qualities, to extract information.

These are the first words of a land title to a huge tract of land bordering on Yro'ysã.

> In the city of the Assumption, on the thirteenth day of the month of December of the year nineteen forty-eight, I proceed to the inscription of a written testimony, presented on this day at seven o'clock and twenty-five minutes, drawn up by notary public Don J. Ronulfo Pérez on the seventh of December of the current year in which he states in writing that on the twenty fifth of November of the current year, the following men appeared before him . . .

Even the surveyor's report, which might seem like the most clearly representational mode that such a document has to offer, was written out in this form before the technique was replaced by maps. One of the first topographical measurements carried out in northern Caaguazú, in 1931, read as follows.

> The operation was begun on the fifteenth of April as had been announced in edicts and flyers, at the southwest corner stake, planted on the Ybycu'i Creek at the point where it crosses the public road from Yhu to Curupucu. No one presented themselves from the company Yerbales, Montes y Estancias, the only property sharing a side with the land being measured. The following results were obtained and are in accordance with the titles of the dominion: from the southwest stake, planted on the left side of the Ybycu'i creek, we proceeded along the length of the creek by a polygon traced along the edge until we met the stake on the northeast corner of the property belonging to the heirs of General Escobar. . . .

And so on, for ten pages. These were not documents created with modern information in mind, and it is an exercise in frustration to try to read them as formal representations of assets whose stability or transparency bears on their relation to the thing represented (a piece of land and a right to ownership).[29] They are the circumstantial sediment of power negotiated elsewhere, the notes between powerbrokers, indexing long strings of gentlemanly agreements in the safe halls of the lettered city, where to write was to rule. They are histories, but excessive histories, their mundane details spilling over the page in a manner that resists reduction to simple rules of possession.

The title is a material object with a certain degree of physical permanence. This, of course, was the promise of such documents at one time—they were gentlemen's agreements with more durability than memory, consensus, or good will. But the title's materiality also makes it capable of surprises. A great deal of the work in the registry was accounting for lost titles, or tracking them down to where they had been taken for some kind of consultation. Titles had to be bound and unbound, and they might go missing for ages before anyone realized it. Bureaucrats worried constantly about who brought titles where, whether marginal notes written in pencil had been tampered with or pages falsified. Even when they weren't touched, they were susceptible to all the other problems of archives: fading, mold, and worms. But it was not just nature's vagaries or the caprices of the unscrupulous that interceded on the qualities of the documents. The writing protocols themselves, those carefully studied ways of sedimenting legal action into the body of the document, could have unforeseen consequences.

The most exquisite of the documents I ran across was the title to Finca 13, or Farm 13. Reputed to be 103,000 hectares in size, Finca 13 was one of the largest properties in northern Caaguazú over which people I knew were struggling. The title followed the standard protocol; it was registered in 1933, during its sale to an investor in the area, making allusions to a title that had existed prior to the registries. The property changed hands several times over the next few decades, and each time a notary recorded in flowing script who was present for the transfer, where it took place, the conditions of sale, quoting the necessary legislation and previous bits of the title that explained the land's layout. Measurements were taken several times, due to disputes over the exact edges of the property or to changes in the laws around surveying procedures, and some of the measurements differed from each other by as much as 15,000 hectares. All of this was recorded in similar flowing script. It was around this time, in the 1970s, that a hereditary battle divided a piece of the property into several dozen smaller segments. In a smaller, more hurried hand, these splits were recorded in black ink over ten pages. The new parcels of land were in turn divided and sold, again creating new properties. Each of these divisions was recorded in red ink over the initial text, angled at 90 degrees to the black descriptions. Moreover, most of the divisions had a small marginal note in pencil or in green ink, describing extra conditions of transfer.

These brilliantly colored pages were extraordinary to look at, but completely illegible. After a few frustrated hours of trying to extract information from

FIGURE 7. Page from a land title in the Public Registry. I was not allowed to take pictures of the documents I worked with, so this comes from a photocopy circulating as part of an expediente in the IBR.

them, I found a note written in 2003, as a new battle for the property was gearing up between state agencies. "Due to the huge number of notes written on the title," the note simply said, "it has become impossible to decipher what is written here. I'm therefore authorizing a new measurement." It was signed and stamped by the director of the section. When I asked the current director about this, she laughed and said such things were done all the time. It was through these sorts of actions that the registry was changing. New interpretations or problems begat new inscriptions in a new format, adequate to the protocols of the day; titles changed shape as new relations were added to them.

As slow and sedimentary as this process was, the registry was inexorably changing, sometimes through ad hoc decisions of individual bureaucrats or the work of guerrilla auditors, at other times through legislation or the concerted interventions of international lenders. In 1931, with the legal creation of "real estate" in Paraguay, inscriptions were translated from an archive in which property was organized according to the claimant to one in which it was organized according to location. These inscriptions followed the same protocol, written in long, flowing script with straight pens, but around 1950 they began to give way to terser phrasing, ballpoint pens, and less accomplished calligraphy. Numbers that had been spelled out in earlier years were replaced by more concise numerals. By the early 1980s, some inscriptions were typed, and in the late 1980s someone had introduced mimeographed pages of protocol with blanks. This had easily been transferred onto computers when notaries started to use them. In 1997, after a corruption scandal in the registry, the most radical change involved the introduction of *fichas*, which altogether eliminated the protocol in favor of a chart; with fichas, the blanks were logically connected not by narrative language, but by gridlines. Titles were becoming more abstract, but abstraction followed the general rule of bureaucratic procedure—the new rules would be progressively applied, sedimented into the existing archives as problems came up, transactions occurred, or more properties were registered. In other words, like the note which declared the Finca 13 title illegible and opted for a new measurement, titles changed shape as new relations were added to them. The archive tranformed and shifted through the constant motion of lawyers, gestores, judges, notaries, and property owners leaving their marks.

The director, a woman with a wry sense of humor and an appreciation of the chaos that I must be experiencing in the room, was pragmatic about what she did. "All of this will change over time," she told me. "But what are you going to do? You can't just throw it out and start again! That would be even worse!" For this reason, among all the corrupt politicians, clamoring lawyers, and groveling notaries and their gestores, whom she despised, she had particular contempt for the folks from the Inter-American Development Bank who were working down the hall on their digitization project. That week, four years after it had begun, the IDB project had been modified because of a serious complication. Although the bank normally refused to hire government employees to reform government institutions, it couldn't find anyone outside the government who could understand the documents well enough to enter them into the database. The IDB had sent a troubleshooting team from Washington to Paraguay to reconfigure the project, allowing them to hire people familiar with the registry to carry out the transfer to computer. In the weeks that I was there, the hiring had just started with a handful of functionaries. When I asked the director, at the end of one of her particularly long rants about the inefficiencies of the registry, she simply smirked. "It's a nice idea," she said, "but there's only one problem." She motioned at the walls with their heaps of decaying documents. "Who do you think is going to read all of this?" Like the expedientes brought out in the meetings at the land agency, one could not expect to read them dispassionately, completely divorced from any particular political encounter. Instead, one carefully figured out what parts of what documents one needed to read at any given moment, then retreated to do so, only to reconvene and start arguing again. The idea that someone might sit down and try to figure the whole thing out once and for all seemed to her derisive.

In fact, the IDB's silver-bullet reform for Paraguay's property woes was the third project of its kind to be undertaken in only twenty years, even though the mythology that circulates among bureaucrats in the registry made these projects seem much older. Only the oldest hands remembered, with some fondness, a similar project from the mid-1980s, funded primarily by USAID, which had produced a set of aerial maps and reformed the municipal registries for the easternmost departments of the country. The new cadastral system produced by the project had no legal standing, but in 2006 it was still being used by municipal bureaucrats for taxation purposes in a handful of border towns, much to the disgruntlement of staff in the capital. Some of the aerial photographs were occasionally used by the national cadastre as well, even though the ground that they depicted had been completely transformed by soybeans over the preceding twenty years. The World Bank had begun a project in 1992 that also promised to overhaul the entire registry. Saddled by funding and organizational problems, however, that team had slowly reduced the scope of the project to cover only about 5 percent of Paraguay's territory and downgraded it to the status of "pilot project," although the $29 million price tag remained the same. For that small area, they produced a fabulous set of maps and a partial cadastre, and introduced a new form of ficha. The project ended in 1999. Aside from some maps stored at the ministry of agriculture, the only evidence of the project that remained in 2006 was that one and a half of the eighteen sections of the registry now used a different kind of form for land titles. There was also the question of $29 million dollars in debt, yet to be repaid. When the IDB arrived, only three years later, to begin research for their project, they found the World Bank documents completely out of date, the technology already antiquated. In short, they contained no information. The IDB consultants convinced state officials that they needed to start over again.

Reading a title like that of Finca 13, one gets a sense of how these new transparency projects are part of a slow shift in the semiotic ideology underpinning the documentation of transactions. The change didn't happen with democratization; it started long before, but picked up noticeably in the late 1980s. Some of the change was technological, from straight pens to typewriters to photocopied forms. But the straight pen hadn't caused writers to write more details about the transactions. This was a change from a culture of documentary excess—in which detailed inscription was a sign of access to the social technologies of inscription—to a culture of parsimony that saw the document itself as something of an embarrassment, in which the quality and accessibility of "information" are critical to making the economy and the state run efficiently. The urge for transparency is, of course, the desire for the document to disappear altogether, and the IDB project saw digitization as a way of doing that. To new democrats, transparency projects should modernize the bureaucracy, dismantle the lettered city (where the letter is power) to make room for the public sphere, where the speed of informational circulation gives the system its legitimacy. But the effect of such projects is the same as the lettered city: it creates the boundaries of an exclusionary economy of documents. And from that point of view, the new rules and new technologies seem primarily designed to shore up a leaky system of privilege. Information is a quality, part of the document's future potential. Taming that is not about creating a stable representation, but about formatting and disciplining who can interpret documents and how.

Ultimately, there is no reason to see such archival reform work as different from what campesinos were doing in the IBR. Or rather, its difference is not in kind, but in the scale of its interpretive ambitions and the resources it could bring to the task. Both groups were equally trying to impose their interpretations on the documents and change the archives to help stabilize those interpretations. Campesinos approached this file by file, forcing tactical interpretations through by bullying, in the hopes of winning small battles. Like guerrilla auditors, the staff hired by the IDB could do no more than try to generate interpretations of documents in their relations with satellite images, survey data, or local bureaucratic knowledge, and to create new documents, in whatever form, that narrowed the possibilities of interpretation more closely around their own. But they did this on a massive scale, using state resources and the legitimacy of their position to reformat the entire archive so as to make access easier for some (bureaucrats and notaries) and far harder for others. The IDB changed the form of the papers themselves, but also changed the legal frameworks within which it was possible to contest interpretations of those documents. Indeed, from the point of view of campesinos, it was the international allies of the new democrats who were the true interlopers in the archive. Campesinos saw their own guerrilla incursions into the country's most inefficient bureaucracy as finally accessing a democratic right, in the outer trenches of the lettered city, that should always have been theirs. As they were doing this, new democrats, and the international reformers they had hired as their own guerrilla auditors, were attempting to update the documents so as to take that right away. In this struggle, what words like *transparency* and *information* mark is not a radically different kind of documentary practice, but merely a claim to universality made by one among many competing interpretive positions.

I remember clearly the first time I was warned about hanging around with Jorge. I was meeting in Asunción with the director of an NGO about funding a crop diversification project that the MAP was shopping around to donors. The director was a well-known sociologist, and in the 1980s, she had been a vocal opponent of the Stroessner regime. She had even done an important study in the area where I now lived, and had met Jorge as a young leader. Campesinos spoke flatteringly of her as one of the few academics they'd met who was willing to get her trousers dirty. But while she spoke nostalgically about those days, her image of Vaquería was far from romantic, and she had clearly dropped the political edge that campesinos remembered from the Stroessner years. "Be careful with what they tell you," she said. "People like Jorge are politicians, probably frustrated that things didn't go his way during the transition. He wants to build up his following [grupo]. He sees everything through politics."

That picture of a man who couldn't be trusted because of his desire for power, and of his devoted, if slightly suspicious flock, was supplemented by much more ominous warnings from less sympathetic quarters. I was told in Vaquería that Jorge was a known con artist with hidden mounds of wealth, and was irresponsible at the head of a mob. People cautioned me to watch myself with *ese vivo* (that live one). Later, when

Jorge had been on television a few times, speaking Guaraní, a number of old friends who had been worried about me in the countryside now felt that their fears had been confirmed. At the very least, the story was that Jorge was a strong-arming blowhard who had duped his followers into supporting him, a *caudillo* opportunist who cowed his flock with rage and might at any moment move them to mass violence. Even the local IBR representative, who knew him quite well, honestly believed that Jorge was a hard drinker who lived lavishly on the backs of his supporters. And even campesinistas from Asunción who considered Jorge a friend and ally were fearful of Antonio, who they thought was liable to lose control at any moment. I will say this for the rumors: Jorge was a big man with a quick tongue who didn't suffer fools easily. He and Antonio had a daily radio show in Vaquería, where they often invited people to talk about environmental and economic issues, but they just as often spent the hour excoriating their opponents. On stage, both were formidable orators who spoke loudly and commanded attention. And there were several occasions, most notably in Tekojoja after the evictions, when one of the brothers marched a crowd of chanting campesinos down the road in an attempt to intimidate those who had just burned down their houses.

But, if anything, all of this struck me as quite a timid response to the pressures that they were under on a daily basis. They were, after all, reacting to the noxious fumigation of entire communities, constant intimidation, arson, arrest, theft of land from people who had nothing else, and even murder. Both Jorge and Antonio received constant death threats, delivered via friends and family members, or implied on the radio, and it was not uncommon for someone to show up at Jorge's house with a gun tucked into his pants, shouting and acting erratic. During particularly tense periods, when Jorge was in Asunción, a group of friends would stay at his house to protect his family.[1] Antonio had three times gone to jail on cooked-up charges, and once even had to wait as the police car he was in stopped by the mayor's house so the officer could collect payment for the "fuel used" during the arrest. For Jorge's part, a man in Tekojoja who worked as an informal real-estate agent for soy farmers accused him of attempted murder, claiming that Jorge had shown up at his house one night, in a drunken rage, and had shot him eleven times at point-blank range (missing every shot) before stumbling off into the darkness, in the process leaving his shoes by the man's well. As a result of these charges, every two weeks both brothers had to spend one day and the equivalent of three days' salary in bus fare to report to a bail officer in Coronel Oviedo until the charges were finally dropped, three years later.

There was no question that Vaquería was a rough place, that parties got out of hand, and that young men periodically murdered each other or young women in jealous rages. Outlying communities were also terrorized by para-police units called civil patrols, groups of young men who ran protection rackets loosely linked to the local police station and who periodically carried out other people's vendettas. And there were plenty of old-style party caudillos in town, running the stores on the *avenida*, organizing civil patrols, the cotton depot, the high school, the local radio station, the municipality, and the district attorney's office, peddling their influence with a combination of economic incentives and bellicose threats. But neither Jorge nor Antonio nor any other campesino leader I knew in the area fit this description. They refused to answer any of this with more than strong words and strategic documents. I often saw both brothers diffuse tense situations, rather than intensify them. The night after the shootings in Tekojoja, it was Antonio who argued against a raiding party that was ready to set off for Santa Clara to burn down soy silos. During the paro cívico, it was Jorge who banned alcohol from the camp, who pleaded with people not to bring weapons, and who repeatedly insisted that people obey the law during protests.

The image of Jorge as caudillo seemed especially bizarre at those moments when he came back from Asunción, walking up from the bus stop, often hobbling a bit from chronic pain in his kidneys that flared up when he was on the road, waving a brightly colored folder that he had been reading on the bus, and eager to show me and a few of his closest friends another sheaf of papers he had collected on his trip. If he was a failed anything, it was not a politician, but a lawyer, fascinated as he was by the minutiae of law and the possibilities of logical argument. As a leader he worried always that he was losing his "base," that he was becoming disconnected from what campesinos call *orerealidad* (our reality) because he spent too much time with his head in the books. He did believe that everything he did was political, but clearly yearned, at some level, for a simpler, more comfortable life for himself and his family, even as a vocational impulse for politics pulled him in another direction.

Far from spending his time strong-arming, Jorge preferred to read and talk about ideas. Judging by my interactions with other highly accomplished campesino leaders on the national stage, there were several styles of leadership, but Jorge was far from an exception. They could all make good fist-pumping speeches in Guaraní, but few were arbitrarily quick-tempered, and most were deeply reflective individuals. Given the chance, and a lighter sense of responsibility, I think many would have been happy to put their talents to other ends, perhaps to live their lives as urban professionals—there was less danger of them spiraling into chaotic rural uprising than there was of them getting a job at an NGO and moving to the city. More often than not, these were the terms in which campesinos talked about their disappointments with former leaders, that is, that they had ended up wearing suits. And yet outside of his immediate circle, most people thought of Jorge, like all those other campesino leaders, as *prepotente* (despotic), deceptively leading an ignorant rabble toward potential violence.

People had different reasons for promoting this image of Jorge, and of campesino leaders in general. Clearly many people feared him politically and legally, and the accusations of corruption, violence, and arbitrary self-interest were the primary ways in which local political actors tried to detract each other's followers. Campesino leaders were no different in this regard. Clearly, as well, the idea of the campesino leader as a short-fused autocrat was an easy stereotype which Asunceños in particular found easy to confirm. In an incident that took place shortly before I arrived, campesinos near Vaquería accosted the minister for the environment with a water-gun full of urine. Jorge hadn't been involved, and though he laughed about it afterward, he nevertheless disapproved of such tactics. He had been forced into damage-control mode for weeks afterward, as riot police visited the houses of everyone connected to the organization. Despite his efforts to defuse the situation, I later heard rumors that Jorge had been branded a "guerrilla" for the incident by none other than President Nicanor and that all government ministers had been warned to avoid him.[2]

But I believe there are deeper reasons for this strange caricature, that, the immediate circles of Jorge's political enemies aside, reveals the extent to which many influential reformers in Paraguay had difficulty seeing politics as anything other than threatening. The vision of democracy which depends on the fragile and evanescent notion of transparency is in constant search of opposites against which to define itself, and the poor, the rural, the Guaraní cannot help but confirm these opposites. To Paraguay's new democrats, campesinos remain an inscrutable and somewhat frightening group that, communicating between themselves in a language of emotions, is capable of spontaneous mass movement against urban reason. The phenomenon is not strictly Paraguayan, but something that arises everywhere alongside liberal aspirations to political rationality, that fear of the irrationality of mobs articulated in the heyday of liberalism in the nineteenth century and revived in the post–Cold War period.[3] In Paraguay, the fear takes on a particular flavor. It is a fear that such crowds are governed by the *ley del mbarete*, or the "law of strength," which causes them to fall in behind caudillo leaders whom new democrats consider crass and violent, for no other reason than their crude charisma. As the premise of the *paraguayología* literary genre shows, part of this fear is self-doubt, the sense that these campesino caprices for authoritarianism infect the whole Paraguayan body politic.

This is what makes the book *El país en una plaza* (Colmán 2004), about the events leading up to the exile of Lino Oviedo in 1999, such a charged portrait of the campesinado. It is not a mean-spirited depiction, but a genuinely ambivalent one. Unlike the students in that tale, who are urged toward martyrdom by nothing more than a primal desire for democracy for all, campesinos appear full of contradictions. One campesino group supports the students in the plaza for purely tactical, "sectarian" reasons, and even then only because their leaders tell them to. The other campesino group supports Oviedo, a vulgar former general and ex-con garbed entirely in the red clothes of the Colorado Party, threatening in his passionate Guaraní speeches to take the state by force and personally murder judges for the good of el pueblo Paraguayo. What unites these two visions of the campesinado is that they are always, irredeemably, political beings, swayed not by reason but by partisanship. And one of the things that makes campesinos indispensable as a foil for new democrats is the way they seem to illuminate the nonpartisan and the apolitical, the universalist ethic that gives rise to a faith in procedural democracy and transparency. New democrats mark as "violent" all politics that threatens to disrupt their bounded ideal of rational, political deliberation.[4]

The problem with guerrilla auditors is that they don't fit well with this profoundly dichotomous view of democracy. Campesinos like Jorge claim to be engaging in a politics of transparency, but they don't obey the ethics of new democratic universalism. At the same time, they don't conform to the stereotype of the campesino so necessary to new democratic mythmaking. They don't approach transparency or law as apolitical spheres. Instead, they are self-consciously political, and so always recall the specter of authoritarianism that the end of the Cold War was supposedly to put to rest. I would suggest that what most new democrats find disturbing in campesinos like Jorge has less to do with their political demands, or anything they do, than with a fear of the past's residue in the present, a fear that, at some level, all politics tends toward authoritarianism. In the image of the caudillo lies the new democrats' struggle to understand the place of politics in a democratic society.

The deep ambiguity surrounding the politics of guerrilla auditing can be explored by examining the way it participates in what Ernesto Laclau calls "populist reason," that form of reasoning that attempts to restate the particular in terms of the universal (Laclau 2005). Campesinos' use of public documents to advance the position of a particular rural constituency seems to flout the very thing documents are supposed to be *for*: making information available for the totality, for the public good of individual citizens. That the difference between universal and particular can be violated in this way throws doubt on the very promise of bureaucratic reform and on the certainties which underlie the new democratic utopia. In combining the narrowly political with the utopian transparent, guerrilla auditors threaten to reveal the political nature of the new democratic project—the possibility that *all* audit is guerrilla audit, and that transparency is always populist. Indeed, the oddest contradiction of new democratic understandings of transparency is that while they require caudillos and campesinos to serve as their opposites, they also require them to do the practical work of making bureaucracies function. More to the point, caudillos and campesinos are the only ones who are capable of making bureaucracies more *inclusive*. Transparency is a technocratic language built on the exclusion of the political from governance, which paradoxically requires excluded political actors to make it work.

PARAGUAYAN POPULISM AND ITS OTHER

The kind of liberalism that washed over Paraguay in the post–Cold War period was not, of course, invented out of whole cloth. It was only the latest iteration of a conversation that dated back to at least the nineteenth century, when European and Latin American thinkers tried to figure out what it would mean to govern a society based on the rational capacities of individuals. Not surprisingly, the very question of what a proper democracy might look like was always dogged by fears of the undemocratic, of the irrational and the uncontrolled. In Latin America, the undemocratic tended to be personified by caudillos, rural men who commanded large followings through violence and duplicity, and by playing on the supposed ignorance of the masses.

Perhaps the first work to describe the divide between democracy and cau-dillismo in such stark terms was *Facundo, or Civilization and Barbarism* (1998 [1845]), written in exile by the Argentine Domingo Sarmiento. Sarmiento's highly idiosyncratic book was ostensibly a biography of a gaucho named Juan Facundo Quiroga, a rural despot in northern Argentina known for his arbitrary violence. The book was a thinly veiled attack on the dictator of the time, Juan Manuel de Rosas, and a masterful piece of political literature that propelled Sarmiento himself to the presidency, two decades later, as a key leader of Argen-tina's liberal period. The book is a fascinating document of transitional logic. In Sarmiento's starkly dichotomous vision, barbarism and civilization mark an absolute divide between violence and reason, despotism and freedom, country and city, backwardness and progress, de Rosas and Sarmiento. Argentine lib-eralism was created out of the polemic view of its opposite: the rural caudillo who ruled by fear and stupidity. Perhaps the most interesting version of this dichotomy is in the book's repetitive slogan, written in (civilized) French: "On ne tue point les idées" (Ideas cannot be killed). Civilization rests in the disem-bodied idea, while barbarism is always a thing of the flesh.[5]

If liberalism has always depended on constitutive exclusions (Mehta 1999), in Latin America the process has perhaps been more bare than in other places, relying on a steadfast dichotomy between reason and violence. In the mid-twentieth century, ideas about the tension between democracy and its opposite took a social-science turn in modernization theory. Democracy was contrasted with "populism," which was epitomized by personalist leaders, who were au-thoritarian, anti-institutional, and adored by the poor.[6] Modernization theo-rists saw these leaders as symptomatic of a dislocation between rapid economic growth and sluggish institutional reform (see Germani 1968; O'Donnell 1979). For modernizers, populism was what happened when liberal ideas could not keep up with industrial change, when rural people arrived in the city in search of work, but without the education or the institutional framework necessary to turn them into proper citizens. In the post–Cold War period, the same figure emerged in the literature on "neopopulism," which created new policies, but reiterated the style of classic caudillismo.[7] In a particularly polarizing diatribe titled "The Return of the Idiot," Alvaro Vargas Llosa (2007) argues that the ghosts of the Cold War are haunting Latin America in the form of ignorant strongmen leading equally ignorant masses of rural migrants. The conclusion to his article brings my discussion full circle, as he calls for "the Latin American idiot [to be] consigned to the archives" (Vargas Llosa 2007, 61).

Throughout this history of hand-wringing about democracy, the undemocratic remains a temporal as well as a spatial problem, a holdover from the past that thrives in "gray zones" of institutional ambiguity in which personalist politics thrives (O'Donnell 1993; Auyero 2007). It also thrives in particular countries, of which Paraguay is a prime example. Even in Sarmiento's time, Paraguay seemed beyond the geography of reason. Sarmiento himself would justify his own country's invasion of Paraguay in the War of the Triple Alliance by claiming that the region needed to eliminate Paraguayan despotism. This same assessment of Paraguay's political disease emerges in the post–Cold War period in writers' attempts to expunge Stroessner's legacy from the nation and to sanitize its newfound democracy.

I use the term *populism* to describe a constellation of political problems of which new democrats wished to rid their nation: "caudillismo," "personalismo," "prebendarismo," and "clientilismo."[8] Caudillismo is that aggressive form of hypermasculine leadership which creates personalist forms of political adulation through arbitrary patronage networks disconnected from formal, public institutions.[9] At the state level, caudillos make good on their blustery promises by directing state resources toward their clients, and these gifts are returned as votes and other forms of political allegiance, but in general the line between public and private is so blurred as to make it hard to even pinpoint where corruption occurs. A key form of gift is patronage appointments which allow allies to collect rents ("prebends") from their office. All of these are seen by new democrats as part of a political disease which must be expurgated for democracy to thrive, that ineffable quality that makes the masses incapable of rational political behavior.

I prefer to use the word *populism* to describe the phenomenon, because while it connotes all of the qualities noted in the last paragraph, its emphasis is different—populism is not simply a condemnation of a particular form of leadership style, but one that draws the caudillo's constituency into the picture in dialectical relation with his (or very occasionally her) constituency. In Francisco Panizza's words, populism is based on "the constitution of the people as a political actor" (2005, 3), and the personalist leader is merely an effect of this constitution. Underlying new democrats' difficulty in coming to terms with Stroessner has always been their inability to understand his enormous popularity as anything more than the cheaply bought adherence of the irrational and the uneducated. This is the same diagnosis that they extend to figures remaining in the official party structure and to campesino leaders like Jorge. Following the tradition of Sarmiento, they see the ability to move masses as political and therefore an inherent violation of technocratic rationality. But the fear that people like Jorge are violent and unreasonable reveals the logic of populism. For it is not so much the caudillo that new democrats fear, as el pueblo that follows his blustery words. Hiding behind the fear of the caudillo is always a fear of the masses of people who have not emerged from the state of ignorance produced by the dictatorship.

STROESSNER AND AGRARISMO

In Paraguay, it is the rural masses of which new democrats have always been most fearful.[10] Stroessner's was an explicitly agrarian populism, what the Colorado Party called *agrarismo*, which sought to build party support by promising land to smallholders.[11] What made the Stronato populist was the way it took shape around a constituency of poor peasants living on the outskirts of Asunción, turning them into "el pueblo Paraguayo." It promised them participation in the state, agency against the manipulation and abuse of outsiders and elites, and thus realigned their aspirations with the developmentalist goals of the nation. In Laclau's (2005) terms, it promised to make the particular universal, not only to include it in politics, but to allow it to engulf the political realm altogether.[12]

Stroessner's rural strategy had two primary political dimensions. First, he and his government addressed the campesinado in the language of national victimization and redemption. Recognizing the reality (*realidad*) of suffering experienced by el pueblo Paraguayo, Stroessner's government used a language of identification that, ironically, was not far removed from that of liberation theology. The movement of radical priests that began several years into Stroessner's rule built a political pedagogy out of the daily lived experiences of rural people, linking the idea of poverty and suffering to a redemptive narrative of liberation from tyranny. Even though completely opposed in its politics, Stroessner's party used the same language as a form of recognition to enlist a massive following. Second, Stroessner equated the land reform with this narrative of liberation and inclusion. His rural deputy, Juan Manuel "Papacito" Frutos was put in charge of personally establishing communities, conducting lavish ceremonies in which, decked out in red scarves and banners, he would repeatedly declare war on the elite *latifundistas* who owned most of the Paraguayan territory.[13] The very existence of frontier colonias, according to this narrative, signaled that Stroessner's government was breaking the hold of these oligarchs and redistributing the state to a previously marginalized community. These communities were then adorned with an office of the land-reform agency, and, as they grew, eventually a party office, or *seccional* through which all patronage could flow (see Turner 1993).

Frutos repeatedly emphasized that giving land to campesinos was part of a "war on the latifundio," which would inaugurate the future of the nation. "In order to confront powerful sectors like the latifundista oligarchy," he wrote in 1974, "we need to count on powerful allies of our own. In Paraguay, the executive of the Agrarian Reform are allied with *el pueblo*, the armed forces, and youth."[14] This latifundista oligarchy against whom Frutos railed so belligerently was actually largely absent and politically powerless. The reform did not target large, functioning haciendas, but took over vast territories of forest, most of them owned by disinterested Europeans, beneficiaries of the venta de las tierras públicas, lands which could be expropriated with little of the complicated confrontation implied by the idiom of war.[15] This allowed Stroessner to sustain the central political contradiction of his administration. Promoting a "war on communists" for international observers, Stroessner was initially loath to even use the words "agrarian reform," finding them too radical (see Pastore 1972). But Frutos found a way to make a land reform that sounded radical without upsetting anyone. By conjuring a mythical latifundista oligarchy he found the elite enemy he needed to consolidate el pueblo Paraguayo without alienating the elite who made up the highest ranks of the party.

Most important, titles were the vehicle through which Stroessner turned peasants into political actors. Titles did not so much grant them citizenship as transform them into rational beings possessed of dignity and a sense of the future. "It is no contradiction to say that 'owning land' is equivalent to owning oneself," wrote Mario Halley in the introduction to one of Frutos's many self-congratulatory books (Frutos 1985, 12). Owning land is "to value one's own labor, to confide in one's own foundation, and on that foundation, to build [*edificar*] that which dignifies human life: house, family, plantation, harvest, bread, peace, love, unity, and dominion." Building on the Lockean premise that land ownership confers special moral characteristics on men, Halley continued,

> The Agrarian Reform, inspired by President Stroessner, HAS TRANS-
> FORMED THE MENTALITY OF THE PARAGUAYAN CAMPESINO. He is
> no longer Lazarus in his grave, but Lazarus on his land. He has left behind
> the moral death that was his disinterest, apathy, and resignation at his own

abandonment, and lives the active and participatory life of he who knows himself to be part of his country [Patria], the proud inhabitant of a free country that has consolidated its national identity, thereby ennobling the identity of its sons. (Frutos 1985, 13, emphasis in original)

Land titling promised to create national subjects, and through them a sovereign and democratic nation and that included el pueblo Paraguayo as participants in the national project.

The key point is that Stroessner did not create el pueblo by merely addressing it. He built it up as a mode of national identification through extensive use of patronage, especially through the doling out favors which linked campesinos directly into the interests of the ruling party. As Javier Auyero (2001) has cogently argued, clientelist politics is not based on a simple market exchange of goods for votes. Instead, it takes the form of gifts that connect people in lasting relationships of influence and reciprocity whose influence works through deferral and expectation.[16] Patronage of this sort was the fundamental logic of political transactions under Stroessner's regime and extended into every aspect of the transactions between Stroessner and el pueblo. The invitation to political membership in the national project was itself a kind of gift, materialized in specific sorts of documents which bore the spirit of the act of giving, demanded loyalty, and promised more gifts in return. Political subjectivity was not an abstract principle or bundle of rights so much as a relationship between people and the state facilitated by documents like identity cards, party-membership cards, military service records (carnets), and birth certificates, which were given by bureaucrats. Like baptismal records and marriage certificates, which indicated that the men and women named belonged to the church, objects like party cards and carnets were markers of belonging to the state, carried primarily by men to facilitate their encounters with bureaucrats and police. Of all these documents, land titles (and the derecheras that preceded them) were the most symbolically laden. As campesinos worked their way toward land titles through careful investments in their household base, the promise of those titles was the shore of Stroessner's populism.

Nearly two decades into the transition campesinos continued to show little interest in the representative qualities of titles, or of other official documents. Instead, they read for indexical traces, the stamps, signatures, and asides that trace a network of relations on the page. In older titles, Frutos's signature was the most important part of the document, because it linked the chain of recognition straight back to Stroessner. Titles were earned, but they were also gifts of recognition, and like all gifts, the title retained something of the giver, thus opening up channels of reciprocity that strengthened the party system. To have title was to be connected to Stroessner in a private network called the state.[17] Stroessner ran his country more like a conglomerate in a frontier boom town than like a democracy, and this system posed little problem for large numbers of party-affiliated campesinos so long as Stroessner *was* the state.[18] Titles worked like a protection racket—by making intelligible and legitimate campesino claims to local party bosses. The rights a title conferred could not be separated from the personality of the giver, nor from the materiality of the document itself, which was useful only if it could be presented to police or bureaucrats during encounters at the periphery of the state.[19]

The importance of the title-gift to Stroessner's rule became most apparent in the waning years of the regime, as the idea of agrarian reform was overshadowed even more by the project of distributing titles as fast as possible. This was Paraguay's first rapid titling scheme, a clear precedent to the kind of projects promoted in the late 1990s by the World Bank and Inter-American Development Bank. The campaign was partially supported by USAID, and even promised a computerized cadastral system that would make land information more efficient. But in practice, it had an overtly personalist edge which eventually led USAID to abandon it. The campaign was promoted on posters which showed Paraguayan progress as a single pyramid of titling accomplishments, at the top of which was the bust of Stroessner, surrounded by agricultural bounty and the IBR icon for the peasant family. In the mid-1980s, Frutos (1985) declared that by 1990, the government would hand out one million titles.[20]

In this first iteration of rapid titling projects, Stroessner and Frutos tried to pursue a sort of land reform on the cheap, to accrue the political benefit that the title-gifts conferred without the costs associated with integral reform strategies. It was a fiscal strategy aimed at generating political, rather than economic, capital: while other countries in the region dealt with recession by printing extra money and causing inflation crises, Stroessner printed titles. Unlike money, titles produced in this way devalued more slowly and bought the government several years before anyone felt the effects.[21] The cover of Frutos's manifesto to this effect showed the nation as a group of young men marching across open ground holding aloft papers. It was titled *Un millión de propiedades para un millión de felices propietarios* (A million properties for a million happy proprietors), and underlined the hope that titles could make men fall in behind the party.

FIGURE 8. Poster from the 1980s promoting Stroessner's land titling campaign. (Courtesy of Editorial El Foro)

FIGURE 9. The cover image from Juan Manuel Frutos's *Un millión de propietarios* (1985). (Courtesy of Editorial El Foro)

The unraveling of the Stronato toward the end of the Cold War can be read in the history of these titles. To expedite their issuance, several bureaucratic steps were removed from the titling process, including measurement and approval from the ministry of public works and the national cadastre. In the last few years of the regime, and well afterward, titles conferred by the land agency stopped going through these offices, which meant that the relationship to the IBR and Stroessner was more direct, but the institutional network that they indexed was less extensive. All of this meant that the IBR was skimping on the complicated bureaucratic work which tied titles into the larger state networks controlled by the party. As the legal apparatus switched hands, and as Stroessner went into exile and Frutos into retirement, the titles that had been issued so quickly in those years became legally suspect, people began demanding new measurements, and the titles were devalued in the new regime. New leaders at the IBR no longer stood by their accuracy, and as the titles had never been vetted by other agencies, they could not be used to call in protection from the national cadastre (part of the ministry of finance) or the ministry of public works. Campesinos owning these titles found them to be a liability, bad assets known to be poorly connected to actual land and transferable only after a series of costly adjustments. On the periphery of Vaquería, for instance, are several roads whose titles, issued in the late 1980s, overestimate by as much as 75 percent the amount of land in the plots to which they correspond.

While the scheme worked, handing out titles solidified the personal relationship between Stroessner and the recipients, a relationship in which the former consolidated his authority as benefactor according to a particular way of gifting citizenship. The title was a political object, that singular material statement that made el pueblo Paraguayo into full political subjects, but it always did so on a hierarchical basis. The transfer of the title was not an institutional gesture, but a personal one; it did not invite participation in a public archive, but invited the receiver into a private club by conferring recognition of his reality and a reward for his work. The rights a title conferred could not be separated from the personality of the giver, and indeed, when the regime collapsed, many of those rights disappeared because they were backed by personal promises rather than institutional ones. The title's work was to offer reassurances that the ruler's knowledge of the beneficiary remained intact. That promise of eventual national inclusion was suspended indefinitely by the coup and the ensuing transition to democracy, but it remained in the rhetoric of those bits of a once important historic bloc—campesino organizations now working independently of the Colorado Party, and a handful of Colorado operatives who continued to build their appeal on the grounds of agrarian populism even while their leadership lost its ideological mooring.[22]

TWO NATIONS

Although they weren't responsible for the 1989 coup, and did not assume power afterward, the new democrats saw Stroessner's departure as an opportunity to assert the sovereignty of the public sphere over the state apparatus, creating a new economy of representation around government. In the new political language, the gift economy sustaining the party came to be called "corruption," and the lack of institutionalized information about the use of state resources became evidence of criminal wrongdoing, to be solved by transparency. What new democrats had perhaps not counted on was the tenacity of rural reality, or the importance that campesinos placed in the documents they'd been given by Stroessner. In the realignment after the coup, the continued alliance between the party and the majority of campesinos was interpreted first as the product of manipulation by elites in the party structure, then, when it stubbornly remained strong, as a symptom of the irrationality of el pueblo and the lack of education in the countryside. Hence the growing divide between that constituency that called itself el público and that which called itself el pueblo. The divide restated the old story of Latin American liberals versus populists, but now with a new language of post–Cold War hopes, which hung largely on the idea of transparency as an epistemological salve to everything from government inefficiency to economic stagnation to corruption and illegality.

The task that new democrats set themselves was enormous. Without throwing out all the documents housed in state buildings and starting from scratch, their project was to carefully reframe existing relationships, transactions, and representations so as to slowly change the way they functioned. In the land archive this meant taking a century of documentary sediment from the land-reform record and making it speak to an entirely new project: the hopes for a perfect land market. Like the movement of the archivo del terror from the police station to the courthouse, bureaucratic reform meant making documents speak to a new national future, imagined as the opposite of the very nation that had created the documents to begin with. Over twenty years new democrats labored on this project, from USAID and World Bank projects and reforms, to the IBR, to the rapid titling bills of 2005 and 2006. But it was not just the materiality of the documents that dogged them in the transition: there were other projects afoot as well. Campesino organizations were emboldened by the coup, but instead of agreeing with reformist ideas, chose to push for a continuation and strengthening of the land reform. Meanwhile, the Colorado Party remained powerful in impoverished areas and sought to maintain that strength while adjusting to the reform. Cold War populism did not disappear with the coup, but continued to exist alongside new democratic institutions, and it was the Colorado Party that was quickest to figure out how to play both sides at once.

The best example of this was President Nicanor Duarte Frutos, elected in 2003, who bore all the trappings of a traditional caudillo, more like Stroessner than any of his democratically elected predecessors.[23] When campaigning for president, Nicanor claimed to be a campesino himself, yelling his speeches in fluent Guaraní, draping himself in the traditional red scarf of his party. He soon showed that he was also adept at turning political slush funds into patronage machines.[24] But his real ingenuity was his ability to simultaneously curry favor with new democrats. He had been Argañista at the time of Marzo Paraguayo, part of the Colorado faction that followed the assassinated vice president, Luís

Argaña. After Marzo Paraguayo, Nicanor was named education minister in the cabinet of González Macchi, from which position he oversaw part of a major World Bank education reform. All of this gave him a plausible connection to the narrative of democratic victory in the plaza after the student massacre. More impressive, he was able to win the approval of international economists and political scientists known for their disdain of Paraguayan party politics (Nickson 2007). He hired a respected economist, Dionisio Borda, also a vocal critic of the Colorado Party, as his finance minister, and quickly signed a previously suspended stand-by agreement with the IMF. He distanced himself personally from those in his party who were the most tainted by scandal, even while he allowed them to continue building the party apparatus.

Analysts of Paraguayan politics during the Nicanor years called this strategy "dual politics."[25] For example, this is the storyline that the *Economist* picked up in its story about Nicanor in the fall of 2004, describing the political tensions in the lead-up to the paro cívico.[26] The notion of duality expressed the sense that Nicanor's team was speaking to two constituencies at once, two publics whose politics were at odds. In this reading, Nicanor's success was based on keeping the two spheres more or less distinct: as long as he showed himself to be transparent to international auditors, then he had accomplished his obligations to new democrats, el público; and as long as he kept the faith among campesinos, he could keep his support among el pueblo. Much of Nicanor's executive, with Dionisio Borda as the primary example, were chosen to speak to the former, while the Colorado-dominated senate and congress, linked to the continuing structure of the party, spoke to the campesinos in a style that had changed little since the 1960s.

This is a good start to understanding politicians like Nicanor, but there was another dimension to the way these constituencies were articulated in the dual project. For both el pueblo and el público were not just constituencies, but modes of address directed at a particular interest group as though it were the sum total of the body politic. This would make both el pueblo and el público populist in Laclau's sense of the word. And yet they also differ in one important way. While new democrats rarely acknowledge their particularity at all, seeing themselves merely as conduits of universal reason, for campesinos, the relationship between the particular and universal is explicit, since they are never allowed to forget their particularity.

The difference can be seen in how each group uses the national flag. Campesino organizations use the flag constantly—usually a simplified ver-

FIGURE 10.
Squatter marking the entrance to a camp to signal to the previous owner and police that the organization was claiming this land for campesinos.

sion of the red, white, and blue stripes, without the emblem in the middle—to mark their political spaces and activities as proper to el pueblo Paraguayo. They even call it "la bandera campesina," carrying it in marches, hanging it in front of squatter tents, wearing it, putting it out on their patios as a sign of solidarity with other campesinos during national political mobilizations. The use of the flag to demarcate land invasion sites and campesino marches makes the point most clearly, and campesinos will say explicitly when raising such flags that they are claiming land for el pueblo Paraguayo. In Tekojoja, where it had the additional advantage of marking the difference between campesinos and Brazilian soy farmers, the flag was used to mark all houses in solidarity with the squatters. In this way, campesinos turn the flag into a threat, and it is understood as such by new democrats and other elites. After a demonstration in Caaguazú that was broken up by police, several campesinos told me they had been arrested because they were wearing tricolor wristbands and hatbands. In the hands of campesinos, the flag ceases to be a celebration of the nation, and becomes instead the threat of a takeover of the nation by campesinos.

FIGURE 11. Picture of student protesters during Marzo Paraguayo, which first appeared in *Última Hora* and was reproduced frequently, including as the cover of Colmán's *El país en una plaza* (2004). (Courtesy of *Última Hora*)

This oscillating conflation between the particular and the totality of the nation would seem to demonstrate Laclau's point perfectly. But, at moments of crisis, new democrats also use the flag for their own project. In the Plaza de Armas during the stand-off with Lino Oviedo (the very apotheosis of caudillismo) students painted themselves with the flag, and were narrated by the press as embodying the dreams of the nation (hence *El país en una plaza*). It was precisely in this moment, which more than any other emblematized the rift in post–Cold War Paraguayan society, that new democrats chose the flag as the defining symbol of their project. The only significant difference between these two brands of nationalism are that one recognizes itself as populist, and is forced to constantly battle the ambiguity of universalist particularism, and the other one doesn't. That is, when campesinos wave the flag, it is both the *bandera Paraguaya* and the *bandera campesina* simultaneously. New democrats do not have to confront this ambiguity, and can leave this dimension of their politics unacknowledged.[27]

These asymmetrical logics force us to move somewhat beyond Laclau's formalist analysis. Laclau celebrates populism and the universalism of "the people" as a pure form of politics that transcends any specific political group or set of demands. For Laclau, new democrats would be populist as well.[28] But at least in Latin America this claim doesn't sound quite right, for those demands and movements named populist are quite precisely located spatially, racially, economically, and, in the liberal narrative, temporally.[29] There is no question who Vargas Llosa's "idiots" are. In the post–Cold War era, el pueblo, far from being successfully elevated to the level of the universal, is asserted and called out as particular as well as universal. Populism is the name of a nagging reminder and a constantly returning interjection, never quite absent but never quite accounted for, in the new democratic public. It is the inescapable suspiciousness of the campesino claim to universality that makes it necessary to name it, even though new democrats, like social scientists, have great difficulty settling on what the name should be (populismo, caudillismo, prebendarismo, etc.). The challenge of my analysis is to return some of this symmetry—to name new democrats as they name populists, to see the public sphere as one among many discursive spheres competing to describe the real.

TWO REALITIES

Campesinos and new democrats each use the nation and its icons to signal their asymmetrical desire to overtake the universal. A similar, but more fundamental, asymmetry lies in the way different Paraguayans use the word reality. Just as there are two nationalisms in Paraguay, so, too, are there two realities, and their political deployments are held to quite different standards. Reality is a universalizing claim and in Latin America it is very frequently connected to populism. But it is also oppositional, a framing device which establishes nonnegotiables, the grounds for incommensurability between divergent political projects and conceptions of the possible. And as with other versions of this confrontation, when campesinos invoke reality, they are labeled as deluded, crass, and populist. By contrast, when new democrats use the word, it remains unmarked.

One often comes to reality through documents, and this is equally true of campesinos and new democrats. For campesinos, as we have seen, most documents exist by and for the elite, and their presence among campesinos is seen as a sign of duplicity. Land titles are something of an exception to this rule, in large part because they do not represent anything: they are objects which can protect the owner from eviction by tying them into networks of state power.

But the disdain for other sorts of documents remains strong. Campesinos use the Spanish word *letrado*, lettered, to mean duplicitous; they mock the use of documents by politicians they dislike; and they will often say, after listening to someone explain something with documents, that the documents "are not our reality." Most important, when they claim that "you can't win anything on paper," they are marking their exclusion from the lettered city, that economy of documents created by and for letrados.

By contrast, campesinos have great praise for politicians who are able to "understand our reality" (*ontende la orerealidad*) or "speak our reality" (*he'i la orerealidad*), which in Guaraní is more or less equivalent to "speak the truth." This ability to speak reality was what made Antonio a great leader, and something which Jorge often praised as well. Speaking reality is an ability to orally invoke the affective landscape of the campesino narrative, to invoke the unremitting bleakness of the material present. Campesinos often told me that they only considered me capable of understanding their reality because I had eaten *mandioca* (cassava) at campesino tables, picked cotton, dug *tũ* (small subcutaneous parasites) out of my toes, faced the police with them, and done my best to speak a stigmatized register of Guaraní. And it was often with reference to these experiences that Antonio would introduce me to his friends, claiming that while I was an academic, these experiences qualified me to write about their reality, a qualification that was always up for questioning. It is by showing signs of this corporeal connection to rural experience, particularly suffering, and weaving them into Guaraní speech that politicians can be commended for speaking reality.

A leader who can speak this reality is very judicious in his or her use of documents covered in Spanish words. Reality is spoken in Guaraní, which also indexes connection to the majority of rural mestizos and the urban poor. Most new democratic parties that emerged after the 1989 coup (particularly Patria Querida and País Solidario) were perennially hampered in the campo by their stilted Guaraní, just as the most effective leaders of the Colorado Party were sneered at by Asunción's elite for their loud discourses in vulgar registers of Guaraní that framed their identification with the rural masses. The evocation of reality in this way, emphasizing the corporeal connection to the hardship of the masses, is the centerpiece of populist discourse in Paraguay. It is anti-elitist, forging a relationship between caudillo and mass that promises to override the economic power of elites and foreign infiltrators who control the lettered city. All of the great caudillos of the second half of the twentieth century—Stroessner,

Frutos, Oviedo, Argaña, Nicanor, and a handful of senators—have had this skill.

This talk of the real is one of the most recognizable elements of caudillo speech, and not surprisingly, most new democrats find it disdainful. They see in it a hint of totalitarianism—that drive to control thought and perception through concentrated executive power. The phenomenon is regional in scope. In a recent critique of this sort of politics, aimed at primarily Latin America's new leftist leaders, Claudio Lomnitz (2007) argues that this politics of reality is a key aspect of populism across the region: "This talk about the real is part of a political language . . . of bawdy transgression, of brown men upsetting protocol and convention. It is a language that instills fear in certain sectors because it is an idiom of identification between leader and marginal follower, an idiom of identification that is generally recognized as a call to class hatred" (26).

Echoing the sentiments of Paraguay's new democrats, Lomnitz sees reality here as an "idiom" with the performative capacity to foment hatred. Lomnitz's critique can be read as an attempt to police the boundaries of legitimate politics along liberal lines: proper opinions are the province of the cool-headed and the well-informed, while the opinions of those who muck around in the ideological fog of "reality" is not politics, but frightening class (and race) hatred. Repeating the fears of Sarmiento and Vargas Llosa, Lomnitz implies that the corruption of politics is marked by the presence of bodies among ideas.[30]

But Lomnitz is careful to point out that the appeal to reality is not only made by traditional caudillos, but also by neoliberals who see economic laws as incontrovertible. This other reality is the one that underpins Paraguayan new democrats' notion of transparency. Pablo Herken Krauer, a well-known economist and public intellectual, provides a useful example. In his weekly appearances on the Channel 9 news throughout Nicanor's term in office, Herken assessed Paraguay's politicians according to whether or not they were paying attention to la realidad económica. During the early years of his presidency, Nicanor's apparent desire to pay attention to macroeconomic indicators, his choice of finance ministers, and his ability to sign agreements with the IMF, all gave Herken some reason for hope. Good government, Herken regularly reminded his audience, is based on transparent fiscal policy responding to this economic reality, which is itself inscribed on documents put out by bodies like the IMF.[31]

La realidad económica is quite clearly a different reality from orerealidad. This reality, as evoked by Herken and others, is not the specialized discourse of economists, but is a public idiom, the reality of a new democratic public that believes that the government's first priority ought to be national growth, a statistic which is produced by economists in NGOs, the government, and international bodies like the IMF. Macroeconomic reality not only can be transparently represented in documents inscribed in Spanish—it is real by virtue of its representation in such documents. Economic reality therefore is also a political language, and an idiom of identification between the educated and the civilized, as against those whose complaints about more mundane issues are merely the bawdy transgressions of brown men. The explosion of documents emanating from the new audit bureaucracies of the World Bank, Transparency International, and the IDB in Asunción are the grounds of new democratic reality, but they refer to a community of interpretation set apart by the walls of the lettered city, the walls guarding the public sphere from the irrationality of the masses. In self-perpetuating representations, they continually seek and affirm a new reality of privilege promised by the transition. Many campesinos see Herken's invocation of reality as a call to class hatred the same way that Lomnitz argues populist politicians use it. It is just slightly more indirect, not called out from the soapbox, but institutionalized, not written in documents to be given as gifts, but written in documents which represent transparently, to be circulated among members of an exclusive public.

Not surprisingly, Herken doesn't speak Guaraní on his television show, and engages in discourse about campo life only in the abstract terms of employment rates or in the occasional despair about another campesino protest ignorantly slowing down the economy. No campesino would ever mistake him as speaking their reality. Herken's use of macroeconomic reality is an idiom of identification, indexing privileged distance from poverty and rurality, just as Oviedo's vulgar Guaraní indexes a corporeal proximity to it. What each of these describes is a different reality, a different way of framing the relationship between particular interests and the universal. Orerealidad is an experiential reality that links the state in a direct relationship with el pueblo in the hopes of mitigating campesino hardship, while "macroeconomic reality" is a technical abstraction which synthesizes many of the hopes of the urban middle class.

During the transition, each of these realities was constituted as the other's opposite. New democrats' inability to see this is one of the reasons their project kept stalling. Not wanting to stoop to what they considered the crass populism of Colorados, too close to the authoritarianism of the Cold War, they constantly excluded campesinos from their project, even those, like Jorge, who wished to join. The political void left by this divide would be filled by reformist Colorados and campesino leaders, who understood how to move between two realities. Theirs was "dual politics" in its most complex form: an ability to speak across mutually exclusive realities. Not surprisingly, it operated with hybrid objects and discourses, and engaged in practices that didn't obey the fundamental dichotomy of transitional Paraguay. One such practice, common to both reform-minded Colorados and guerrilla auditors, is what I call "populist transparency," in which transparency is consciously presented by a leader as a gift to his followers.

THE GIFT OF TRANSPARENCY

One of the few times I saw Jorge and Antonio openly collaborating with the Colorado Party was during complicated negotiations for a community called Mariscal López. Mariscal López was a huge squatter settlement northwest of Vaquería and Tekojoja, a place where soybeans had yet to make a significant appearance. The first time I went there was in January 2005, when they invited me to a political gathering which they had been arranging for several weeks. A neighbor named José agreed to take me to the meeting on his motorcycle, and we arrived early in the morning, in time to join a crowd of several hundred residents waiting expectantly for the arrival of famous politicians from Asunción. Eventually, the president of the IBR, Érico Ibáñez, and a popular Colorado senator named Bader Rachid Lichi arrived on a rickety Cessna to address the crowd. Their big announcement that day was that Mariscal López was about to be legalized, which would mean that residents could stop worrying about the threats of eviction that they had faced for twenty years. Rachid Lichi had devised a plan whereby he would "regularize" the colony and make it possible for everyone to receive titles to their land. The leadership of the MAP was primarily responsible for organizing the event, but they'd been helped by a local *seccionalero*—the representative of the ruling Colorado Party in Mariscal López. He had outfitted the space behind his sawmill with tables draped in red cloth and arranged for members of the Colorado chapter (*seccional*) to wear the red shirts and scarves of the party.

Even though the meeting was about a purely technical and legal matter regarding the land—regularization—it had all the trappings of a party event, with as much red displayed for the admiration of the party representatives as possible. Rachid Lichi delivered a long and boisterous speech dominated by references to his own party as the savior of the people and by vicious attacks on Liberals, elites, technocrats, and foreigners. It was strange to see Jorge and Antonio in this setting. Like most campesino leaders, they considered themselves nonpartisan and had great disdain for these sorts of color displays. One thing they shared with the new democrats was the feeling that the Colorado Party was manipulative and corrupt and that it needed to be defeated. After the meeting, they even joked about how much like the Stroessner years the meeting had seemed. When I asked José, whose family was Liberal, what he thought of the meeting, he said, "It was a bit boring, but it makes me laugh, just like the old days. My dad would take us to meetings to hear Papacito Frutos talk about land, and he would just repeat over and over again, Stroessner is great, the Colorados are great."

Nonetheless, Jorge brought home a red object that day: a binder full of documents that the senator had given Jorge after presenting its contents to the crowd. As a gift dressed in the unmistakeable symbols of party patronage, the binder was just one of a history of populist gestures that had been made in this area for decades. But unlike common patronage, this gift was not economic, nor did it confer any particular rights or privileges on the receiver or the assembled crowd. In fact, Rachid Lichi said, the binder contained documents to which anyone had access; he was simply helping people to see them and so to understand what he was doing. It showed, he said, that his regularization plan was completely transparent—"Che transparenteite!"

Like so many documents copied from the public archive, this binder eventually found its way into Jorge's personal archive. That night I took one look through it and put it aside, unimpressed, having already seen all of the documents it contained in other folders and binders in Jorge's cabinet. When I asked Jorge what good he thought had come from the meeting, however, he said the binder was an impressive accomplishment. "But you already have copies of those documents," I objected, knowing that he had gone to great lengths to get them in preparation for this very meeting, that he had traveled to Asunción and asked for a favor from a friend who worked in the senate. As information, the binder was redundant. "Yes," he said, "but it's not every day that a senator comes in person to the campo and gives a binder full of documents like that." For Jorge, it was the binder's function as a gift, rather than the specific information that it contained, that made it so valuable. He might have disdain for the party and no use for the photocopies that the binder contained, but he saw important significance in the act of giving, that is, in what Rachid Lichi claimed was the gift of transparency.

"The gift of transparency" has a somewhat dissonant, if not outright absurd ring to it. Gifts, after all, are objects that stubbornly refuse to be abstracted from the people who transact them. They entail forms of reciprocity which link the recipient back to the giver, and therefore confer power on the person of the giver, unlike transparency, which is predicated on the logic of democracy as political marketplace, and therefore of the transaction of ideas in commodity form.[32] To give transparency is therefore simultaneously to create the grounds for citizens to make informed choices free of political influence, and to bind those citizens into an obligatory relationship with the giver. But this is exactly what was happening in Mariscal López that day. I want to resist the urge to dismiss the talk of transparency as duplicitous rhetoric, the same sort of talk that allowed Lino Oviedo to call himself "ethical" while handing out bundles of cash from his military helicopter in the years before the 1998 election. Instead, I want to open it up as an analytic question: in what ways was Rachid Lichi's gift of transparency formally similar to new democratic projects for bureaucratic reform? I have suggested that one think of the IDB's bureaucratic streamlining activities as a kind of "transparency project" which, while flawed, builds toward the new democratic dream of a democratic public sphere. Here I want to explore other projects in which the gift of transparency is not only coherent, but actually necessary. If the representational hubris of large-scale transparency projects seems utopian, at a small scale such projects seem flawed and inconsistent, but possible. If at the scale of the state they seem designed to exclude campesinos, then transparency projects conducted around specific political concerns can have surprisingly inclusive effects. It is around these sorts of projects, carried out by populists, caudillos, and guerrilla auditors, that transparency regains some of its radical democratic potential. And this is how I see what Rachid Lichi was doing in his effort to "regularize" Mariscal López.

REGULARIZATION

"Regularization" is a crucial but utterly unglamorous transparency project, the little sibling of registry streamlining and rapid titling. It refers to the process of cleaning up legal or representational idiosyncrasies in specific land titles which, for whatever reason, have become impossible to trade. The practice was introduced as a legislative tool during the reform of the Estatuto Agrario, which lasted through the 1990s and was finally ratified in 2002. The new estatuto opened up a new office in the IBR called the "office of regularization of state land," which in 2004 was handling a dozen or so very complicated cases.

Most of these cases dealt with massive properties, estates which campesinos would consider tierra malhabida. In the legislative language of the estatuto, they were called "irregular," a designation which encompassed land that was poorly mapped, properties that overlapped drastically with others, and most often land so hopelessly mired in legal disputes as to make it either legally impossible to transfer or to make the cost of transferring it prohibitive. Finca 13, or Farm 13, one of the largest and most intractable of these properties, had been out of the market since 1981. This title supposedly corresponded to the land on which Mariscal López sat.

Most campesinos who attended the meeting in Mariscal López went there hoping the speaker would solve a problem that was almost twenty years old. They described the history of their woes this way: the community had been founded by pioneers in the mid-1980s, when young families moved north into forests that for a long time had been "idle."[33] Mariscal López had never been formalized as a colony by the IBR, and as a consequence its residents had not been able to receive occupancy permits, let alone titles, for the land they lived on. The settlement was now home to several thousand residents, and the main road sported two gas stations, a police post, several schools, and a bull-fighting ring. Nonetheless, the residents were legally still land invaders living on lotes precarios, and since they had started building here, a military unit, a financier, a bank, and a powerful Colorado organizer had all claimed to own the land. With each new claim came the threat of dispossession. None of these claims had ever stuck, and Mariscal López's residents said the main reason for this was that they had fought off each of the claimants, often violently. When I was told this story by Don Marcelo, one of the original residents, who didn't understand the legal reason he still couldn't get title to this land, he ended with a shrug: "Pe'a la orerealidad," he said. "That is our reality."

The primary problem this caused residents was not strictly a "market" problem in the sense imagined by the proponents of the de Soto solution to rural poverty, which lies in creating a streamlined public registry and providing informal landowners with regular titles. According to de Soto, titles are necessary to reviving the "dead capital" of the poor by making it possible to use land as collateral against loans. But orerealidad rarely has anything to do with an abstractly envisioned "market," and none of the people with whom I spoke in the colony expressed any desire to mortgage their land. They were already able to get small amounts of credit using cattle, motorcycles, and future agricultural product as collateral, and few campesinos were in any hurry to deepen their debt load and risk losing their land.[34] Instead, they said, the lack of kuatia (papers) meant that they lived in constant fear of eviction from powerful people better connected to the state apparatus than they were. What campesinos wanted was not an efficient land market, but a document to say that the state recognized their labor and was behind their claim. They went to the meeting because they had been convinced that Rachid Lichi and the IBR could provide these guarantees by trumping the claims of powerful land speculators.

Derlis, the local representative of the MAP, had done most of the legwork prior to the meeting, going house to house to convince his neighbors to show up. It was no small feat. Although there was a core of Colorado supporters willing to come simply to see their party leaders, most residents were suspicious of the land agency and the party, even afraid that appearing in person would jeopardize their precarious claims by revealing them as squatters. There had been two periods in the early and late 1990s in which settlers had been promised titles and had even begun to pay quotas to the IBR for land titles. But in both cases residents had stopped payments when they became convinced (correctly) that the IBR was unable or unwilling to issue titles to this particular tract. After that, most campesinos avoided the IBR. As far as they were concerned, the land remained tierra malhabida; they had no doubts about their right to be there, but no longer trusted that the IBR could fix the situation for them. But given that tensions were increasing between campesinos and indigenous people on the western edge of Mariscal López, between campesinos and loggers to the north, and with Brazilian speculators on the eastern edge, Derlis was able to make the case to several hundred people that they should come listen to what the senator would say.

For all but a handful of those in attendance, "regularization" was a completely foreign concept. What most people expected of Rachid Lichi was a speech about expropriation—the familiar idiom from the land reform. But the senator explained at the beginning of the meeting that it was impossible to expropriate the property because it in fact belonged to the state—or, more accurately, it belonged to the National Development Bank, the Banco Nacional de Fomento (BNF). Rachid Lichi's primary task was therefore to explain regularization and convince people that it was an appropriate political response to their problems. Rachid Lichi was trying to get approval from campesinos for a project of a kind that most had never heard of, by manufacturing a plausible link between the regularization of someone else's enormous, legally convoluted estate and ore-realidad. And in order for campesinos to accept that regularization was in their

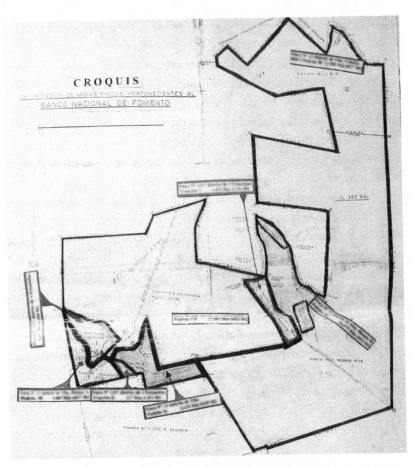

FIGURE 12. Copy of the polygon, originally drawn in 1981, retraced and colored for the red binder, showing the four properties to be regularized.

interests, they first had to accept that Finca 13, this bureaucratic abstraction arriving in their midst for the first time, was actually a representation of Mariscal López.

This is where the binder came in. Before handing it to Jorge, Rachid Lichi opened it, holding up several survey maps that had been reproduced inside, with the main fractions of the property traced in bright colors. He introduced the polygon quickly, stating that it represented the land they were standing on, and then quickly showed that there were hundreds more pages of text in the binder proving the research that had gone into the regularization project. Not much in this binder was new for someone with a cursory understanding of the legal problem. Most the pages were copied from a draft senate bill, authored by Rachid Lichi, generically titled "Bill _____, which increases the national budget for the fiscal year 2005." It was followed by a short summary of the convoluted documentary history of the land and a map of the land in question. The bill itself covered one page, the explanation fit on two pages, and the supporting documents, most concerning the bureaucratic history of Finca 13, amounted to approximately 170 pages photocopied from an old land title in the public registry.

What was so irregular about this documentary history that it needed regularization? According to the binder, Finca 13 was part of an old estate that had once covered over 200,000 hectares, but the photocopied pages of the title only covered the most recent transactions. In 1965, 71,000 hectares of land had been acquired by a company called Financiera Picollo (FINAP), whose owner was the son-in-law of a general. It was transferred, in 1967, to another "financiera" called Capiibary, owned by the same person. Shortly thereafter, the owner died, leaving both companies to his wife, who dissolved the latter and transferred the property back to FINAP, in 1973. In 1981, the land was seized and transferred to the BNF. What FINAP had done with the title in the eight intervening years was not clear from the title itself, but it had accumulated thirty-seven embargoes resulting from lawsuits filed by individuals, lawyers, other financiers and two banks, an airline, and the national electric company, and no less than four separate suits filed by the Instituto de Prevision Social (IPS), the state social insurance company and well-known slush fund. Since then, the title had become impossible to trade, so mired in bureaucratic loops and lawsuits as to make the cost of figuring it all out unreasonable to any potential buyer. While there were the difficulties of reading the title itself, which had been overwritten so many times, the problems were not confined to a single document, instead involving the interplay of dozens of titles, court depositions, and political interventions.

This strange bureaucratic history, of documents piling up and overshadowing each other to the point of suspending the land market for decades, was all the stranger to imagine in the shade behind the sawmill where Rachid Lichi gave his speech, and where people were concerned not with legal histories but with the daily grind of smallholder existence: orerealidad. Almost every word in the binder referred to other documents or to pronouncements made by judges in the lettered city, a space of rarefied notarial protocols traded back and forth on increasingly dog-eared documents between bureaucrats, notaries, and lawyers, in efforts to arrive at some sort of equilibrium between assets and credits, and, presumably, between favors, debts, and grudges that didn't quite make it onto the page. Although the meeting was supposed to be about land security in Mariscal López, the gift which conveyed Rachid Lichi's solidarity was a record of a litany of transactions between people who had no interest whatsoever in the campesino colony of Mariscal López itself and no connection to orerealidad. The tone of the documents contained in the binder is represented well by the text of the first page copied from the title.

> NUMBER SIX HUNDRED AND NINETEEN: In the city of Asunción, Capital of the Republic of Paraguay, on the twelfth day of August of the year nineteen eighty-one, I, J.J.B.R., Public Notary, owner of registry number eighty, with two witnesses, received the following people: On the one hand is doctor P.C.B.A., Paraguayan, married, judge of the first circuit civil court of commerce and labor in Coronel Oviedo, living at 11 Manduvira Street (Asunción); and on the other hand is Doctor Don Julio M. Rejis Sanguina, Paraguayan, married, living for the purposes of this transaction on the corner of Independencia Nacional and Presidente Francia [also Asunción]; both are of legal age and have complied with all the relevant laws of the country as far as I know and to which I will testify. Dr. Julio M. Rejis Sanguina is here in representation of the Banco Nacional de Fomento in his character as the president of that institution, a position for which he was named according to the Presidential Decree no. 20 331 on the 26 of January 1976, which states: "DECREE NO. 20 331, BY WHICH DR. JULIO M. REJIS SAN-GUINA IS NAMED AS THE PRESIDENT OF THE BANCO NACIONAL DE FOMENTO.—Asunción, January 26th, 1976. . . . THE PRESIDENT OF THE REPUBLIC OF PARAGUAY DECREES: Article 1. That Dr. Julio. M. Rejis Sanguina be named President of the Banco Nacional de Fomento, for the period 1976/1981.—Art 2. That thanks be given to Mr. Alberto Gonzalez for services rendered as Interim President of said Institution. . . . Signed: ALFREDO STROESSNER. I testify that this is an exact copy."

Most of the text contained in the 170 pages is of this nature: high-protocol, scene-setting encounters between important men vouching for each other's legal status, the very foundation of the lettered city.

Most striking about this faraway place of legal negotiations is that it was a place where hectares of land were abstract units traded more like money than real estate. In sharp contrast to the highly personal way in which campesinos understand ownership, the title here is currency, not a fixed commodity, but an abstract and fungible one, its primary use being as collateral. In an odd way, Finca 13's nontransferability resulted from the creation of a perfect land title—a representation that the different parties involved assumed to be so secure that they rarely checked its accuracy or even its readability. People continued transacting on the representation without apparently caring much what was going on in the forests to which it referred. So abstract were these financial transactions that no mention was made of physical investments on the land, much less to the existence of at least a dozen indigenous communities, several squatter communities, and even a military base established near the northern edge.

Finca 13 was certainly not the only property in eastern Paraguay that before the 1980s was based on this rather tenuous relationship between a piece of paper and a vast piece of territory. In the first decades of the twentieth century, most of the land in this area was registered to elites living in Asunción or Villarrica, or even abroad, and most bore the name of a company. Finca 13 had been nominally controlled since the previous century by a huge company called simply Yerbales, Montes y Estancias (Yerba Stands, Forests and Ranches), and bordered to the north by an even larger company, La Industrial Paraguaya, which owned 2.65 million hectares (Kleinpenning 1992).[35] These companies used the land for extraction, primarily of yerba mate, which was collected by indigenous pickers and sold along a line of contractors until it was ready for export (Reed 1995; Ramirez 1975).[36] As the export yerba market fell apart in the mid-twentieth century, the companies and their assets were slowly sold off to speculators and investors like FINAP.

The apparent disconnection between the language of property ownership in these documents and any actual practices on the ground was in part an artifact of a genuine disinterest in actual land by its owners in this period. But it was also enabled by complicated practices of framing which increased the abstraction of the land title, making the relationship between the title and the land more distant. In the early decades, the text in the title referred to several of the fixed assets on the land. The survey that Yerbales, Montes y Estancias commissioned to title the property included references to the presence of yerba, forest, and pasture, features from which economic value could be directly extracted. (What was completely lacking in these survey descriptions was reference to the near-captive indigenous labor that the company used to perform that extraction.) By 1950, this had been somewhat simplified, but the yerbales were still mentioned. By 1967, even the yerbales had disappeared from the description, and by the time the polygon was drawn, the company was owned by a financier rather than a forestry company. Little was left in the descriptions to identify the land as a *particular piece* of land, or to suggest what kind of agriculture or extraction it might support.

Until the late 1960s, the pattern of frequent trading and repossession of land without much physical investment remained common. At that point, though, the land reform put pressure on "unused" latifundios to either start producing something or face expropriation.[37] And this is where Finca 13 began to diverge from other properties in the area, because while other titles were being expropriated, this title was repossessed by the BNF, making it more politically complicated to redistribute. The BNF's ownership effectively shielded the title from expropriation after 1981.[38] Much of the land in this area was beginning to acquire a more complex legal history, most of it, in one form or another, being bought up and distributed through the IBR either to campesinos or to high-ranking Colorados. Finca 13, in contrast, was suspended in its abstraction by BNF owners, the relationship between title and land being almost completely severed.

As the IBR's redistribution of idle land accelerated, the abstractness of Finca 13 from the land to which it referred became a liability. The growing land market, and new buyers in the area looking for land on which to plant soy, all increased interest in the material assets behind the title, and the value of the title shifted from the reams of notarial testimony to the physical terrain to which that testimony only alluded indirectly. The two key shifts that gutted the title of transactable value were the transition to democracy and the moment of frontier consolidation: the former made it more difficult for government to arbitrarily move assets between different funds and made buyers suspicious of the very protocols that had brought the title into being; the latter increased the number of parties interested in the land, and hence the amount of vigilance paid to the accuracy of the documents.

What had turned Finca 13 into a bad asset was not the lack of representation of the property, but rather that the representation had become abstracted from its referent. The BNF was unwilling to simply write off the title, which it now claimed was worth $13 million, and it was also unwilling to invest in fixing the legal problems associated with the title or in doing a proper audit to figure out what the title referred to. This meant that no private buyer was likely to buy the land, since the costs of acquiring it had become unfathomable. Anyone actually visiting the land would have encountered hints of these costs in the form of orerealidad. Even a cursory visit would have revealed what the title did not:

ten thousand hectares of the land were likely to be expropriated and declared indigenous territory as part of a World Bank project, and the rest of the land was home to tens of thousands of organized campesinos planting cotton (and in a growing number of places, marijuana). It was impossible to ignore these people or evict them by force, so the only way to take control of the property would have been to divide it and sell the inhabited parcels to its inhabitants, none of whom would be able to pay close to market value, and then to rent it or buy it back from them.[39] This sort of arrangement was not entirely unheard of, but it had never been undertaken at such a scale, and there simply weren't buyers around willing to undertake that kind of risk.[40] Rachid Lichi and the IBR understood full well that the only way to fix Finca 13's "irregularity" was for the IBR to buy it from the BNF at asking price, then to undertake the work of measuring it and settling disputes with people who still had claims against it—all at huge expense. The IBR could then assess the value of the title and accept its devaluation, before divvying it up and handing it out on credit to campesinos, few of whom were likely to pay off all of their quotas. For the project to succeed at all, it needed to receive the support of the BNF, both houses of congress, the ministry of finance (which would approve the payment of $13 million), the IBR, and at least some campesino organizations on the land.

This is a fascinating political gambit if one compares it to the legal sleight of hand for turning lotes precarios into propiedad privada, outlined in chapter 3: land in Tekojoja, which fell under the purview of the Estatuto Agrario, was being surreptitiously transferred into the legal regime defined by the Civil Code. This was enabled in part by the argument, associated with the de Soto solution, that the Civil Code presented a more complete, more rational form of property law. The Estatuto Agrario, by contrast, was merely a populist relic of the Cold War which needed to be done away with. In Mariscal López almost the reverse was going on. A title which, under Civil Code rationality, had become so unmoored from the very land it was supposed to represent as to become nontransferable could only be fixed by processing it through the Estatuto Agrario. In other words, the title's problem could only be solved by buying it out of the public registry in which it had bogged down, then giving it to campesinos under the legal regime of the land reform. Campesinos, who were busy building up their bases and mejoras in the hope that the state would begin recognizing their claims, could then turn the land into titlable property again through the convoluted rules of the Estatuto Agrario. For the land to become transactable once more, it needed not a better, more transparent title, but actually to be removed from the market by political decree and laundered back through orerealidad by giving it to campesinos as land reform. Only then, once titled to campesinos, could the land reenter the market.

As an attempt to give the BNF's problem title to campesinos, Rachid Lichi staged a populist spectacle exactly as Papacito Frutos had when giving out land titles. He first established the context as orerealidad, by speaking for over half an hour about the hardship of campesino life, about the hard work of men and women in their fields, the difficulty of accessing education and health care, the terrible road into town, the lack of running water, the indignities heaped on the campesinos by Asunción elites, and the constant threat of dispossession by powerful absentees, which compounded all of the other problems. In the midst of this, he picked up the binder and told the crowd that their problems were associated with Finca 13. He opened the binder, showing the polygon to all those present, explaining that the potential for tenure security lay just beyond Finca 13's transfer to the IBR. Then he presented the local MAP leader with the document. In so doing, Rachid Lichi connected the binder to campesino reality and with campesino interests in a way not envisioned by proponents of transparency reforms.

The binder therefore fulfilled two functions. On the one hand, it fulfilled what one might call a gift function, in which a party operative creates a personal relation between himself and a group of followers; it is in the giving of a gift that the binder becomes part of orerealidad. But beyond the binder's gift function lay what one might call its audit function. The binder, filled with photocopies of Rachid Lichi's work product in the senate, was offered as proof of his deeds, proof of the legal possibility of his promises. If the land title was meant to evoke a personal connection between receiver and the giving authority, the binder of administrative documents evoked the openness of the process, the symmetry of giver and receiver, and the capacity of the receiver to double-check the oral claims of the giver against a written record. Whether it was authoritative was a different question, for rather than affirming the unquestionability of oral pronouncements, it served primarily to preempt accusations of corruption. The audit function is not just about extending recognition, but about inviting the gift's recipient to scrutinize the government. This is unmistakably a new democratic way of reckoning political legitimacy, a transparency project in which relations of visibility are reversed. Instead of saying, "I see you and therefore you are good," the audit function says, "You see me, and therefore I am good." In so doing, it also displaces authority to the depersonalized sphere of law, and to an archive which is open, in principle, to consultation by any citizen.

Most important, the audit function was only possible in conjunction with the gift, as the lines of visibility couldn't be opened if the crowd weren't convinced that the transaction was being carried out in the realm of orerealidad. The document alone would not be part of reality, but giving it as a gift made it so. And in that hybrid act, Rachid Lichi presents a new kind of politics, something like a populist transparency that seeks self-consciously to draw politically expedient lines of visibility and to find new ways of linking documents to reality. This may be a dual politics that plays on segregated constituencies, on different realities, in a calculated attempt at building senate influence. It may also be an ingenious form of accounting which uses a bifurcated reality to create a land market. But it is also an attempt to be transparent to both realities simultaneously, and to find a documentary bridge between them.

POPULIST TRANSPARENCY

Rachid Lichi's regularization bill stalled for several years because he was never quite able to make the project speak properly to the new democrats, who now controlled the government purse strings. The asking price of $13 million was not negotiable, and the ministry of finance refused to hand the money to the IBR for the purchase of bad assets. From the beginning it was fairly clear this was a possibility. Even at the meeting, one of the campesino leaders raised his hand to ask how the plan to regularize Mariscal López could possibly proceed, given Finance Minister Dionisio Borda's position on overspending. Rachid Lichi gnashed at this suggestion, his voice became louder, and his hands gesticulated more wildly. "Borda is a condom [*tembofóro*]!," he railed. "He is not even a Colorado, and he can't stop us." Throwing a few more epithets at the minister, he ducked the question successfully amid raucous laughter. Within a month, Borda had been forced out of his position, showing that the caudillos had won out over the technocrats in internal government squabbling. But the question remained, and over the next two years, the IBR was unable to get the land transfer approved. Just as surely as the materiality of the archive interposed itself on the IDB's streamlining project, here the reality of the market showed itself to be too rigid for the populist accounting game.

More to the point, what Rachid Lichi showed that day was that transparency reforms are both more partial than most purport to be and more politically interesting than many critics claim. Regularization aspires to transparency of the sort that new democrats say they desire. But it does so on the bawdy and boisterous margins of technocracy, in those anti-institutional gray zones which new democrats will not enter because they are too steeped in politics. This is a highly compromised transparency, one which is bartered for votes over tables bearing the color of Stroessner's old party. It speaks to a campesino reality that seems to defy reason, that is suspicious of documents and of the expert knowledge of economists. It is vulgar, sentimental, and contains hints of authoritarianism. And yet it is more radically inclusive than anything the IDB might devise in the land agency or the public registry—because this is a dual politics that shuttles between two realities, manufacturing points of contact and recognition of mutual interests. Despite all appearances, this is a sophisticated politics of mediation which has the potential to open new forms of political dialogue and new forms of democracy.

Jorge and Antonio understand full well that they are engaged in a form of mediation between worlds, and often speak in precisely these terms, for campesinos don't seem to have trouble recognizing multiple realities the way that new democrats do. What matters to campesinos is orerealidad, "our reality," a grounding which is at once particular and universal. They rarely talk about new democrats as unknowledgeable, which is the way new democrats speak about them, but rather as living in a different world. Perhaps this is always a feature of subaltern discourse, which, as Gyan Pandey (1991) puts it, is always necessarily fragmentary, never quite able to fulfill its aspiration to hegemony (see Chatterjee 1993; Chakrabarty 2002). Campesino populism is grounded in an understanding of opposing realities, while new democrats continue to ground their politics in the opposition between reality and delusion or ignorance. And it's in that closed view of the universal—perhaps a relic from the moment, in 1989, when new democrats thought their Cold War understanding of the truth had finally become politically incontrovertible—that leaders like Jorge or Rachid Lichi continue to seem so threatening and distasteful. Even so, it is clear that large bureaucratic problems like Finca 13 could never be fixed without them. The caudillo's function in a liberal democracy is precisely to find bridges over the technocratic gaps by connecting realities, exchanging economic promises for political influence, connecting land and documents, creatively mixing legal inconsistencies and rhetorical bluster in order to bring about change.[41]

None of this is confined to Paraguay. Rather, it is a feature of all liberal democracies, in which certainty in the procedural fix is always accompanied by the echo of the arbitrary, of those despised political creatures on whose words we nonetheless rely to heal the fissures in the technocratic. Francisco Panizza describes the fear of populism: "Populism reminds us of the totalitarian ghosts that shadow democracy. But it also reminds us that all modern democratic societies are compromises between democratic and non-democratic logics. . . . In modern global society, populism raises uncomfortable questions about those who want to appropriate the empty site of power, but also about those who would like to subordinate politics to technocratic reason and the dictates of the market" (Panizza 2005: 30).

Consider, for a moment, how many of these same themes emerged during the U.S. financial crisis in 2008, right in the center of the global network that defines new democrats' understanding of reality. Like the problem with Mariscal López, the Wall Street financial crisis was rooted in bad real-estate assets whose precipitous devaluation threatened the liquidity of the banks that owned them. The bad debt was incurred primarily by the trading of two highly abstracted representations of real estate: mortgage-backed securities and asset-backed commercial papers. Both were considerably more abstract than the Finca 13 title, constructed at so many levels of remove from the homes and land that "backed" them, and reconstructing the link required a complex, virtually impossible process of disaggregation of the representations themselves (unlike individual titles which only requires measuring, assessment, and some legal actions). Financiers, convinced that real-estate assets were always secure, traded these documents among themselves in completely legal ways within a relatively small community of like-minded people, without noticing that their value was in fact vanishing. President George Bush pled with the Senate to appropriate the money for a massive, publicly funded purchase of the bad assets, which could then be sold at a loss.

The crisis seemed genuinely to have caught U.S. lawmakers unawares, and their flustered responses said much about the underside of American technocracy. Three particularly strong, if vague, discourses emerged. The first was a metaphorical division between Wall Street and Main Street, or between the "fictitious" and "real" economies. Main Street is the American equivalent of orerealidad, a language of populist appeal that in moments of crisis suddenly becomes unstuck from the reality of Wall Street. The second discourse, in part due to the simultaneous presidential election campaign, emerged as people called for more "leadership." None of the proposals on the table were purely technocratic or rationally economic, but rather political calculations, power plays, and leaps of faith associated with the persons of the presidential candidates. In that moment, leadership was the ability to convincingly say, "This is our reality, and this is how I am going to make it better." The third common complaint about the payout to Wall Street banks brings this all back to the beginning: in the absence of any clear technical solution to the problem, all sides of the debate bemoaned the lack of "oversight" and "transparency." Transparency emerged as the ethical language of governance, without being accompanied by any real sense of what it was or what it might accomplish. What, exactly, needed to be transparent, and to whom? Who needed to have seen what for problems to have been averted?

Transparency is not a form of representation that fixes mistakes, deters corruption, and finally puts the state at the service of the common good. What transparency actually is—and Rachid Lichi demonstrates this beautifully—is a political negotiation between disparate points of reference that have become unmoored, between documents, people, bodies, laws, circulating stories, plotted ground, the intransigent material objects and processes littering the landscape, the habits of the past and the looming uncertainties of the future. Transparency is nothing more than the name for a negotiation that forges a momentary agreement about representations and that aims to facilitate future connections.

Seeing transparency as populist is critical to an anthropology of post–Cold War development in Latin America. It provides an analytic that resists developmentalist temporalities by refusing to see procedural democracy as an antidote to and natural successor for populism and caudillismo. Rachid Lichi's gift of transparency—obviously partisan, blustery, and flawed—neither conforms to the demands of new democratic reformers, nor simply subverts them. Instead, it complicates them by assuming the situatedness of realities and engaging in tactical articulations between them. If transparency is a relationship that is formed and reformed between documents and reality, then it is an open relationship always under political negotiation, not only because documents are inherently slippery and their creators prone to occlusion, duplicity, and error, but because the real is itself always open. Like the guerrilla auditors with whom Rachid Lichi occasionally works, his is a politics of uncertainty and contingency, whose very existence is a constant reminder of the deep ambivalences of any democracy.

A book about open-ended documents can hardly be tied up at the end with something so pat as a conclusion. Moreover, to suddenly rest my case on a stable ending would also be to jump the political ship onto which I was invited after the shootings in Tekojoja. After all, ethnography as a form of stabilizing representation played a central role in solidifying the distinction between campesinos and new democrats during the Paraguayan transition. The popular literary genre of paraguayología, at times satirical, and at times quite earnest, traced a portrait of the nation from which Paraguay's middle-class urbanites could distinguish themselves as they yearned for democracy. The objectification of Paraguay as a largely rural mass, stuck in the past and prone to authoritarianism, established new democratic subjectivity just as it created a new slot and function for the campesinado as the foil for transparency. Ironically, that very exclusionary practice was necessary to the belief that all of Paraguay could, at some level, be represented as information, and that this would inevitably bring about a more just, more inclusive, and more efficient democratic society. Into such a mix, it would hardly seem advisable to claim that I could settle things ethnographically once and for all.

But then history is full of moments when the clocks stop, moments of rupture and rearticulation when the terms that made sense in the past no longer seem adequate to explain the present, and the future is suddenly murky enough to allow for some sort of stock-taking. These are not moments of closure and conclusion, so much as moments of suspension, in which analysis is shifted to the register of the conditional. In these final pages, therefore, I look to the future, to the realm of hope. A shift to the method of hope, as Hirokazu Miyazaki (2004) puts it, comes in part from a recognition of the limitations to human agency. It is to step back from the desire to cause good outcomes, and to put faith instead in the possibility that the conditions one helps to cobble might play out favorably. For campesinos in Paraguay, the future is always the product of labor in the present, but since labor itself is always in conflict with the labor of others, the future is mediated through the storm of politics. Unlike risk, which reifies the uncertainty of the future in order to make it representable, hope sees the future as nontransparent. A shift to the conditional tense is only therefore a reflection on what one's work might make possible given a new set of circumstances. And a new set of circumstances is precisely what Paraguayan political actors have been dealing with since 2008, when the Colorado Party was voted out of power for the first time in sixty-one years.

To explain the change, I need to return to the beginning of this story and pull out one more narrative thread. During most of the paro cívico of November 2004, I was hunkered in a tent on the outskirts of Caaguazú by the main highway leading from Asunción to Ciudad del Este. The protest had been billed as a nationwide general strike against Nicanor's government, but within a day it had resolved itself into a specifically campesino protest in several camps like the one I was in. For nine days I watched the campesino movement fail to make a concerted national statement, to seize the idea of "tierra malhabida," and to use it to fundamentally change the political landscape in Paraguay. It was a demoralizing moment for many campesino leaders, and in the months and years that followed, the paro cívico become something of an embarrassment for many of those involved. No one realized at the time that the apparent defeat of that week would contribute to the most transformational moment in Paraguay's recent history, a moment that many have now come to see as the final fruition of the long transition to democracy.

The Caaguazú camp was the second largest of the paro cívico camps, and was kept calm by Jorge Galeano's legal posturing and his insistence on fighting force with documents. The campesinos at no point pushed against the police, and though they were threatening to block the road, they never did. But protestors at the largest camp, near General Resquín, in the more combative department of San Pedro, north of Asunción, did at one point cross the line. On the second day of the protest, campesinos blocked the road and were beaten back aggressively by mounted riot police and a military unit using rubber bullets and tear gas. The camp was set on fire, blankets and mattresses systematically destroyed by riot police.[1] Several people were injured in the operation, and two of those who were dragged off in handcuffs by police were local priests, longtime local sympathizers with the campesino movement, and vestiges of the days when priests versed in the "option for the poor" teachings of liberation theology were at the forefront of campesino mobilization.

In April 1976, in what is still remembered as one of the darkest months in the history of campesino protest, Stroessner had rounded up, imprisoned, killed, or exiled most of Paraguay's Left-leaning clergy, all but forcing liberation theology out of the church and out of the country (Equipo Expa 1981). Most of those who remained were outliers, defrocked priests running NGOs and consulting agencies, or quiet priests in small parishes like those who were suddenly noticed during the paro cívico.[2] Many priests returned from exile in 1989, but few of them rejoined the church, which was by then wary of political involvement; even there liberation theology was considered a slightly dangerous vestige of the Cold War. When I was in Paraguay, the two most prominent clergymen who did not conform to this pattern were the bishops of the departments of Caaguazú, Monseñor Juan Bautista Gavilán, and of San Pedro, Monseñor Fernando Lugo. They had entered the clergy as young men in the late 1970s and spent much of the remainder of the dictatorship abroad; on their return, they practiced a nonmilitant version of liberation theology in their respective dioceses. On the eve of the paro cívico, Lugo and Gavilán both tried to head off the conflict, getting the Episcopal council to meet with Nicanor to request that he demobilize the army that had been deployed preemptively to the country's interior. Their efforts failed.

In the years after the paro cívico, Gavilán was a crucial ally for moderate campesino leaders like Jorge. He visited Vaquería and Tekojoja frequently while I was there, and his house in the city of Coronel Oviedo was always open to those of us who needed a place to stay during difficult or uncertain moments. I got to know him when he became interested in the rapid titling schemes promoted by the Liberal Party, and he asked me to help him articulate an argument against them. His approach to politics was always quiet, reflective, and usually quite private. He continued to sermonize on the option for the poor, and counseled his primarily urban congregation to think about what caused campesino protests, just as he counseled against the dangers of abortion and gay marriage.

But it was Lugo's path that took a most surprising turn. When the army and police attacked the camp at General Resquín, Lugo spoke out against the government, and less than a month after the paro cívico ended he officially renounced the bishopric and returned to his rural parish as a priest. Publicly he said he had tired of his duties and preferred the quieter life of a rural priest. Privately it was rumored that he had been forced to resign by the Episcopal council led by Asunción's conservative archbishop, with whom he had been disagreeing for years. For a while, Lugo disappeared from the national stage. But a year later, his name began to circulate again in Vaquería, for he had returned to confronting the government, making public speeches about the corruption of the Colorado Party. And by May 2006, he had quietly formed a committee to begin researching the possibility of running for president in 2008, when Nicanor's mandate ended.

Jorge Galeano was one of about twenty-five people who met with Lugo monthly to discuss the possible run for office. At first, the idea sounded rather unlikely. With no party behind Lugo, and the impressive Colorado Party showing signs of strengthening under Nicanor, even Jorge saw the campaign as largely symbolic. But the campaign increased in strength, and soon named itself the Movimiento Popular Tekojoja.[3] As that year progressed, Lugo led three impressive marches in Asunción against Colorado corruption, including one that effectively prevented Nicanor from passing a constitutional amendment that would have allowed him to run for a second term. Lugo later separated himself somewhat from the Movimiento Tekojoja to head a much broader coalition of social movements and political parties, eventually including even the old-guard Liberal Party and the new democratic Partido Patria Querida, both of which had campaigned on free-market reforms in the previous election.

For many of us watching from afar, it came as a great, and welcome, surprise that Lugo won the 2008 election in a landslide. He had faced down the Vatican, which initially refused to defrock him (a necessity for him to run for office legally). He had beaten Blanca Ovelar, Nicanor's hand-picked successor for the Colorados (she had also been education minister in his cabinet), and Luís Castiglioni, the petulant vice president who had broken away from the Colorados to promote his own platform of bilateral trade with the United States and transparency reforms like rapid titling. And he had beaten Stroessner's grandson, who had changed his name to Alfredo Stroessner in order to run for the

presidency and festooned the city with the ominous graffiti "Stroessner 2008."
In a bizarre twist, in September 2007 Nicanor pardoned Lino Oviedo—the man
who until then had been characterized as the demon figure of Paraguayan politics and kept in solitary confinement in the Chaco desert—and allowed him to
run for the presidency, presumably hoping in this way to split the opposition.
But Lugo soundly beat Oviedo's UNACE party as well.[4]

Lugo's victory was immediately hailed in the international media as a victory
for the "Left" in Paraguay over the Colorados' "far Right" leanings.[5] The interpretation fit a regional narrative of leftist governments regaining power over
the past decade in Venezuela, Bolivia, Brazil, Argentina, Chile, and Ecuador. For
all his public claims to be a centrist, Lugo also fanned this story somewhat.
His platform included redistributionist tax increases on large landholdings and
soybean exports, renegotiation of the Itaipú Dam's uneven hydroelectric deal
with Brazil, and a call for "integrated land reform" that went far beyond titling.
Lugo ran as the "bishop of the poor," and having accepted Venezuelan president Hugo Chávez's offer of cheap oil, he danced with Chávez on election night.
Bolivia's Evo Morales went so far as to welcome Lugo to the "Axis of Evil."

But as I hope this book has made clear, the Left-Right distinction is something of a red herring in this case. A much more instructive parallel in recent history is not Chávez's victory in Venezuela, but Vicente Fox's victory, in 2000, over
Mexico's Partido Revolucionario Institucional (PRI), which had held power,
under different names, since 1928.[6] The trajectories of the Colorado Party and
the PRI were quite different, but involved many similar elements and settled
into similar patterns of rule. If the Colorados started out as a conservative
agrarista party in the late nineteenth century (in opposition to the laissez-faire
Liberal Party), the PRI began as a member of the Socialist International and
as heir to the Mexican Revolution. Both, however, consolidated their power
through sweeping land reforms under populist leaders, and after several decades in power ceased to have much in the way of ideological content.[7] They
were corporatist machines, prebendary organizations that maintained power
through patronage, rents, and violence, all activities which eventually came
to be categorized as "corruption" after the Cold War ended. And just as Fox
cracked the PRI electoral machine with a convincing promise of transparency
and anticorruption reforms, so, too, was "transparency" the central plank of
Lugo's campaign in Paraguay.

On that count, perhaps most telling are the people who rose to public
prominence under Lugo who had, throughout my research, introduced new

democratic ideals into national politics. Dionisio Borda, who had been the finance minister for the first year and a half of Nicanor's rule (until his new democratic ways rubbed too strongly against Colorado insiders), was once again named finance minister, this time with unprecedented power to reorganize the ministry and to control other ministries by proxy. Borda, the squeaky-clean U.S.-trained economist, became the country's top technocrat, the bureaucratic tsar of the executive branch. Efraín Alegre, the congressman responsible for the tierras malhabidas document, became Lugo's minister of industry, charged with the crucial task of revisiting the Itaipú agreement. And if Chávez was the most boisterous international visitor to the inauguration, bearing the sword of Simón Bolívar to signal Lugo's membership in a pan-American socialism, the more interesting visitor was Joseph Stiglitz, the Nobel Prize–winning economist at the center of the "economics of information." Stiglitz made a huge public splash, delivering a speech and giving several interviews to the mass media in which he offered his services pro bono as an economic consultant to the new government.

Still, just as in Mexico in 2000, Lugo's transparency platform was populist through and through. Lugo and Fox both campaigned as men out-of-joint with the country's political establishment, impressive charismatic figures who could convincingly claim to be incorruptible, though for very different reasons (Fox because of his corporate record, Lugo for being a priest). They consolidated in their personal figures the widespread disdain for the ruling group and desire for a new national body organized around a vision of the state as transparent. Lugo's was a dual politics of the highest order. He appealed to some because his message was procedural, more in keeping with that view of democracy being promoted by international development agencies and the rule of law. To others, he was compelling because he could genuinely speak to their reality. But more to the point, he spoke across both groups, found things on which they more or less agreed, and brought them together in a national narrative that suggested an overlapping of realities.

Lugo's win was soon qualified, of course. While he might have taken the executive, the congress and senate remained largely controlled by the Colorado Party. Even many cabinet positions were filled by Liberal Party members who received their posts in return for entering the coalition. The high drama of coalition members dividing up the prebendary spoils would dominate political headlines for the next two years, as Liberal Party members, technocrats, and social groups vied for plum positions. Perhaps predictably, new democrats got the ministry of finance, Liberals got industry and agriculture, and campesinos were given their choice of presidents for the IBR. Just as after the coup against Stroessner, the IBR was the piece of the state that most interested campesinos, but by the time Lugo took power, they were hoping for much more. Shortly thereafter, campesinos staged the largest demonstrations in Paraguay since the paro cívico, concerned that they were already being forgotten in the fray of new political alignments; during these protests, they were viciously beaten back by police on the streets of Asunción. Only weeks after his assumption of office, Lugo learned that coalitions are difficult to manage and that new hegemonic formations are unstable and fractious. His biggest immediate problems, however, would come in the form of more personal attacks: early rumors of coup attempts, highly politicized paternity suits from women who claimed he had fathered their children, and finally a diagnosis of non-Hodgkin's lymphoma leading to aggressive chemotherapy.

Moreover, transparency politics, as I have shown in this book, is a fickle thing. Lugo would discover this less than a year into his mandate, when Transparency International's *Corruption Perception Index* came out, and *ABC Color* could announce that Paraguay was once again the third most corrupt country on earth. When Lugo tried to counteract this by questioning the methods behind the index, *ABC Color* delighted "Lugo is using the same excuses as Nicanor."[8] Campesinos watching what happened to the IBR after they took it over had to deal with a far more serious problem. The new president of the institution, chosen by campesino groups, was a well-known campesinista sociologist. Although an ally of campesinos, he was a new democrat by temperament, and shortly after he took the head office in the IBR, he declared all employees of the institution to be corrupt; he quickly found it impossible to work with any of them, and the entire bureaucracy ground to a halt, with long-serving bureaucrats sitting idly under humming air conditioners just so they could collect their pay. Moreover, his bold plan to revive the land reform based on the reversion of those millions of hectares of tierra malhabida soon bogged down in onerous legal fights for small patches of unusable land on the margins of soy fields. After insisting on paying the requisite fees for expropriation and canceling many campesino debts, the new leaders soon found that the institution was bankrupt. Although they were able to prevent a restructuring of the institution proposed by the World Bank, they created enemies in the ministry of finance in the process. It seemed unlikely that the IBR would be able to accomplish anything without experimenting with the law, which Lugo's high-minded rhetoric about corruption had made far more difficult. In the IBR, the transparency project began to look as though it would destroy the institution, shutting campesinos out of the state once and for all. After a year and a half, the campesino-appointed president of the IBR was forced aside, and the institution handed over to a rapid-titling Liberal.

Despite these problems, there is no question that Lugo's election was a transformational moment in Paraguayan politics. When I returned to visit friends in Paraguay six months after the election, many campesinos and new democrats I knew were already deeply frustrated with the pace of change, but none would understate or express regret for the enormous joy, surprise, and shock they had felt on the night the election results were announced. This mix of emotions was not unlike that felt by new democrats when Stroessner was first removed from power. This time, however, these feelings were shared by many campesinos, who understood it to be their transformative moment as well. The change that Lugo promised was therefore somewhat different than the change brought about by the coup of 1989. Lugo's victory was not about division, but consolidation, however fleeting, of the new democratic dream of *el público* with *el pueblo* deeply felt by campesinos. Like guerrilla auditors and reformist senators, but at a much larger scale, Lugo's election created a flash of genuine openness at the margins of transparency, a view of a political way forward on the very terrain of a deeply technocratic and antipolitical way of thinking. Lugo's victory should be read in this way—as a momentary joining of forces, a moment of clarity, when transparency seems to provide multiple lines of visibility to different realities and different possible futures.

In April 2009, the very month when the possibility of the IBR's closure first became real, I asked Jorge if he still had hope that Lugo's election would bring change to Paraguay. "We have to have hope," he said, "that's why we keep fighting [luchando]." Hope, for someone like Jorge, is the opposite of rest or of waiting. Jorge's life had changed radically since the election. His work was much the same as it had been, only at a much higher intensity. He was now more or less living in a jeep paid for by the Movimiento Tekojoja, now an official party with a campesino leader named Sixto Pereira in the senate. Jorge was the group's chief political mobilizer, driving all over the countryside holding meetings to try to keep the rural parts of the coalition together. He shuttled between dozens of communities, archives, and offices, and had a handful of students helping him with paperwork, outfitting him with the documents he needed for the meetings in which he tried to help people see across a new and fluctuating set of realities. He rarely knew exactly what the payoff of any of these meetings would be, but he knew he had to participate in them. Jorge's work continues to be a politics of transparency, but this is transparency not in the procedural sense favored by new democrats during the transition, the sense that seeks to close the state to certain kinds of representational practices, to certain realities and the people that embody them. It is a politics of transparency in the radically open sense of guerrilla auditing, a dogged, argumentative, and always out-of-place practice, and a politics of hope that the work done to make vision possible in the present might serve as a base for a better future.

INTRODUCTION

1. This literature has focused overwhelmingly on two aspects of the neoliberal period: the economic consequences of neoliberal reform in the global south, and the formation of new kinds of subjectivities, both market-ready entrepreneurs and the alternative cultural and indigenous categories that have been produced by these new strategies of government (see Hale 2006; Shever 2008; Colloredo-Mansfield 1998). The literature is by turns bleak about the economic prospects for much of the world's population (e.g., Gill 2000; Gledhill 1995) or sanguine about the possibilities opened up by contestatory practices (e.g., Postero 2007; Sawyer 2004).

2. Joseph Stiglitz (1998) began using the term "post–Washington Consensus" in 1998, a sign that mainstream international development practitioners were entering a period of autocritique. In Latin America, Taylor (1999) and Hershberg and Rosen (2006) have used "post-neoliberalism" as a lens for exploring current economic and political conditions. An alternative reading is that provided by Peck and Tickell (2002; also Hart 2002), which suggests that neoliberalism has not really ended, but can be divided into two phases, a "roll-back" phase of drastic cuts to public spending, and a "roll-out" phase in which policy and public spending is aimed at reconfiguring state institutions. Although I don't use the same language, it should be clear from the pages ahead that I largely agree with this latter view.

3. Figures are from the Ministerio de Agricultura y Ganaderia agricultural census of 2006. This was the first census to be undertaken in Paraguay since 1991, and the figures are striking

in that they show a considerable concentration of land occurring over that period, with a decrease of 6 percent in the overall number of smallholdings and a remarkable drop of 27 percent in the number of medium-sized farms between twenty and fifty hectares.

4. Campesino struggles date from much earlier, but with considerable changes over time. As I argue herein, campesino struggles in the post–Cold War period are related directly to strategies undertaken in the 1960s.

5. Just as, for a time, Soviet scientists claimed that the Western obsession with information was a symptom of idealism, and therefore complicit with capitalism (Gerovitch 2002). This was an ideological battle that the West would win, with many claiming that it was information that killed the Soviet Union (see Stiglitz 1994; Shane 1994).

6. In this respect one of the most damaging mistakes of Stroessner's in the waning years of his regime was not so much the repression of dissidents, which had become routine, but the censorship of the country's major national newspaper, ABC Color, in 1983, which won him international condemnation.

7. Economics of information was not formalized until the early 1960s (Stigler 1961; Vickrey 1961).

8. One of the most common ways to "fix" information gaps is the commodification of risk in the form of insurance. See chapter 4 for a more extended discussion.

9. For examples of this line of argument, see the articles in O'Donnell et al. 1986 and Diamond, Linz, and Lipset 1988. The fall of the Berlin Wall was accompanied by a flurry of writing that celebrated the fusion of democracy and capitalism, including articles in the *Washington Quarterly* by Diamond (1989), de Soto (1989a), Gershman (1989), and Fukuyama's (1989) infamous article on the end of history. For an excellent review of all of this ideological production, see Abrahamsen 2000. Transparency had its role to play in mature democracies as well, as the audit explosion of the 1980s and 1990s created new forms of bureaucratic rituals meant to regularize and technicalize governance in Europe and North America (Power 1997; Strathern 2000; Miller 2003).

10. In Latin America the most influential version of this argument appeared in Hernando de Soto's best-selling book, *The Mystery of Capital* (2000), which argued that the greatest problem faced by the slum-dwellers of Third World megacities was "missing information."

11. This peculiar formalistic definition comes from midcentury information theory and cybernetics, and has had enormous influence in a number of disciplines, from economics to psychology to biology (see especially Mirowski 2002). I explore its workings in Paraguay in much more depth elsewhere (Hetherington forthcoming).

12. See especially Day 2008. It is not that economists believe that it is possible to have complete knowledge of the economic world, nor do they forget that written information is different from information in the mind, and many in fact build complex models of mediation between these different forms of information (see Rasmusen 1994). But the entire model, often called the "economics of uncertainty" (Hirshleifer

and Riley 1992) or the "economics of imperfect information" (Stiglitz and Arnott 2003), implies as an analytic grounding the possibility of perfect knowledge, or complete access to the real. In short, the economics of information is an analytics premised on the difference between real social relations and transparency.

13. The mechanical or computational view of market society is another inheritance from cybernetics, which makes possible the view of economic behavior as a growth machine, democracy as an apparatus for choosing optimal governments (see especially Mirowski 2002).

14. In addition to the aforementioned literature on representationalism and on information in economics, some trenchant critiques of transparency include Žižek 1997, West and Sanders 2003, Morris 2000, Levine 2004.

15. See, for example, Dreyfus and Rabinow 1982, Ferguson 1990, Scott 1998, Barry 2001, Rose 1999.

16. See especially Riles 2000, Riles 2006, Miyazaki 2004, Brenneis 2006, Hull 2003, Barrera 2008, Latour 2002.

17. This is why technocrats like Hernando de Soto are obsessed with the technical elements of document use, with constructing better registries, better databases, more streamlined protocols for access to information. They are not denials of the material, but attempts to control and overcome the materiality of documents in order to stabilize the meanings they carry (e.g., Barata and Cain 2001). De Soto does not peddle in abstract representations per se; instead, he peddles the desire for abstraction against the obduracy of the world.

18. Michael Power's seminal work, The Audit Society (1997), makes the point that audit is a response to lack of trust, but it can never entirely fill that lack. Audits can also be audited (see also Strathern 2000; Miller 2003).

19. For an example of the most sordid descriptions of Paraguay in popular literature, see Gimlette 2003.

20. It's telling that I cannot find the original citation for this often-repeated quote. The quote can most easily be found now in the evocative opening passages of political tracts in Paraguay, UNESCO reports, satirical pieces, and travelogues of the 1990s.

21. Geography is often held to blame for national impoverishment, as Timothy Mitchell (2002) has noted of development discourse in Egypt.

22. The Chaco entered Paraguayan history during the war with Bolivia (1932–1935), but still resides outside of the primary national narrative. It is a space controlled largely by Mennonites, who emigrated from Canada in the 1930s and continue to speak Plattdeutsch. It is also home to dozens of non-Guaraní-speaking indigenous groups. In the twenty-first century, the Chaco has become a space of intensive beef and soybean development, and its national role is therefore being redefined.

23. After the devastating War of the Triple Alliance against Argentina and Brazil (1865–1870), Paraguay also fought a devastating war with its other neighbor, Bolivia, in the 1930s.

24. Paraguay's linguistic peculiarity is only emphasized by the fact that *diglossia* normally refers to the relationship between closely related languages (French and

Creole in Haiti) or registers of the same language (High German and regional dialects). In Paraguay, despite significant lexical borrowing, Guaraní and Spanish are completely different languages.

25. Of course this is a simplification. In the 1990s new democrats tried to rescue Guaraní as a national language by creating a new orthography and introducing it into elementary and high schools. Ironically, the standardization of Guaraní turned it into a language very different from that which campesinos speak, which came to be known as Jopara, a kind of stew, because it included so many Spanish loanwords. The formal rescue of Guaraní in the democratic project was clearly, therefore, also a rescue of the language from campesinos, in whose vernacular mouths the language was degrading.

26. See Carter Center and Council of Freely Elected Heads of Government 1993 for a report of international monitors in Paraguay's first democratic elections. Analysis since then has generally agreed that although the Colorado Party maintained power through corrupt practices, vote-rigging in the national elections was not one of them. The Colorado Party was finally voted out in 2008, nineteen years after Stroessner was deposed. The new president, Fernando Lugo, was a former bishop from outside of the party system, and as such it is unclear how his victory can be transformed into long-term support. I will touch briefly in the epilogue on the structural forces that brought Lugo to power.

27. Throughout this book I write Guaraní words using the standards established in the 1990s during the education reform. Among other things, this means that Guaraní words without accents almost always place the emphasis on the final vowel (as opposed to the second-to-last syllable in Spanish). There are two exceptions to this. The first is place names, many of which, like Caaguazú, have conventionalized spellings that predate the reform. The second are Spanish loanwords; many argue for spelling these words phonetically when incorporated into Guaraní (i.e., kampesíno rather than campesino), but people rarely follow this practice in published texts. I have retained the Spanish spelling unless the word's pronunciation has been significantly altered and is generally understood as a Guaraní word (i.e., kuruzu rather than cruz).

28. The Spanish word base was initially used by the Jesuit agrarian leagues, also known as the Christian Base Organizations. It has come to refer to a local organization or constituency, to the rural household economy, and to the sense of "grounding" of politics in the travails of the countryside.

29. This image, and many others throughout this book, are taken directly from Gramsci 1971. My use of his work and vocabulary is close to the poststructuralist readings by subaltern studies theorists (e.g., Guha 1983) and in Laclau and Mouffe 1985, rather than a specifically materialist one.

30. See especially Power 1997, Strathern 2000, Miller 2003, Harper 1998, Riles 2000, Riles 2006, Miyazaki 2004, Hull 2003, Maurer 2005, and the special issues American Ethnologist 33.2 and Journal of Legal Anthropology 1.1.

31. The same problems attend to anthropologists writing about relations (Strathern 1991; 1996), exchange (Maurer 2002; 2005), hope (Miyazaki 2004), duplicity (Nelson 2009), and of course transparency itself (Amy Levine 2004).

32. Nigel Thrift (2007) and Bill Maurer (2005) call this a kind of "lateral" reasoning, which moves by making connections rather than by synthesizing. An early proponent of such an approach was Michel de Certeau (1984), whose metaphors of walking and tactical thinking were often on my mind as I learned to come to terms with my own ignorance in Paraguay.

33. See Última Hora, 26 June 2005.

34. See, for instance, Thrift 2007 and Whatmore 2002 for analytic usages of the term entanglement which are meant to defy representationalist theory.

35. Nor will it satisfy those many activists and scholars I have met who would like to see in campesinos a set of age-old traditions under threat.

CHAPTER ONE: THE TRANSITION TO DEMOCRACY

1. Gutmann 2002, Paley 2001, Nelson 2009, and Coronil 1997 all make powerful ethnographic cases about the polysemy of "democracy" in other parts of post–Cold War Latin America.

2. This echoes a point made by other ethnographies of transition (e.g., Grant 1995; Verdery 1999; Yan 2008).

3. Burawoy and Verdery 1999 makes the point for Eastern Europe that many analyses of transitional failure place blame on socialist cultural holdovers for elements of the state that could just as easily be explained as adaptations to current conditions (see also Paley 2002).

4. By dispassionate, I mean most Paraguayan sociology, which uses the word campesino to talk about a demographic group, a constituency made up of people whose primary source of family income is derived from farming on plots under twenty hectares, whether or not they own those plots. This group, which includes landless households that make their money by working in agriculture, numbers as much as half a million households, close to half of the national population (see Toledo 2010).

5. As such, campesinos fit Ranajit Guha's (1983, 4) famous dictum that peasants are those people who, in social analysis, are not subjects of their own history.

6. Particularly notorious are Gaspar Rodríguez de Francia (1811–1839), Francisco Solano López (1862–1869), and of course Alfredo Stroessner (1954–1989).

7. Estatuto Agrario, Ley no. 854/63, "Que establece el estatuto agrario," Ministerio de Agricultura y Ganadería, Asunción, Paraguay, 1963. In 2002, the IBR changed its name to INDERT, the Instituto de Desarrollo Rural y de la Tierra. Although the change was not insignificant, I use IBR throughout this volume, for the sake of continuity.

8. Brazilian frontier expansion toward the Paraguayan border included overt references to "flexible borders," and was seen by many Paraguayans, then and now, as

a drive to complete a de facto takeover of the country that had been thwarted in 1870. Frutos also liked to rail about how redistribution also fought communism and achieved the Pope's vision of the earth. The IBR's annual reports from 1963 until the mid-1980s all contain long propagandistic rants by Frutos attesting to these many goals.

9. The party closest in form to the Colorados in Latin America may have been Mexico's Partido Revolucionario Institucional (PRI), which began on the Left, but after years in power calcified into a self-serving private association. See epilogue.

10. The 1976 crackdown followed the military coup in Argentina, marking the beginning of the Dirty War in that country. Although Paraguay's crackdown was not so violent as Argentina's, it was a particularly nasty chapter in a much longer national history of dictatorship and repression.

11. The best overviews in English are Americas Watch 1985, Lewis 1980, Miranda 1990.

12. The term historic bloc, along with much of the vocabulary used to describe alliances and fields of force in this chapter, is of course taken from Gramsci 1971. I intend this vocabulary to underline both the complexity and the fragility of these sorts of provisional historical alliances.

13. The "residual" here is also from Raymond Williams (1977), who characterizes cultural formations as being divided into residual, dominant, and emergent properties.

14. These opinions, common among Paraguayans on the frontier, were almost exactly the same as those of Brazilian soy producers described by Albuquerque 2005.

15. This point is similar to the analysis of the American middle class by Barbara Ehrenreich (1989), who claims that that group has trouble recognizing itself as a group, because the primary role of its members, as professionals, is to produce an analysis of their entire country in their own self-image.

16. Nicolas Guilhot has described all of these as core beliefs of the international group of reformist cosmopolitans he refers to as The Democracy Makers (2005).

17. The term engaged universal is taken from Judith Butler (2000), but I have picked it up from Anna Tsing, whose Friction (2005) deals ethnographically with universals in much the same way I do. I take this to be the most useful way out of the analytic paradox posed by new democrats. Writers such as Strathern (1991), Riles (2000; 2002; 2004), and Levine (2003) have shown the epistemological difficulties attending analyses of discourses that are about their own self-description. I do not claim to escape these, but I do try, using Tsing as a guide, to situate universal claims as they arise in the text by adopting a site from which to speak that is different from the one already given by the subject.

18. El público, a singular space of civic identification, is very similar to what social scientists call "the public sphere," so long as one understands this term to be socially and culturally grounded. This implies a historicist approach to public spheres, rather than the normative abstract approach which dominates much of the literature. That is, this is the Habermas of The Structural Emergence of the Public Sphere

(1989), rather than that of his subsequent work on communication and law (e.g., 1996). The approach adopted here sees the public sphere as *a public* which differs from other publics in its claim to being separate from the state but coterminous with the nation, and a space from which democratic citizens can exercise their sovereignty. But the public sphere's putative inclusiveness is only ever an aspiration, and it is limited by the political economy of information as it circulates materially in Paraguay. Indeed, *el público* is really that sphere of identification that is called forth by new democrats addressing each other.

19. New democrats therefore position themselves as proponents of a specific form of liberal democracy which authors like Chantal Mouffe (1993) and Jacques Rancière (1998) have critiqued for ironing out or excluding the difficult, sometimes insurmountable disagreements of a more open and pluralistic form of political agonism.

20. I had a lot of trouble spotting them at first. Indeed, while most of my friends in Asunción were young professionals and students, I didn't see them as a sociologically interesting category until I noticed a troubling pattern in my own fieldnotes: some people were always quoted, while the words of others made it into my notes as if they were my own words, bits of analysis that I had thought of in the course of conversation. Quite unintentionally, I had begun to treat campesino utterances, often in Guaraní, as *data*, while the utterances of some of my friends in Asunción already counted as analysis. To put it another way, campesino utterances counted as bits of social reality, while what new democrats told me were already reflections about that reality, akin to the ethnographic practice I was engaged in.

21. Asunción's elite families are small in number, and most know each other quite well. During the dictatorship and shortly thereafter it was not uncommon for family members of people who had been tortured to have to endure dinner parties with the families of the torturers, if not the torturers themselves. This has changed considerably in the last two decades, but remains a part of Asunción's system of elite civility, which dictates that the more embarrassing political details of one's life should not be aired in the salons of one's friends.

22. In fact, the novel is so difficult that few people I've met, other than literary scholars, claim to have finished it. But it is still often referred to.

23. Like artistic and literary figures all over Latin America, Roa Bastos and others carried out folkore studies, uncovering all that was good and bad in the inscrutable beliefs of the country's barefoot rural masses. In fact, Roa Bastos's other great work, *Hijo de hombre* (Son of Man) (1960), which is much more widely read and beloved in Paraguay, finds its criticism of the dictator in the "collective conscience" of the masses, a historical consciousness to which the middle-class narrator only has fleeting access.

24. There is little criticism available about these books, although in a somewhat oblique reference Bartolome Meliá, the figurehead of Paraguayan Jesuit anthropology, says he finds them demeaning (Meliá 2000).

25. Terere is the cold version of yerba maté, a tea drunk by most people throughout the region. The cold form is drunk only in Paraguay, and rarely by the elite.

26. The other group to be blamed for the continued success of the Colorados were slum dwellers in and around Asunción's *bañados*, the floodplain between downtown and the Paraguay River. Like campesinos, the slum dwellers, due to their lack of education, their poverty, and their cultural backwardness, remained out of touch with Paraguay's democratic progress, which left them vulnerable to the manipulation of old-style autocrats.

27. This language is taken from Guilhot's (2005) excellent book on the international movement of "democracy makers" that was established at the end of the Cold War with the World Bank as its institutional center. According to Guilhot, "This form of political virtue is exactly the opposite of the pursuit of private interest through politics—which the classical political tradition equated with corruption. . . . Yet, this conception of civic virtue has always been the ideology of an aristocratic form of politics. For it is those who have raised themselves above material contingencies who can be trusted not to put their own interest before the common good and who represent the best guarantee against corruption" (6).

28. The Centro de Estudios Paraguayos Antonio Guash also publishes a monthly protest magazine called Acción.

29. The diglossic relationship between Guaraní and Spanish helps to index a relationship between populism and transparent democracy as a function of the relationship between orality and inscription. The project of CEPAG and of other anthropologically inspired Jesuit organizations (and later of a group of linguists, the neologists, led by the public intellectual Ramón Silva and by an education reform, funded by the World Bank, that standardized and taught written Guaraní in elementary schools) was to elevate Guaraní to the level of a public language. Despite this, these projects also made it clear that Guaraní was unrecognized as public speech and therefore had to be translated into Spanish to help "give voice to the voiceless," as the adage from that period goes. Guaraní remains strongly associated with the oral and the vulgar, and ultimately with el pueblo rather than el público.

30. Paraguay's constituent assembly participated in a global moment, when dozens of states around the world adopted new constitutions as a kind of legal therapy for states recovering from the Cold War. Although Latin America had a long history of constitutionalism, fully thirteen countries in the region ratified new constitutions in the years between 1990 and 1996 (Van Cott 2000), a move that was echoed across much of Eastern Europe, as well as in South Africa (see Borneman 1997; Wilson 2001). The goal of all of these constitutions was to effect a renovation of states whose legitimacy had been marred by Cold War politics, to call a truce between warring factions, and to draw the previously excluded into more complete citizenship. In most cases, the constitutions built on advances in international law to include provisions for more inclusive multiculturalism (Van Cott 2000). But their primary role was to establish again the rule of law (*estado de derecho*) as the highest

principle in running the state, and to provide a new, untainted procedural framework for making that rule work. The constitution actually constitutes Paraguay as an "estado social de derecho," which involves a combination of "estado de derecho" (rule of law) and "estado social" (welfare state). Daniel Mendonca (2000) offers a much more nuanced reading of what this might mean in the Paraguayan context than I can offer in this book.

31. Habeas Data is a new constitutional provision, based on German and then European Union standards of data transparency enacted in the 1980s. It was first adopted by Brazil's constitution, in 1988, then by Paraguay, and is now a common legal right in most of Latin America. Not surprisingly, the procedural code for enshrining the right has lagged behind its enactment, and behind that the legal systems needed to carry out the procedure (Guadamuz 2001).

32. Although the Cold War produced many sinister variants of this sort of information gathering, the epistemological conceit which underlies it has been a central feature of modern governance since at least the nineteenth century (see Mitchell 1988; Richards 1992; Rama 1996).

33. Stroessner's police, politically inured to the threat that democracy posed by decades of rule, were the only ones in the region to make this mistake. This is why Paraguay's archive of terror is also a vital resource for researchers from Argentina, Chile, and Brazil, who are more likely to find records of their own citizens in Paraguay than they are in their own countries, where the cleanup was better managed (see Nickson 1995; Blanton 2008).

34. As the good Pastor wrote on a notecard for a presentation to party brass about the radical Organización Política y Militar, "With 'Human Rights' or without 'Human Rights,' we will continue in power, building and progressing, proud of our government and party" (Centro de Documentación y Estudio 1993, 121).

35. The archivo's stability is, of course, apparent only from the outside, or in a brief and superficial visit, where it serves its most important public function. As soon as one gets inside, it is full of all the contradictions, slippages, and decay of any archive (e.g., Derrida 1996; Buckley 2005).

36. There's another argument to be made about news media. The primary national papers, ABC Color, Última Hora, La Nación, and Noticias (which folded while I was there) had little readership among the poor. The papers that were more accessible were cheaper tabloids. The paper with the widest readership, by contrast, was called Popular, and was written in a register of Spanish sprinkled with Guaraní morphemes. It rarely published political stories, and certainly didn't print the reams of text of the archivo.

37. I was first in Paraguay from August 1998 to January 1999, working as a volunteer intern for an Asunción-based NGO.

38. See Classen 1996 for a description of malls as the new public plazas in Formosa. The other somewhat more cynical metaphor I heard expressed in Asunción around this time was the mall as cathedral.

39. In 2006 Wasmosy's long trial on corruption charges was thrown out in a process run by his own Colorado Party protégés.

40. On Oviedo's messianic appeal, see especially Morínigo and Brítez 2004.

41. The landscape was complicated considerably by the fact that Paraguay's most important news source, the newspaper *ABC Color*, was owned by Aldo Zucolillo, a vocal supporter of Oviedo. While the other papers (*Última Hora, Noticias, La Nación*) all toed a strictly new democratic line, *ABC Color* played at both professional journalism and explicit political agitation, giving over much space to explicitly supporting Oviedo and other camps.

42. See Gupta 1995 and Lomnitz 1995 for similar analyses of corruption discourse in India and Mexico, respectively.

43. Arguably this is the very meaning of charisma, which Weber famously defined as that form of authority which founds law and ethics but is not itself subject to them.

44. While there is general agreement that national elections after the coup in Paraguay were clean affairs, internal Colorado elections were notorious for dirty tricks (Brítez and Morínigo 1993).

45. Cubas, like Wasmosy, was not really a politician, but an engineer who had risen in the party by not offending anyone while making his fortune during the construction boom of the Itaipú Dam. They and a handful of others are popularly known as the Barons of Itaipú.

46. Argaña was the perfect antonym for Oviedo, for he had indeed been one of Stroessner's closest supporters. Argaña was not only Stroessnerian in form, but also personally wedded to Stroessner's project and legacy.

47. González Macchi's consensus cabinet comprised an even more fractious group of representatives from different parties. In this case, the vice presidency was actually held by an even more unlikely collaborator, the head of the Liberal Party.

48. This is meant to echo one of Gramsci's better-known statements about civil society: "In the West, there was a proper relation between State and civil society, and when the State trembled a sturdy structure of civil society was revealed. The State was only an outer ditch, behind which there stood a powerful system of fortresses and earthworks" (1971, 238).

49. *ABC Color*, the largest national newspaper, had a more complex relationship to the events, given that they were allied with Oviedo.

50. Yhu, which sits on the road just south of Vaquería, is one of the oldest towns in eastern Paraguay. It is, in fact, Colmán's hometown. For the book, however, the choice of towns may owe more to the name itself, which is virtually unpronounceable to any but the most fluent Guaraní speakers and is the butt of many jokes on both sides of the linguistic divide.

51. In Paraguayan history, *pynandi* connotes the blind and ferocious allegiance given by volunteer campesino armies to populist leaders, most notably to the barefooted battalions led by Stroessner in the 1947 civil war.

52. By far the best of these analyses is Morínigo 1999. A committed ally of the campesinado and an unsurpassed commentator on national politics, Morínigo nonetheless finds no redemptive meaning in campesino participation—it is only an accident of history.

53. That the Colorado Party and other corrupt organizations were stealing from the public was certainly true. For instance, most of a half-billion-dollar economic startup loan from Taiwan in 1998 found its way into foreign banks. And many of these same political elites took advantage of a banking crisis between 1995 and 1998 to steal international bailout money (see Albert Berry 2010a; Borda 2010).

54. Economists calculate the openness of an economy by dividing the sum of imports and exports by the GDP. By this standard, Paraguay has long been, and continues to be, an extremely open economy, even while it remains socially and politically isolated.

55. This is in contrast to the Colorado Party, run as a clientilist machine, which consolidated admirably through the land reform and was able to use international money to its advantage.

56. The figures for this are unreliable and hard to systematize. The best recent source explaining the two decades of recession are the chapters in Albert Berry 2010b. Perhaps the most telling single figure is that between 1981 and 2005, per capita GDP fell by 16 percent, making Paraguay one of the worst performing economies in the Americas (see Albert Berry 2010a).

57. See chapter 5 for a further analysis of Nicanor's "dual politics."

58. The "standby" loan of $73 million was created to buffer potential foreign currency shortfalls, which make it difficult to keep up to date with debt servicing. It was therefore the precondition of receiving more credit from the World Bank and the Inter-American Development Bank.

59. Borda 2010 describes these policy decisions in glowing third-person terms.

60. There are a number of reasons for this. To begin with most of the farmers in western Brazil originally came from Germany and brought with them knowledge of grain production on midsized farms. But more important, their experience with Brazilian extension support for planting mint, tobacco, and soybeans was far greater than anything offered in Paraguay. Finally, though poor by Brazilian standards, most began farming in Paraguay with more capital to invest in inputs and tools than even the richest of Paraguayan campesinos (see Souchaud 2002).

61. All of this is explored in more technical terms in Albert Berry 2010a. This economic phenomenon is usually referred to as the "resource curse" or "Dutch disease," a reference to the increase in unemployment that accompanied the rise of the natural-gas sector in the Netherlands.

62. The change in land use since the beginning of the recession is most dramatically expressed in the following numbers. In 1980, smallholder cotton production accounted for 33.6 percent of primary exports, while soybeans accounted for only 13.5 percent. By 2005, this had more than reversed, with soybeans accounting for

33.5 percent, and cotton having fallen to 2.4 percent. The other big winner in this transition was beef, another sector requiring extensive land use but very little labor, which rose from 0.3 percent to 15 percent over the same span. All figures from Ministerio de Agricultura y Ganaderia 2006.

63. In 2004, soy farmers were offering up to 10,000,000 guaranis per hectare, while the state price was 450,000.

64. Research on Roundup Ready soy production in Argentina suggests that Roundup soybeans require a more complex array of chemicals in the Southern Cone than they do in the United States, whereas Monsanto claims that they require very little other than a couple of applications of the relatively benign glyphosate (Branford 2004).

CHAPTER TWO: ILL-GOTTEN LAND

1. In Paraguay it is common to omit the usual space between the words mal and habida. Although some people retain the space, I have standardized the contracted version here. In Spanish, the plural and masculine form of the adjective is occasionally used, as in bienes malhabidos, but its most common usage remains singular feminine, following the Guaraní convention (which does not differentiate gender in this way and marks plurals only when absolutely necessary).

2. In the comisión's larger project of awarding reparations for past abuses, victims could make a claim by bringing together oral testimony with written support in the archivo.

3. Centurión's story is detailed in the tomes of oral testimony put out by CEPAG in 1990 and 1991.

4. In these cases, the land was owned by the Instituto de Previsión Social (IPS) and the Banco Nacional de Fomento (BNF). The IPS is the national public health and social insurance fund. It is also, historically, the government's biggest slush fund. Colorado Party operators are notorious for channeling IPS funds through various state banks, such as the BNF and the Banco de Desarrollo, to fund populist programs with no hope of return. Several have also used the IPS funds for direct investment in personal boondoggles, or used the IPS as collateral on shady loans. For examples, see Miranda 2001, Miranda 2002, and Pangrazio 2001.

5. The postposition -kue in Guaraní marks an absence, so Zapatini kue literally means "where Zapatini was." The -kue becomes one of the easiest ways of finding tierra malhabida in eastern Paraguay, although it can also be used to designate land owned by a respected figure.

6. This assertion draws on literature about the phenomenology of injustice (see Fraser and Honneth 2003). Judith Shklar (1990), the best-known proponent of this position, claims that injustice is an affective state which cannot be arrived at through the deductive sense of injustice proposed by liberalism (most notably Mill 1998 [1863]). She suggests that a sense of injustice is the "natural core" of morality, which liberal forms of law are ill-advised to ignore. I use this basic argument, with the anthropological caveat that the sense of injustice is historically constituted, as are the subjects who sense it.

7. Interestingly, though, the classic nude is no longer the standard graphic icon of the nation, having been replaced in political cartoons by a character in the shape of the national territory.

8. U.S. intervention in Guatemala, in 1954, was a direct result of Guatemala's attempts at land reform. But only seven years later the American government had completely changed its policy in the region, in large part because of the Cuban revolution. Many aspects of Punta del Este charter were abandoned in the late 1960s and 1970s, but several key institutions remain, including the Organization of American States (OAS) and the Inter-American Development Bank (IDB).

9. In Paraguay, *latifundio* is usually used to refer to a large tract of land, although its legal definition is land that is not being "rationally exploited" and that is usually covered in forest.

10. These provisions appear in articles 50 and 75 of the Estatuto Agrario.

11. All of the generals who took over after the 1989 coup controlled large tracts of land in the east (Kleinpenning and Zoomers 1991), and even in 2008 the majority of senators and congresspeople were large landowners.

12. William Thiesenhusen (1995) estimates the Gini coefficient for land in Paraguay at 0.95. The World Bank (2008) put the coefficient at 0.93. However, these are highly suspect numbers, since they are based on confusing data about land ownership, and a huge array of official and unofficial land-tenure arrangements which are not systematically recorded anywhere.

13. See Lewis 1993 for an overview.

14. I mean this to echo Arjun Appadurai's (1986) discussion of the social lives of commodities which pass through different regimes of value. In this case, I'm talking about the social life of a document, and with it snippets of political discourse, as it travels through, and is deployed in, different political spheres.

15. See the report put out in 2005 by the Contraloría General de la República del Paraguay titled "Informe Examen Especial a la verificación del inventatio nacional de tierras públicas del Instituto Nacional de Desarrollo Rural y de la Tierra (INDERT) ejercicios fiscales 1994 al 2003."

16. See for example "Revelan grosero reparto político que hizo IBR de tierras públicas," *ABC Color*, 1 October 2004.

17. See Fraser and Honneth 2003 for an excellent discussion.

18. Positive law is a pervasive aspect of constitutional democracies, and it is hard to imagine an appeal to "rule of law" that does not rely on it. To affirm the rule of law one must obey the rule of law (see Cotterrell 1984). These terms are not, of course, absolute, as even the most conservative theories of law must leave some room for change. Still, in moments of consolidation of the rule of law, the claustrophobia of positivism is enhanced. It also necessarily tends "to displace criminality from the centre to the margins, away from political leaders to border regions and provincial actors" (Borneman 1997, 4).

19. Labor was always very weak in Paraguay, mainly because of its lack of an industrial sector. The important unions comprise primarily public employees, still strongly

tied to the Colorado Party. The Frente Nacional was an unusual alliance for reasons that I can only hint at here, and not surprisingly it only lasted a few months.

20. Among the national credit banks was Crédito Agrícola, the primary national body for distributing cotton credit, and therefore the way in which campesinos were able to get their debts canceled in bad years was also affected.

21. The idea of such a Gabinete was not unprecedented. Campesinos had often seen their most successful pressure tactics answered with the creation of a special committee on "rural crisis." The special committee was a way to open up an exceptional space of campesino participation in policymaking, with two ramifications: first, because it was exceptional, it could funnel funds more freely without the approval of congress (though in this case that didn't work); second, it meant that campesinos were kept separate from official deliberative processes.

22. Ruta 5, the highway that links Asunción to Brazil via Ciudad del Este, was built in the 1950s and is generally considered the economic backbone of the country (see Vázquez 2006). The city of Caaguazú sits about 180 km from the capital and 100 km from the border. Any prolonged blockage of this road at Caaguazú would deal an important economic blow to Asunción. And although the periodic blockages of this road have never lasted more than a few hours, the possibility of cutting it off remains one of the most effective threats the campesino movement has at its disposal.

23. Shortly before the demonstration, the daughter of the former president Raúl Cubas was kidnapped just outside her home. Cubas, who had spent years in exile after the Marzo Paraguayo, had recently returned with his family to his mansion in Asunción, but remained something of a pariah. After the paro cívico, though, the government turned the hunt for Cecilia Cubas into a matter of national concern, and when her body was found decomposing in an underground lair, the Cubas family was rehabilitated as national martyrs. Most of Patria Libre's leadership was arrested or chased into exile, and many campesino organizations that had been in some way associated with the party felt the taint of this event for years afterward.

24. Executive decree no. 167 of 27 August 2003 allowed the army to be employed internally in matters of "internal security." Until this point the army had not been used against civilian demonstrations. However, it had become a common fixture during the soybean harvest, after campesinos began burning soy in 2003 to dispute the use of pesticides near campesino homes. In the aftermath of the paro cívico, the military presence in the campo increased substantially. And although the decree in question was probably unconstitutional, the campesino movement didn't have the resources to fight it in court.

25. With regard to the beating of the protestors, see "Repriment a campesinos cuando intentaban cerrar ruta en Resquín," *ABC Color*, 20 November 2004.

26. The two stories that made this plan seem reasonable were those of the Marzo Paraguayo, on the one hand, and the Movimento Sem Terra (MST) march to Brasília, which had happened a few months before. In later months, the leadership would

admit that having their own march to the capital would have highlighted just how small and disorganized their movement was in comparison to the MST, which had supported thousands of people walking for months.

27. Outside of a few key exceptions, like the truth commissions in Guatemala, this is standard fare in Latin America, Africa, and Eastern Europe (see Wilson 2001; Borneman 1997). Truth commissions are a key ritual technology, with constitutional reform, of post–Cold War democracy, with its emphasis on accountability and rule of law.

28. See Dagnino 2003.

29. Or so said Fukuyama 1989.

CHAPTER THREE: PRECARIOUS LOTS

1. On customary land, see, for example, Sara Berry 2001. For postsocialist agrarian reform see Katherine Verdery's (2003) impressive ethnography, and Hann 2003. Latin American cases are somewhat less stark, with perhaps the best-known being the privatization of the Mexican *ejido* system (e.g., Deere and León 1997). In much of this work the temptation is to understand the current moment of neoliberal agrarian reform as a recapitulation of the enclosure laws of the eighteenth century, in which a formalized system of enclosure overtakes a customary (sometimes communal) one (e.g., Thompson 1975). But in most of Latin America, the transition has been more subtle than this. The state has backed away from land reform (Kay 2002), but, as this book shows, it has usually accomplished this through subtle legal changes which ultimately have important effects on agrarian relations, and through World Bank– and IDB-funded reforms of land bureaucracies.

2. There is an important difference between American and Latin American anthropological approaches to peasantries. In the latter tradition, especially in certain national contexts like Peru and Bolivia, there is a huge literature describing peasant economics as its own logical space. These span the gamut from adaptive strategies (the "verticality" of John Murra [1980]) to cultural logics inherited from indigenous predecessors (for example Frank Salomon's [1986] work in ethnohistory). Another important exception to this rule is Michael Taussig's exemplary *Devil and Commodity Fetishism* (1980), which I leave aside here because it does not focus on the role of land in economic thinking. In Paraguay there has been very little work that tries to translate campesino thought in a coherent way, and most of that relies on rescuing exotic indigenous elements of campesino mestizaje (e.g., Chase-Sardi 1998; Meliá and Temple 2004).

3. See, for example, Wolf 1969, Mintz 1974, Roseberry 1976, Edelman 1999, Fogel 2001, Quintín Riquelme 2003.

4. Examples of this can be found in Collier 1994, Jonathan W. Warren 2001, Postero 2007, and Hale 2006.

5. American anthropologists have long thought of rural Paraguayans as essentially Spanish mestizos who had accidentally adopted an indigenous language while

maintaining a medieval Spanish culture (Service and Service 1954), differentiating them from indigenous forest dwellers and Chaco hunter-gatherers, who remained completely outside of the nation until the early 1980s (Prieto 1994). This view is rejected by most Paraguayan anthropologists (e.g., Meliá 2000; Chase-Sardi 1998). But politically speaking, the divide between campesinos and indigenous peoples couldn't be more stark.

6. See Arens 1976, Reed 1995, Clastres 1972.

7. Physiocracy was an economic theory which based all economic wealth in the productivity of land. It was largely abandoned in the nineteenth century, but it laid important groundwork for classical economics by emphasizing the role of self-interest and private property in the economic growth of nations.

8. See Ng'weno 2007 and Catherine LeGrand's (1986) historical study of the Colombian frontier for a jarringly different take on the politics of property rights in that country.

9. Repeated constantly in speeches, this discourse appears in the dozens of books and introductions to annual reports written by the land agency's head (e.g., Frutos 1982; 1985). The materiality of the land titles as populist gifts was also continuously reinforced in title-giving ceremonies and in depictions of campesino men holding papers aloft, a point to which I return in some detail in chapter 5.

10. Even as late as 2004, most campesinos I met equated the presence of forests with a lack of solid property claim, often using the terms of the 1963 reform to explain that even if someone owned it, the fact that it was *improductivo* (nonproductive) and *ocioso* (idle) made the claim contestable.

11. See, for example, Riquelme 2003 for a discussion of branches of the Asociación Rural del Paraguay (ARP) which argued that property was an absolute and inviolable right, and therefore objected to the agrarian reform. Other branches of the ARP, which remains the largest organization of large landowners in Paraguay, recognized agrarian reform as a good way of quelling rural dissent.

12. Increasingly, through the 1970s and 1980s, campesinos claimed Colorado and church land and ran into military repression. And when, in 1989, the rules changed completely, undermining the legitimacy of many old Stronista landowners and introducing tierra malhabida into the mix, the relationship between land invasion and expropriation exploded, making almost every new colony one born of violent conflict.

13. The word *derecheras*, until very recently, did not appear in legal documents. Where I have seen the word used in legal settings, it is usually placed in inverted commas, separating it from the flow of legal language, objectifying the vernacular as a particular mode of speech, rather than as a term of analysis.

14. People were also barred from receiving land more than once from the IBR. By forbidding these sorts of transfers, land-reform planners hoped to avoid land speculation by people buying at IBR prices and selling again privately. Since these rules were never enforced, people bought and sold plots all the time. But seriously prof-

itable speculation of a smallholder kind was kept in check by the fact that in most areas of the country the openly haphazard land reform prevented the emergence of much of a private smallholder market at all. The only speculation that was very successful was carried out by large land buyers along the Brazilian border, who then sold to Brazilian pioneers looking for land which was for them comparatively very cheap (see Souchaud 2002; Nickson 1981). That original transfer of land to Brazilian migrants would form the social basis for the soy frontier of the 1990s and 2000s.

15. The idea was that an enforced delay would keep pioneering families on the land long enough to put down roots (*arraigarse*) and start building their base.

16. Although it should be noted that local creditors often charged interest rates of 70 to 100 percent.

17. This feeling goes back to the work of Elman Service and Helen Service (1954) and Ramiro Domínguez (1995 [1967]), who argued that the frontier movement of campesinos was creating an entirely new culture. One of the primary goals of the Ligas Agrarias in the 1960s and 1970s was the creation of stable communities, a pastoral catholic ideal which they felt was necessary to maintaining a spiritual life (Fernández 2003; Telesca 2004). More recently it has become important in the campesino movement itself, which is in a significant moment of soul-searching, to consider whether it is campesinos, with their constant movement and their illegal traffic in nontransferable derecheras, who are in fact responsible for the onslaught of soybeans. In recent years this has been expressed in a common discourse about fostering *arraigo campesino* (campesino rootedness).

18. Courtesy of Cecilio Mareco; translation by author.

19. Colloquial Guaraní, often referred to by the disparaging term Jopara (named for a campesino stew), includes many Spanish loanwords, some dating from the conquest and others of much more recent borrowing. This is an open process in which words are constantly being incorporated, a process accelerated by the fact that most Paraguayans also speak or at least understand Spanish. Words slowly take on a Guaraní pronunciation, particularly the movement of emphasis from the second-to-last syllable to the last syllable, and characteristic shifts in certain consonants. The best work on Paraguayan diglossia is still Rubin 1968, and the work of scholars like Bartomeu Meliá (1988; 1986) has extended this diglossia into the cultural realm in provocative ways.

20. When I suggested this interpretation to the author he corrected me and said the song should be heard as "offering advice" to those who violate private property. I think that the song's power resides, in large part, in the ambiguity about whether the situation is unjust or not—even when heard as a warning to potential invaders, it doesn't ever claim that the rules are justified.

21. Most of the women came as wives or daughters of landless men, although there were many young single men, and two or three unattached women claiming land for themselves as well.

22. The IBR rate for land in the area at the time was 450,000 guaranis per hectare, or about $75 per hectare, to be paid off over ten years. Soybean farmers were offering upwards of 10,000,000 guaranis per hectare on a regular basis in Tekojoja. In other communities I heard reports of offers of 12–15,000,000 guaranis.

23. In this scenario is a familiar background story about urban migration, which one might argue would have happened regardless of the soybeans. It would be hard to dispute, though, that the soy farms presented a strong push-factor, convincing many families to leave who might not otherwise have considered it.

24. See "Matan a dos labriegos en un confuso incidente en Vaquería," *ABC Color*, 25 June 2005.

25. See *Última Hora*, 26 June 2005.

26. Criminal proceedings were also initiated, but did not result in any convictions.

27. See the special issue of the Centro de Documentación y Estudio's *Informativo Campesino* (2006) on this debate among campesino organizations. Internationally, organizations like Via Campesina and the Foodfirst Information and Action Network have also opposed land-titling initiatives for similar reasons.

28. One way to clarify this position is to distinguish it from Stephen Gudeman's (2001; 2008), which takes abstraction and materiality (as well as market and community) as pre-given analytic categories. But nothing necessitates reading these transactions in this way. In fact, with regard to the indigenous people from whom they originally took the land, campesinos might very well claim superiority for the Estatuto Agrario on the basis of its abstract legality in relation to indigenous people's long-standing use of land and forests. In this view, politics takes up available economic languages, rather than being produced by underlying economic tensions.

29. This opinion is implicit in most of the material about the state of agricultural governance in Paraguay (e.g., Inter-American Development Bank 2004; United States Agency for International Development 2004; World Bank 1995). The question of modernity and premodernity was made explicit to me during an interview I conducted with an IDB economist (see also Inter-American Development Bank 2002).

30. The best general discussions of the constitutive exclusions of liberalism and social contract theory are by Carole Pateman (1988) and Uday Singh Mehta (1999). Both of these authors show that Locke, among others, built his theory of social contract on the necessary exclusion of women, the poor, and the "uncivilized."

31. For one thing, according to the Estatuto Agrario, it was almost impossible for women to get occupancy permits. Rectifying this was one of the more salutary changes to the Estatuto Agrario in 2002. Restrictions on women's ownership of property are not explicit in the Civil Code.

32. See especially the World Bank's "Land Use Rationalization Project" (1992) and the IDB's *Cadastre and Property Registration Program* (2002), which I will address more in chapter 4.

33. The first interviews were published 4–5 July 2005 in *ABC Color*, which has continued to revisit the theme at least once a year since.

34. The name change was significant, if awkward, as the IBR became the INDERT, the Instituto de Desarrollo Rural y de la Tierra. There were a few significant and long-overdue amendments, including the inclusion of women as equal beneficiaries and special provisions for indigenous territories. Perhaps the most significant change, though, was a new council made up of large landowning interests and industrialists who were able to veto expropriations.

35. Three versions of this bill were introduced, and the one which was finally passed was Castiglioni's version, which was the least radical. It stipulated that campesinos could solicit unconditional title to their land once they had paid 25 percent of their IBR quotas. In other words, it didn't freely hand out titles, but it made them far more accessible.

36. A civil code may be developed out of a prior conception of natural law and usually is. That is the tradition of the French and American constitutions, and by extension the Paraguayan one as well. But the code itself does not rely on these claims; it is merely a code instituted by the sovereign for the purpose of creating order, regardless of how the principles of that order are determined. This is why utilitarians like Jeremy Bentham (who was influential in the construction of Latin American first constitutions) argued against the natural-law principles of the French constitution, but for a purified version of the civil code that that tradition had created (Bentham 1789; Williford 1980).

37. Again, it is worth underlining that, in their relations with indigenous people, campesinos precisely reverse this relationship: they see their own labor as a form of "mejora," which communicates to other campesinos their rights to be there, but they do not consider indigenous labor to be constitutive of rights. This merely shows that the language of abstraction and materiality are not stable targets, but get taken up politically in the context of different struggles over land.

38. In a common strategy of ignoring the line between empirical description and policy proposal, economists seemed to ignore the fact that the models they used to assess campesino tenure are also implicitly descriptions of how the state ought to be organized (Mitchell 2007; Callon 1998). For certain politicians and landowners, the ignorance was far more willful.

39. The awkward passive voice in this translation is meant to capture something of the Spanish, in which reflexive verbs allow statements like these to be completely passive. It is also interesting to note here that in the same month a lawyer from the IBR did a similar visual inspection of the place. The word "precario" is absent from her report, and the houses, gardens, and electrical lines are classified as "mejoras" and "actos posesorios."

40. The most serious of these was an attempted murder charge against Jorge, Antonio, and one other man, which never made it to trial. All of these charges were subsequently dropped, but while they were in effect, those members of the organization most capable of making public pleas were legally barred from speaking on behalf of others.

41. Arguably the pages were *too* striking, the logo too large, and didn't conform to a sort of bureaucratic restraint that accompanies elite political performances. It was a sign of the organization's maturity that years later, when they did finally achieve official recognition, they began using a much more modest logo.

42. Guaraní appears on Paraguayan television primarily in snippets of interviews during the news, in speeches by politicians in the countryside, on shows devoted to national folklore, or on comedy shows. Rubín, who showed that night that he understood the language well, nevertheless claims that he cannot speak it. It should be said, however, that new democrats I knew who were sympathetic to campesinos from Tekojoja thought Jorge had damaged his case by speaking Guaraní on television.

43. On how discourses of corruption are opposed to ideas of political purity in other contexts, see Verkaaik 2001, Gupta 1995, Bratsis 2003, and Lomnitz 1995.

44. Kachaka is a form of popular dance music related to the Colombian cumbia.

45. That a majority of legislators voted for the bill despite campesinos' fierce opposition was one of the more serious political defeats for campesinos in recent years, but the law was later vetoed by the president. In 2008 the World Bank tried to introduce similar legislation, which was again blocked by campesino organizations, this time through the INDERT. Jaeggli reintroduced the legislation in 2009. While this particular fight has been surprisingly successful, it seems likely that some version of one of these bills will eventually be approved.

46. One important connotation of this was that a title given by the state with no labor would be *undeserved*, and thus, were someone to try to take it away, the organization would not stand up for the owner.

47. There is every reason to remain wary of romanticizing agrarian populism. Certainly, Paraguay's indigenous populations and other impoverished minorities have as much reason to fear a continuation of the land reform as they do any rights-based legalism that might replace it. But campesino struggles to hold that blurry line should give one pause about current property arrangements favored by most development experts in the twenty-first century. For they are unlike the frail, hackneyed titles once offered by the IBR, which gave campesinos the smallest tools for building new kinds of states and suggested systems of ownership that might remain perpetually open and flexible.

48. This also does not work in practice, leading to its own kind of violence and to predatory speculation by soy farmers and campesinos themselves.

CHAPTER FOUR: DUPLICITOUS DOCUMENTS

1. The IBR, as far as I could tell, was not the site of heavy bribe-taking, since most of the clients of the institution were campesinos. Favors were exchanged frequently in the field, and there were different sorts of informal "fees" levied for particular professional services (surveyors, for example, often expected their gas to be paid for and a good lunch, even though they also billed the institution for these expenses).

But cash for bureaucratic attention was unusual. This was not true in other bureaucracies, as I would discover over the following year, when, for example, I helped a number of campesinos acquire passports.

2. For excellent examples of these sorts of practices from different national contexts see Feldman 2008 and Hull 2003.

3. See Barrera 2008 for a sophisticated analysis of a similar experience in the Argentine Supreme Court.

4. This argument is made in greater detail by Ronald Day (2008) and by the contributors to *Documents: Artifacts of Modern Knowledge* (Riles 2006). I have also elaborated on it in Hetherington 2012.

5. The number has changed over the years, but has remained in the top ten since Transparency International started publishing the indexes, in 1995, and it rose to number 2 in 1999. The joke that year was that Paraguay had sold the number 1 spot to Cameroon.

6. "El Gobierno pretende desmentir lo que esta a la vista de todos," *ABC Color*, 3 October 2006.

7. See Marcus-Delgado 2003, Haber 2002, Hasty 2005, World Bank 2000, United States Agency for International Development 2004, Tulchin and Espach 2000, Pangrazio 2001; Haarhuis and Leeuw 2004.

8. In other publications and studies, Transparency International has defined corruption much more specifically and tried to measure the frequency of such activities as bribe-taking. But the organization's public showcase internationally has always been the *Corruption Perception Index*, which is both far less rigorous (and therefore easier to produce) and far more circular in its tacit definitions of corruption and transparency.

9. See Diane Nelson's (2009) excellent ethnography on post–Cold War Guatemala for an extended discussion of the role of duplicity in popular understandings of the state there.

10. See the introduction on the critique of representationalism in the social sciences (see, for example, Thrift 1996; Thrift 2007; Foucault 1966; Mitchell 2002). More recently, the social effects of representationalist ideology have come to be recognized as social facts themselves (Rabinow 1996; Law 2004; Latour 1993; Whatmore 2002).

11. For examples of this sort of argument, see Comaroff and Comaroff 2003, Sanders 2003, Morris 2000, Freidberg 2004.

12. Marx is clear: "The religious reflections of the real world can, in any case, vanish only when the practical relations of everyday life . . . generally present themselves to him in a rational form" (1867, 173). See McCarthy Brown 2003 and Pietz 1988.

13. For examples of this kind of argument, see Taussig 1992, 1997; Coronil 1997; Mitchell 1991; and Abrams 1988 [1977]. There are good reasons to be wary of deploying the notion of the fetish for talking about the state at all. Talal Asad is adamant: "The reification of social relations of production that characterizes the

commodity," he says, "is quite different from the abstract character of the modern state. The commodity form hides the productive power of the laborer. It is merely inert material falsely taken to be alive. The abstract structure of the state, on the other hand, is the essential condition for the exercise of specific kinds of legal power" (2004, 281).

14. I should clarify here that in Taussig's original formulation, from which I draw the quote, this problem does not occur. In that essay, Taussig (1992) is clear that it was not the natives who were in the thrall of the state fetish, but the post-Durkheimian sociological school. But Taussig's state fetish has been reread and quoted in a less reflexive manner by writers like Gaston Gordillo (2006).

15. For an overview of the early literature, see Hirshleifer 1973.

16. The most apposite example of this kind of argument was provided by Joseph Stiglitz (1974) to explain the persistence of sharecropping in much of the developing world, despite strong evidence that sharecropping was a poor profit-maximization strategy for both landlords and the peasants using their land. Stiglitz argued that sharecropping was not the result of economic irrationality, but of imperfect information in risky agricultural markets. Given the inherent uncertainty of agricultural income, the risks associated with entering into a fixed-price rental contract were simply too much for a peasant farmer to bear; at the same time, a landlord was unlikely to want to assume the risk by owning the crop and paying the peasant a wage, without being able to monitor the peasant's labor. Sharecropping (in which "rent" is paid as a percentage of the crop) became a way of sharing the risks and incentives between peasant and landlord in an inherently uncertain situation. The corollary to this argument was that if one could fix the uncertainty problem (improving information), those concerned would stop sharecropping and start renting, and returns would go up. In this case the fix meant creating better information about risk, so that risk itself could be represented, commodified, and insured against.

17. The two key papers are Arrow and Debreu 1954, which argued that under conditions of perfect information markets reached optimal distributions, and Greenwald and Stiglitz 1986, which showed that even assuming all real markets to be imperfect, it was nonetheless possible to improve information and thereby improve optimality.

18. Philip Mirowski (2002) and Ronald Day (2008) have extended discussions of this ambiguity, but it is even acknowledged by leading economists like Stiglitz (2000) and Kenneth Arrow (1996).

19. As I've argued elsewhere (Hetherington 2012), the other reason for this is that in the mathematical model, information is treated as a ratio between *all possible* signals that can be made between participants in a market and the ones that actually are. This is the much more precise definition of information in electronics, which measures signals in ratios like bits, where information is the relationship between possible signals (2) and actual signal (1). For example, the information contained by any given letter in English can be described in such terms as 26:1. Any given bureaucratic file can then, in principle, be described as the relationship between what it actually says and all the things it could possibly say.

20. The report is instructive in that it conflates the idea of "information"—a technical economic term for a quantifiable market signal—with "knowledge" which is the product of research.

21. In 1967 Stroessner passed a new constitution which was mainly intended to allow him to continue governing, but which also enshrined his development ambitions, including the agrarian reform begun in earnest in 1963.

22. Ley 2419/04. "Que crea el Instituto Nacional de Desarrollo y de la Tierra (INDERT)." Congreso Nacional, Asunción, Paraguay, 2004.

23. It's worth noting that inflation was negligible during this period.

24. Indeed, the Tekojoja case was escalating at this point over the very problem of non-transferability.

25. Ley 2051/03. "De Contrataciones Públicas." Congreso Nacional, Asunción, Paraguay, 2003.

26. The World Bank seems to rely on models which are framed in less abstract ways. Klaus Deininger's (2003) much more nuanced approach to property reform is good example of this. It is nonetheless predicated on the same basic principles.

27. I don't have the space here to discuss the challenge to materiality presented by digitization. For obvious reasons, digital information is appealing to those who wish to circumvent the document's materiality. Of course, what they do is introduce another material form with a different set of potentialities and resistances (see Harper 1998; Sellen and Harper 2002).

28. Everyone, from the clients to the functionaries, hated gestores, but they all depended on them. Even the World Bank, which dubbed them "special agents" in its latest institutional review of Paraguay, couldn't quite figure out what to do about them.

29. See Rama 1996 and Messick 1993 on forms of bureaucratic inscription that are meant to demonstrate authority, rather than to inform.

CHAPTER FIVE: POPULIST TRANSPARENCY

1. Nor was any of this mere paranoia. During my interviews with soy farmers, two people told me openly that they were "just waiting" for someone to kill the brothers; later, one of them was involved in the drive-by shooting that narrowly missed both brothers.

2. I heard this claim repeated both by campesinos and bureaucrats, and it's certainly true that after this incident no minister responded to the MAP's requests for visits.

3. One only needs to think about Gustave Le Bon's The Crowd, written in 1895, for an example of classic liberal attempts to deal with the supposed irrationality of mobs (see Laclau 2005). In the post–Cold War period, the fear of rising populism has been a feature of transitional societies from post-Soviet republics to Latin America and Southeast Asia (see Panizza 2005; Chari and Verdery 2009).

4. This depends on the subtle distinction between "politics" and "the political" made by authors such as Chantal Mouffe (1993) and Jacques Rancière (1999). Politics, in this view, is the practice of adopting distinctive positions within the framework of

liberal deliberation, while the political is the form of disagreement that threatens to radically reformulate the conversation.

5. Sarmiento would also symbolize for many the fear that liberalism could be contaminated by the nonliberal. Juan Bautista Alberdi, a contemporary, complained that *Facundo* was merely "a fable decked out as a document . . . a sort of *political mythology* with a political base" (quoted in Stavans 1998, xxi–xxii). What bothers Alberdi here is the way in which *Facundo* confuses representations of the real (what would later come to be called "information") with sentimental fiction.

6. The standard examples are Juan Perón in Argentina, Getúlio Vargas in Brazil, and Lázaro Cárdenas in Mexico.

7. For key examples of this argument, see Weyland 1996, 2003; O'Donnell 1996; Demmers, Jilberto, and Hogenboom 2001.

8. See, for examples of this type of analysis, Helio Vera 1990, Brítez and Morínigo 1993, Romero Sanabria 1998.

9. This is a familiar argument across a number of contexts, most famously articulated by Marx in the 18th Brumaire (1852), wherein he argued that Bonaparte's rise was a result of the French peasantry's disorganization and preference for personal relationships with a strong leader. In Asunción, the rationale behind this argument takes different forms, from deeply racist suspicions about blood to sympathetic Marxist arguments about political disarticulation, all of which ultimately shore up the notion that campesinos are incapable of rational politics.

10. Stroessner sought out corporatist ties with labor unions, but the unions were so inconsequential that the more important strategy was to build peasant communities through land reform. This is in contrast to countries like Argentina and Venezuela, where populism has largely been understood as a product of recent rural-urban migration.

11. In academic debates about agrarian structure, the term *agrarian populism* connotes a Chayanovian approach to understand rural labour relations. The debates on this are enormous, and they have persisted well into recent decades, with both romantic reassertions of Chayanovian ideals (Netting 1993; Francis 1994) and quite pointed attacks on their political consequences (Bernstein 1998; Brass 2000). I have largely avoided this debate; my discussion is not about the economics of this kind of arrangement so much as the ways in which agrarian economic strategies become part of larger national populist strategies (e.g., Boyer 2003; Gupta 1998).

12. This kind of agrarian populism goes back to the late nineteenth century. (A compelling but tangential argument could be made in favor of considering Paraguay's first president, Rodríguez de Francia, to be the first true populist, although his own anti-elitist tendencies may have had as much to do with personal paranoia and maintaining control of his peers as it had to do with any commitment to the concept of the "pueblo.") But it began in earnest with a surprise coup by the Febrerista Party over both the Colorados and Liberals, in 1936, shortly after the Chaco War against Bolivia. This was the only time during the twentieth century that a third party took the Paraguayan presidency. Capitalizing on wartime xenophobia and on

the sense of entitlement of returning troops, General Rafael Franco sustained a popular revolution for three years by addressing the masses publicly in Guaraní, reviving a history of national victimization, and promising to redistribute lands lost during the venta de las tierras públicas (Lewis 1968). Though Franco was soon overthrown, the popular appeal of land reform remained the foundation on which the Colorado Party would rebuild its success.

13. I don't know when or why Frutos picked up the nickname Papacito, "little father," but it couldn't be more apt. In the campo Paraguayo, Frutos served perpetually as Stroessner's "mini me," dispatched to deliver paternal speeches and patronage, but never allowed to overtake his boss. I have heard it suggested that Frutos was removed from the presidency of the IBR shortly before the coup in order to prevent him from becoming Stroessner's successor in the event of a revolt within the party.

14. This quote comes from the Memoria of 1974 of the Instituto de Bienestar Rural (33), a publication which Frutos used yearly to rehearse the rationale of the reform. Quotes similar to this can be culled from any time during Frutos's tenure, from 1963 to 1989.

15. This marks an important contrast between Paraguay and better-known cases like Mexico or Peru. Critics of the reform have since shown that despite the combative language, the immense latifundios in eastern Paraguay today were actually created by the land-reform agency, which was really a colonization project, taking over tracts of unexploited forest and dividing them up into campesino colonies and new logging and ranching grants for Colorado elite (see Morínigo 1999; Kleinpenning and Zoomers 1991). The new rural land inequality created by the reform, one of the worst in the world, was one of the key reasons for the eventual weakening of the historic bloc linking the Colorado Party to the campesinado.

16. Auyero's analysis is built from a standard reading of Marcel Mauss's classic The Gift (1945), in which gifts retain the aura of the giver and thereby create relations of reciprocity. The idea of strategic deferral he takes from Bourdieu's reinterpretation (1977).

17. Here the signature stands in for the spirit of the gift, and by that I hope to acknowledge the capacity of the signature, as much as any other part of the document, to become unmoored, for the indexical chain to be cut (Derrida 1978). Indeed, this tension, between the inalienability of the gift and the fundamental separability of the signature, speaks to the central political tension that I see growing in a post-Stroessner political environment.

18. Nickson and Lambert (2002) have called the Colorado system of rule a "privatized state," in which the entire apparatus of what would ideally be public was organized as though it were party property.

19. See Poole (2004) for a similar example in Peru.

20. It is hard to reconstruct the influences that went into this shift, given the lack of public reflection on ideological changes among Colorados, but one can assume three important factors. The first was the increasing division between the party and campesino organizations in the early 1980s. After the purge, in 1976, of the Jesuit

agrarian leagues, campesino organizations took a decidedly radical turn, many of them openly espousing agrarian reform as Marxist strategy (see Borda 1990). The second was the severe recession that hit Paraguay in 1982, making the costly job of measuring colonies and building infrastructure almost impossible. And the third was that agrarian reform had lost its cachet internationally. USAID was by then promoting rapid titling programs in the region as an alternative to redistributive land reforms (beginning with Honduras, in 1983), ushering in a new period of neo-liberal thinking about land policy (Fandino 1993; Zoomers and van der Haar 2000). In 1985, USAID began a comprehensive attempt at reforming Paraguay's cadastre, a project that was soon abandoned.

21. The devaluation of these titles was slower, but nonetheless followed the same basic pattern as simple inflation. Inflation occurs as it becomes clear that there is more currency in circulation than domestic product. Land titles lost value after the coup, when it became clear that in many areas there were more titles than there was land. Around Vaquería, most campesinos who tried to sell the ten-hectare plots that had been given to them in the 1980s found that formal measurements indicated that their plots were more like six to eight hectares.

22. When Stroessner was removed, causing his party to slowly disintegrate, the system that he had developed operated parallel to the formal legal system. Paraguay's notorious black market was less a product of unscrupulous underground operators than it was a product of soft institutionalization, which appeared disconnected and arbitrary to institutional reformers bent on making the bureaucracy operate around a strengthened constitution and civil code. This wouldn't change overnight in 1989, and the Colorado Party had a long list of caudillos waiting in the wings who would vie for power over the next decade, as the party won election after election (see Paredes 2001).

23. The two first Colorados to win presidential elections, Juan Carlos Wasmosy and Raúl Cubas, were two of the richest men in the country, chosen as consensus candidates by factions within the party, rather than for their oratorical skills. González Macchi, who was also no caudillo, did not win a presidential election, but as president of the senate, he was appointed to the presidency after Raúl Cubas resigned and the vice president was murdered. González Macchi wasn't particularly rich at the time of his election, although he made himself so during his time in office.

24. This is what Nicanor did with the royalties from the sale of Itaipú hydroelectricity, for instance. Instead of rolling the money into state revenue, Nicanor set up a separate agency which distributed Itaipú royalties in the campo in the form of small government handouts disguised as agricultural start-ups (goats, chickens, bee-hives, and so on).

25. Paraguayan "dual politics" was essentially the same as what was known elsewhere in the region as "neopopulism," a politics that recapitulates classical populism in style, but trades in import substitution for neoliberal structural adjustments (see Weyland 1996; 2003; Demmers, Jilberto, and Hogenboom 2001).

26. See "Caught in the triangle; Discontent in Paraguay." *The Economist*, 23 October 2004.

27. There are of course other nuances in these use of flags which bear underlining. The first is that many of the students of Marzo Paraguayo clearly took their use of the flag as part of a political idiom modeled on campesino marches. The second is the historical point that Stroessner's hegemony over campesinos was by no means complete. The use of the flag's three colors in campesino marches may historically have begun as a protest against the ubiquitous red of the Colorado Party, which until 1989 was the single color of all official political spaces.

28. This is the source of some confusion in recent literature, with Erik Swyngedouw (2009), for example using the term "populism" to describe the "postpolitical" technocratic age.

29. Lest it be forgotten in Laclau's celebration, populism also strongly connotes fascism (Žižek 2006), a specter that in Paraguay is never entirely exorcised from either the history of the official parties or land reform.

30. For Jacques Rancière it is precisely this disturbance that makes campesino politics properly political. For Rancière, "the political act consists in the exclamatory interjection of affective bodies as they enter a pre-existing public, or, rather, as they reveal that they have been there all along as an unaccounted-for part" (Bennett 2010, 105; Rancière 1998).

31. Herken would later change his mind about this, calling Duarte Frutos out as a populist, authoritarian charlatan (quoted in Pepe Escobar, "Part 2: Lost *paraguayos*: The Yankees Are Coming," Asia Times Online, 4 August 2006).

32. The distinction draws on readings of Mauss, such as Gregory 1982 and Weiner 1992, which conceptualize gifts as the opposite of commodities.

33. In land-reform language, idle meant that the land was not being used for agriculture. There were indigenous groups using the forest for hunting and gathering and some swidden horticulture, but these were not considered "economic" activity by campesino pioneers, nor were indigenous people considered even to have claims on the land by land-reform legislation, in which they remained invisible until 2002.

34. The credit relationship was extremely complex, and its reliability is one of the cornerstones of campesino organizing that I have not been able to properly address in this book. Most cotton in eastern Paraguay was planted on credit that could eventually be traced back to Crédito Agrícola, and most years campesino organizations attempted to have part of this debt forgiven in March as the season drew to a close. This was one of the precipitating factors of the Marzo Paraguayo in 1999. But since that time campesino ability to pressure the government into forgiving debt had been diminishing, which was one reason that campesino organizations were shifting their tactics. Those campesinos who knew that regularization and rapid titling were intimately connected to the project of banking reform, which would have closed the Crédito Agrícola altogether were deeply suspicious of these projects.

35. The name Yerbales, Montes y Estancias is interesting because it is nothing but a list of the three most common uses of extensive property in this period of Paraguayan history: yerbales, or regions of forest with wild yerba mate to be harvested; estancias, or ranch lands; and montes, or "bush," which refers to the potential, usually for logging, of virgin forest.

36. The Paraguayan tea once commanded a high value on international markets, but now is generally produced only to supply the national demand.

37. It is important to note the difference between Paraguayan latifundios and the better-known examples of semi-feudal haciendas in places like Mexico and the Andes on which arguments about "inefficiency" were based. In Paraguay, the majority of the properties repossessed as latifundios were not giant ranches, but yerbales, huge forested concessions with little infrastructure, inhabited by indigenous groups. When the yerba trade ceased to be profitable, the lands were generally bought up for logging, but even that industry didn't get up to speed until the land reform began to put pressure on the owners to produce something.

38. The only pages attached to the title after that year were a handful of requests from different government officials asking for copies, and then usually asking for a concise interpretation of those copies. This first happened in 1990, when CONCODER, the body established by the transitional government to "fix the rural problem" once and for all, was looking for land to quickly redistribute, but there is no record of what happened after that request. A similar request took place in 2002, when the IBR started looking into buying the land again, and this review resulted in the director of the registry putting a note on the title saying that it had to be re-measured because the title was no longer legible.

39. And this could be accomplished only after complicated negotiations with the various organizations operating on the territory and after first investing the high cost of measuring and plotting. By far the most negotiable community was Mariscal López, but it was surrounded to the north and west by strongholds for Patria Libre (a recently outlawed Marxist party) and several communitarian Protestant sects, none of which was likely to relocate for the foreseeable future.

40. The Estatuto Agrario has a provision for this sort of arrangement, called a "private colonization," which was fairly common in the 1970s and 1980s as a way for owners to avoid expropriation. There were very few buyers in Paraguay capable of this scale of real estate investment, and none would have been willing to assume the extra costs and risk of a property like this one.

41. A similar point was originally made by Max Weber (1946), who argued that charisma was functionally necessary to even the most rational of governmental systems in order to make it change.

EPILOGUE

1. See "Gobierno reprime marcha y anuncia más mano dura," ABC Color, 19 November 2004.

2. The NGO Comité de Iglesias para Ayudas de Emergencia (CIPAE) was formed by people associated with the progressive church to react to the crisis and to support the huge numbers of people incarcerated in 1976. CIPAE continues to be one of the most helpful organizations for campesinos, housing people like Digno Brítez (who introduced the concept of tierra malhabida into the proceedings of the Truth and Justice Commission). The organization took on a largely secular tone in the 1980s, and became one of those rare institutional links between professional new democrats and campesino organizations.

3. The name was meant to connote more than the violent evictions at Tekojoja. Indeed, the word *Tekojoja* became popular in the wider campesino movement after the shootings because it roughly translates as "living together harmoniously."

4. Oviedo seemed to be off his game in campaigning for this election, attempting to reinvent himself as a relatively staid neoliberal reformer. In perhaps the most shocking change of course, after his defeat in the election, Oviedo, who had once threatened to "bury" members of the Supreme Court, took his grievances to the courts, suing the government for mistreatment during his years in jail.

5. See Patrick J. McDonnell and Paul Richter, "Paraguay Moves Left with President-elect Fernando Lugo," *Los Angeles Times*, 22 April 2008; Oliver Balch and Rory Carroll, "Leftist Former Bishop Set for Victory in Paraguay Election," *Guardian*, 18 April 2008. The same narrative was prominent on alternative leftist news sources like www.upsidedownworld.org and the U.S. radio show *Democracy Now!* For more thorough analysis along the same lines, see O'Shaughnessy and Ruiz Díaz 2009.

6. Few international newspapers drew the parallel with Mexico. The most sustained analysis was Alexei Barrionuevo, "An Outsider's Victory Allows Jubilant Paraguayans to Look Past Dictatorship," *New York Times*, 22 April 2008. The one analysis I read shortly after the election which seriously questioned the "leftist" narrative appeared the on the World Socialist web site, which saw in Lugo a victory for "neoliberal reforms" (Bill Van Auken, "Paraguay: Election Ends Six Decades of One-Party Rule," 23 April 2008). Matthew Gutmann's (2002) ethnography of Mexican democracy also seriously complicates the comparative example, suggesting among other things that Fox did not have nearly as broad-based support as did Lugo.

7. The PRI's Lázaro Cárdenas is often presented as an iconic example of Latin American populism, one of the early leaders to perfect the genre.

8. See "Lugo recurre a excusas iguales a las de Nicanor," *ABC Color*, 26 November 2009.

BIBLIOGRAPHY

Abrahamsen, Rita. 2000. *Disciplining Democracy: Development Discourse and Good Governance in Africa*. London: Zed.

Abrams, Philip. 1988 [1977]. "Notes on the Difficulty of Studying the State." *Historical Sociology* 1.1: 58–89.

Albuquerque, José L. C. 2005. "Campesinos Paraguayos y 'Brasiguayos' en la frontera este del Paraguay." *Enclave Sojero: Merma de soberanía y pobreza*, ed. Ramón B. Fogel and Marcial Riquelme, 149–82. Asunción: CERI.

Alegre Sasiain, Efraín, and Aníbal Orué Pozzo. 2008. *La tierra en Paraguay 1947–2007: 60 años de entrega del patrimonio nacional: Stroessner y el Partido Colorado*. Asunción: Arundarã Editorial.

Americas Watch Committee. 1985. *Rule by Fear: Paraguay after Thirty Years under Stroessner*. New York: Americas Watch Committee.

Appadurai, Arjun. 1986. *The Social Life of Things: Commodities in Cultural Perspective*. Cambridge: Cambridge University Press.

Arditi, Benjamín. 2005. "Populism as an Internal Periphery of Democratic Politics." *Populism and the Mirror of Democracy*, ed. Francisco Panizza, 72–98. London: Verso.

Arens, Richard. 1976. *Genocide in Paraguay*. Philadelphia: Temple University Press.

Arnold, Adlai F. 1971. *Foundations of an Agricultural Policy in Paraguay*. New York: Praeger.

Arrow, Kenneth J. 1996. "The Economics of Information: An Exposition." *Empirica* 23.2: 119–28.

Arrow, Kenneth J., and Gerald Debreu. 1954. "Existence of an Equilibrium for a Competitive Economy." *Econometrica* 22: 265–90.

Asad, Talal. 2004. "Where Are the Margins of the State?" *Anthropology in the Margins of the State*, ed. Veena Das and Deborah Poole, 279–88. Santa Fe: School of American Research Press.

Auyero, Javier. 2001. *Poor People's Politics: Peronist Survival Networks and The Legacy of Evita.* Durham: Duke University Press.

———. 2007. *Routine Politics and Violence in Argentina: The Gray Zone of State Power.* Cambridge: Cambridge University Press.

Baer, Werner, and Melissa H. Birch. 1984. "Expansion of the Economic Frontier: Paraguayan Growth in the 1970s." *World Development* 12: 783–98.

Banck, Geert Arent. 1997. "The City That We Desire after 2000: Political Participation and the Construction of an Urban Image in Vitoria, Brazil." *City and Society* 9.1: 73–95.

Barata, Kimberly, and Piers Cain. 2001. "Information, Not Technology, Is Essential to Accountability: Electronic Records and Public-Sector Financial Management." *Information Society* 17.4: 247–58.

Bardhan, Pranab K. 1991. *The Economic Theory of Agrarian Institutions.* Oxford: Oxford University Press.

Bareiro, Line. 1999. *El costo de la libertad: Asesinato y heridas en el marzo paraguayo.* Asunción: Centro de Documentación y Estudios.

Barrera, Leticia. 2008. "File Circulation and the Forms of Legal Experts: Agency and Personhood in the Argentine Supreme Court." *Journal of Legal Anthropology* 1.1: 3–24.

Barry, Andrew. 2001. *Political Machines: Governing a Technological Society.* London: Athlone.

Benhabib, Seyla. 1996. *Democracy and Difference: Contesting the Boundaries of the Political.* Princeton: Princeton University Press.

Benjamin, Walter. 1978 [1920]. "Critique of Violence." *Reflections*, ed. Peter Demetz, 277–300. New York: Schocken.

Bennett, Jane. 2010. *Vibrant Matter: A Political Ecology of Things.* Durham: Duke University Press.

Bentham, Jeremy. 1789. *An Introduction to the Principles of Morals and Legislation.* London: T. Payne and Son.

Bernstein, Henry. 2004. " 'Changing Before Our Very Eyes': Agrarian Questions and the Politics of Land in Capitalism Today." *Agrarian Change* 4.1–2: 190–225.

Berry, Albert. 2010. "Elements of an Employment Strategy for Paraguay." *Losing Ground in the Employment Challenge: The Case of Paraguay*, ed. Albert Berry, 11–30. New Brunswick, N.J.: Transaction Publishers.

———, ed. 2010b. *Losing Ground in the Employment Challenge: The Case of Paraguay.* New Brunswick, N.J.: Transaction Publishers.

Berry, Sara. 1997. "Tomatoes, Land, and Hearsay: Property and History in Asante in the Time of Structural Adjustment." *World Development* 25.8: 1225–41.

———. 2001. *Chiefs Know Their Boundaries: Essays on Property, Power, and the Past in Asante, 1896–1996.* Portsmouth: Heinemann.

Blanton, Thomas S. 2008. "Recovering the Memory of the Cold War: Forensic History and Latin America." *In from the Cold: Latin America's New Encounter with the Cold War*, ed. Gilbert M. Joseph and Daniela Spenser, 47–75. Durham: Duke University Press.

Block, Fred. 2003. "Karl Polanyi and the Writing of the Great Transformation." *Theory and Society* 32.3: 275–306.

Boccia Paz, Alfredo, Myrian Angélica González, and Rosa Palau Aguilar. 1994. *Es mi informe: Los archivos secretos de la policía de Stroessner*. Asunción: CDE.

Borda, Dionisio. 1990. *Estado y políticas públicas: Aportes para una reforma agraria*. Asunción: CEPAG.

———. 2010. "Recent Reforms: Results and Challenges." *Losing Ground in the Employment Challenge: The Case of Paraguay*, ed. Albert Berry, 295–323. New Brunswick, N.J.: Transaction Publishers.

Borda, Dionisio, and Fernando Masi. 1998. *Los límites de la transición: Economía y estado en el Paraguay en los años 90*. Asunción: Universidad Católica Nuestra Señora de la Asunción.

Borneman, John. 1997. *Settling Accounts: Violence, Justice, and Accountability in Postsocialist Europe*. Princeton: Princeton University Press.

———. 2004. *Death of the Father: An Anthropology of the End in Political Authority*. New York: Berghahn.

Bourdieu, Pierre. 1977. *Outline of a Theory of Practice*. Cambridge: Cambridge University Press.

Boyer, Christopher R. 2003. *Becoming Campesinos: Politics, Identity, and Agrarian Struggle in Postrevolutionary Michoacán, 1920–1935*. Stanford: Stanford University Press.

Boyle, James. 1996. *Shamans, Software, and Spleens: Law and the Construction of the Information Society*. Cambridge: Harvard University Press.

Branford, Sue. 2004. "Argentina's Bitter Harvest." *New Scientist* (April): 40–43.

Brass, Tom. 2000. *Peasants, Populism, and Postmodernism: The Return of the Agrarian Myth*. London: F. Cass.

Bratsis, Peter. 2003. "The Construction of Corruption, or Rules of Separation and Illusions of Purity in Bourgeois Societies." *Social Text* 21.4: 9–33.

Bray, David, and Dionisio Borda. 1988. "Internalizing the Crisis of Cotton: Organizing Small Farmers in Eastern Paraguay." *Grassroots Development* 12.2: 16–23.

Brenneis, Donald. 2006. "Reforming Promise." *Documents: Artifacts of Modern Knowledge*, ed. Annelise Riles, 41–70. Ann Arbor: University of Michigan Press.

Brítez, Edwin, and José Nicolás Morínigo. 1993. *Democracia tramparente*. Asunción: RP Ediciones.

Brown, Wendy, and Janet E. Halley. 2002. *Left Legalism/Left Critique*. Durham: Duke University Press.

Buckley, Liam. 2005. "Objects of Love and Decay: Colonial Photographs in a Postcolonial Archive." *Cultural Anthropology* 20.2: 249–70.

Burawoy, Michael, and Katherine Verdery. 1999. *Uncertain Transition: Ethnographies of Change in the Postsocialist World*. Lanham, Md.: Rowman and Littlefield.

Butler, Judith. 2000. "Restaging the Universal." *Contingency, Hegemony, Universality: Contemporary Dialogues on the Left*, ed. Judith Butler, Ernesto Laclau, and Slavoj Žižek, 11–43. London: Verso.

Caballero Aquino, Ricardo. 1985. *La segunda república paraguaya 1869–1906: Política, economía y sociedad*. Asunción: Arte Nuevo.

Calhoun, Craig J. 1992. *Habermas and the Public Sphere*. Cambridge: MIT Press.

Callon, Michel. 1998. "An Essay on Framing and Overflowing, Economics and a Market: The Case of the Cement Industry." *The Laws of the Markets*, ed. Michel Callon, 244–69. Oxford: Blackwell.

Caplan, Jane, and John C. Torpey. 2001. *Documenting Individual Identity: The Development of State Practices in the Modern World*. Princeton: Princeton University Press.

Carter, Michael R. 1997. "Intellectual Openings and Policy Closures: Disequilibria in Contemporary Development Economics." *International Development and the Social Sciences: Essays on the History and Politics of Knowledge*, ed. Frederick Cooper and Randall M. Packard, 119–39. Berkeley: University of California Press.

———. 2000. "Old Questions and New Realities: Land in Post-liberal Economies." *Current Land Policy in Latin America: Regulating Land Tenure under Neo-liberalism*, ed. E. B. Zoomers and Gemma van der Haar, 29–43. Amsterdam: KIT Publishers.

Carter Center and Council of Freely Elected Heads of Government. 1993. *The May 9, 1993 Elections in Paraguay*. Atlanta: Carter Center.

Cavallo, Guglielmo, and Roger Chartier. 1999. *A History of Reading in the West*. Amherst: University of Massachusetts Press.

Centro de Documentación y Estudio. 1999. *El costo de la libertad*. Asunción: CDE.

CEPAG. 1990. *Ko'ãga roñe'ẽta (ahora hablaremos): Testimonio campesino de la represión en Misiones (1976–1978)*. Asunción: CEPAG.

Chakrabarty, Dipesh. 2000. *Provincializing Europe: Postcolonial Thought and Historical Difference*. Princeton: Princeton University Press.

———. 2002. *Habitations of Modernity: Essays in the Wake of Subaltern Studies*. Chicago: University of Chicago Press.

Chari, Sharad, and Katherine Verdery. 2009. "Thinking between the Posts: Postcolonialism, Postsocialism, and Ethnography after the Cold War." *Comparative Studies in Society and History* 51.1: 6–34.

Chase, Jacquelyn. 2002. *The Spaces of Neoliberalism: Land, Place, and Family in Latin America*. Bloomfield, Conn.: Kumarian.

Chase-Sardi, Miguel. 1998. "Cultura Guarani y cultura campesina: Nexos apenas estudiados." *Realidad social del Paraguay*, ed. J. N. Caballero Merlo and R. Cespedes Ruffinelli, 263–22. Asunción, Paraguay: Centro de Estudios Antropológicos de la Universidad Católica Nuestra Señora de la Asunción.

Chatterjee, Partha. 1993. *The Nation and Its Fragments: Colonial and Postcolonial Histories*. Princeton: Princeton University Press.

Choy, Timothy K. 2005. "Articulated Knowledges: Environmental Forms after Universality's Demise." *American Anthropologist* 107.1: 5–18.

Classen, Constance. 1996. "Sugar, Coca-Cola, and Hypermarkets: Consumption and Surrealism in the Argentine North-West." *Cross-Cultural Consumption: Global Markets, Local Realities*, ed. David Howes, 39–54. London: Routledge.

Clastres, Pierre. 1972. *Chronique des Indiens Guayaki*. Paris: Libraire Plon.

Collier, George Allen. 1994. *Basta! Land and the Zapatista Rebellion in Chiapas*. Oakland: Food First.

Colloredo-Mansfeld, Rudi. 1998. "'Dirty Indians,' Radical Indígenas, and the Political Economy of Social Difference in Modern Ecuador." *Bulletin of Latin American Research* 17.2: 185–205.

Colmán Gutiérrez, Andrés. 2004. *El país en una plaza: La novela del marzo paraguayo.* Asunción: El Lector.

Comaroff, Jean, and John Comaroff. 1999. "Occult Economies and the Violence of Abstraction: Notes from the South African Postcolony." *American Ethnologist* 26.2: 279–303.

———. 2000. "Millennial Capitalism: First Thoughts on a Second Coming." *Public Culture* 12.2: 291–343.

———. 2003. "Transparent Fictions; or, The Conspiracies of a Liberal Imagination: An Afterword." *Transparency and Conspiracy: Ethnographies of Suspicion in the New World Order,* ed. Harry G. West and Todd Sanders, 287–300. Durham: Duke University Press.

Coronil, Fernando. 1997. *The Magical State: Nature, Money, and Modernity in Venezuela.* Chicago: University of Chicago Press.

Cotterrell, Roger. 1984. *The Sociology of Law: An Introduction.* London: Butterworths.

Crapanzano, Vincent. 1981. "Text, Transference, and Indexicality." *Ethos* 9.2: 122–48.

———. 2000. *Serving the Word: Literalism in America from the Pulpit to the Bench.* New York: New Press.

Dagnino, Evelina. 2003. "Citizenship in Latin America: An Introduction." *Latin American Perspectives* 30.2: 3–17.

———. 2005. "Meanings of Citizenship in Latin America." *IDS Working Papers* 258: 1–33.

Day, Ronald E. 2008. *The Modern Invention of Information: Discourse, History, and Power,* 2nd ed. Carbondale: Southern Illinois University Press.

de Certeau, Michel. 1984. *The Practice of Everyday Life.* Berkeley: University of California Press.

Deere, Carmen Diana, and Magdalena León de Leal. 1997. *Women and Land Rights in the Latin American Neo-liberal Counter-Reforms.* East Lansing: Michigan State University Press.

Deininger, Klaus W. 2003. *Land Policies for Growth and Poverty Reduction.* Washington: World Bank.

de la Cadena, Marisol. 2000. *Indigenous Mestizos: The Politics of Race and Culture in Cuzco, 1919–1991.* Durham: Duke University Press.

de la Torre, Carlos. 1992. "The Ambiguous Meanings of Latin American Populisms." *Social Research* 59.2: 385–414.

Demmers, Jolle, A. E. Fernández Jilberto, and Barbara Hogenboom. 2001. *Miraculous Metamorphoses: The Neoliberalization of Latin American Populism.* London: Zed.

Derrida, Jacques. 1978. "Structure, Sign, and Play." *Writing and Difference,* 278–94. Chicago: University of Chicago Press.

———. 1996. *Archive Fever: A Freudian Impression.* Chicago: University of Chicago Press.

de Soto, Hernando. 1989a. "The Informals Pose an Answer to Marx." *Washington Quarterly* (winter): 165–72.

———. 1989b. *The Other Path: The Invisible Revolution in the Third World.* New York: Harper and Row.

———. 2000. *The Mystery of Capital: Why Capitalism Triumphs in the West and Fails Everywhere Else.* New York: Basic.

Dezalay, Yves, and Bryant G. Garth. 2002. *The Internationalization of Palace Wars: Lawyers, Economists, and the Contest to Transform Latin American States.* Chicago: University of Chicago Press.

Diamond, Larry Jay. 1989. "Beyond Authoritarianism and Totalitarianism: Strategies for Democratization." *Washington Quarterly* (winter): 141–62.

Diamond, Larry Jay, Juan J. Linz, and Seymour Martin Lipset. 1988. *Democracy in Developing Countries.* Boulder: Lynne Rienner.

Domínguez, Ramiro. 1995 [1975]. "Culturas de la selva." *El valle y la loma: Comunicación en comunidades rurales y culturas de la selva,* 187–243. Asunción: Editorial EMASA.

———. 1995 [1967]. "El Valle y la Loma: Comunicación en comunidades rurales." *El Valle y la Loma: Comunicación en comunidades rurales y Culturas de la Selva,* 17–186. Asunción: Editorial EMASA.

Dorner, Peter. 1992. *Latin American Land Reforms in Theory and Practice: A Retrospective Analysis.* Madison: University of Wisconsin Press.

Dreyfus, Hubert L., and Paul Rabinow. 1982. *Michel Foucault: Beyond Structuralism and Hermeneutics.* Chicago: University of Chicago Press.

Edelman, Marc. 1999. *Peasants against Globalization: Rural Social Movements in Costa Rica.* Stanford: Stanford University Press.

Ehrenreich, Barbara. 1989. *Fear of Falling: The Inner Life of the Middle Class.* New York: Pantheon.

Equipo Expa. 1981. *En busca de "la tierra sin mal."* Bogota: Indo-American Press Service.

Espeland, Wendy Nelson. 2002. "Commensuration and Cognition." *Culture in Mind: Toward a Sociology of Culture and Cognition,* ed. Karen Cerulo, 63–88. New York: Routledge.

Espeland, Wendy Nelson, and Mitchell Stevens. 1998. "Commensuration as a Social Process." *Annual Review of Sociology* 24: 313–43.

Fabian, Johannes. 1983. *Time and the Other: How Anthropology Makes its Object.* New York: Columbia University Press.

Fandino, Mario. 1993. "Land Titling and Peasant Differentiation in Honduras." *Latin American Perspectives* 20.2: 45–53.

Feldman, Ilana. 2008. *Governing Gaza: Bureaucracy, Authority, and the Work of Rule, 1917–1967.* Durham: Duke University Press.

Ferguson, James. 1990. *The Anti-politics Machine: "Development," Depoliticization, and Bureaucratic Power in Lesotho.* Cambridge: Cambridge University Press.

Fernández, David. 2003. *La herejía de seguir a Jesús: Intrahistoria de las Ligas Agrarias Cristianas del Paraguay.* Madrid: IEPALA.

Fogel, Ramón B. 1990. *Los campesinos sin tierra en la frontera.* Asunción: CIPAE.

———. 2001. *Las luchas campesinas: Tierra y condiciones de producción.* Asunción: CERI.

Fogel, Ramón B., and Marcial Riquelme, eds. 2005. *Enclave Sojero: Merma de soberanía y pobreza.* Asunción: CERI.

Foucault, Michel. 1970. *The Order of Things: An Archeology of the Human Sciences.* London: Tavistock.

———. 1977. *Discipline and Punish: The Birth of the Prison.* New York: Pantheon.

———. 1991. "Governmentality." *The Foucault Effect: Studies in Governmentality,* ed. Graham Burchell, Colin Gordon, and Peter Miller, 73–86. London: Harvester Wheatsheaf.

Foweraker, Joe. 1981. *The Struggle for Land: A Political Economy of the Pioneer Frontier in Brazil from 1930 to the Present Day.* Cambridge: Cambridge University Press.

Francis, David G. 1994. *Family Agriculture: Tradition and Transformation.* London: Earthscan.

Franco, Jean. 1987. "Afterword." *Son of Man,* ed. Augusto A. Roa Bastos, 265–79. New York: Monthly Review Press.

———. 2002. *The Decline and Fall of the Lettered City: Latin America in the Cold War.* Cambridge: Harvard University Press.

Fraser, Nancy. 1993. "Rethinking the Public Sphere: A Contribution to the Critique of Actually Existing Democracy." *The Phantom Public Sphere,* ed. B. Robbins, 1–32. Minneapolis: University of Minnesota Press.

Fraser, Nancy, and Axel Honneth. 2003. *Redistribution or Recognition?: A Political-Philosophical Exchange.* London: Verso.

Freidberg, Susanne Elizabeth. 2004. *French Beans and Food Scares: Culture and Commerce in an Anxious Age.* New York: Oxford University Press.

Fretes Carreras, Luis A. 2003. *Descentralizacion y participación ciudadana: Reto a la transición democrática del Paraguay.* Asunción: CIDSEP.

Freud, Sigmund. 1930. *Civilization and Its Discontents.* Translated by Joan Riviere. London: Hogarth.

Friedman, Milton, and Rose D. Friedman. 1962. *Capitalism and Freedom.* Chicago: University of Chicago Press.

Frutos, Juan Manuel. 1982. *Con el hombre y la tierra hacia el bienestar rural.* Asunción: Cuadernos Republicanos.

———. 1985. *Un millión de propiedades para un millión de felices propietarios.* Asunción: Editorial "El Foro."

Fukuyama, Francis. 1989. "The End of History?" *National Interest* (summer): 3–18.

Germani, Gino. 1968. *Política y sociedad en una época de transición, de la sociedad tradicional a la sociedad de masas.* Buenos Aires: Editorial Paidós.

Gerovitch, Slava. 2002. *From Newspeak to Cyberspeak: A History of Soviet Cybernetics.* Cambridge: MIT Press.

Gershman. 1989. "The United States and the World Democratic Revolution." *Washington Quarterly* (winter): 127–39.

Gill, Lesley. 2000. *Teetering on the Rim: Global Restructuring, Daily Life, and the Armed Retreat of the Bolivian State.* New York: Columbia University Press.

Gimlette, John. 2003. *At the Tomb of the Inflatable Pig: Travels through Paraguay.* London: Hutchinson.

Gledhill, John. 1995. *Neoliberalism, Transnationalization, and Rural Poverty: A Case Study of Michoacán, Mexico.* Boulder: Westview.

Gordillo, Gaston. 2006. "The Crucible of Citizenship: ID-Paper Fetishism in the Argentinean Chaco." *American Ethnologist* 33.2: 162–76.

Graeber, David. 2006. "Beyond Power/Knowledge: An Exploration of the Relation of Power, Ignorance, and Stupidity." *Malinowski Lecture*. London: London School of Economics and Political Science.

Gramsci, Antonio. 1971. *Selections from the Prison Notebooks of Antonio Gramsci*. London: Lawrence and Wishart.

Grant, Bruce. 1995. *In the Soviet House of Culture: A Century of Perestroikas*. Princeton: Princeton University Press.

Greenwald, Bruce, and Joseph E. Stiglitz. 1986. "Externalities in Economies with Imperfect Information and Incomplete Markets." *Quarterly Journal of Economics* 90: 229–64.

Gregory, Chris A. 1982. *Gifts and Commodities*. London: Academic Press.

Grow, Michael. 1981. *The Good Neighbor Policy and Authoritarianism in Paraguay: United States Economic Expansion and Great-Power Rivalry in Latin America during World War II*. Lawrence: Regents Press of Kansas.

Guadamuz, Andreas. 2001. "Habeas Data: An Update on the Latin American Data Protection Constitutional Right." Presented at the Annual Conference of the British and Irish Law, Education, and Technology Association. Edinburgh, 9–10 April.

Guano, Emanuela. 2002. "Spectacles of Modernity: Transnational Imagination and Local Hegemonies in Neoliberal Buenos Aires." *Cultural Anthropology* 17.2: 181–209.

Gudeman, Stephen. 2001. *The Anthropology of Economy: Community, Market, and Culture*. Malden, Mass.: Blackwell.

———. 2008. *Economy's Tension: The Dialectics of Community and Market*. New York: Berghahn.

Gudeman, Stephen, and Alberto Rivera. 1990. *Conversations in Colombia: The Domestic Economy in Life and Text*. Cambridge: Cambridge University Press.

Guha, Ranajit. 1983. *Elementary Aspects of Peasant Insurgency in Colonial India*. Delhi: Oxford University Press.

Guilhot, Nicolas. 2005. *The Democracy Makers: Human Rights and International Order*. New York: Columbia University Press.

Gupta, Akhil. 1995. "Blurred Boundaries: The Discourse of Corruption, the Culture of Politics, and the Imagined State." *American Ethnologist* 22.2: 375–402.

———. 1998. *Postcolonial Developments: Agriculture in the Making of Modern India*. Durham: Duke University Press.

Gutmann, Matthew C. 2002. *The Romance of Democracy: Compliant Defiance in Contemporary Mexico*. Berkeley: University of California Press.

Haarhuis, Carolien M. Klein, and Frans L. Leeuw. 2004. "Fighting Governmental Corruption: The New World Bank Programme Evaluated." *International Development* 16.4: 547–61.

Haber, Stephen H. 2002. *Crony Capitalism and Economic Growth in Latin America: Theory and Evidence*. Stanford: Hoover Institution Press.

Habermas, Jürgen. 1989. *The Structural Transformation of the Public Sphere: An Inquiry into a Category of Bourgeois Society*. Cambridge: MIT Press.

————. 1996. *Between Facts and Norms: Contributions to a Discourse Theory of Law and Democracy*. Cambridge: MIT Press.

Hacking, Ian. 1983. *Representing and Intervening: Introductory Topics in the Philosophy of Natural Science*. Cambridge: Cambridge University Press.

Hale, Charles R. 2006. *Más que un Indio = More than an Indian: Racial Ambivalence and Neoliberal Multiculturalism in Guatemala*. Santa Fe: School of American Research Press.

Handelman, Don. 2004. *Nationalism and the Israeli State: Bureaucratic Logic in Public Events*. Oxford: Berg.

Hann, C. M. 2003. *The Postsocialist Agrarian Question: Property Relations and the Rural Condition*. Münster: Lit.

Hansen, Thomas Blom. 2001. "Governance and State Mythologies in Mumbai." *States of Imagination: Ethnographic Explorations of the Postcolonial State*, ed. Thomas Blom Hansen and Finn Stepputat, 221–53. Durham: Duke University Press.

Haraway, Donna Jeanne. 1988. "Situated Knowledges: The Science Question in Feminism and the Privilege of Partial Perspective." *Feminist Studies* 14.3: 575–99.

Harper, Richard. 1998. *Inside the IMF: An Ethnography of Documents, Technology and Organisational Action*. London: Academic Press.

Hart, Gillian. 2002. "Geography and Development: Development/s beyond Neoliberalism? Power, Culture, Political Economy." *Progress in Human Geography* 26.6: 812–22.

Hasty, Jennifer. 2005. "The Pleasures of Corruption: Desire and Discipline in Ghanaian Political Culture." *Cultural Anthropology* 20.2: 271–301.

Hayek, Friedrich A. von. 1945. "The Use of Knowledge in Society." *American Economic Review* 35: 519–30.

Hershberg, Eric, and Fred Rosen. 2006. *Latin America after Neoliberalism: Turning the Tide in the Twenty-First Century*. New York: New Press / NACLA.

Herzfeld, Michael. 1992. *The Social Production of Indifference: Exploring the Symbolic Roots of Western Bureaucracy*. New York: Berg.

Hetherington, Kregg. 2008. "Populist Transparency: The Documentation of Reality in Rural Paraguay." *Legal Anthropology* 1.1: 48–72.

————. 2009. "The Strategic Incoherence of Development: Marketing Expertise in the World Development Report." *Peasant Studies* 36.3: 665–73.

————. 2012. "Promising Information: Cadastral Reform in Post–Cold War Latin America." *Economy and Society*.

Hirshleifer, Jack. 1973. "Where Are We in the Theory of Information?" *American Economic Review* 63.2: 31–39.

Hirshleifer, Jack, and John G. Riley. 1992. *The Analytics of Uncertainty and Information*. Cambridge: Cambridge University Press.

Hobsbawm, E. J. 1959. *Primitive Rebels: Studies in Archaic Forms of Social Movement in the Nineteenth and Twentieth Centuries*. Manchester: Manchester University Press.

Hull, Matthew S. 2003. "The File: Agency, Authority, and Autography in an Islamabad Bureaucracy." *Language and Communication* 23: 287–314.

Hultin, Niklas. 2007. "'Pure fabrication': Information Policy, Media Rights, and the Postcolonial Public." *POLAR* 30.1: 1–21.

Instituto de Bienestar Rural. 1974. *Memoria*. Asunción: IBR.

Inter-American Development Bank. 2002. *Cadastre and Property Registry Program* (PR-0132). Washington: Inter-American Development Bank.

———. 2004. *The Bank's Country Strategy with Paraguay (2004–2005)*. Washington: Inter-American Development Bank.

Kay, Cristóbal. 2002. "Agrarian Reform and the Neoliberal Counter-Reform in Latin America." *The Spaces of Neoliberalism: Land, Place and Family in Latin America*, ed. Jacquelyn Chase, 25–52. Bloomfield: Kumarian Press.

Keane, Webb. 2001. "Money Is No Object: Materiality, Desire, and Modernity in an Indonesian Society." *The Empire of Things: Regimes of Value and Material Culture*, ed. F. R. Myers, 65–90. Santa Fe: School of American Research Press.

———. 2005. "Signs Are Not the Garb of Meaning: On the Social Analysis of Material Things." *Materiality*, ed. Daniel Miller, 182–205. Durham: Duke University Press.

Kearney, Michael. 1996. *Reconceptualizing the Peasantry: Anthropology in Global Perspective*. Boulder: Westview.

Kleinpenning, J. M. G. 1987. *Man and Land in Paraguay*. Amsterdam: CEDLA.

———. 1992. *Rural Paraguay, 1870–1932*. Amsterdam: CEDLA.

Kleinpenning, J. M. G., and E. B. Zoomers. 1991. "Elites, the Rural Masses, and Land in Paraguay: The Subordination of the Rural Masses to the Ruling Class." *Development and Change* 22: 279–95.

Kopytoff, Igor. 1986. "The Cultural Biography of Things: Commoditization as Process." *The Social Life of Things: Commodities in Cultural Perspective*, ed. Arjun Appadurai, 64–91. New York: Cambridge University Press.

Laclau, Ernesto. 2005. *On Populist Reason*. London: Verso.

Laclau, Ernesto, and Chantal Mouffe. 1985. *Hegemony and Socialist Strategy: Towards a Radical Democratic Politics*. London: Verso.

Lambert, Peter. 2005. "Paraguay's Enigmatic President." *NACLA* 38.1: 10–12.

Latour, Bruno. 1993. *We Have Never Been Modern*. Cambridge: Harvard University Press.

———. 2002. *La fabrique du droit: Une ethnographie du Conseil d'Etat*. Paris: La Découverte.

Law, John. 2004. *After Method: Mess in Social Science Research*. London: Routledge.

Le Bon, Gustave. 1926 [1895]. *The Crowd: A Study of the Popular Mind*. London: T. Fisher Unwin.

LeGrand, Catherine. 1986. *Frontier Expansion and Peasant Protest in Colombia, 1850–1936*. Albuquerque: University of New Mexico Press.

Levine, Amy. 2004. "The Transparent Case of Virtuality." *POLAR* 27.1: 90–113.

Levine, David K., and Steven A. Lippman. 1995. *The Economics of Information*. Aldershot, U.K.: E. Elgar.

Lewis, Paul H. 1968. *The Politics of Exile: Paraguay's Febrerista Party*. Chapel Hill: University of North Carolina Press.

———. 1980. *Paraguay under Stroessner*. Chapel Hill: University of North Carolina Press.

———. 1993. *Political Parties and Generations in Paraguay's Liberal Era, 1869–1940*. Chapel Hill: University of North Carolina Press.

Li, Tania. 1999. "Compromising Power: Development, Culture, and Rule in Indonesia." *Cultural Anthropology* 14.3: 295–322.

———. 2007. *The Will to Improve: Governmentality, Development, and the Practice of Politics.* Durham: Duke University Press.

Locke, John. 1963 [1689]. *Two Treatises of Government.* Cambridge: Cambridge University Press.

Lomnitz, Claudio. 1995. "Ritual, Rumor, and Corruption in the Constitution of Polity in Modern Mexico." *Latin American Anthropology* 1.1: 20–47.

———. 2007. "Foundations of the Latin American Left." *Public Culture* 19.1: 23–27.

López, Miguel H. 2003. *Los silencios de la palabra: Lo que dijeron y callaron los diarios en las memorias de la dictadura durante la transición paraguaya.* Asunción: Servilibro.

Mackenzie, Donald, Fabian Muniesa, and Lucia Siu. 2007. *Do Economists Make Markets?: On the Performativity of Economics.* Princeton: Princeton University Press.

Marcus-Delgado, Jane. 2003. "Trust, Corruption, and the Globalization Tango." *Social Text* 77: 139–44.

Marx, Karl. 1964 [1852]. *The 18th Brumaire of Louis Bonaparte.* New York: International Publishers.

Massey, Doreen. 1994. *Space, Place, and Gender.* Minneapolis: University of Minnesota Press.

Maurer, Bill. 2002. "Anthropological and Accounting Knowledge in Islamic Banking and Finance: Rethinking Critical Accounts." *Journal of the Royal Anthropological Institute* 8.4: 645–67.

———. 2005. *Mutual Life, Limited: Islamic Banking, Alternative Currencies, Lateral Reason.* Princeton: Princeton University Press.

McCarthy Brown, Karen. 2003. "Making Wanga: Reality Constructions and the Magical Manipulation of Power." *Transparency and Conspiracy: Ethnographies of Cuspicion in the New World Order,* ed. Harry G. West and Todd Sanders, 233–57. Durham: Duke University Press.

Mehta, Uday Singh. 1999. *Liberalism and Empire: A Study in Nineteenth-Century British Liberal Thought.* Chicago: University of Chicago Press.

Meliá, Bartomeu. 1986. *El Guaraní—conquistado y reducido: Ensayos de etnohistoria.* Asunción: Centro de Estudios Antropológicos de la Universidad Católica Nuestra Señora de la Asunción.

———. 1988. *Una nación, dos culturas.* Asunción: RP Ediciones / CEPAG.

———. 2000. "Y al final, ¿qué es un campesino paraguayo?" *Acción* 202.

Meliá, Bartomeu, and Dominique Temple. 2004. *El don, la venganza y otras formas de economía guaraní.* Asunción: CEPAG.

Mendonca, Daniel. 2000. *Estado social de derecho: Análisis y desarrollo de una fórmula constitucional.* Asunción: Konrad Adenauer Stiftung / Centro Interdisciplinario de Derecho Social y Economía Política de la Universidad Católica Nuestra Señora de la Asunción.

Messick, Brinkley Morris. 1993. *The Calligraphic State: Textual Domination and History in a Muslim Society.* Berkeley: University of California Press.

Mill, John Stuart. 1998. Utilitarianism. Oxford: Oxford University Press.

Miller, Daniel. 2003. "The Virtual Moment." Journal of the Royal Anthropological Institute 9.1: 57–75.

Ministerio de Agricultura y Ganadería. 2006. El sector agropecuario y forestal en cifras. Asunción: Ministerio de Agricultura y Ganadería.

Mintz, Sidney. 1974. "The Rural Proletariat and the Problem of Rural Proletarian Consciousness." Journal of Peasant Studies 1: 291–325.

Miranda, Carlos R. 1990. The Stroessner Era: Authoritarian Rule in Paraguay. Boulder: Westview Press.

Miranda, Anibal. 2001. Crimen organizado en Paraguay. Asunción: Miranda y Asociados.

———. 2002. Partido Colorado: La máxima organización mafiosa. Asunción: Miranda y Asociados.

Mirowski, Philip. 2002. Machine Dreams: Economics Becomes a Cyborg Science. Cambridge: Cambridge University Press.

Mitchell, Timothy. 1988. Colonising Egypt. Cambridge: Cambridge University Press.

———. 1991. "The Limits of the State: Beyond Statist Approaches and Their Critics." American Political Science Review 85.1: 77–96.

———. 2000. Questions of Modernity. Minneapolis: University of Minnesota Press.

———. 2002. Rule of Experts: Egypt, Techno-politics, Modernity. Berkeley: University of California Press.

———. 2005. "The Work of Economics: How a Discipline Makes Its World." European Journal of Sociology 47.2: 297–320.

———. 2007. "The Properties of Markets." Do Economists Make Markets? On the Performativity of Economics, ed. Donald Mackenzie, Fabian Muniesa, and Lucia Siu, 244–75. Princeton: Princeton University Press.

Miyazaki, Hirokazu. 2004. The Method of Hope: Anthropology, Philosophy, and Fijian Knowledge. Stanford: Stanford University Press.

Morínigo, José Nicolás. 1999. "La disolución del podel dual y el origen de una nueva legitimidad política." Marzo de 1999: Huellas, olvido y urgencias, ed. Luis Galeano and José Nicolás Morínigo, 29–97. Asunción: Universidad Católica Nuestra Señora de la Asunción.

———. 2005. "La matriz histórica del problema de la tierra en la sociedad paraguaya." Novapolis 10: 4–12.

Morínigo, José N., and Edwin Brítez. 2004. La construcción de la opinión pública en el Paraguay. Asunción: Ediciones PROMUR/GES.

Morris, Rosalind C. 2000. "Modernity's Media and the End of Mediumship?: On the Aesthetic Economy of Transparency in Thailand." Public Culture 12.2: 457–75.

Mouffe, Chantal. 1993. The Return of the Political. London: Verso.

———. 2005. "The 'End of Politics' and the Challenge of Right-Wing Populism." Populism and the Mirror of Democracy, ed. Francisco Panizza, 50–71. London: Verso.

Murra, John V. 1980. The Economic Organization of the Inka State. Greenwich, Conn.: JAI Press.

Nelson, Diane M. 2009. *Reckoning: The Ends of War in Guatemala*. Durham: Duke University Press.

Netting, Robert M. 1993. *Smallholders, Householders: Farm Families and the Ecology of Intensive, Sustainable Agriculture*. Stanford: Stanford University Press.

Ng'weno, Bettina. 2007. *Turf Wars: Territory and Citizenship in the Contemporary State*. Stanford: Stanford University Press.

Nickson, Andrew. 1981. "Brazilian Colonization of the Eastern Border Region of Paraguay." *Latin American Studies* 13.1: 111–31.

———. 1995. "Paraguay's Archivo del Terror." *Latin American Research Review* 30: 125–30.

———. 2010. "Political Economy of Policymaking in Paraguay." *Losing Ground in the Employment Challenge: The Case of Paraguay*, ed. Albert Berry. New Brunswick, N.J.: Transaction Publishers.

Nickson, Andrew, and Peter Lambert. 2002. "State Reform and the 'Privatized State' in Paraguay." *Public Administration and Development* 22.2: 163–74.

Nikiphoroff, Basilio. 1994. *El subdesarrollo rural paraguayo: La problemática algodonera: Estrategias para el desarrollo*. Asunción: Fundación Moisés Bertoni / Intercontinental Editora.

North, Douglass Cecil. 1990. *Institutions, Institutional Change, and Economic Performance*. Cambridge: Cambridge University Press.

Ocampos, Genoveva. 1990. *Mujeres campesinas y estrategias de vida*. Asunción: Base Ecta.

Oddone, Pancho. 1998. *La transición a pedal: Artículos periodísticos*. Asunción: Ediciones Colihue / Editorial Arandurú.

O'Donnell, Guillermo. 1979. *Modernization and Bureaucratic-Authoritarianism: Studies in South American Politics*. Berkeley: Institute of International Studies, University of California.

———. 1993. "On the State, Democratization and Some Conceptual Problems: A Latin American View with Glances at Some Postcomunist Countries." *World Development* 21: 1355–69.

———. 1996. "Illusions about Consolidation." *Democracy* 7.2: 34–51.

O'Donnell, Guillermo A., Philippe C. Schmitter, and Laurence Whitehead. 1986. *Transitions from Authoritarian Rule*. Baltimore: Johns Hopkins University Press.

Olinto, Pedro. 1997. "Land Tenure Insecurity, Credit Rationing, and Household Asset Accumulation: Panel Data Evidence from Rural Paraguay." PhD diss., University of Wisconsin, Madison.

Ollman, Bertell. 1971. *Alienation: Marx's Conception of Man in Capitalist Society*. Cambridge: Cambridge University Press.

O'Shaughnessy, Hugh, and Edgardo Venerando Ruiz Díaz. 2009. *The Priest of Paraguay: Fernando Lugo and the Making of a Nation*. London: Zed.

Palau Viladesau, Tomas. 2005. "El movimiento campesino en el Paraguay: Conflictos, planteamientos y desafios." *Observatorio Social de América Latina* 46.16: 35–46.

Paley, Julia. 2001. *Marketing Democracy: Power and Social Movements in Post-Dictatorship Chile*. Berkeley: University of California Press.

———. 2002. "Toward an Anthropology of Democracy." *Annual Review of Anthropology* 31: 469–96.

Pandey, Gyanendra. 1991. "In Defense of the Fragment: Writing about Hindu-Muslim Riots in India Today." *Economic and Political Weekly* 26.11–12: 559.

Pangrazio, Miguel Angel. 2001. *Corrupción e impunidad en el Paraguay*. Asunción: ServiLibro.

Panizza, Francisco. 2005. "Introduction: Populism and the Mirror of Democracy." *Populism and the Mirror of Democracy*, ed. Francisco Panizza, 1–31. London: Verso.

Pappalardo Zaldívar, Conrado. 1990. *Estrategias y políticas de desarrollo rural*. Vol. 1, *El desarrollo rural en el Paraguay*. Asunción: Universidad Nacional de Asunción.

Paredes, Roberto. 2001. *Los colorados y la transición*. Asunción: Etigraf.

———. 2004. *Stroessner y el Stronismo*. Asunción: Servilibro.

Pastore, Carlos. 1972. *La lucha por la tierra en el Paraguay*. Montevideo: Editorial Antequera.

Pateman, Carole. 1988. *The Sexual Contract*. Stanford: Stanford University Press.

Peck, James, and Adam Tickell. 2002. "Neoliberalizing Space." *Antipode* 34.3: 380–404.

Phlips, Louis. 1988. *The Economics of Imperfect Information*. Cambridge: Cambridge University Press.

Pietz, William. 1988. "The 'Post-Colonialism' of Cold War Discourse." *Social Text* 19–20 (fall): 55–75.

———. 1993. "Fetishism and Materialism: The Limits of Theory in Marx." *Fetishism as Cultural Discourse*, ed. Emily S. Apter and William Pietz, 119–50. Ithaca: Cornell University Press.

Polanyi, Karl. 1944. *The Great Transformation*. New York: Farrar and Rinehart.

Poole, Deborah. 2004. "Between Threat and Guarantee: Justice and Community in the Margins of the Peruvian State." *Anthropology in the Margins of the State*, ed. Veena Das and Deborah Poole, 35–66. Santa Fe: School of American Research Press.

Postero, Nancy Grey. 2007. *Now We Are Citizens: Indigenous Politics in Postmulticultural Bolivia*. Stanford: Stanford University Press.

Povinelli, Elizabeth A. 2002. *The Cunning of Recognition: Indigenous Alterities and the Making of Australian Multiculturalism*. Durham: Duke University Press.

Power, Michael. 1997. *The Audit Society: Rituals of Verification*. Oxford: Oxford University Press.

Prieto, Esther. 1994. "Indigenous Peoples in Paraguay." *Indigenous Peoples and Democracy in Latin America*, ed. Donna Lee Van Cott, 235–58. New York: St. Martin's.

Rabinow, Paul. 1986. "Representations Are Social Facts: Modernity and Post-Modernity in Anthropology." *Writing Culture: The Poetics and Politics of Ethnography*, ed. James Clifford and George E. Marcus, 234–61. Berkeley: University of California Press.

Radin, Jane. 1993. *Reinterpreting Property*. Chicago: University of Chicago Press.

Rama, Angel. 1996. *The Lettered City*. Translated by John Charles Chasteen. Durham: Duke University Press.

Rancière, Jacques. 1999. *Disagreement: Politics and Philosophy*. Minneapolis: University of Minnesota Press.

Rasmusen, Eric. 1989. *Games and Information: An Introduction to Game Theory*. Oxford: Basil Blackwell.

Reed, Richard K. 1995. *Prophets of Agroforestry: Guaraní Communities and Commercial Gathering*. Austin: University of Texas Press.

Richards, Thomas. 1992. "Archive and Utopia." *Representations* 37: 104–35.

Riles, Annelise. 1994. "Representing In-Between: Law, Anthropology, and the Rhetoric of Interdisciplinarity." *University of Illinois Law Review* 3: 597–650.

———. 1999. "Wigmore's Treasure Box: Comparative Law in the Era of Information." *Harvard International Law Journal* 40.1: 221–83.

———. 2000. *The Network Inside Out.* Ann Arbor: University of Michigan Press.

———. 2002. "User Friendly: Informality and Expertise." *Law and Social Inquiry* 27.3: 613–19.

———. 2004. "Real Time: Unwinding Technocratic and Anthropological Knowledge." *American Ethnologist* 31.3: 392–405.

———, ed. 2006. *Documents: Artifacts of Modern Knowledge.* Ann Arbor: University of Michigan Press.

Riquelme, Marcial. 2005. "Notas para el estudio de los de los causas y efectos de las migraciones brasileñas en el Paraguay." *Enclave Sojero: Merma de soberanía y pobreza,* ed. Ramón B. Fogel and Marcial Riquelme, 113–48. Asunción: CERI.

Riquelme, Quintín. 2003. *Los sin tierra en Paraguay: Conflictos agrarios y movimiento campesino.* Buenos Aires: CLACSO.

Rivarola, Milda. 2001. *Marzo Paraguayo: Una lección de democracia.* Asunción: Última Hora.

Roa Bastos, Augusto Antonio. 1960. *Hijo de hombre.* Buenos Aires: Editorial Losada.

———. 1987. "Fragments from a Paraguayan Autobiography." *Third World Quarterly* 9.1: 212–28.

———. 1988. *Yo el Supremo.* Mexico: Siglo Veintiuno Editores.

Roett, Riordan, and Richard Scott Sacks. 1991. *Paraguay: The Personalist Legacy.* Boulder: Westview.

Romero Sanabria, Aníbal A. 1998. *De la tierra sin mal a la republiqueta bananera y de la republiqueta bananera a la tierra sin mal.* Asunción: A. Romero Sanabria.

Rorty, Richard. 1979. *Philosophy and the Mirror of Nature.* Princeton: Princeton University Press.

Rose, Carol M. 1994. *Property and Persuasion: Essays on the History, Theory, and Rhetoric of Ownership.* Boulder: Westview.

Rose, Nikolas S. 1999. *Powers of Freedom: Reframing Political Thought.* Cambridge: Cambridge University Press.

Roseberry, William. 1976. "Rent, Differentiation, and Development of Capitalism among Peasants." *American Anthropologist* 78.1: 45–58.

———. 1996. "Hegemony, Power, and Languages of Contention." *The Politics of Difference: Ethnic Premises in a World of Power,* ed. Edwin N. Wilmsen and Patrick McAllister, 71–103. Chicago: University of Chicago Press.

Rowe, William, and Teresa Whitfield. 1987. "Thresholds of Identity: Literature and Exile in Latin America." *Third World Quarterly* 9.1: 229–45.

Rubin, Joan. 1968. *National Bilingualism in Paraguay.* The Hague: Mouton.

Salazar, Arnaldo Ricardo. 2003. *Retrato de la transición: Album de la memoria (1989–1993).* Asunción: A. R. Salazar.

Salomon, Frank. 1986. *Native Lords of Quito in the Age of the Incas: The Political Economy of North-Andean Chiefdoms.* Cambridge: Cambridge University Press.

Sánchez González, Bartolomé. 1997. *Políticas agrarias y desarrollo, Paraguay: 1954–1994.* Asunción: Amambay.

Sanders, Todd. 2003. "Invisible Hands and Visible Goods: Revealed and Concealed Economics in Millennial Tanzania." *Transparency and Conspiracy: Ethnographies of Suspicion in the New World Order,* ed. Harry G. West and Todd Sanders, 148–74. Durham: Duke University Press.

Sarmiento, Domingo Faustino. 1998 [1845]. *Facundo, or Civilization and Barbarism.* New York: Penguin.

Sawyer, Suzana. 2004. *Crude Chronicles: Indigenous Politics, Multinational Oil, and Neoliberalism in Ecuador.* Durham: Duke University Press.

Scott, James C. 1998. *Seeing Like a State: How Certain Schemes to Improve the Human Condition Have Failed.* New Haven: Yale University Press.

Sellen, Abigail J., and Richard Harper. 2002. *The Myth of the Paperless Office.* Cambridge: MIT Press.

Service, Elman Rogers, and Helen S. Service. 1954. *Tobatí: Paraguayan Town.* Chicago: University of Chicago Press.

Shane, Scott. 1994. *Dismantling Utopia: How Information Ended the Soviet Union.* Chicago: I.R. Dee.

Shever, Elana. 2008. "Neoliberal Associations: Property, Company, and Family in the Argentine Oil Fields." *American Ethnologist* 35.4: 701–16.

Shklar, Judith N. 1990. *The Faces of Injustice.* New Haven: Yale University Press.

Silverstein, Michael. 1979. "Language Structure and Linguistic Ideology." *The Elements: A Parasession on Linguistic Units and Levels,* ed. Paul R. Clyne, William F. Hanks, and Carol L. Hofbauer, 193–247. Chicago: Chicago Linguistic Society.

———. 2001 [1981]. "The Limits of Awareness." *Linguistic Anthropology: A Reader,* ed. A. Duranti, 382–401. Malden: Blackwell.

Sorel, Georges. 1910. *Réflexions sur la violence.* Paris: Rivière.

Souchaud, Sylvain. 2002. *Pionniers brésiliens au Paraguay.* Paris: Karthala.

Spivak, Gayatri Chakravorty. 1988. "Can the Subaltern Speak?" *Marxism and the Interpretation of Culture,* ed. Cary Nelson and Lawrence Grossberg, 271–313. Urbana: University of Illinois Press.

Stavans, Ilan. 1998. "Introduction." *Facundo, or Civilization and Barbarism,* by Domingo Sarmiento, vii–xxxii. New York: Penguin.

Stigler, George. 1961. "The Economics of Information." *Political Economy* 69: 213–25.

Stiglitz, Joseph. 1974. "Incentives and Risk Sharing in Sharecropping." *Review of Economic Studies* 41: 219–55.

———. 1991. "Rational Peasants, Efficient Institutions, and a Theory of Rural Organization: Methodological Remarks for Development Economics." *The Economic Theory of Agrarian Institutions,* ed. Pranab K. Bardhan, 18–29. Oxford: Oxford University Press.

———. 1994. *Whither Socialism?* Cambridge: MIT Press.

———. 1998. *More Instruments and Broader Goals: Moving toward the Post-Washington Consensus.* Helsinki: UNU World Institute for Development Economics Research.

———. 2000. "The Contributions of the Economics of Information to Twentieth-Century Economics." *Quarterly Journal of Economics* 115.4: 1441–78.

———. 2002. *Globalization and Its Discontents*. New York: W.W. Norton.

Stiglitz, Joseph E., and Richard Arnott. 2003. *Economics for an Imperfect World: Essays in Honor of Joseph E. Stiglitz*. Cambridge: MIT Press.

Strathern, Marilyn. 1991. *Partial Connections*. Savage: Rowman and Littlefield.

———. 1996. "Cutting the Network." *Journal of the Royal Anthropological Institute* 2.3: 517–35.

———. 1999. *Property, Substance, and Effect: Anthropological Essays on Persons and Things*. London: Athlone.

———. 2000. *Audit Cultures: Anthropological Studies in Accountability, Ethics, and the Academy*. London: Routledge.

Swyngeouw, Erik. 2009. "The Antinomies of the Postpolitical City: In Search of a Democratic Politics of Environmental Production." *International Journal of Urban and Regional Research* 33.3: 601–20.

Taussig, Michael T. 1980. *The Devil and Commodity Fetishism in South America*. Chapel Hill: University of North Carolina Press.

———. 1992. *The Nervous System*. New York: Routledge.

———. 1997. *The Magic of the State*. New York: Routledge.

Taylor, Lance. 1999. *After Neoliberalism: What Next for Latin America?* Ann Arbor: University of Michigan Press.

Telesca, Ignacio. 2004. *Ligas Agrarias Cristianas: Orígenes del movimiento campesino en Paraguay*. Asunción: CEPAG.

Thiesenhusen, William C. 1995. *Broken Promises: Agrarian Reform and the Latin American Campesino*. Boulder: Westview.

Thompson, E. P. 1975. *Whigs and Hunters: The Origin of the Black Act*. New York: Pantheon.

Thrift, Nigel. 1996. *Spatial Formations*. London: Sage.

———. 2007. *Non-representational Theory: Space, Politics, Affect*. Abingdon, U.K.: Routledge.

Toledo, Ricardo. 2010. "Farm Size-Productivity Relationships in Paraguay's Agricultural Sector." *Losing Ground in the Employment Challenge: The Case of Paraguay*, ed. Albert Berry, 85–101. New Brunswick, N.J.: Transaction Publishers.

Tsing, Anna Lowenhaupt. 2005. *Friction: An Ethnography of Global Connection*. Princeton: Princeton University Press.

Tulchin, Joseph S., and Ralph Espach. 2000. "Introduction." *Combating Corruption in Latin America*, 1–12. Washington: Woodrow Wilson Center Press.

Turner, Brian. 1993. *Community Politics and Peasant-State Relations in Paraguay*. Lanham: University Press of America.

United States Agency for International Development. 2004. *An Assessment of Corruption in Paraguay*. Washington: USAID.

Van Cott, Donna Lee. 2000. *The Friendly Liquidation of the Past: The Politics of Diversity in Latin America*. Pittsburgh: University of Pittsburgh Press.

Vargas Llosa, Alvaro. 2007. "The Return of the Idiot." *Foreign Policy* 160: 54–61.

Vázquez, Fabricio. 2006. *Territorio y población: Nuevas dinámicas regionales en el Paraguay.* Asunción: ADEPO.

Vera, Helio. 1990 [1988]. *En busca del hueso perdido (Tratado de paraguayología).* Asunción: ExpoLibro.

Vera, Saro. 1993. *El Paraguayo: Un hombre fuera de su mundo.* Asunción: El Lector.

Verdery, Katherine. 1994. "The Elasticity of Land, Problems of Property Restitution in Transylvania." *Slavic Review* 53.4: 1071–109.

———. 1999. *The Political Lives of Dead Bodies: Reburial and Postsocialist Change.* New York: Columbia University Press.

———. 2003. *The Vanishing Hectare: Property and Value in Postsocialist Transylvania.* Ithaca: Cornell University Press.

Verkaaik, Oskar. 2001. "The Captive State: Corruption, Intelligence Agencies, and Ethnicity in Pakistan." *States of Imagination: Ethnographic Explorations of the Postcolonial State,* ed. Thomas Blom Hansen and Finn Stepputat, 345–64. Durham: Duke University Press.

Vickrey, W. 1961. "Counterspeculation, Auctions, and Competitive Sealed Tenders." *Finance* 16: 8–37.

Viveiros de Castro, Eduardo Batalha. 1992. *From the Enemy's Point of View: Humanity and Divinity in an Amazonian Society.* Chicago: University of Chicago Press.

Wagner, Carlos. 1990. *Brasiguaios: Homens sem pátria.* Petrópolis: Editora Vozes.

Warner, Michael. 2002. *Publics and Counterpublics.* New York: Zone.

Warren, Harris Gaylord, and Katherine F. Warren. 1985. *Rebirth of the Paraguayan Republic: The First Colorado Era, 1878–1904.* Pittsburgh: University of Pittsburgh Press.

Warren, Jonathan W. 2001. *Racial Revolutions: Antiracism and Indian Resurgence in Brazil.* Durham: Duke University Press.

Weber, Max. 1946. *From Max Weber, Essays in Sociology,* ed. H. H. Gerth and C. Wright Mills, 196–244. New York: Oxford University Press.

Weiner, Annette B. 1992. *Inalienable Possessions. The Paradox of Keeping-While-Giving.* Berkeley: University of California Press.

Weisskoff, Richard. 1992. "The Paraguayan Agroexport Model of Development." *World Development* 20.10: 1531–40.

West, Harry G. 2003. "'Who Rules us Now?': Identity Tokens, Sorcery, and Other Metaphors in the 1994 Mozambican Elections." *Transparency and Conspiracy: Ethnographies of Suspicion in the New World Order,* ed. Harry G. West and Todd Sanders, 92–124. Durham: Duke University Press.

West, Harry G., and Todd Sanders. 2003. *Transparency and Conspiracy: Ethnographies of Suspicion in the New World Order.* Durham: Duke University Press.

Weyland, Kurt. 1996. "Neopopulism and Neoliberalism in Latin America: Unexpected Affinities." *Studies in Comparative International Development* 31.3: 3–31.

———. 2003. "Neopopulism and Neoliberalism in Latin America: How Much Affinity?" *Third World Quarterly* 24.6: 1095–115.

Whatmore, Sarah. 2002. *Hybrid Geographies: Natures, Cultures, Spaces.* London: Sage.

Williams, Raymond. 1977. *Marxism and Literature*. Oxford: Oxford University Press.

Williford, Miriam. 1980. *Jeremy Bentham on Spanish America: An Account of His Letters and Proposals to the New World*. Baton Rouge: Louisiana State University Press.

Wilson, Richard. 2001. *The Politics of Truth and Reconciliation in South Africa: Legitimizing the Post-apartheid State*. Cambridge: Cambridge University Press.

Wogan, Peter. 2003. *Magical Writing in Salasaca: Literacy and Power in Highland Ecuador*. Boulder: Westview.

Wolf, Eric R. 1969. *Peasant Wars of the Twentieth Century*. New York: Harper and Row.

World Bank. 1989. *Sub-Saharan Africa: From Crisis to Sustainable Growth: A Long-Term Perspective Study*. Washington: World Bank.

———. 1992. *Land Use Rationalization Project (3445 PA)*. Washington: World Bank.

———. 1995. *Paraguay Agricultural Sector Review*. Washington: World Bank.

———. 1998–1999. *World Development Report: Knowledge for Development*. Washington: World Bank.

———. 2000. *Helping Countries Combat Corruption: Progress at the World Bank since 1997*. Washington: World Bank.

———. 2005. *Breaking with Tradition: Overcoming Institutional Impediments to Improve Public Sector Performance*. Washington: World Bank.

———. 2008. *World Development Report: Agriculture for Development*. Washington: World Bank.

Yan, Hairong. 2008. *New Masters, New Servants: Migration, Development, and Women Workers in China*. Durham: Duke University Press.

Yashar, Deborah J. 2005. *Contesting Citizenship in Latin America: The Rise of Indigenous Movements and the Postliberal Challenge*. Cambridge: Cambridge University Press.

Žižek, Slavoj. 1997. *The Plague of Fantasies*. London: Verso.

———. 2006. "Against the Populist Temptation." *Critical Inquiry* 32.3: 551–74.

Zoomers, E. B. 1988. *Rural Development and Survival Strategies in Central Paraguay: The Policy of Agricultural Colonization as an Instrument for Alleviating the Situation of the Rural Poor*. Amsterdam: CEDLA.

Zoomers, E. B., and Gemma van der Haar. 2000. *Current Land Policy in Latin America: Regulating Land Tenure under Neo-liberalism*. Amsterdam: KIT Publishers.

Note: *Page references in italics indicate illustrations. All place names and institutions, unless otherwise indicated, are in Paraguay.*

ABC Color: on corruption, 152–53, 229; documents' excesses used by, 173; on land, 80–81, 124, 250n33; Marzo Paraguayo and, 242n49; Oviedo supported by, 242n41, 242n49; readership among the poor, 241n36; shut down by Stroessner, 42, 234n6; on Tekojoja raid, 119

abstraction vs. materiality, 120–21, 125–26, 138, 250n28, 251n37

Acción, 240n28

activists. *See* guerrilla auditors

agrarian populism, 192–98, 256–57nn11–12

agricultores (farmers by profession), 32, 73, 107

agricultural exports, 58

Alberdi, Juan Bautista, 256n5

Alegre, Efraín: documents' excesses used by, 173; Itaipú Dam corruption exposed by, 77; as minister of industry, 228; tierra malhabida report by, 75–82, 79, 95

Alliance for Progress, 28, 72, 100–101

Almada, Martín, 43

Alto Paraná, 61

anthropology, 154–55, 159, 237n31

Appadurai, Arjun, 245n14

Aquino, Miguel Ángel, 67–68, 75, 92–93, 96

archive of terror: the democratic transition and, 43–48, 44, 57, 241n33, 241n35; vs. IBR's tierra malhabida documentation, 76–77, 92; used in forum on tierra malhabida, 66–67, 92, 244n2; U.S. funding for, 45–46

Arendt, Hannah, 35

Argaña, Luís María, 51–52, 59, 199–200, 242n45

Argentina, 62, 190, 238n10

army, internal deployment of, 87, 246n24

ARP (Asociación Rural del Paraguay), 248n11

arraigo campesino (campesino rootedness), 249n17

arriero porte transactions (gentlemanly agreements), 106

Arrow, Kenneth J., 254n17

Asad, Talal, 94, 253–54n13

Asunción: elites/intellectuals in, 33–35, 239n21 (*see also* campesinistas); NGO sector in, 13; reactions to democratic transition in, 25–26; reform in, 13 audits, 159, 218–19, 235n18. See also guerrilla auditors

authoritarianism and information control, 6

Auyero, Javier, 194, 257n16

Banco Nacional de Fomento. See BNF

Barons of Itaipú, 242n46

base (local organization/constituency/grounding), 19, 103–5, 236n28

beef, 244n62

Benjamin, Walter, 94

Bentham, Jeremy, 251n36

black market, 58, 258n22

BNF (Banco Nacional de Fomento), 211, 213–14, 216–18, 244n4

Borda, Dionisio, 60, 85, 91, 200, 219, 228

Borneman, John, 96, 245n18

Bourdieu, Pierre, 257n16

brasiguayos (Brazilian pioneers in Paraguay), 61–62, 243n60, 249n14

Brazil: frontier expansion by, 28, 237–38n8; hydroelectric dam built by, 58; indigenous politics in, 101; soybean production in, 62

bribes, 252–53n1

Brítez, Digno, 92–93, 162, 261n2

Brítez, Edwin, 56

Burawoy, Michael, 237n3

bureaucracy, generally, 7–9, 91, 147–48, 174. See also under IBR

Bush, George W., 221

Caaguazú, 66, 86, 224–25, 246n22

Caballero, Bernardino, 71

campesinistas: on Alegre's report, 78, 81; Borda, 85; on Brazilian migrant communities, 62; Brítez, 92; as campesino allies, 38, 42, 127; as dated, 39; the Estatuto Agrario and, 124; on frontier land, 112; on lotes precarios, 127; on tierra malhabida, 80

campesinos (peasants): agrarian-reform goals of, 29–30 (see also property); Alegre's tierra malhabida report used by, 78, 79, 80; citizenship of, 101–2; Colorado Party and, 29–30, 40, 198–99, 257n15, 257–58n20; definition/meanings of, 2, 27, 31–32, 100, 102–3, 237n4, 238n14; democracy as undermined by, 2–3, 189–90; during the democratic transition (see under democratic transition); economic thinking by, 99–100, 102–4; fear of, 187–89; identity politics of, 27, 237n5; vs. indigenous people, 100–102, 141, 247–48n5, 251n37; land struggle and, 2, 102–3 (see also tierra malhabida); leadership of, 186–87 (see also guerrilla auditors); marginalization of, 8, 21, 56, 93, 101; Marzo Paraguayo role of, 52–56, 243n52; national flag used by, 200–201, 201, 259n27; political history of (see Ligas Agrarias Cristianas); population of, 2, 233–34n3; populism of, 14, 27, 76 (see also populism/caudillismo); as el pueblo, 14, 26, 33, 192; rational politics of, capacity for, 191, 256n9; relationship with new democrats of, 12–14, 20 (see also under new democrats); repression of, 47, 52, 83; rootedness of, 249n17; soybean farming's impact on, 56, 61–65, 244n63; struggles of, generally, 234n4; testimonies by, 42–43; on the universal vs. the particular, 200–202

"Campesinos y Tierra Malhabida" forum, 66, 92. See also tierra malhabida

Canada, corruption in, 153

Canindeyú, 61

capitalism, 4, 60, 234n5, 234n9

Cárdenas, Lázaro, 256n6, 261n7

Castiglioni, Luís, 84, 124, 139, 226–27, 251n35

caudillismo. *See* populism/caudillismo

censorship, 3, 33, 234n6

census, agricultural (2006), 233–34n3

Centro de Documentación y Estudio, 52

Centro de Estudios Paraguayos Antonio Guash (CEPAG), 42–43, 240n28–240n29

Centurión, Victoriano ("Centú"), 67–68, 91–93

CEPAG (Centro de Estudios Paraguayos Antonio Guash), 42–43, 240n28–240n29

CEPAL (Economic Commission on Latin America), 28

Chaco hunter-gatherers, 247–48n5

Chaco war, 235n23, 256n12

charisma, 242n43, 260n41

Chávez, Hugo, 227–28

Chayanovian ideals, 256n11

CIPAE (Comité de Iglesias para Ayudas de Emergencia), 261n2

citizenship, 101–3, 140–41

civic virtue, 40, 240n27

Civil Code (Paraguay): campesinos excluded by, 122, 137, 143; vs. Estatuto Agrario, 122–23, 125, 128, 217; land titles and, 109, 111, 121, 124, 217; laws as contractual under, 125; membership in society assumed by, 125–26; on women's ownership of property, 250n31

civil codes, generally, 251n36

Civilization and Its Discontents (Freud), 42

civil patrols, 186

civil society, 52, 242n48

clientelism, 26, 29, 149, 194

Cold War: indigeneity and, 100–101; information control during, 6; new constitutions following, 43, 240–41n30; transparency after, 3–9, 234n6, 234n9

Colmán Guttiérrez, Andrés: El *país en una plaza*, 53–56, 188, 202, 202, 242n50

colonies: agricultural vs. ranching, 73; IBR's role in, 106–8, 248–49n14; land-reform, property in, 104–8, 140–41, 248–49nn11–14; March to the East, 28–29, 106; private colonization provision, 260n40

Colorado Party, 257n18; *agrarista* wing of, 28, 227; Argañista wing of, 59, 199; campesinos and, 29–30, 40, 198–99, 257–58n20, 257n15; congress/senate controlled by, 228; corruption of, 75, 136–37, 198, 207, 226, 243n53, 244n4; coup by insiders of, 11–12; dual politics of, 206–7; elections within, 242n44; election wins/losses by, 224, 258nn22–23; factions within, 48; founding of, 71; Guaraní spoken by members of, 204; land reform/distribution by, 71–74, 243n55; vs. Liberal Party, 28–29, 71, 75, 227; Mariscal López and, 207–8; patronage and, 11; political orientation of, 29; power of, 13, 25–26, 28, 40, 48, 236n26, 240n26

Comisión de Verdad y Justicia (Truth and Justice Commission), 66–68, 91–92, 96, 244n2

communist countries, intelligence gathering in, 3

CONAMURI, 86

CONCODER, 260n38

constitutions, 43, 95–96, 240–41n30, 251n36

Conversations in Colombia (Gudeman and Rivera), 103–4

corn cobs vs. toilet paper, 136

Coronel, Pastor, 44, 241n34

corruption: of caudillos, 191; *la crisis* and, 58; definition/meanings of, 33, 152, 253n8; legislation for curbing, 60; media coverage of, 152–54, 229; Oviedo's anticorruption platform, 48–49; in the public registry, 180; tierra corruption (cont.)

malhabida and, 70–71, 77–78, 81, 95; transparency as a cure for, 13, 48, 152–55; of Juan Carlos Wasmosy, 48–49, 242n39. *See also under* Colorado Party; tierra malhabida

Corruption Perception Index, 152–54, 229, 253n5, 253n8

cotton, 50, 52–53, 58, 61, 103, 243n62, 259n34

credit, 109, 210–11, 243n58, 249n16, 259n34

credit banks, 84, 246n20

Crédito Agrícola, 109, 246n20, 259n34

la crisis (recession), 57–59, 243n56, 258n20

crony capitalism, 60

The Crowd (Le Bon), 255n3

Cuban revolution, 245n8

Cubas, Cecilia, 87, 246n23

Cubas, Raúl, 51–53, 242n46, 246n23, 258n23

cybernetics, 234n11, 235n13

Dagnino, Evelina, 140

Debreu, Gerald, 254n17

de Certeau, Michel, 20, 237n32

deferral, strategic, 194, 257n16

Deininger, Klaus, 129, 255n26

democracy: campesinos and, 2–3; capitalism and, 4, 234n9; the free market and, 57; as a global project, 33; knowledge through documentation and, 45; vs. populism, 14, 190–91; poverty cured via, 2; procedural, 4, 43, 95, 188, 222; via rural development, 2; via transparency, 3–4, 6–7, 234n9

democratic transition, 3, 25–65; the archive of terror and, 43–48, 44, 57, 241n33, 241n35; campesino anachronism and, 26–27; campesino exclusion from, 56–57; campesino pioneering/

homesteading, 30–31, 58–59, 101–2; campesino populism during, 27–28; corruption during, 13; via the coup, 11–12; *la crisis* (recession) during, 57–59, 243n56; cynicism about, 25; economic recovery during, 60–62; euphoria over, 12; first elections, 13, 236n26; land reform during (1960), 28–31, 237–38n8; the Marzo Paraguayo (March 1999) and, 51–57, 243n52, 246n26; new democrats' rise, 26, 32–40; overview of, 25–27; protests following Luís María Argaña's assassination, 51–52; el público and, 33, 49, 238–39n18, 240n29; soy boom during, 56, 61–65, 243–44nn62–64

derecheras (occupancy permits), 108–10, 120, 122, 128, 135, 248n13, 249n17

de Rosas, Juan Manuel, 190

Derrida, Jacques, 41–42, 45, 175

de Soto, Hernando: on documents, 235n17; *The Mystery of Capital*, 157–58, 234n10; on property, 99, 124, 131, 136, 174, 250n33; on tenure security, 129; on titles, 210

development: via democracy, 2; evidence-based research as basis for, 157; as politicized, 7–8; Stroessner's projects, 58, 255n21; transparency model of, 1, 3–5

diglossia, 11, 235–36n24, 249n19

doctors, 160

documents, 143–83; authenticity as representations, 132, 134, 159; bureaucracy and, 147–48, 174; campesinos' strategy involving, 165, 182–83; citizenship/inclusion via, 102–3, 161; desire/reverence for, 160–61, 162; excess of, 172–73, 182; as exclusionary, 140–41; as fetishes, 155; fichas, 180, 182; IBR handling of, 144–50, 167–71, 173–74, 177; inefficient systems of,

158; information and, 150–51, 158–59, 165–66, 173–74; materiality of, 165–67, 172, 178, 255n27; networks of, 132, 137; overview of, 143–44; reading of, 148, 176–77; reality and, 203–4; social life of, 76–77, 245n14; technologies and, 182; transparency and, 8–9, 16, 150–51, 174, 182, 235n17 (*see also* archive of terror); universal vs. particular uses of, 189; usefulness of, 160–67; writing protocols for, 178, 179, 180. *See also* archive of terror; guerrilla auditors; IBR; public registry; titles

Domínguez, Ramiro, 249n17

Dorner, Peter, 72

dual politics, 199–200, 206–7, 228, 258n25

Duarte Frutos, Nicanor: Borda hired as finance minister by, 60; dictatorial tendencies of, 89; dual politics of, 199–200; economic recovery under, 60–61; as education minister, 200; election of, 59; Herken on, 259n31; vs. Lugo, 226; Oviedo pardoned by, 227; the paro cívico and, 85, 91; patronage used by, 199, 258n24

Dutch Disease, 243n61

Economic Commission on Latin America (CEPAL), 28

economics: of information, 4, 228, 234–35n12, 234n7; peasant, 99–100, 102–4, 247n2; physiocracy, 103, 248n7

economy: la crisis (recession), 57–59, 243n56, 258n20; open, 58, 243n54; recessions, global, 60

Ehrenreich, Barbara, 238n15

ejido system (Mexico), 247n1

elites. *See* intellectuals/elites

En busca del hueso perdido (H. Vera), 37

enclosure laws, 247n1

Encuentro Nacional (National Encounter Party), 12, 17, 38

Enlightenment, 6

Estatuto Agrario: campesino use of, 83; vs. Civil Code, 122–23, 125, 128, 217; establishment of, 28, 72; guidelines regarding unused lands, 72–73, 77, 245n10; importance to campesinos of, 31; indigenous land use and, 250n28; occupancy permits regulated by, 107–8, 250n31; private colonization provision, 260n40; on private property, 111; reform of, 209; titles regulated by, 109; as a transitional institution, 111

ethnographic entanglement, 20–23

executive decree no. 167 (2003), 246n24

exiles, 35–38

expedientes. *See* documents

Facundo (Sarmiento), 190, 256n5

Febrerista Party, 71, 256n12

Federación Nacional Campesina. *See* FNC

Fernández, José Agustín, 43–44

fetishes, 154–55, 253–54nn13–14

FINAP (Financiera Picollo), 69, 213, 215, 244n4

Finca 13 (Caaguazú), 178, 180, 210–13, 215–18, 221, 260nn38–39

flag, national, 200–201, 201, 259n27

FNC (Federación Nacional Campesina), 52–53, 56, 82–83, 87, 144, 161

Fogel, Ramón, 62

folklore studies, 239n23

Foodfirst Information and Action Network, 250n27

Foucault, Michel, 7

Fox, Vicente, 227–28

Francia, José Gaspar Rodríguez de, 35–37, 237n6, 256n12

Franco, Jean, 40

Franco, Rafael, 256–57n12

free speech, 42

French constitution, 251n36

French legal tradition, 125

Frente Nacional por la Defensa de la Soberanía y la Vida, 83–87, 90–91, 246n19

Freud, Sigmund: *Civilization and Its Discontents*, 42

Friedman, Milton, 129

Frutos, Juan Manuel ("Papacito"): communities established by, 192–93; Estatuto Agrario instituted by, 28; as IBR head, 72, 74, 257n13; land holdings by, 73; on land reform, 28, 74, 162, 167, 238n8; land titles signed by, 194–95; on latifundios, 193, 257n14; *Un millón de propiedades*, 195, 196

Gabinete de Crisis Rural, 84–85, 90, 246n21

Galeano, Antonio, 16–19, 88, 161, 185–86, 204, 207–8, 251n40, 255n1. *See also* MAP

Galeano, Jorge, 47; archive of, 16, 132, 144–45, 208; background/success of, 16–17; on the Civil Code, 137; dangers faced by, 184–87, 255n1; documentary expeditions by, 18–20, 146–47, 161–62; elites' disapproval of, 18–19, 187, 191, 255n2; at IBR meetings, 163–65, 173; on neoliberal hegemony, 64; paro cívico role of, 86–87, 89, 186, 224; Tekojoja conflict role of, 117–19, 122–23, 126–27, 130–32, 135, 169, 252n42. *See also* MAP

Gavilán, Juan Bautista, 225–26

General Resquín, 224, 226

geography and national impoverishment, 10, 235n21

gestores, 41, 76, 175–76, 180–81, 255n28

The Gift (Mauss), 257n16, 259n32

gifts, 191, 194–95, 208–9, 218–19, 257nn16–17, 259n32

González Macchi, Luís, 52–53, 57–60, 200, 242n47, 258n23

governance: agrarian or rural, 99, 111, 141, 250n29; bureaucratic reform and, 1, 3, 7, 121, 143, 234n9; "good," 4, 12, 123, 138, 147; information and, 6, 12, 241n32; multicultural, 101; transparency and, 57, 189, 222. *See also* democracy

Gramsci, Antonio, 64–65, 236n29, 238n12, 242n48

Greenwald, Bruce, 254n17

Guaraní language: accents in, 236n27; diglossic relationship with Spanish, 10–11, 114–15, 236nn24–25, 236n27, 240n29, 249n19; at IBR meetings, 164–65, 169; in public documents, 42–43; reality spoken in, 204; in schools, 62, 240n29; on television, 135, 252n42

Guatemala, 72, 101, 245n8

Gudeman, Stephen, 250n28; *Conversations in Colombia*, 103–4

guerrilla auditors: definition of, 9; vs. documentary pedagogy, 166–67; documents produced by, 163–67, 173–74, 182–83; elites'/bureaucrats' disapproval of, 19–20; goals of, 151; vs. official auditors, 20, 151; politics/fear of, 188–89

Guha, Ranajit, 237n5

Guilhot, Nicolas, 38, 238n16, 240n27

Guttman, Matthew, 261n6

Habeas Data, 43, 241n31

Habermas, Jürgen, 238–39n18

haciendas, 260n37

Halley Mora, Mario, 193–94

Handelman, Don, 68, 91

Hayek, Friedrich, 4, 6, 156

hegemony, 64–65

Herken Krauer, Pablo, 205–6, 259n31

Hershberg, Eric, 233n2

Hijo de hombre (Roa Bastos), 40, 239n23

historic bloc, 30, 102, 238n12

Ibáñez, Érico, 207

IBR (Instituto de Bienestar Rural; *later named* INDERT): approaching the table at meetings of, 169–70, 172; bankruptcy of, 229; bureaucracy of, 121, 124, 174, 183; campesino-appointed president of, 229–30; campesinos' distrust of, 211; colonization by, 28–29, 106; criticism/attempted dissolution of, 124, 135; document handling by, 144–50, 167–71, 173–74, 177; favors/informal fees for services of, 252–53n1; founding of, 28, 72; gerente general (general manager), 162–65, 167–68, 173; gestores' access to information held by, 76; vs. the IDB, 174–75; importance to campesinos, 31; land redistribution by, 69, 73–75, 80–81, 84; land-reform colonies of, role in, 106–8, 248–49n14; name changed to INDERT, 124, 251n34; office in Asunción, 146; vs. public registry, 110; rate for land set by, 250n22; records of its abuses of law, 76–77; Tekojoja conflict role of, 117–20; on titles, 111; as a transitional institution, 111. *See also* Estatuto Agrario

IDB (Inter-American Development Bank), 99, 180–81, 245n8; credit from, 243n58; on derecheras and titles, 123–24; economists/planners from, 137; vs. the IBR, 174–75; registry reform project of, 174–75, 181–83

IMF, 60–61, 200, 205–6

INDERT (Instituto de Desarrollo Rural y de la Tierra). *See* IBR

indigenous people: vs. campesinos, 100–102, 141, 247–48n5, 251n37; exclusion/dispossession of, 122; recognition of, 141; reserves for, 141, 252n48

indigenous politics, 100–101

Industrial Paraguaya, 71, 215

inflation, 255n23, 258n21

information: as communication, 5, 234n11; completeness of, 5–7, 156–57, 234–35n12, 254nn16–17; definitions of, 5, 156–57, 234n11, 254–55nn19–20; digital, 181–82, 255n27; documents and, 150–51, 158–59, 165–66, 173–74; economics of, 4, 228, 234nn7–8, 234–35n12; gathering of, 43–47, 241n32; vs. knowledge, 255n20; market role of, 156, 158, 254nn16–17; poverty eased by, 9–10, 157, 234n10; provision for privacy of, 43, 241n31; for the Third World, 157–58; transparency and, 156–57, 183. *See also* transparency

information age, 4, 8–14

injustice, sense of, 70, 74, 76, 81, 95–96, 244n6

institutional ethics, 50

Instituto de Bienestar Rural. *See* IBR

Instituto de Desarrollo Rural y de la Tierra (INDERT). *See* IBR

Instituto de Previsión Social. *See* IPS

intellectuals/elites: in Asunción, 33–35, 239n21 (*see also* campesinistas); encounters with campesinos in the countryside, 136; on guerrilla auditors, 19–20; Stroessner's purging of, 34–35, 239n21

Inter-American Development Bank. *See* IDB

IPS (Instituto de Previsión Social), 85, 213, 244n4

Itaipú Dam, 58–59, 77, 227, 242n46

Itapúa, 61

Jaeggli, Alfredo Luís, 124, 139, 252n45

Jesuits, 36, 42, 236n28, 239n24, 240n29, 257–58n20

Jopara language, 236n25, 249n19

Kachaka music, 139, 252n44

Ka'iho, 69, 244n4

Keane, Webb, 5–6, 165–66, 172
Kearney, Michael, 100
Keynesian policies, 138
Ko'ãga roñe'ẽta (CEPAG), 42
kuati'a (papers), 109–10, 121, 129–30, 160–61, 210–11

labor unions, 83–84, 245–46n19, 256n10
Laclau, Ernesto, 189, 192, 202–3, 259n29
Lambert, Peter, 257n18
land: changes in use of, 62, 243–44n62; colonization of, 28–29, 106; concentration of, 2, 233–34n3; idle, 210, 259n33; invasion of, 107, 112–16, 201, 210, 248n12; irregular, 210 (*see also* Finca 13); progressive tax on, 60. *See also* latifundios; property; tierra malhabida
land reform: campesino goals of, 29–30 (*see also* property); citizenship via, 101, 140–41; by the Colorado Party, 71–74, 243n55; during the democratic transition (1960), 28–31, 237–38n8; Frutos on, 28, 74, 162, 167, 238n8; land inequality created by, 257n15; popular appeal of, 256–57n12; property in colonies, 104–8, 140–41, 248–49nn11–14; by Stroessner, 28, 72, 101, 192–98, 196, 255n21. *See also* colonies; Estatuto Agrario; IBR
land titles. *See* titles
language, 5–6, 159. *See also* Guaraní language
lateral reasoning, 237n32
latifundios (large tracts of unused land), 28, 72–73, 105–6, 192–93, 216, 245n9, 257n15, 260n37
El *Látigo*, 71
Le Bon, Gustave: *The Crowd*, 255n3
Left-Right distinction, 227, 261n6
legal positivism, 82, 93–94, 141–42, 245n18
letrados, 204

lettered city, 140, 143–44, 160, 170, 182. *See also* documents
ley del mbarete (law of strength), 36, 39–40, 50, 188
Li, Tania, 8
liberalism, 14, 190, 199, 244n6, 256n5. *See also* neoliberalism
Liberal Party, 28–29, 71, 75, 226–29
liberation theology, 29, 83, 192, 225
Ligas Agrarias Cristianas, 29, 36, 38, 74, 83, 144, 249n17
Locke, John, 120–22, 193, 250n30
Lomnitz, Claudio, 205–6
lotes precarios (precarious lots), 99, 111, 124, 127–29, 133, 251n39
Lugo, Fernando, 225–30, 236n26, 261n6
lumber, 58

Main Street (U.S.), 221
MAP (Movimiento Agrario y Popular): charges against leaders of, 134, 251n40; founding/goals of, 18; land invasions by, 82; leadership of, 134, 144, 162, 251n40 (*see also* Galeano, Jorge; guerrilla auditors); letterhead/logo of, 132, 134, 252n41; the Tekojoja conflict and, 116, 134–35
maps, 7, 181–82
March to the East (Paraguay), 28–29, 106
March to the West (Brazil), 28, 237–38n8
Mareco, Cecilio: "Propiedad Privada," 113–14, 139, 249n20
Mariscal López (Caaguazú), 207–14, 217, 219, 260n39
market society, computational view of, 6, 235n13
Marx, Karl, 155, 253n12, 256n9
Marzo Paraguayo (March 1999), 51–57, 202, 243n52, 246n26, 259n27, 259n34
materiality: vs. abstraction, 120–21, 125–26, 138, 250n28, 251n37; of documents, 165–67, 172, 178, 255n27; of land titles, 104–5, 178, 195, 248n9; of

representation, 129–37, 133; of rights, 123–37

Maurer, Bill, 237n32

Mauss, Marcel: *The Gift*, 257n16, 259n32

MCNOC (Mesa Coordinadora Nacional de Organizaciones Campesinas), 78, 80, 82–84, 86, 144

MCS Grupo Consultor, 152, 154

Mehta, Uday Singh, 250n30

mejoras (improvements), 105–8, 110, 121, 125, 248n10, 251n37, 251n39

Meliá, Bartolome, 239n24

Memoria (IBR), 257n14

Mennonites, 39, 107, 235n22

Mesa Coordinadora Nacional de Organizaciones Campesinas. *See* MCNOC

middle class, American, 238n15

Un millión de propiedades (Frutos), 195, 196

Minga Guazu, 112

mint, 61

Mitchell, Timothy, 6, 154, 235n21

Miyazaki, Hirokazu, 224

mobs, irrationality of, 27, 50, 187–88, 255n3

modernization theory, 190

Monsanto, 63, 244n64

Morales, Evo, 227

Morínigo, José Nicolás, 56, 243n52

Mouffe, Chantal, 239n19

Movimiento Agrario (Vaquería), 91

Movimiento Popular Tekojoja, 226, 230, 261n3

MST (Movimento Sem Terra), 246–47n26

multiculturalism, 100–102

Museum of Justice (Asunción), 46

The Mystery of Capital (de Soto), 157–58, 234n10

La Nación, 241n36

nation, graphic icons of, 71, 245n7

national cadastre, 76, 124, 175, 181–82, 197–98, 258n20

nationalism, 91

natural law, 120, 125, 251n36

neoliberalism, 1, 4–5, 60, 64, 233nn1–2

neopopulism (dual politics), 199–200, 258n25

networking, 21

new democrats: campesino culture objectified by, 34, 37; campesinos' alliance with, 38–39, 68, 74, 83; campesinos opposed by, 38; vs. campesinos, overview of relationship, 12–14, 20, 206–7; definition/meanings of, 32–33; democratic transition rise of, 26, 32–40; as engaged universals, 32–34, 238n17; vs. ethnographers, 21; exiled, 12–13; as liberal democrats, 239n19; Marzo Paraguayo role of, 51–52; on modernization, 174, 182; national flag used by, 202; in NGOS, 38; as populists, 203; professionalization of, 38–39; as el público, 33, 199–200, 230, 238–39n18; on reality, 205; rituals of affirmation by, 96; as social scientists, 32, 34, 239n20; sociological makeup of, 12–13. *See also* campesinistas; democratic transition

newspapers, 46–47, 52, 241n36. See also *ABC Color*; *Última Hora*

NGOS, 38, 42

Nicanor. *See* Duarte Frutos, Nicanor

Nickson, Andrew, 61, 257n18

Noticias, 52, 241n36

OAS (Organization of American States), 245n8

Ocho de diciembre, 116

Odilio Román y los Románticos, 113

'óga (dwelling), 126–27

orality and inscription, 42–43, 240n29

Organización Política y Militar, 241n34

Organization of American States (OAS), 245n8

Orwell, George, 35

Ovelar, Blanca, 226
Oviedo, Lino: *ABC Color*'s support of, 242n41, 242n49; anticorruption platform of, 48–49; following Argaña's assassination, 51–52; charisma/popularity of, 47–51, 59, 242n43; conviction/imprisonment of, 50–51, 261n4; corruption of, 48–49, 209; criticism of, 50; exile of, 52, 188; Guaraní spoken by, 206; institutional ethics and, 50; pardon for, 51, 227; presidential campaign of, 227, 261n4; student demonstrators and, 202; vs. Juan Carlos Wasmosy, 48–50, 152

El país en una plaza (Colmán), 53–56, 188, 202, 202, 242n50
Palacio de Justicia (Asunción), 41, 45, 175
Pandey, Gyan, 220
Panizza, Francisco, 191, 221
papers. See documents; titles
Paraguay: as "an island surrounded by land," 9–10, 235n20; authoritarian history of, 36; bilingualism/diglossia of, 10–11, 235–36nn24–25; the Chaco, 235n22; constitution of, 43, 95–96, 240–41n30, 255n21; crackdown on dissidents in, 29, 238n10; despotism in, 191; economy of, 57–61, 243n54, 243n56; foreign loans to, 59–60, 243n58; geography of, 10; image/politics of, 9–10, 235n20; independence from Spain of, 28; isolation of, 9–10; map of eastern, 15; wars with Argentina, Brazil, and Bolivia of, 235n23
El Paraguayo: Un hombre fuera de su mundo (S. Vera), 36–37, 39–40
paraguayología, 37, 223, 239n24
Pariri, 70, 117, 122
paro cívico (general strike; 2004), 83–95, 88, 186, 200, 224–26, 229, 246n24, 246–47n26

Partido Patria Querida, 38, 204, 226
Partido Revolucionario Institucional (PRI; Mexico), 227, 238n9
party cards, 194
Pateman, Carole, 250n30
Patria (political cartoon figure), 71
Patria Libra, 86–87, 246n23, 260n39
patronage, 11, 191, 193–94, 199, 258n24
peasantries, literature on, 100, 247n2
peasants. See campesinos
Peck, James, 60, 233n2
Pereira, Sixto, 230
Perón, Juan, 256n6
physiocracy, 103, 248n7
politics vs. the political, 255–56n4
Popular, 241n36
populism/caudillismo, 189–222; agrarian, 192–98, 256–57nn10–12; in Argentina and Venezuela, 256n10; corruption of caudillos, 191; definition of, 27, 191, 203, 259n28; vs. democracy, 14, 190–91; fascism and, 259n29; fear of, 221; history of, 28; the irrationality of mobs and, 27, 50, 187–88, 191–92, 255n3; land titles and, 193–95; liberalism and, 190, 199; populist leaders, 190, 256n6, 261n7 (*see also* Stroessner, Alfredo); populist reason, 189; reality and, 203–7; regularization and, 207, 209–20, 212 (*see also* Finca 13); romanticizing, 252n47; transparency as a gift, 207–22; transparency as populist, 189, 219–22
Portuguese language, 62
positive law, 82, 93–94, 141–42, 245n18
post-neoliberalism, 1, 233n2
post-Washington Consensus, 233n2
poverty: democracy as cure for, 2; de Soto solution to, 124, 129, 131, 136, 157–58, 210; information as easing, 9–10, 157, 234n10; nonmembership signified by, 140
Power, Michael, 159, 235n18

precarious lots (lotes precarios), 99, 111, 124, 127–29, 133, 251n39

priests, radical, 192, 225

private property (propiedad privada), 111–15, 249n20

privatization of property, 97–99, 115–17, 120, 123, 137–38, 140–41

productores (soy farmers), 32, 111–12

propaganda, 3, 105

property, 97–142; abstraction vs. materiality and, 120–21, 125–26, 138, 250n28, 251n37; acts of possession and, 122–23, 125–26, 128, 251n39; credit and, 109, 249n16; derecheras (occupancy permits), 108–10, 120, 122, 128, 135, 248n13, 249n17; de Soto on, 99, 124, 131, 136, 174, 250n33; dignity of land ownership, 193–94; economic growth of nations and, 248n7; empirical descriptions of vs. policy proposals about, 251n38; forest land as nonproductive and, 210, 248n10; frontier mobility and, 112, 249n17; the IDB and, 99; inalienable, 112; via labor, 104–5; in land-reform colonies, 104–8, 140–41, 248–49nn11–14; Locke on, 120–22, 193; lotes precarios (precarious lots), 99, 111, 124, 127–29, 133, 251n39; materiality of land titles, 104–5, 178, 248n9; materiality of representation, 129–37, 133; materiality of rights, 123–37; mejoras (improvements), 105–8, 110, 121, 125, 248n10, 251n37, 251n39; occupancy permits for, 107–8, 250n31; overview of, 97–99, 138–42, 247n1, 252nn45–48; premodernity vs. modernity and, 121, 250n29; privatization of, 97–99, 115–17, 120, 123, 137–38, 140–41; propiedad privada (private property), 111–15, 249n20; rights to, 99; sovereignty and, 141–42; speculation and, 248–49n14; Tekojoja conflict over, 99,

116–20, 122, 126, 128, 130–32, 134–40, 249–50nn21–23; títulos (titles), 104–5, 108–11, 119–20, 124, 127–30, 248n9, 249n15, 250n27, 251n35 (see also rapid titling law); women's ownership of, 250n31

"Propiedad Privada" (Mareco), 113–14, 139, 249n20

propiedad privada (private property), 111–15, 249n20

el público (the public), 33, 49, 199–203, 230, 238–39n18, 240n29

public registry: corruption in, 180; vs. IBR, 110; land titles handled by, 109, 124, 178, 179, 180; organization of information in, 174–76, 176; reform projects for, 174–75, 181–83

public sphere, 46–47, 238–39n18

el pueblo: campesinos as, 14, 26, 33, 192; vs. el público, 199–203; Stroessner's creation of, 14, 192, 194

purahéi jahe'o (lament song), 113–14

pynandi (allegiance to leaders), 55, 242n51

qualities of things, 165–66, 172

Rachid Lichi, Bader, 207–9, 211–14, 217–20, 222

radical politics vs. rights/law-based strategies, 93–94

Rama, Angel, 140

ranching colonies, 73

rancho (hut), 126–27

Rancière, Jacques, 239n19, 259n30

rapid titling law, 124, 129, 137, 139–40, 195, 196, 252nn45–46, 258n20. See also titles

reading rights, 43

reality: ability to speak it, 204; economic, 205–6; as felt in the body, 22, 192; gifts and, 218–19; meanings of, 203–7; orerealidad (our reality), 186, 205–6,

reality (cont.)
210, 213, 216–21; populism and, 203–7;
vs. representation, 154
regularization, 207, 209–20, 212. See also
Finca 13
representationalism, 154–55, 158–59,
174, 177, 253n10
resource curse, 243n61
rights: free speech, 42; human, 38, 94;
materiality of, 123–37; political membership through land, 105; to property, 99; radical politics vs. rights/
law-based strategies, 93–94; reading,
43. See also under property
Riles, Annelise, 21
Riquelme, Marcial, 62
Riquelme, Quintín, 248n11
Rivera, Alberto: Conversations in Colombia,
103
Roa Bastos, Augusto, 37–38; Hijo de
hombre, 40, 239n23; Yo el Supremo,
35–37, 239n22
Rodríguez, Andrés, 12
roll-out neoliberalism, 60
Roseberry, William, 9
Rosen, Fred, 233n2
Roundup, 63, 244n64
Rubín, Humberto, 135, 252n42
Rubin, Joan, 11
rule of law: the archive of terror and, 45–
46; constitutions as establishing, 240–
41n30; established via democratic
transition, 94; positive law and, 82, 93–
94, 245n18; truth commissions and,
247n27. See also under tierra malhabida
rural mestizo population, studies of, 36,
239n23
Ruta 5 (highway), 86–87, 246n22

Santa Clara, 70
Sarmiento, Domingo, 191–92, 205;
Facundo, 190, 256n5

semiotic ideology, 6, 154–55, 159, 166, 182
Service, Elman Rogers and Helen, 249n17
setentistas (seventies-ists), 39, 62
shantytown (bordering Caaguazú), 86–87
sharecropping, 254n16
Shklar, Judith, 244n6
signatures and gifts, 257n17
signification, 159. See also semiotic
ideology
Silva, Ramón, 240n29
slum dwellers, 240n26
social contracts, 120–21, 138, 250n30
Solano López, Francisco, 237n6
Somosa, Anastasio, 74
Soviet Union, 4, 157, 234n5
soybeans, 56, 61–65, 97–98, 243–44nn62–
64, 249n14, 249n17, 250nn22–23. See
also property, Tekojoja conflict over
Spanish language. See under Guaraní
language
squatter organizations, 86–87
state as fetish, 155, 253–54nn13–14
Stiglitz, Joseph, 157, 228, 233n2,
254nn16–18
strikes, 94. See also paro cívico
Stroessner, Alfredo, 191, 237n6; ABC
Color shut down by, 42, 234n6;
agrarian populism of, 192–98, 256n10;
anticommunism of, 29, 193; constitution passed by, 255n21; criticism of,
35–36; development projects of, 58,
255n21; economy under, 59; exile of,
49; historic bloc created by, 30; information controlled via spying/torture,
44–45; intellectual opposition purged
by, 34–35, 239n21; land holdings by
his family, 73; land reform by, 28, 72,
101, 192–98, 196, 255n21 (see also IBR);
on the March to the East, 106; overthrow of, 11–12, 30, 42, 59, 258n22;
patronage used by, 194; popular support for, 14, 191–92; populist project

of, 101; power of, 11; repression by, 11, 30, 43–45, 225; Roa Bastos on, 36; Somosa and, 74; unions and, 256n10; U.S. support for, 11; youth movement against, 16–17

Stroessner, Alfredo (grandson), 226–27

structures of feeling, 31

subaltern discourse, 220

sugarcane, 61

surveying, 177

Swyngedouw, Erik, 203, 259n28

Taussig, Michael, 155, 254n14

tax reform, 60

Taylor, Lance, 233n2

la Técnica (Asunción), 44

Tekojoja (Caaguazú), 255n24; Brazilian land holdings in, 70, 116–17; police raid on/shootings in, 21–22, 119, 134, 138, 250n26 (see also under Galeano, Jorge; property); privatization in, 116–17; productores in, 112; settlement of, 106–7; squatter camp in, 14, 16

tenure security, 129

terere, 39, 240n25

Thiesenhusen, William, 72, 245n12

Thrift, Nigel, 237n32

Tickell, Adam, 60, 233n2

tierra del estado (state land), 113

tierra malhabida (ill-gotten land), 66–96, 244n1, 244n5; agricultural colonies vs. ranching colonies and, 73; Alegre's report on, 75–82, 79, 95; archive of terror used in forum on, 66–67, 92, 244n2; Centurión's testimony at forum on, 67–68, 91–93; Comisión de Verdad y Justicia's forum on (2006), 66–68, 91–92, 96, 244n2; corruption's role in, 70–71, 77–78, 81, 95; definition/meanings of, 69–70, 80; as 11 million hectares, 80–81; land distribution, uneven, 71–74, 245nn11–

12, 257n15; lands misappropriated, 69–70, 77, 244n4; new democratic narrative of, 70–71, 75; overview of, 66–69, 93–94, 244n2; the paro cívico (general strike; 2004) and, 83–95, 88, 186, 200, 224–26, 229, 246n24, 246–47n26; propiedad privada as, 113; public lands sold as war reparations, 71–72; recognition vs. redistribution and, 82; the rule of law and, 82–83, 85–87, 90, 93–95; size vs. legality of land holdings, 70, 81–82; the venta de las tierras públicas and, 71–72, 74

tierra ociosa (idle land), 113

titles (títulos): accuracy of, 197–98, 258n21; the Civil Code and, 109, 111, 121, 124, 217; devaluation of, 195, 258n21; as gifts, 195; IDB on, 123–24; materiality of, 104–5, 178, 195, 248n9; populism and, 193–95; property and, 104–5, 108–11, 119–20, 124, 127–30, 248n9, 249n15, 250n27, 251n35; public registry's handling of, 109, 124, 178, 179, 180; World Bank on, 123–24. See also rapid titling law

tobacco, 58, 61

toilet paper vs. corn cobs, 136

totalitarianism, 3, 35–36, 42, 45, 96, 205, 221

transitional failure, analyses of, 237n3

transition period. See democratic transition

transparency: after the Cold War, 3–9, 234n6, 234n9; vs. corruption, 13, 48, 152–55; democracy via, 3–4, 6–7, 234n9; as a development model, 1, 3–5; documents and, 8–9, 16, 150–51, 174, 182, 235n17 (see also archive of terror); as exclusive, 2–3; as fetish, 154–55; information and, 156–57, 183; of language, 11; as a negotiation, 222; opacity of, 152–59, 253n5, 253n8; political economy of, 47; politics of,

transparency (cont.)
7–9, 16, 155–56 (see also under populism/caudillismo); representationalism and, 154–55, 159, 177; as a universal good, 2
Transparency International, 13, 152–54, 159, 253n5, 253n8
Triple Alliance, War of the (1865–1970), 71, 191, 235n23
truth commissions, 66–68, 91–92, 244n2, 247n27
Tsing, Anna, 238n17
Turner, Brian, 112

Última Hora, 52, 119, 135, 202, 241n36
UNACE (Unión Nacional de Colorados Éticos), 49–50, 227
United States: archive of terror funded by, 45–46; financial crisis in (2008), 221–22; Guatemala invaded by, 72, 245n8; soybean production in, 62
Universal Declaration of Human Rights, 94
USAID (United States Agency for International Development), 45–46, 152, 181, 195, 258n20

Van Cott, Donna Lee, 95
Vaquería (Caaguazú), 186
Varela, Nelly, 119, 134–37
Vargas, Getúlio, 256n6
Vargas Llosa, Alvaro, 190, 203, 205
vendettas, 186
venta de las tierras públicas, 71–72, 74, 193, 257n12

Vera, Helio: En busca del hueso perdido, 37
Vera, Saro: El Paraguayo, 36–37, 39–40
Verdery, Katherine, 237n3
Via Campesina, 250n27

Wall Street (U.S.), 221–22
Wasmosy, Juan Carlos, 48–50, 69, 152, 242n39, 258n23
Weber, Max, 7–8, 147, 242n43, 260n41
Williams, Raymond, 31, 238n13
Wilson, Richard, 96
World Bank, 255n26; credit from, 243n58; on derecheras and titles, 123–24; economists/planners from, 137; education reform funded by, 38, 200, 240n29; on gestores, 255n28; on good governance, 3–4; hydroelectric and agricultural projects of, 10; on information as easing poverty, 9–10; on land distribution, 245n12; rapid titling legislation introduced by, 252n45; registry reform project of, 181–82
World Development Report, 157, 255n20

Yerbales, Montes y Estancias, 215–16, 260n35
yerba mate, 71, 215, 240n25, 260nn35–37
Yhu, 52, 242n50
Yo el Supremo (Roa Bastos), 35–37, 239n22

Zapatini, Colonel, 69
Zapatini Kue, 57, 69, 244n5
Zucolillo, Aldo, 242n41